Celebrating What Is Important to Me

West
Grades 3-12
Spring 2012

Celebrating What Is Important to Me
West
Grades 3-12
Spring 2012

AN ANTHOLOGY COMPILED BY CREATIVE COMMUNICATION, INC.

Published by:

PO BOX 303 • SMITHFIELD, UTAH 84335
TEL. 435-713-4411 • WWW.POETICPOWER.COM

Authors are responsible for the originality of the writing submitted.

All rights reserved. No part of this book may be reproduced or transmitted in any form or by any means, electronic or mechanical without written permission of the author and publisher.

Copyright © 2012 by Creative Communication, Inc.
Printed in the United States of America

ISBN: 978-1-60050-495-2

FOREWORD

Dear Reader:

Is writing meaningful to your life? The greatest gift that my mother ever gave me was her writing. For over 70 years, she kept a record of every moment that was meaningful in her life. Taking these stories, she created several books which allow me to remember and relive moments in my childhood and the life my mother had as she grew up. She got into the habit of writing and has now left a great legacy.

As a parent, I know that my children bring home samples of their writing from school assignments each week. However, after a few days on the school bulletin board or fridge at home, these slices of their lives often get thrown away.

The books we publish create a legacy for each of these students. Their work is recorded to show friends, family and future generations. We are glad to be part of capturing their thoughts, hopes and dreams.

The students that are published have shared a bit of themselves with us. Thank you for being part of this process, as every writer needs a reader. We hope that by recognizing these students, writing will become a part of their life and bring meaning to others.

Sincerely,

Thomas Worthen, Ph.D.
Editor
Creative Communication

WRITING CONTESTS!

Enter our next POETRY contest!

Enter our next ESSAY contest!

Why should I enter?
Win prizes and get published! Each year thousands of dollars in prizes are awarded throughout North America. The top writers in each division receive a monetary award and a free book that includes their published poem or essay. Entries of merit are also selected to be published in our anthology.

Who may enter?
There are four divisions in the poetry contest. The poetry divisions are grades K-3, 4-6, 7-9, and 10-12. There are three divisions in the essay contest. The essay divisions are grades 3-6, 7-9, and 10-12.

What is needed to enter the contest?
To enter the poetry contest send in one original poem, 21 lines or less. To enter the essay contest send in one original non-fiction essay, 250 words or less, on any topic. Please submit each poem and essay with a title, and the following information clearly printed: the writer's name, current grade, home address (optional), school name, school address, teacher's name and teacher's email address (optional). Contact information will only be used to provide information about the contest. For complete contest information go to www.poeticpower.com.

How do I enter?

Enter a poem online at:
www.poeticpower.com
or
Mail your poem to:
  Poetry Contest
  PO Box 303
  Smithfield, UT 84335

Enter an essay online at:
www.poeticpower.com
or
Mail your essay to:
  Essay Contest
  PO Box 303
  Smithfield, UT 84335

When is the deadline?
Poetry contest deadlines are December 6th, April 4th, and August 15th. Essay contest deadlines are October 18th, February 19th and July 16th. Students can enter one poem and one essay for each spring, summer, and fall contest deadline.

Are there benefits for my school?
Yes. We award $12,500 each year in grants to help with Language Arts programs. Schools qualify to apply for a grant by having 15 or more accepted entries.

Are there benefits for my teacher?
Yes. Teachers with five or more students published receive a free anthology that includes their students' writing.

For more information please go to our website at **www.poeticpower.com**, email us at editor@poeticpower.com or call 435-713-4411.

TABLE OF CONTENTS

WRITING ACHIEVEMENT HONOR SCHOOLS   1

LANGUAGE ARTS GRANT RECIPIENTS   5

GRADES 10-11-12 HIGH MERIT ESSAYS   7

GRADES 7-8-9 HIGH MERIT ESSAYS 43

GRADES 3-4-5-6 HIGH MERIT ESSAYS 137

INDEX 195

STATES INCLUDED IN THIS EDITION:

Arizona
California
Colorado
Idaho
Texas
Utah

Spring 2012 Writing Achievement Honor Schools

Teachers who had fifteen or more students accepted to be published

The following schools are recognized as receiving a "Writing Achievement Award." This award is given to schools who have a large number of entries of which over fifty percent are accepted for publication. With hundreds of schools entering our contest, only a small percent of these schools are honored with this award. The purpose of this award is to recognize schools with excellent Language Arts programs. This award qualifies these schools to receive a complimentary copy of this anthology. In addition, these schools are eligible to apply for a Creative Communication Language Arts Grant. Grants of two hundred and fifty dollars each are awarded to further develop writing in our schools.

Athens Christian Preparatory Academy
Athens, TX
Phyllis Walker*

Bios Christian Academy
Higley, AZ
Kelly Maguire*

Cypress Ranch High School
Cypress, TX
Jason Bannahan
Wendy Baron*
Susan Credeur*
Katherine Cunningham*
Jon R. McIntyre
Candice Smith

Dingeman Elementary School
San Diego, CA
Leigh Morioka*

Excelsior Academy
Erda, UT
Paul Bey*

First Baptist Academy
Universal City, TX
Cynthia Baxter*

Foothills Academy
Scottsdale, AZ
Nancy Bleasdale*

Foothills Elementary School
Colorado Springs, CO
Barbara Peters*

Horn Academy
Bellaire, TX
Lisa Miller*
Lizbeth Ueckert

Lampasas Middle School
Lampasas, TX
Judy Kennedy
Tamra Warner*

League City Intermediate School
League City, TX
Tracy Steiner*

Lindale Jr High School
Lindale, TX
    Kristine Brown*
    Debbie Dugger
    Julie Steen*

Margaret Landell Elementary School
Cypress, CA
    Brian Gary
    Melinda Pfafflin*
    Fernando Sintora
    Eric Watanabe

Monte Vista Christian School
Watsonville, CA
    Janice Renard*

North Star Academy
Redwood City, CA
    Elisabeth Stitt*

Outley Elementary School
Houston, TX
    Jayati Sengupta*

Saint Mary's Hall
San Antonio, TX
    Breanne Hicks*
    Dr. Teri Marshall
    Megan Soukup
    Amy Williams-Eddy

Salida Middle School
Salida, CO
    Jacque Fisher*

Santa Clara Elementary School
Oxnard, CA
    Michelle Mullen*

Seven Lakes High School
Katy, TX
    Jonathan Frishman*

South Jordan Middle School
South Jordan, UT
    Jill Jenkins*

St Ferdinand Catholic School
San Fernando, CA
    Vanessa Arellano*

St Gregorys Catholic School
Phoenix, AZ
    Baron Silva*

St Joseph Catholic School
Auburn, CA
    Kristen Mendonsa*
    Georgia Stempel

St Pius X Catholic School
Corpus Christi, TX
    Kathi Urbis*

St Raphael School
Santa Barbara, CA
    Terri Breton*

St Matthew Catholic School
San Antonio, TX
    Kathy Dylla*

Vacaville Christian Schools
Vacaville, CA
    Valerie Marchione*

Vista Charter School
Ivins, UT
    Elizabeth Bowler*

Vista Ridge High School
Cedar Park, TX
    Ellen Bickling
    Penny Billingsley*
    Renli Montoya

White Pine Charter School
    Ammon, ID
        Dr. Chad Harris*

Woods Cross High School
    Woods Cross, UT
        Brooke Gregg
        Jessica Heck*

Young Scholar's Academy
    Bullhead City, AZ
        David Martinez*

Language Arts Grant Recipients 2011-2012

After receiving a "Writing Achievement Award" schools are encouraged to apply for a Creative Communication Language Arts Grant. The following is a list of schools who received a two hundred and fifty dollar grant for the 2011-2012 school year.

Annapolis Royal Regional Academy, Annapolis Royal, NS
Bear Creek Elementary School, Monument, CO
Bellarmine Preparatory School, Tacoma, WA
Birchwood School, Cleveland, OH
Bluffton Middle School, Bluffton, SC
Brookville Intermediate School, Brookville, OH
Butler High School, Augusta, GA
Carmi-White County High School, Carmi, IL
Classical Studies Academy, Bridgeport, CT
Coffee County Central High School, Manchester, TN
Country Hills Elementary School, Coral Springs, FL
Coyote Valley Elementary School, Middletown, CA
Emmanuel-St Michael Lutheran School, Fort Wayne, IN
Excelsior Academy, Tooele, UT
Great Meadows Middle School, Great Meadows, NJ
Holy Cross High School, Delran, NJ
Kootenay Christian Academy, Cranbrook, BC
LaBrae Middle School, Leavittsburg, OH
Ladoga Elementary School, Ladoga, IN
Mater Dei High School, Evansville, IN
Palmer Catholic Academy, Ponte Vedra Beach, FL
Pine View School, Osprey, FL
Plato High School, Plato, MO
Rivelon Elementary School, Orangeburg, SC
Round Lake High School, Round Lake, MN
Sacred Heart School, Oxford, PA
Shadowlawn Elementary School, Green Cove Springs, FL
Starmount High School, Boonville, NC
Stevensville Middle School, Stevensville, MD
Tadmore Elementary School, Gainesville, GA
Trask River High School, Tillamook, OR
Vacaville Christian Schools, Vacaville, CA
Wattsburg Area Middle School, Erie, PA
William Dunbar Public School, Pickering, ON
Woods Cross High School, Woods Cross, UT

Grades 10-11-12 Top Ten Winners

List of Top Ten Winners for Grades 10-12; listed alphabetically

Molly Brinkley, Grade 10
Germantown High School, TN

Shelby Brooks, Grade 11
Lovejoy High School, TX

Eesha Choudhari, Grade 11
Grafton High School, VA

Kym Goodsell, Grade 11
Woods Cross High School, UT

Savanna Johnson, Grade 11
Lone Peak High School, UT

Paul Kleier, Grade 12
Covington Catholic High School, KY

Elizabeth Kunz, Grade 12
Allegan High School, MI

Catherine Niu, Grade 11
Walton High School, GA

Pauline Truong, Grade 10
Gabrielino High School, CA

Stacy Wang, Grade 11
Mt Hebron High School, MD

All Top Ten Essays can be read at www.poeticpower.com

Note: The Top Ten essays were finalized through an online voting system. Creative Communication's judges first picked out the top essays. These essays were then posted online. The final step involved thousands of students and teachers who registered as the online judges and voted for the Top Ten essays. We hope you enjoy these selections.

Childhood Memories

The thrill of youth. The enjoyment of the simple, warm summer air. I take a deep breath, filling my lungs with excitement, ecstasy, and adventure. My first time exploring the wooded part of the golf course's 13th hole. This place is a little bit outside of my backyard, and I wanted to see what it's like in there. This would become my new place to imagine all kinds of different worlds. The air smells like old oak leaves, and fresh vegetation. I explore, navigating through trees as I make new discoveries. As I look around, I notice a family of quail. I watch as the fat little birds find their way through the forest floor. As they wander off, I experience the feeling of appreciation for all the wildlife around me, and I feel the joy of experiencing this new occurrence. After the pleasure and wonder of my new friends, I climb a tree that looks sturdy and big. The wise and magnificent tree supports me as I climb to a bright and blue sky. I look around and I see the world in a whole new way. I can see my home from here, and I notice my mother is looking for me. I climb down from my new tower and start heading towards home. I look back and see my new friend, the woods. As I look back, I can't help but smile.

Michael Thompson, Grade 10
Woods Cross High School, UT

The Ocean

I slowly shut my eyes and can hear the sound of the dark blue ocean waves splashing on the shore in perfect sequence. The Earth is making the music that whispers sweetly to my soul. I can smell the aromas of the salty water and feel the sand scratching softly between my toes. I stretch out my arms to soak up the sun's golden rays. The warmth is comforting. A soft smile appears on my face as I start to spin around. As my feet dig deeper and deeper into the silky beach beneath my feet, the warm water washes the sand away, right from underneath me. Just like the sand, the ocean washes away my imperfections. It takes my worries, makes me feel as if I could be young forever. As the grin on my face grows bigger, my heart begins to fill the emptiness it has been longing to get rid of. I have never felt so alive and happy.

Laney Sayer, Grade 11
Woods Cross High School, UT

Never Say Die!

Never quit! Never give up. No matter what you're going through or what you're battling, just keep pushing on. Every dark tunnel we go through in life will always have light at the end of it. One of the best sayings I've heard is: "Hold on just a little longer; it may be stormy now but it can't rain forever." God is always watching over us and He knows exactly what we're going through. Many of the mountains we have to climb in our lives are mountains that God has put here. He tests us to see if we will trust him even in our difficult times. God will carry you over every mountain, and the way to tell if God had placed that mountain in your life is to ask yourself: "Am I a better or bitter person because of that mountain?"

Madison Weatheread, Grade 10
Athens Christian Preparatory Academy, TX

Teen Pressure

Society today makes everyone crazy, especially teenagers. One main stresser that teenagers have is fitting in. Teenagers feel pressured into looking and acting a certain way. Teenagers feel the need to be accepted by everyone. What influences a teenager to work hard at fitting in with society? A teenager may respond that going the distance is the answer. For what you might ask. To feel accepted. Teenagers shouldn't be stressing over anything because they are still kids.

Acceptance is what stresses teenagers. They feel they need to fit in doing things like joining gangs, doing drugs, and ditching school. Parental authority is the key to changing a teenager's life. Parents need to step up and be more involved in their teen's life instead of trying to be just a child's friend. One example of being more involved in a teenager's life is asking questions. Teenagers need someone to talk to and that's when parents should take the initiative to become a friend and parent guiding the teenager toward the right path.

Another example is music videos. The majority of teenagers spend at least two or three hours a day watching music videos. Some videos are not only offensive, but are very vulgar. They demean women and young teens by showing them in nontraditional roles.

In conclusion, society has played a huge role in teenager's lives and their perspectives toward life. Unfortunately, it has not been very positive. New regulations should be enacted to turn the tide of teenage control to teenage self-control.

Samantha Diaz, Grade 12
Plato Academy, TX

Certain Someone

Rarely do you find someone young who has lost a parent through death, or at least I don't anyway. Two years ago, however, I did. Our meeting was so brief I can't recall his name, but I'll never forget his face. That face, only a year older than mine, was withdrawn, tired-looking and serious. Through a strange turn of conversation we came to the topic of parents. He asked about mine, I said they were good, annoying at times, but good. I asked about his own.

"My mom's messed up," he answered bluntly, "cause my dad died last year. Overdose." Shock and embarrassment quickly overcame me. "That bites," I mumbled. It didn't seem like something I should've said, but to my surprise he cracked a wide smile.

"That was refreshing," he said with a snicker, "Everyone usually just says they're so sorry. Whatever, you know?" "Oh, yeah," I answered dumbly.

The rest of our conversation didn't include dead parents and it didn't last long. I left soon after with one last look at the guy, who smiled again and waved goodbye.

A couple years and thousands of other small conversations later, I still remember him. Like I said, it's not often you meet someone young who lost a parent through death. I guess it's not often those same someones would smile after you responded poorly, either.

Katie Barney, Grade 12
Woods Cross High School, UT

One Little Decision Makes a Big Difference

Standing quietly with its shape distorted as if a thousand well-trained infantry had attacked it, the car showed its scars from the tragic accident, which not only took the life of a potential news reporter, Alexandria Brown, but also broke countless hearts. Not knowing the risk of texting and driving, Alexandria did not make a wise decision before she picked up her phone while she was driving; this misstep led her to the final destination of her existence, death. It seemed like Alexandria was just one of those teenagers who were careless of the risks in texting and driving; however, people never learn lessons from these tragedies that are happening every day. No matter how often teachers warn students of the consequences of texting while driving, these words of advice are usually like air to teenagers because they think they are professionals who can easily handle texting while driving. Nevertheless, no one's safety can be guaranteed when one hand is typing and the other hand controlling the wheel, just like Alexandria Brown who paid for those few words on the phone with her life. However, teenagers are not the only victims of these accidents, but also their families who suffer from these tragedies even if they are innocent. Experiencing the death of Alexandria, Alexandria's sister Katrina states that she envies her friends for having siblings to play with because she no longer has one; and, most importantly, she has to accept the fact that the person who always sleeps next to her will never come back because of those few words on the phone. Katrina's pain proves that her family's suffering and Alexandria's death are not worth a few words; therefore, people should think before they put their thoughts into actions because one little decision may cause disastrous consequences.

I-Chia Huang, Grade 10
Saint Mary's Hall, TX

The Double Side

Splash! Swoosh! My feet skip from puddle to puddle, dancing to a soundless beat. The warm breeze whistles a tune of spring in my ear as my yellow pocket buttons accompany it with the clicking of true lead percussionists.

The yearly springtime showers have finally ceased and I was sure dear old Earth was pleased. For she was like me at the age of three — reluctant to take a shower, no matter how much Mother (Nature) would plead. But mother had won as she always did.

In the end, I was never angry, though. What harm could a little sprinkle bring? After the rain showers, poppies were sure to bloom and lift their sleepy lids to reveal vibrant orange irises. The vineyards would be sprinkled with drops of purple grapes, and the orchards would be painted with dollops of more varieties of citrus than one could name. Limes and lemons. Oranges and clementines. And even the peculiar tangelo, a cross between a tangerine, grapefruit, and orange.

Yet, as I look closer among the crowds of gleaming, clean, washed faces, the world isn't entirely happy. Upon the rain-softened sidewalk sits the only being upon which the rain had done no justice. His face is still coarse. Still smudged with dirt. His eyes don't sparkle, but are hardened with pain and packed with wrinkles of sleepless nights. The markings on his cardboard sign are dripping away. And his home…Where was it? Was it that pile of drenched boxes blown down by the wind? Soaked by the rain?

Ever wonder why some people say that it rains in spring, and others say that Mother Nature is crying? It was my mother and the Earth's that gave me the answer (as mothers always do): Even the happiest things have an unhappy side.

Nikisha Vaghjiani, Grade 10
Quartz Hill High School, CA

Who Are You?

Brachial Plexus Palsy is a paralysis of the arm due to an injury to the brachial plexus, a network of spinal nerves that originate in the back of the neck. I always knew I was different, growing up asking myself, "What's wrong with my arm?" I knew that no matter how hard I tried, I would never truly fit in, but I don't think I ever realized the disrespect I would receive. From kids to adults alike, the nicknames were astounding, "Crip, Gimpy, Lefty, Baby Arm, One Arm Willy, and One Arm Bandit." I was told that if I let people's words get to me, then I was weak-minded, but how do you withstand 18 years of constant name-calling and disrespect? You have to be more than mentally strong. You can't be afraid to wear short sleeve shirts, you can't try to hide your arm, and you have to learn to embrace who you are. Learn to brush everything off. I've learned to do that, I've learned to be a man. You won't stop me from playing basketball with the best. I won't ever give up. I've learned to keep my chin up, knowing your whispers are directed at me. You stare, but never ask questions, laugh when no words are said, and whisper when I enter the room. Who am I? I think the real question is, who are you?

Devin Nichols, Grade 12
Ridge View Academy, CO

Lack of Tears

I always feel bad when I look at people around me in the dark movie theater with faces wet with tears. I feel bad because my eyes are dry and I'm just blankly staring at the sad movie before me. I never cry during movies, no matter how sad they are. I think the reason that I don't is because I can't relate any of my own situation to the character's. My mom says it's because I have a cold heart, but I disagree. I get the feeling of crying, my throat catches, I bite my lip like I always do when I'm sad, but no tears come. The only times that I am in danger of crying is when a man cries on the screen. More like men than women, I cry at night into my pillow, where no one can hear or see my tear-stricken face. When a man cries, on a movie or not, you know the issue is probably serious. The same goes for me. I hate showing emotion in front of people because I don't want to seem weak. Men who cry in movies, at least their characters, have let all their guards down. The event, whatever it was, has affected them so much that there is nothing in the world but sadness. When that sadness hits me, it will be like a tidal wave, and those tears that I've never shed will all come out at once.

Morgan McGrath, Grade 12
Vista Ridge High School, TX

Ballroom Dancers

The heat kissed my skin, as the swirls of amber danced closer to me. The crackling of the walls thundered in my ear, whispering their destruction. I pressed myself deeper in the warming corner, afraid of the fire dancers that drew closer. My six year old mind could not process what was going on, and all I did was stare into the glare of the fire. Those two minutes seemed like an eternity.

Flames cascaded from the ceiling, and oddly enough, the flames became hypnotizing, as if they wanted me to play. Their pirouettes swirled the different shades of orange, red and yellow into a tornado of vile spirits being sucked out of thin air. The flames, the ballroom dancers, swaying from wall to wall, swallowing the apartment whole.

Suddenly, a hand wrapped around my wrist, jerking me into the fire. The blaze stroked my skin as I flew past the elegant fire dancers; their strokes became bites, as I neared the entrance. The hallways were coal black; the stair cases became vague as we made our way to the lobby. I could still hear the walls crumble as we neared the last steps. There was a feeble ray of light that bore through the black blizzard of ashes.

Could it be daylight or just more dancers? I thought.

Regardless what it might be, the hand compelled me toward it, and as we neared, we could hear sirens blasting and people shouting. As the sun's rays touched my face, I heard a familiar voice. And then I knew. I was safe. I was Alive.

Elizabeth Rodriguez, Grade 11
Alief Early College High School, TX

Nearing Neverland

In the neurotic subconscious of my mind, I have a strange neurosis to be a nonconformist. Conformity is the nauseous nature of our nitwit society, where everyone nonchalantly falls into nothingness. Some people are the exception, but they are a Nobody that has sunk away into a black abyss until the day they die. My nomadic mind has the nerve to narrate my life. And instead of falling into the flow of things, I've decided to cast away the nasty comments and pursue what comes naturally to me: a novelist. I have neglected my ability by not finishing a novel, but short narratives and poems flow better. I know the world is a nightmare, and to chase my dream is nonsensical, but it is my life. It numbs me and infuriates me when narrow-minded people shoot down my notion of what I want to do. Let me nestle in a corner and nibble on whatever food I have. Being a nonpartisan, I don't care what you want to do. I will not be a narcotic for your apparent nonexistent life, so don't be one for me.

Nowadays, nuisances such as yourself do not belong in this nation, and yet you are somehow taking over. Maybe, you are a necessary evil, just like our faithful government. But I love living my life sober, despite the not-so-neat world around me. I refuse to take your drugs and will instead enjoy my life. I do not need your negative thoughts disrupting my existence. My soon-to-come nostalgia will thank me later without you putting a notch in my dream.

Kaitlin Wood, Grade 12
Kingman High School, AZ

Deteriorating Human Capability

Ralph Waldo Emerson once said, "The civilized man has built a coach, but has lost the use of his feet." I agree with Emerson's belief that technology makes man's basic skills increasingly obsolete. Although its purpose is to make life easier and more enjoyable, technology makes humans duller by giving people an "easy way out," instead of forcing them to use their mental and/or physical skills to solve problems. As a result, people, especially students, increasingly rely on their phones, computers, and electronic sources on the Internet to find information. In a comic satirizing the effects of technology, a student asked his teacher, "Now that we have these [smart phones], isn't knowing things obsolete?" This shows the profoundly negative effect technology has on the intellectual development of America's future generation. Electronic technology does not allow people use their intelligence to their full potential.

Advancements in transportation also render people helpless to the lure of getting places without physical exertion. For the past century, cars, trains, and buses have all but replaced the bike and feet as the most common means of travel.

Transportation is not the only area where laziness is an unwanted byproduct of improved technology; nowadays, many people do not know how to cook. This is why the Carl's Jr. company created their concise catch-phrase: "Without us, some guys would starve." Fast-food restaurants and drive-thru joints allow people to obtain food quickly and at an affordable price, making a lot of people reluctant to learn how to cook — a necessary life skill — and making America obese. Although technology aims at improving the modern standard of living, it actually prevents humans from using their full capabilities and expanding on their basic skills to develop intellectually.

Vanessa Lam, Grade 11
Downey High School, CA

In the Darkness of the Room

I put my headphones on. Then I turn the radio on and find the song that fits the moment. It is sometimes sad, sometimes pumped up but it helps me to find the way I feel. I remain lying in bed for a few minutes. It feels so peaceful, so quiet and so mine that I can barely feel the beat of my heart. The music is still playing on, it's always the same songs, does not matter the station, but that helps me to really find the meaning of the song and adjust it to my life. I focus on the lyrics, not that much on the music. What really matters for me right now is to find the perfect words, the perfect quote. Then I try to figure out my real feelings. I have been trying to hide them from people all day long because most of the time I don't want them to see my crying. I sometimes do cry just for myself though, when it is just me and I don't have to smile all the time to seem happy "twenty-four-seven." I wish I could also scream, but that is not always possible. it just feels so good when it is just yourself and you don 't have to care about anything else. The time is off. It is time to go to bed. I knew it was going to be short, but fortunately there is always a "tomorrow."

Cristina Mendez, Grade 10
Woods Cross High School, UT

Home Is Where the Heart Is

I stare out the window as the bus makes its usual route around the city, frequently stopping to pick up another batch of passengers. As I watch the passing stores and restaurants, I can't help but think that this is the way it's going to be for a long while. Now that I have moved to California, I will no longer see the passing trees, cornfields, and farms. The Wisconsin farm town I once lived was now replaced with the hustle and bustle of the city.

I suffocate in the exhaust from the traffic. I feel squished with the many buildings built so close together so that there's room for one more shopping center or fast-food chain. I gaze up at the night sky, only to count up to four or five stars. As the bus nears my stop, I find myself longing for my home out in the country. The white, snowy winters, the fresh country air, and the wide open space will always have a place in my heart. And as I walk off the bus and onto the sidewalk, I know that one day I'll be back there again.

Heather Alexis Wicks, Grade 11
Washington High School, CA

Soldier

He went away, sometimes for days. Why did he go? I was told it was his job. Why didn't he call? I was told he didn't have a phone where he went. He always came back. It seemed strange to me, why he left. My mom told me that it was a good cause. I never understood it. He always came home to me, in green and brown. I never understood, but I was told it was his job. He told his little girl that she didn't need to worry, he would come home. He would hug and kiss Mom and me. Then he went away for a week. I thought he was gone forever. I was told again that it was for a good cause and that he would come home to me. When he came home to me that time, it was different. I understood, he was in the Army. I never though that my dad was a soldier. A hero. I understood now why he went away, and came back in brown and green. It was because my dad was a Green Beret. He fought for this country, and he always would. My dad is a hero. A soldier.

Aubree Peterson, Grade 10
Woods Cross High School, UT

You Will Never Change Something That You Are Willing to Tolerate

Bad habits come from examples people see as they are growing up. These habits are often things that one was allowed to get away with at a young age. Their parents tolerated this behavior, and later it became viewed as acceptable.

Manners are the same way; rarely does one see a young person voluntarily help the elderly or be respectful to them in public. This is because the society of the modern world allows this behavior, and accepts it widely. Common courtesy is just a footnote of what has suffered because of this toleration and will continue to suffer if society continues down its current path toward apathy and ignorance.

Katie West, Grade 11
Athens Christian Preparatory Academy, TX

Perfection

Perfection. Expectations. Expectations to be perfection. I am expected to be perfect…and I was, or thought I was. Expectations are the energy drink I use to keep me going, to keep me perfect. But they are also my wardens, keeping me isolated, keeping me barred from anything but perfection.

For me, perfection is like religion. I'm sworn to it, devoted to it, bound to it…blessed with it…cursed with it, whichever. Although many would like it, being faultless at everything, they have no idea what that life really entitles. The thing about the philosophy of perfection is that it's only understood by the few who possess it…the few like me. I know that I had to give up everything to be the flawless girl expected of me. I know that I can't let anyone down. I know that I have to be perfect. So I became a slave…a slave to expectations. But the thing about my indentured servitude is that I am my own slave holder. I'm the voice that rouses me from my two second nap and that locks me in my room until I finish my project. I'm the voice that keeps me perfect, that keeps me moving forward, that keeps me improving, that keeps me where I want to be. It's not perfection…but it's not that far away.

Patricia Dasilva, Grade 10
Cypress Ranch High School, TX

Talent

Every person on this planet was given a talent, somehow in some way. When I was a young girl, my mom put me in dance. I never really liked it much, and I would always be bored in dance class. I would not pay attention the whole time. As I grew older, I began to enjoy dance more. I would actually pay attention in dance class and try my hardest to do the dance moves to the best of my ability. I realized that dance was not easy for me, and it was not my talent. Even though I did not have a natural talent, I worked my hardest every day in dance class. Now, I am on my school dance team. Working hard at something you love, even though you are not the best at it definitely pays off in the end. My natural talent is the ability to work my hardest at all times, no matter what. Everyone has a talent, somehow in some way.

Taylor Chapman, Grade 10
Cypress Ranch High School, TX

In the System

On paper I am the offender, but in reality I am the victim. I am the victim of a situation I have no say in. I didn't have a dad to be a father and I didn't have a mom to be a mother. I am a victim, a victim of the system. I have been placed under lock and key for a good portion of my life. The choices were mine, but the foundation of those choices were not. I was born into the system. There are a lot of names the system hides behind, but I can quickly spot the workings of the system. I would love to be optimistic, but how? How are you suppose to force a smile when you know that no matter what you do or how hard you try, your future is still in the hands of the man with the gavel?

Rueben Marquez, Grade 11
Ridge View Academy, CO

Ai Wa Sensou

Mom and Brother are arguing again. They're in the kitchen. I'm playing on the laptop. The laptop is in the kitchen. I don't want to ask Mom if I can move it somewhere else. I'm not touching that argument with a forty foot pole. Why can't they just knock it off? They argue over the stupidest things. I can't even remember what they're arguing about, it's that insignificant.

I discovered a new song today. With headphones firmly in place, I turn up the volume. The singer is screaming, the lyrics throaty, belted, with what seems to be every inch of capacity his lungs have. The song isn't metal and the singer isn't growling or roaring, but the music flows with a mad intensity just the same. The guitar chords are sharp, quivering, the kind that make you want to jump on your bed and play the most chaotic, on-stage-at-a-concert air guitar of your life.

Mouth moving silently, head discretely bobbing, I turn up the volume once more. I don't want to hear them. I can't scream. This song will do it for me. The music ends. I hit replay.

With no other outlet for the emotions swirling inside me, tamed and focused by the music, they find their way onto paper. The pencil skritch-scratches over the surface, pressing harder with each darkening line. My drawings will scream for me too. The pencil acts as a conducting rod. The dark storm within me drains to my fingertips and is funneled out through the graphite. All that's left is an image on paper, shades of gray pulsing with negative emotions cast aside by their owner.

The yelling stops, so does the song. My drawing is done.

Molly Tapken, Grade 12
Washington High School, CA

Emptiness

She took in her last breath of air from this Earth. There, the grandmother I adored more than life itself was gone in the blink of an eye, and my world came crashing in. My Mimi was now in the place I longed to be, Heaven, and I was stranded here with a new normal. It swept me up like a hurricane and never let me go. It was do or die.

I hate what I have been given and am constantly surrounded with emptiness. The emptiness of her presence. There is nothing I can do to escape it. I go to her home, the place where I have many memories of her being happy, and I completely crumble. No matter how many of her things are there, I feel as though there is nothing. Her presence made the home, and without that I am alone. Her empty chair is the worst. It's the place I would always find her. Seeing that chair empty reminds me I am basically in a "home" with nothing, because it lacks the presence of my precious Mimi.

Words cannot describe the hatred I have towards the aftermath of my great loss. It has taught me that the presence of people is more important than anything, which breaks my heart, because that is what I lack. I don't have the presence of my Mimi to make me the happy girl I once was. I long to be with her again, but until that day I will fight the crashing waves and live in a world that is empty of her presence.

Madison Owen, Grade 10
Cypress Ranch High School, TX

Pirate Football Rewind 2011

With only eight returning seniors we thought it was going to be a rough season for West Side football, but it became even more frightening with so many injuries plaguing our team. With Brett Thornley sustaining injures in the first game against Firth, we were still able to hold the Cougars 14-13 for the win. Our next game was away against the Rich County Rebels. We ended up severely beating them 34-20. With that win under our belt, we would have no problem against Layton Christian, or that's what we thought. To the team's surprise, it was revealed to them that JD Cook's knees had again taken quite a beating in the Rich County game, leaving Trevor Montes the huge responsibility of filling his shoes. He and the team did an incredible job of pummeling Layton Christian 36-14. With the American Falls game fast approaching, Brett had finally recovered from his injury and was able to join his teammates on the field, which was much needed for the game against the undefeated Beavers. However the team came up just shy, 14-16 for the Beavers. With the Homecoming game fast approaching, JD Cook had finally recovered. He led the team to a grand victory over the Bear Lake Bears 27-6. Our next two games were close but went without incident; we iced Aberdeen 14-12 and beat Soda Springs 20-14. Finally, it was time for the long awaited district title game against our longtime rivals, the Malad Dragons. This game started with us scoring first and staying in the lead. Needless to say, we slaughtered the Malad Dragons 33-8, ending our regular season as district champions. Now it is time to RELOAD and take it to state!

Daz Buttars, Grade 12
West Side Sr High School, ID

Forever Hope

A wave of terror hits me. In an instant I feel the rush of heat flood my veins. My body moves only to tremble, my voice speaks only to cry. I stare at my reflection in my bedroom mirror. All I see is the stain of wet mascara and salty tears streaking my porcelain skin. Like a snap of my fingers I grab hold of myself. Now is not a time to show weakness, but to show strength. Now is the time to step up to the plate, rather than to back down.

Finding out my grandma would be fighting cancer for a third time was devastating. My grandma's everything to me. She has bright, mesmerizing eyes filled with life, spirit, and love. She has gentle wrinkles creasing her aged face and hair resembling the purity of new fallen snow on Christmas day. She even has a large bellowing laugh that could place a grin on Scrooge's face. I can't imagine her glorious smile wiped away, but with cancer I can.

Bearing witness to this uninvited guest twice before, I know how physically and emotionally draining it is. Cancer comes through and washes away every bit of life that exists inside you. It's on its own agenda and if not caught soon enough your body becomes its new grounds for exploration. Terror is just the beginning of my emotions, but I won't let it consume me. I stare again at my reflection in the mirror, this time seeing my eyes illuminating with hope.

Emily Gordon, Grade 11
The Woodlands College Park High School, TX

Nothing

Some people will complain about essays and then do an essay on nothing. If they are actually able to do an essay on nothing, wouldn't that be the same as not doing anything? You are not capable of imagining nothing because no one has been or is able to imagine nothing. Some people will say that they can imagine nothing, but when most people imagine nothing, they think of a void.

A void is something.

When talking about nothing, which politicians do well, it can become confusing since we have grown up thinking that nothing is simply the absence of anything entertaining. Even when someone tells us that there is "nothing" on TV, we just go with it. Thinking that there would ever truly be nothing on TV is not possible either, for if there was "nothing" on TV then the TV wouldn't exist either. There are several parts to this statement. Firstly; by saying that there would be "nothing" on TV you have left enough open with poor wording, so that anything in contact with the TV would be considered something. Secondly, if there was "nothing" on the TV, it would not be a TV; they are built to receive signals transmitted over the air. When there are no signals to receive there is still a blank screen. So, if no signals are being received, and nothing can be displayed, the TV no longer would function as it was intended and would not serve the strict purposes that TV's were designed for. When something that is invented by humanity loses its purpose or becomes obsolete, we get rid of it and it is quickly forgotten.

Caleb Schallenmuller, Grade 12
Rock Solid High School, CO

Dairy Scare

The dry Oklahoma air blew against my young face, forcing dust into my green eyes. The night had just begun and my brother Jordan and I were looking for something exciting to do. We were staying with my uncle Arlyn in his ranch home for the month of June and so far there was nothing to do. Uncle Arlyn, our great uncle pushing seventy, never wanted to play with us. Every night we would sit with him and watch the uninformative news, his face serious and intent.

His neighbor behind him had a large collection of dairy cows whose pasture connected to our uncle's fence. Looking out of his small one-story home, you could see the assortment of brown- and black-spotted dairy cows. On the third night of our visit, once uncle Arlyn had fallen asleep, Jordan came up with a great plan. "Let's go cow tipping!" He said ecstatically. I had heard about cow tipping, but I had never done it myself.

We snuck out wearing our PJ's and carefully climbed over the low wire fence to the soft fertilized grass. The cows were all sleeping, not moving at all, so Jordan went right up to one of the black spotted cows and began pushing almost effortlessly, before the hefty cow fell over on its side. It woke up frantic and started mooing excitedly. Jordan and I ran away with uncontrollable laughter, over the wire fence and back into our beds before anyone heard the chaos in the pasture. Thirty minutes later, our stern uncle came in with worry on his face. He told us about how a couple of kids had gone next door and disturbed the cows. He then winked at us and asked with a wide grin, "They're pretty funny, right?"

Rachel Bridgers, Grade 11
Seven Lakes High School, TX

Surroundings

It all started when the entire country became aware that an extremely dangerous hurricane was heading to the Gulf of Mexico. I remember asking my parents, "Is Hurricane Katrina going to hit us?" They told me, a curious little 10 year old, "We have no idea honey, it looks as if it will hit somewhere in Louisiana." It was a terrible feeling anticipation during the days before it hit land. My entire family lives in New Orleans and it really scared everyone around me. Finally, Hurricane Katrina made landfall in New Orleans while all my family and I got to do was watch. Knowing that your family could be in trouble and that there is nothing you can do is one of the worst feelings. As the storm progressed and weakened later in the week, we got news that all of my family was okay. All of this hurricane drama caused me to become a nervous wreck.

It wasn't until a few months later that I actually got to see the destruction that had resulted from this catastrophe. Seeing how everything had changed was really eye-opening. All of the things that I was used to seeing weren't there anymore. A lot of trees were destroyed and everything was gone. Seeing all of my family was truly a special moment. My mom's side of the family wasn't hit as hard, but was seriously affected. This hurricane really scared thousands of people and changed their personalities, including me.

Ross Hedges, Grade 10
Cypress Ranch High School, TX

Smart Man's Burden

What is the nature of the smart individual? This is difficult to answer. One could argue that the thinker spends so much time answering questions that only produce further questions, and, in this vain search, loses sight of his or her own desires, leaving the person forever unsatisfied. The same could also be said for the psychologist, who, like a mathematician, attempts to create equations, but for behavior, with individuals as variables, and repeats a pattern of life of their own creation. For them, seeing life as a system is enlightening, but sadly living in it is often melancholy.

However, the economist, another great mind, could and should argue that where one man loses, another gains. Often, in history, it is seen that the common man enjoys the fruits of the labor of the intellectual. For, the "smart" people of the world are usually the most profound shapers of it, and the shapers of the lives of other, perhaps less ingenious men. While this may not always be for the better, one cannot argue the magnitude of their effect.

Once again this raises further questions for the thinker. If we wish to inquire as to the nature of the intellectual, we must question the nature of the average man, as well. Each side envies the other to a degree. After all, a fool did not coin the phrase "Ignorance is bliss."

Alex Alberts, Grade 11
Plano West Sr High School, TX

Blindfold

"I really like this one guy." Typical words making up the normal conversations between middle school girls. "Who is it?" Typical response. "Lee Fulton!" Not so typical. I had had a crush on my best friend, Lee, since we first met. I had never had the courage to confess my feelings, and here was my close friend telling me that she wanted me to get them together. I couldn't breathe. I felt like Lee was getting farther from my grasp with that one phrase. "What are friends for?"

I took my usual seat in my next class and waited for my crush to sit beside me like always. However, I didn't feel my usual fluttering heart; instead I fell deeper into the dark that threatened to consume me completely. He walked into the room with his usual goofy smile. What if he smiled like that for her? I smiled back and we began our normal conversations. I couldn't take it! "Do you like someone?" It was all over his face that he did. The dark threatened to burst out of me as he described his dream girl. I left school that day numb to try and run from that terrible feeling.

When I saw him again, I couldn't look him in the eye, and when I remembered the image of the girl he described, a strange feeling replaced the dark taking over me. I felt that 'last chance' feeling and finally confessed everything. He gave me a serious look. I'VE RUINED EVERYTHING! Then he did something unexpected; he laughed. I began to feel an embarrassment that would have given me the courage to smack him, but then, he kissed me on the forehead. I stared back in shock. He smiled and said, "That girl I was talking about…was you."

Ashley Garrett, Grade 12
Seven Lakes High School, TX

The Truth On the Wise

Going into world history, my hopes were escalated high for my teacher; mother raved and brother adored his mighty wisdom. However, expectations were a little too high for I became disappointed and lost hope quickly. I began to derogate the "brash" teacher, dreading the end of the day and depriving seventh period of an upbeat personality. During Thanksgiving break, I was picking up cough medicine at Target when I saw Coach Metcalfe and his son dressed in basketball shorts and t-shirts. Because of my shock and blunt excitement of seeing him I quickly blurted, "What are you doing here?" with a huge hint of rude connotation, leading to a very awkward conversation. Honestly I did not realize my bitter remorse towards this man till the realization of negative comments and released tension through my actions and words. After the confrontation and the hate I had been hiding became evident, I slowly began seeing the good and accrediting how wonderful a teacher he really is. Now Coach Metcalfe has become my favorite teacher and my love for history has ascended for now I want to minor in History. People have always told me to look with open and new eyes for you never know who will surprise you. Little did I know how true the quote was until I experienced the truth on my own.

Madison Scott, Grade 11
Seven Lakes High School, TX

Wal-Mart Chocolate

Chocolate, its deliciousness discovered years ago, is a beautiful product of the theobroma tree's seeds; however, when I was younger, my foolish mother did not allow me to indulge in consuming the treat. Hence, I took matters into my own hands.

At the ripe age of four, my mother took me on a journey to the magically foreign land of WalMart. After an hour or so of searching for the best deals on items ranging from apples to Windex, my mother decided it was time to check out. Sitting in the cart, I watched in a state of melancholy as the boring healthy foods and cleaning items slid by the scanner while the candy by the register remained stationary. Suddenly, a beautiful plan hatched in my mind.

I climbed down to the bottom part of the cart, eyeing the young couple standing behind us in line. I realized that on this lower level, neither my mother nor the cashier could see if I hastily took some beloved Reese's mistakenly left on the lowest shelf. Giving the couple the death stare as they gawked over my baby-like face, I adeptly stuck my hand out, grabbed a handful of the beloved peanut butter cups, and shoved them in my pocket in one swift movement. Suddenly the cart started moving backwards, and I stayed in my hiding place as my mother rolled me away, keeping my eyes on the young couple laughing together, thinking: "She's going to be on America's Most Wanted one day."

I have never been caught for the WalMart incident, but every time I return to the store I keep away from the cameras, and try to forget the desperate measures I took for chocolate.

Madeline Kotarski, Grade 12
Seven Lakes High School, TX

Hero

What is a hero? Is a hero always a grown man wearing a cape? Or even the man who arrests the bad guys? No, a hero can be anybody. Whether it be your local firemen or the lady next door who survived cancer. And believe it or not, it can even be a toddler, and in this case, the toddler was me.

I am proud to say my dad is a firefighter. With him being a firefighter, his schedule made him pretty much a stay at home dad. On this particular day my dad was not completely there, he had a rough night at the fire station, but as a three year old I couldn't tell the difference until it was too late. My dad was serving my sister and me breakfast when all of a sudden he was laying on the floor with his mouth covered in blood.

I rushed to get him a paper towel to absorb the blood; it wasn't long until I realized that it was not helping. A sudden impulse had rushed over me to take my one year old sister and try and find a neighbor to help. Once we found a neighbor to call the paramedics everybody could breathe again.

Unknowingly, I had taught myself that even I could be a hero. I wasn't aware of this discovery until many years later, but I am humbled by the fact I could teach myself that lesson. I am thankful because of it and I am also sure that in the eyes of my dad I am a hero to him.

Alexa Trujillo, Grade 10
Cypress Ranch High School, TX

The Battle of Thermopylae

The Battle of Thermopylae was a shining example in human history where the few challenged the many and triumphed. A meager 300 Spartans challenged the overwhelming forces of the Persian Empire and annihilated a considerable portion of their forces over three grueling days.

Prior to 480 BC, Greece enjoyed a ten-year peace; it had successfully resisted against Persia before. Peace ended abruptly when Emperor Xerxes I decided to exact revenge upon the free people of Greece, sending hordes of soldiers to conquer the lands. Hastily preparing to counter the invasion, the Greeks sent a small army to hold the line against their Persian assailants.

The Greeks would not go down without a fight. Led by King Leonidas I, the force stood determined to fight off their enemies. By using the Phalanx Formation (where each warrior shielded the warrior to his right whilst brandishing his spear), the Spartans slaughtered the front line with a mere two casualties. They would continue their onslaught by defeating Xerxes' Immortals.

The next day held as much bloodshed against the Persian invaders as the previous. However, an unexpected element was placed into the equation; a traitorous Greek showed the Persians a route to flank the Spartans, ensuring their defeat. In what would become one of the greatest last stands in history, Leonidas and his men faced death with dignity and repelled a number of Persian soldiers. Eventually, their final act of bravery would drive the Greeks to rebel against the Persian Empire and ultimately triumph.

Grant Davis, Grade 12
Plano West Sr High School, TX

An Adventure of Fulfillment

It was the summer of 2011 as we marched on. The hot weather caused sweat to drizzle down our unprotected faces, our backs ached from the weight of our massive packs, and our water bottles swished back and forth, creating constant noise. We were at Philmont Scout Ranch, another day, and another mile to go.

It was day 6 of our long trek in the wastelands and acres of nothingness Philmont has to offer. Even though desolate with desert and drought conditions, Philmont still was beautiful. But the true beauty of Philmont we still had yet to see. Day 6 was special because out of our 10 day expedition, it was the day we were supposed to hike to the top of Mt. Baldy. Mt. Baldy is one of the foremost destinations at Philmont, and on day 6, the summit of Mt. Baldy would be ours.

We slowly dragged ourselves up the faceless mountain that was Baldy. Even though we were shaded by some tree cover, the sun still gave off intense rays that burned our skin. All that went through the minds of the 10 members of my crew was "One step forward...one step forward...one step forward." But as we got closer to the top, it seemed more and more worth it. We could see for miles, the desolate land of Philmont was shown, but also the patches of grass and the great river in the center of Philmont. But nothing could prepare us for the top of Baldy. We could see everything, Philmont's glory was at full force and we could see it all.

Reaching the top of Baldy and of Philmont shows you the world and its inherent beauty. It is fulfilling and entirely worth the slow drudge up.

Ben Stover, Grade 10
Cypress Ranch High School, TX

Fill in the Blank

Several years ago I met a girl named Theresa. At the time, I had been rather caste-less, without a specific niche that we all know our society is "secretly" made up of. In an unlikely turn of events, she and I began talking and eventually a friendship emerged. Over the course of a year this girl and I grew closer and, eventually, secrets began to become revealed. Theresa had lived a hard life filled with many atrocities. As I grew closer to her, I also began to slide into a depression.

A strange thing began to happen: while I became more indifferent and sad, Theresa became happier and more outgoing. Though she was not fully happy, she was much less depressed than she had been when we met. Even through the haze of my unhappiness, I caught glimpses of the good I was doing for her and it made me glad to be able to help her.

To this day, I remember her fondly. The times we were happy together and very close are some of the most memorable. We knew more about each other than we knew about ourselves and I still regret my part in her end. In my existence, I try to make those I love smile and ease whatever pain they may feel. Though the means for this change is dire, the end is not bad, I live my life based on the principles I gained from my time with Theresa, my closest and dearest friend.

William Laney, Grade 11
New Waverly High School, TX

Ignorance Is Quickly Spreading

In the south, racial tensions have always been high, but I never really thought anything of it until it directly affected me. Playful remarks between races are not always playful; some may think them benign, but I know the truth. There is always a facade covering the intended crippling pain beneath the words and the hatred inside the heart. That hatred is the spawn of ignorance and stereotypes. Some believe ignorance is not contagious. However, if that is true, then why do children of racist people turn out racist too? The most horrifying case occurred in my own family. My younger brother always hears my dad speak ill of black people, so one day he uttered a remark that nearly brought me to my knees. The worst part was the fact that at the time, my heart belonged to someone of a different race. Needless to say, my family members were not the only ones to judge me for it. Numerous close friends of mine shunned me in a sense. I became marked with a social stigma. Several friends of mine began to completely ignore me. When questioned, all they would answer was that it was because of my choices. I still lack the ability to grasp the concept of interracial relationships being wrong, and that is how I plan to raise my children. I want them to judge only by the kind of person someone really is, not what their race is.

Rebecca Kilgore, Grade 11
New Waverly High School, TX

Man's Best Friend

As a young girl, and an only child, I've always had a dog to be my companion. It wasn't until I lost that friend, that I realized how much I needed him. Chloe and Zach were my childhood companions and my best friends. I could tell them everything and never be judged.

Dogs are always important in a person's life. Especially for me, a dog was someone who wouldn't judge, was sad when I was, and always there to protect me. But, it also helped that they were big and strong as well. When both of them left me, I was devastated just as if I had lost a member of my family, because to me they were a member of my family. Today, they both still hold a special place in my heart, even though I have my little Prince now.

What makes a person so attached to their dog though? The idea that a dog could be so important it that they will love you unconditionally. Dogs don't need a fancy home and a home cooked meal every night. They are utterly loyal to their owners without asking questions. A dog will protect their owner from home even if they don't get their own bed in the house. But every dog is not the same in personality as well. Some are bratty, some are spoiled, and some are proud. There is the perfect dog for every person and for every personality type. Dogs may not always want the best things in the house, but they capture you heart so well that they certainly do deserve the best.

Lisa Lopez, Grade 11
La Serna High School, CA

What Comes with Seventeen

I find it really difficult to find out what I want to be when I grow up. Being a junior and seventeen, my parents want me to be a man about it and to just know. I don't. I'm afraid I never will. I don't want to be anything but a teenager. I know that as soon as I pick out and settle for that dream and tell my parents, I'll eventually lose whatever naive qualities that comes with being a teenager.

"Well, if you want to be a so-and-so then you have to study harder and work hard for it and to stop goofing around with your friends and blah blah blah." I can picture my dad saying with his heavy Filipino accent.

Like he already doesn't say it enough. I try to talk to my mom about it, and even though she's gentler and calmer about it, she still ends up saying the same thing as my dad.

"Boy that was pointless." I always take away from my conversations with my mom, saying it in my head because if I said it out loud then that would lead to another conversation and then to another and it would be all bad.

Back to the topic at hand, I don't know what I'm going to be in five years. I don't where I'm going to apply for college next year. I don't even know what I'm going to do tomorrow. The point is, I love where I am right now. I love not paying for insurance, rent, gas, and food. I love being a kid and spending money that was given to me. I love being young and I love enjoying it while it lasts.

Joshua Laquian, Grade 11
Washington High School, CA

July 1st

It was July 1 when I got the news. I had just gotten home from a fun day at my church camp, and that's when my day changed. I opened the door and saw my mom on the couch crying. She told me about the situation and we packed and my family headed towards San Antonio. The entire way the car was dead silent. We were thinking about what happened and we found out when we arrived. My aunt had been run over by a truck next to the hospital and now was in the hospital. We were heartbroken when we heard the news. We also found out that the driver was an elderly man who got angry and drove out of the hospital as fast as he could and lost control and hit my aunt. He was not even supposed to be driving. We spent the rest of the week in the hospital, praying for my aunt and spending time with our family. When my aunt got out of surgery and we got the okay to see her, we ran as fast as we could to see her. When we saw her, it didn't even look like her. She was in pain and looked horrible. We said our goodbyes, because the doctor told us she was not going to make it. We told her we loved her and left in tears. We comforted our family until they were fine to leave, and we started planning the funeral.

Fernando De Jesus, Grade 10
Cypress Ranch High School, TX

God Sees the Big Picture

Sometimes I think that we need to think about what we're doing before we do it, because we could do something that we might regret later and God says to have no regrets.

My family is going through a rough time right now and it's hard on all of us. I don't know what the truth is but I do know that God does and that whatever happens that God will be there with my family every step of the way. God is a miracle worker; He has the power and all the love in the world for you and me. Sometimes God does things in our lives that we cannot explain, or we ask Him, "Why me? Why did this happen to my family?" Only God knows the answer to that, and we just have to trust that He knows what He's doing and remember that He's the only one who can judge us, not anyone else.

Brianna Matero, Grade 11
Athens Christian Preparatory Academy, TX

Attraction vs Love

Attraction is just a feeling that you would get when you think someone is beautiful or handsome; love is a deep feeling and it doesn't matter if that person is an attractive person. Attraction is all about what meets the eye, but love is deeper. Love goes deeper than skin; it goes to the soul. When you are attracted to somebody you only like them because of what you see; it has nothing to do with that person's personality. When you love someone, you love them because of who they are inside, not who they are on the outside. So many people confuse these two things, because they think to love they must have attraction, but if they really loved that person they would not have to be attracted to them. Sadly, these days most people fall into attraction rather than fall in love.

Callie Moltz, Grade 10
Athens Christian Preparatory Academy, TX

Threads of Life

At the beginning of life for each individual human, the soul winks into existence, an endless treasure chest filled with priceless gems of emotion: glistening obsidian for anger, sparkling diamonds of joy, murky rubies of confusion, and many others. Every emotion that has ever been felt by man rests in the confines of the soul, tranquil for the time being, but capable of escaping in wild torrents or barely noticeable trickles. From birth to death, every second of life is a new experience, for each moment in time adds on to prior experiences and influences one's views of life. As soon as man is affected by an event, one, two, or many emotion-gems escape their boundaries and embed themselves onto the box, immediately transforming into brilliant threads of color that weave together. Depending on the experience, the emotion-gems may be of various size and quality; for instance, if one suddenly discovered that a tragic accident had befallen a close friend, an enormous, shimmering opal — the overwhelming sadness that is felt — might slip out. Over time, more opals may emerge from the bottomless box, but as the sadness recedes, the opals diminish in size and luster. However, all of these emotion-gems, as soon as they leave the box, decorate the outside of the treasure chest — the soul — as memories, building up an intricate mosaic of colors that will influence the rest of one's life. Of course, over time, the gem-threads fray and dull; most become forgotten memories, too insignificant in the complex tapestry of life to consider anymore. The more important memory-threads retain their beauty longer, leaving a greater impact on how one acts and thinks in the future.

Ivonnie Shih, Grade 11
Mission San Jose High School, CA

A Grateful Hero

"Heil Hitler!" rang through the streets of the Netherlands in the year 1940. The terrible wrath of the Germans had just begun, and Ralph Hamburger was only a junior in high school. He needed to make a decision quickly. Would he join or fight? Every day, busloads of Jews were dragged off the streets and driven away to their deaths. Ralph knew in his heart that he had to fight. Against his parents' wishes, he joined a peaceful resistance group, determined to do what was right. His task was recruiting willing Dutch families and building hiding places for Jews to stay in their homes. In addition, he was assigned the dangerous job of making new registration cards for the Jews in hiding. This was a high-stakes task. Everything had to be just right or he would be responsible for an innocent death. Becoming an expert forger, Ralph made many types of documents. On one occasion, he forged hospital release papers to save a disabled girl from death, and even drove the taxi that helped her escape! How could a man so close to danger and death survive? The answer to this question is the fact that God was on his side. He was, and still is, a deeply devoted Christian. He gives credit to God for everything in his life. Today, eighty-eight-year-old Ralph Hamburger simply describes himself as "the most grateful man alive."

Katie Blackmore, Grade 10
Whittier Christian High School, CA

You Were A Warrior Once

You've probably forgotten, but you were a warrior once. You had the sky at your command, the earth beneath your feet, the world at your fingertips, and the voice of thunder. You led your people to war and then to peace. You were fearless, strong, and resilient.

But somehow, somewhere along the way, you lost an angel. You had forgotten how to be fearless, so your heart turned dark under that tanned skin and your eyes grew cold under those warm pupils. Fear replaced strength, and soon you had lost your grace.

Still, you fooled yourself into thinking you were forging stars from the fallen, when in fact, you were racing to rescue your own. You were afraid, deathly afraid, that someone would pull you too hard and your joints would pop apart like a paper figurine, your fingers would be dancing on the floor, and you would be such a mess — still fighting, fighting to keep your past.

But never again did you regain your grace, your sense of gravity. Fear had lifted your heels off the ground, off balance, and thrown you to fend for yourself, your sky, your earth, and your thunder.

So now you speak. You converse, politely. In a civilized manner. Fear has crippled your strength, so now your fingertips no longer touch the sky and your arms no longer embrace the weight of the world.

You've probably forgotten by now, but you truly were a warrior once.

Ke Zhao, Grade 11
Amador Valley High School, CA

How Can You Possibly Understand?

We all have times in our lives where we're having a bad day and don't want to be messed with. But how can you possibly understand what it's like to feel that way for the rest of your life? I don't understand why people think they can relate to you when you're diagnosed with depression.

A mental disorder that takes away everything you love and care about, as if it didn't matter. That blasted disorder took away my friends, my family, and finally all my efforts of trying to smile. You took away the ability to finally find happiness after each disaster in my life. I deal with you every day of my life and I survive somehow, but when the average human being comes up and yells, "It's all your fault!", that's where I draw the line!

Every emotion we feel and pain we endure, no human feels the same, so how can you tell me that I'm being the spoiled brat? We all experience many disasters, heartaches, and drama differently and attempt to fix the situations, so how can you sit there, with the love of your life and friends by your side supporting you, accusing me that I do not try! You'll never fully understand what happens in my life behind the closed doors, the truth behind the pain, the people I've been forced to say goodbye to for their happiness, because you will never know what true depression possibly means.

Ruby-Ann Tran, Grade 11
Vista Ridge High School, TX

Words

When I was young my parents told me to always look for the good in others. I'll tell someone when they have spinach in their teeth in a polite and private way only because I know that is what most people want you to do. However it has never occurred to me to tell another person to fix their hair, or eyebrows, or tell them that they need to lose weight. Maybe because my parents told me to look for the good when I was younger, the thought never crossed my mind, and after an incident I had with a close friend I learned words really do hurt and what you say really does matter.

My close friend and I were sitting in the back during gym class chatting away like we always did. The previous night I got my eyebrows done and she was complimenting them.

Suddenly she looked at me as though she was examining my face and critically said "they're a little uneven though." Then she searched my face again and spoke "and you have some acne on your forehead you need to get rid of, and your face is getting a little chunky."

All of my insides seemed to fall and I suppose she saw the disappointment cross my face because she laughed as if to lighten the mood.

Then in an attempt to get the sad look out of my eye she laughed out an "oh baby I'm just kidding you know I think you're pretty," but it was too late I was already insecure and ready to hide under a rock where no one could see my hideous face.

The words she spoke produced insecurity in me. She did not look for the good in me and I felt worthless.

Leah Moonesan, Grade 12
Seven Lakes High School, TX

Abortion: Does Legal Mean Right?

Abortion is the deliberate murder of an unborn child by surgical means, through the removal of an embryo or fetus from the womb. At this stage, a fetus is more than just a piece of tissue inside a mother's womb; it is a human life ready to walk the face of the Earth. Abortion proves otherwise. Imagine if you were the baby about to be aborted and no one could hear you. Silenced, afraid, and pain-stricken. After all, what did an innocent child do to deserve death?

Abortion has quickly become among the leading causes of death in America. Although abortion is legal in America under Roe v. Wade, we must keep in mind that what is legal is not always justified. Abortion has quickly become a norm in society, and those who agree with abortion share one thing in common: they have all been born. Humans do not have the right to intervene in authoritatively judging the beginning or ending of life, but do so regardless. Is this justice, is this equality, is this destiny? We are given the gift of free will to discern right from wrong. We shall not kill; rather, we should love with the fullest of affection. To nurture is kindness, to kill is hatred. The golden rule is "Do unto others as you would have others do unto you." Is this how you would want to be treated by others? I did not think so.

Kassandra Diaz, Grade 12
Bourgade Catholic High School, AZ

On Love and Loss

Love and loss are one and the same. When you love someone, the inevitability of losing them is wrenching. And when one loses, feelings of compassion and love surface in the people around the devastated friend. This past winter break our community lost one of its cherished youth. A tragic car accident robbed him of his life. The effects of this event on the community were abundant. Even many people who did not personally know this young man have participated in the grieving. The overwhelming pain that radiated off of his mother was enough to open up any one's heart and send them into a state of depression. It is inspiring to see how much one boy, one number, one talent, one night could change an entire community. The effects are withstanding. It has reunited old friends, raised a cautious hand, and reminded all of us that death knows no age. So as tragic as this event was, did it have some positive effects? For with loss also comes strength. So through this horrible loss we have become strong enough to pick ourselves back up and carry on as a community in our everyday lives. Our love forever lives in his name and our strength grows forever in his memory.

Kylie Nunmaker, Grade 11
Seven Lakes High School, TX

Hourglass

The glass shakes.

Inner discussions twist inside my head like a sandstorm, raging and railing against each other with good and bad reasons, pros and cons, but no clear outcome. Who knows which one, which course of action, is one of those grains of sand that will manage to stay on the surface when the weather subsides?

With conflict writhing within me, I emerge from my room, noticing only that which will consume. I discard the ideas, the drops of sand, one by one, ignoring them as they go. Which precious grain will remain on the top, I do not yet know.

The sand settles.

But it does not matter. The raging sandstorm will always be within me; each idea is not deleted but put aside. I may choose to focus on one for the moment, but the others will always be there in my mind, waiting.

And then the glass will shake again, and the sand will settle once more.

Kyra Jensen, Grade 12
Edison High School, CA

The Rest of My Life

Today is the first day of the rest of my life. In a way, if the rest of my life was a huge timeline, then this day would be at the beginning, making this day the first day. But on another hand, my life has, in fact, already begun. A long time ago I started living every day with a purpose. My purpose for each day may vary. But the fact that this may be the last day of the rest of my life is why I have a purpose for every day. Living through Christ is my purpose in life.

Caroline Perryman, Grade 10
Athens Christian Preparatory Academy, TX

Oh No He Didn't

"Lindsey you have to do this for me! Please! I want to know if Beau can tell! Lindsey please!" After hearing this constant nagging for four days I finally agreed to the task my sister Sarah wanted me to perform. Sarah and I look exactly alike, or so we have been told, though I have never understood the confusion people feel when we both walk in a room. Sarah wanted me to walk into the store her ex-boyfriend worked at and see if he could tell the difference between us, because he has never actually seen me in person.

When we got to his store, I prayed that he wasn't working today, because even though Sarah and I look alike, we're completely different. I wasn't sure how I was going to pass as her. To my misfortune, he was working. Sarah told me she would wait in the car and after ten minutes she was going to walk in. I took a gulp and walked into the store. After walking around for a few minute eye-stalking Beau and Beau eye-stalking me, he finally approached me.

"Sarah, I miss you! I know that I was the one that ended it, I was wrong and I am so sorry, I realized after we broke up that not having you in my life was a big mistake. I really hope that over time we can get back to what we had before." Then without warning he leaned over and kissed me! I didn't know what to do, and was relieved when my sister walked up to him and tapped him on the shoulder. She smacks him across that face and took my hand and we walked out of the store, without me having to say a word.

Lindsey Kreitlein, Grade 11
Seven Lakes High School, TX

From Boy to Man

The summer of 2011 proved to have an extreme amount of difficulty for not just myself but my sister as well. After everything that happens to people in this world, becoming strong has become mandatory. Once my mother went into the hospital, I knew that it was time for me to become a man.

After becoming pregnant again, my mother had complications and became a permanent guest at the hospital for over three months. While my mother stayed in the hospital, I became the caretaker of my little sister Keanna because my father didn't have the time. After my mother stayed in the hospital for two days, my sister realized she was not coming home for a while, and that did not settle well for her.

Weeks went by, and still no mommy at home, and the situation became harder and harder. From getting only two hours of sleep, doing my homework and helping with hers, it was by no means a trouble-free accomplishment. When it became apparent that I kept burning the candle at both ends, I looked to my mother for some serious strength. "Tristan, you have grown up so much stronger than I expected and I know you can do this."

After all the groaning and moaning for mommy, I finally had proven that I could take care of myself and that I was a man. Once my mother came home with my baby brother Devan, I knew that she had never been so proud of me.

Tristan Price, Grade 11
New Waverly High School, TX

Earth's Children

Earth's children see much, hear much, and know much yet somehow humankind foolishly refuses the insights of the young. "They are naive, inexperienced, and have seen next to nothing of how our world works," high-nosed elders scoff while shaking their prestigious minds. "What have they to tell us of the world in which we ourselves live?" Due to these stubborn views from previously implied superiors, children remain an untapped treasure, an unclaimed wealth, a forgotten lore to disappointed people. We ignore these immensely creative, imaginative, under-appreciated souls by narrowing our focus to established human restrictions given precedence by our wise yet distinctly dissimilar ancestors. In precious early years of development, we as human beings encounter this world equipped with an enviable open mind, limitless imagination (nearly always lost later), and innovative and thereby coveted ideas. Why do we irresponsibly lose these crucial keys to our world? Why must we imprudently misplace these items of intrinsic value? A child's eyes penetrate even the deepest and most dangerous depths of your soul and silently record their findings. Beware: for these little ones hold some of the true underlying meanings beneath our too human world.

Shelby Brooks, Grade 11
Lovejoy High School, TX

Nothing Is Impossible

I can do all things through Christ who strengthens me. Anything is possible through Jesus. A man who was about to be taken off of life support and die somehow managed to pull through, even though many doctors and specialists said he had no hope. This was a miracle that can only happen because of our Lord and Savior, Jesus Christ. Many of the famous basketball players, baseball players, and football players have tragic upbringings and it is only through miracles of God that they have come out on top, and been so successful. They were in the dumps and nothing was right, yet Jesus Christ came through when they doubted. Even in the worst situations nothing is impossible. All one has to do is trust in Jesus and ask for help. Jesus is the answer, the key to making anything possible.

Jordan San Miguel, Grade 10
Athens Christian Preparatory Academy, TX

Inspiring Sounds

Music is our universal language, it's who we are. You hear it on the street, on your phone, even in your head. Some of us think of it as entertainment, others may see it as an escape. All of us, though, share one thing: the inspiration music provides for us. Have you ever heard a song where you wanted to get up, jump around and go crazy? We can all relate. Some of us are blind though, not seeing the true genius behind it. Music is artwork, believe it or not. Those certain sounds fill you with joy. It not only inspires me, but thousands of others to follow their dreams. It relaxes you and helps you think beyond whatever it might be. That's why I love music so much.

Evan Boneta, Grade 10
Cypress Ranch High School, TX

Where the Wind Blows

Birds chirping, a cool breeze on my back, and the spray of cool water against my legs, in other words: paradise. Once I visited Yosemite National Park, I fell in love with the scenic waterfall area. The sound of the water crashing down the rocks and gurgling down the mountain in a creek transports you to a site nearby the ocean. As it tumbled down, the water glinted with the shine of the brilliant sun. Crisp, clean air filled my nose as I breathed in the sweet smelling spray of pristine water. I pulled off my shoes and dipped my toes into the chilly water that sent a shiver down my spine. Water washed over my toes as if cleansing my body of its impurities. Nearby trees danced in the wind as their leaves jostled from the power of the waterfall. As I surveyed the scene, I imagined it could have been something as fantastical as the beautiful cascades of Shangri-La. Animals bounded around the falls and grazed on the green, lush meadows of grass. Deer roamed the surrounding area and birds chirped mating calls to each other from the treetops. I climbed the rocks that lined the outside of the waterfall and tried to go behind it. To my delight, I saw a lush abundance of green plants and beautiful flowers that grew nurtured behind the waterfall. Bright sunlight and an easy supply of water allowed the flowers and plants to grow to their maximum potential and create a garden of paradise to add to the beautiful scene. I remember vividly the day when I first visited the beautiful waterfall at Yosemite National Park, and I shall never forget it.

Suhitha Veeravelli, Grade 11
Desert Vista High School, AZ

Perception

I live a fairly mundane life; attention to the nature of social interactions between my fellow human beings never was a key purpose of my existence—in all honestly I found it quite exhausting to pay any mind to others' daily interactions. Racial profiling, by no means seemed prominent in our society when I acquired a moment to make observations.

This all changed once I started dating my Arabic boyfriend: Omar. To me Omar was just a run-of-the-mill teenage guy. His racial fabrication of Arabic and British never fazed me. He was different, and in my opinion different did not have a negative connotation, for difference is what makes human beings individuals. Months later, a woman I had known for many years began to make racist comments about the Arabic culture; claiming they all had terroristic thoughts of destruction. Soon I found myself infuriated as I viewed a post littered with an abundance of profanity. I seemed to vibrated from rage within as likes and comments appeared underneath. This wasn't a limited view quarantined within an area; it was indeed a widespread hatred of a people. The same breed of hatred that influenced so many German citizens to eradicate the Jewish population without a second thought. Before I met Omar, I was blind to the hatred that still lingered like the smell of smoke after a forest fire. I am forever indebted to him for changing my perception of racism.

Katelin Herzog, Grade 11
New Waverly High School, TX

The Shortcut

I am lazy. I'll be the first to admit it. All my life I've been lazy.

Even at six years old, I was lazy. My mom, on the other hand, was not: in fact, she would only wash dishes by hand— she would not allow dishwasher use in her house. Luckily, the chore of washing dishes never fell on my six-year-old shoulders.

Until one day. Being lazy, I did not want to wash dishes. Instead of complaining, though, I sucked it up and did the chore. Except I was secretly plotting my revenge: I would never let this happen to me again. But how best to exact vengeance upon my mother? That was the ultimate question.

Then the answer hit me. It was simple; it was perfect.

Armed with sponge and soap, I set to work. My hands were soaked with water, and the bowl was slick with soap, so it was perfectly plausible that the bowl simply slipped from my grip. Nevertheless, my mother forbade me from ever washing dishes again.

Just what I wanted!

So I cleaned up the shattered bowl fragments and scampered away cheerfully. As irony would have it, my right foot happened upon an overlooked shard of glass — a jagged piece which stuck deeply into the flesh. I had never felt such pain in my short life!

Howling in agony, I was dragged to the bathroom by my parents, who hoisted my foot into the sink and promptly ripped out the interloping glass. Gallons of crimson blood filled the basin, and my brief life flashed before my eyes.

Well, that was the end of that. My foot healed up fine, leaving a decent scar; I didn't even get stitches, though I probably needed them. Ah, but I haven't washed a single dish since.

Brett Connors, Grade 12
Seven Lakes High School, TX

Kendo

The art of Kendo has always interested me. Kendo is an sword form that is a direct descendant of the sword schools seen when the samurai became dormant in Japan. Kendo was practiced as a non-lethal way of fighting with the sword. Using only shinai (bamboo swords) and sometimes bokken (wooden swords) as well as bogu (sparring armor), it teaches the students to have absolute respect for each other, bushido (the way of the samurai), and to have fun.

Kendo may seem like just a fighting system with a sword but it really isn't. It's a art form. It's an art of peace. The creators of Kendo created it to have the same components as any sword school; the only difference is its non-lethal nature. They wanted everyone to enjoy and learn from Kendo, without the risk of dying.

Today, Kendo is still practiced as it was back then. It is a international sport, obtaining many students of Kendo from Japan to the U.S. Kendo is possibly the last remnant of the noble samurai and the inheritor of a tradition of honor and glory.

Jamie Tran, Grade 12
Fossil Ridge High School, TX

On Nestle (Honestly)

It was the cool summer of '06, and while my friends were biking in the breeze that carried a touch of winter, I stayed in a cramped living room, waiting impatiently for the full hour. Every devoted fan knows that Teen Titans starts at exactly 4:02 pm; and, as a devoted fan, I was always on the television by 3:58, when I can catch the end of Martin Mystery, and the introduction to my favorite cartoon. Setting down a plate of chocolate cookies, I curled up on the brown couch with a mug of iced hot chocolate. During that first commercial break, I pulled out the envelope for the drink. Nestle, figures. My mother always bought Nestle; no matter how much I protested with arguments of "Child Labor" or "Unethical Planting," a box of Nestle products always ended up at home.

I took a bite of the cookies, and I swallowed without thinking. Sweet, bitter, potently fragrant, the taste reminded me of the past. I forced myself from the memories when the show returned, but like those chunks of dark chocolate, bitter memories stayed heavily on my tongue. The half hour passed with a blur, and as I pulled myself away from that screen, I dropped my mug on the kitchen table, and threw the plate into the sink. I knew I couldn't stay alone forever.

Memories, dreams, childhood and wishes all came flooding in, and I allowed them. So many years later, I barely accepted those years of life. However, when I took that bite of Nestle chocolate, I can only remember that icy summer when I pulled out my bike to join my friends as I came to terms with myself.

Shuyin Yu, Grade 10
Seven Lakes High School, TX

A Simple Inspiration

At a very delicate age, I learned from my grandmother that life was not always going to be easy. My father worked, my mother lived in America and my aunts and uncles lived in their separate houses. My grandmother and my grandfather were the ones that took care of me. They fed me, clothed me, and sheltered me. Though I loved my grandfather, he was somewhat harsh when he spoke. He was a very blunt man. He told me I couldn't sing. I cried for awhile, but it was something I had to get over. I couldn't base my whole life over one failure. I looked for a reason to keep singing and found that reason in my grandmother.

The funny thing is she didn't even attempt to make me look up to her, all she did was live her life. My grandparents owned a shop and a farm which they both monitored, but incidents occurred and my grandfather had difficulty walking. My grandmother took her role as provider seriously and did not complain as she cared for me, my grandfather, the shop, the farm, and any other relatives that came to visit us. I admired the way she kept smiling though she worked hard day and night. She was the one who taught me that life might be hard at times, but as long as I apply myself I could be anything I wanted. Now I am the alto section leader of my Varsity Choir and I have her to thank. I am extremely grateful for her inspiration, dedication, and sweet words of kindness.

Monique Morris, Grade 12
Kerr High School, TX

On Aimless Tomfoolery

We were waltzing about town, as tangoing about town required too much effort and none of us had the right rhythm. It was a midsummer-night's afternoon and our unfocused, unorganized and objective-less wandering was going exactly as planned. It was just me, and few of my friends.

Eventually, we ran into a book store, but they threw us out for running in the store, so we went into a Walgreen's instead.

I don't know what Walgreen's was implying by exclusively putting toys in the "Office Supplies" aisle, but it spoke negatively of the productivity of the regional office workers. I also don't know what they were implying by exclusively putting office supplies in the "Toys" aisle, but it spoke negatively of the capability of the guy who puts up signs.

Despite these issues, one of my friends and I managed to find the most essential office supply of all, the toy foam sword. There were several different copies of this invaluable tool, along with associated products such as the toy foam shield, the toy foam mace, and the toy foam piece of foam, which, now that I think about it, may have been just a piece of foam.

Regardless, as classy sophisticated connoisseurs of toy foam weapons, we did what any cultured and well-mannered person would do in our position; start a toy sword fight.

Kicking us out of the store was their second mistake, (their first mistake was letting us in), as outside the store, we had access to the wonderful world of shopping carts. Now, the underground shopping cart drag races as depicted in movies are as untrue and made up as the existence of movies that depict them, but that did not stop us from trying to recreate them. The brick wall, however, did.

Kyle VanderHeyden, Grade 12
Seven Lakes High School, TX

Brief Paradise

The California sun peeked through a small clear patch in the overcast sky. We all stopped our bikes and reveled in the glowing warmth that we had missed so much throughout the day. There on the pathway between the shimmering beach and the beautiful little beach houses we found a brief paradise like we had expected to come from our vacation.

We continued our ride down the path, watching the ocean glisten and the waves crash lightly along the shore in the low tide. The beach houses glowed with a new beauty with the help of the sun's rays. The large bay windows reflected the beach and ocean and we could see ourselves on our bikes as we rode by the mirror-like glass.

People began to step out of their little homes on their balconies and patios, many with drinks in hand and friends or relatives accompanying them, and we would simply wave as we rode by.

We stopped at a pier with a shake shack at the far end and parked our bikes. As we reached the small structure, the sun dipped back behind the clouds and the sky reverted back to overcast, but the memory of paradise stayed locked in our minds.

Tim Lawrence, Grade 12
Woods Cross High School, UT

Is the Practice of Abortion Ethical?

Abortion, a highly controversial topic, limits itself to one question: should we continue to merely listen and watch as unborn, innocent children die without the dignified right to life? Abortion has become a norm and has become accepted in modern-day society, although it is deliberate murder of an unborn child. Abortion is unfair because it takes away an infant's right to life and is ethically wrong, although the controversy is subjective. I question your stance, and wonder, is abortion prudent, is it moral, is it just? We were all meant to live; therefore, no human should have the right to disturb this or choose the destiny of another person. We should respect the dignity of all people in this way, no matter how small they are, or even if they have not been born into this world yet.

Imagine awaiting birth but, instead, being thrust out of your home with cruelty, the hatred of your own mother surrounding you: clueless, there you are, feeling unloved, only to know that you are silenced and can do nothing about your fatality. Through the actions of abortion, one is intending death for an unborn, innocent infant who has done nothing to deserve the punishment of death. Immoral, impractical, inane — these are the words that describe the practice of abortion. Nothing good can come from the cruel, undignified practice of abortion. Abortion, as it is, is deliberate murder. If you believe that abortion is a choice on behalf of the mother, then think again, because, with abortion, death is always around the corner. There is no way that any deliberate murder can be justified, because there should never be an exception or legitimate reason for any form of fatal means.

Priscylla Diaz, Grade 12
Bourgade Catholic High School, AZ

Is Photography Me?

Images, photographs, pictures. No matter what you call them, I take them. I am a notches when it comes to pictures. Just ask people that know me, if you don't believe me. My camera is on me 24:7. I am constantly whipping it out and clicking the button. The button itself, to me, has a bright flashing neon sign above it, even though that isn't possible. It's just my imagination running wild. My use of a camera can sometimes scare people, infuriate them, or make them happy that I am documenting a memory. People who don't know me are completely confused as to why I am always taking pictures. People who know me, on the other hand, sometimes run before I can catch them, or they will attempt to hide. Neither of those works well, because I can manipulate those things into realistic photographs. Every image I capture, I will in some way use in the art of my photography. I'm not sure exactly when I became obsessed with my camera, but it has been going on for four plus years. With my camera, I create what different people call different things, whether it is art, crap, beauty, essence, perspective, creative, pure, or of the world around us. Photography is a part of my life, my world, and me. In fact, photography is, in a way, actually me. So, what do you think? Is photography me, or am I photography?

Alexandra Berrett, Grade 11
Woods Cross High School, UT

The Video Game Designer

The game designer is a position that I, along with a lot of teenagers around the world who have a passion for gaming, would like to have when we are older and thrust into the open world. Even though I know the hardships, I still wish to see my ideas come to life in a video game.

The video game designer has a very hard job, and this is not well known. It takes many hours of hard work to make a high quality game, like the big franchises are known for. Bethesda spent 5 years working on their latest installment of The Elder Scrolls. The amount of work that goes into these games is amazing. First off, the designer has to make an initial design of the game, through rough stories and story boards. Once that is over with, they start by making a very detailed plan called a design document. In this document, they think of everything they can and put it into this document. This may include the maps of the levels, the setting and flow chats to show how the events may take place. It may also include all of the sound design and visual design, the plot and characters with drawings. Once they take that to the rest of their team, they can start designing the best part of the game, what makes it a challenge, this may come in the form of puzzles, bosses, or cunning AI. Once they do this, they can start cramming in hours as deadlines come and go, and the finished product is put on shelves.

All in all, the video game designer can have a rough job at times, with long hours and working weekends to meet deadlines, but it can still be a very fun experience.

Marco Marioni, Grade 10
Cypress Ranch High School, TX

Helpless

The worst sight in the world is seeing someone you love in pain. The most difficult feeling is being helpless; knowing there is absolutely nothing you can do for them, except be there — no matter how difficult.

I walked out of my math class to answer the fourth call I had received from my dad in ten minutes. I pressed the green button and immediately heard screams of "Call 911. I need an ambulance. Come home NOW!" I ran back into the class, grabbed my stuff, and told my teacher I was leaving. I sprinted to my car as fast as my body could carry me. The rest of the experience feels surreal. Seeing him in his bed, screaming. Dialing those three little numbers. Seeing four paramedics and a cop walk into my house. Feeling quick, hot tears roll down my face and hearing sobs, not recognizing them as my own. Watching my dad get three doses of morphine just so he could stand, and still screaming the whole way to the ambulance. The sight of him being loaded onto a gurney, then into the back of that red truck will never leave my mind. Jumping in my car to follow the wailing sirens to the emergency room. Seeing him screaming in the hospital bed, with no one trying to help him. Though I was a distraught mess, I had to put that aside and be strong for him. I let everything else go, and simply held his trembling hand.

Kassidy Beckstrand, Grade 12
Woods Cross High School, UT

Time Crunch

I glanced around nervously, wiping my sweaty hands on my jeans. Trying to write while surrounded by a classroom full of loud noise is not easy. A plastic ball flew around the room between people, slapping against each person's palm. The teacher came through the door and the room fell to a low buzz.

"Jacob, give me the ball," the teacher's voice boomed. "Some people are still working on —"

"I'll be back!" a shrill voice pierced the air and a short girl left the room.

"Quick! Lock her out," Derek whispered. But before the teacher could move, a shadowy figure seeped through the door and snuck to his seat.

"Darius, late again," the teacher murmured. "Back to work everyone."

A few minutes later, the short girl reappeared at the door and scurried to her desk. Groans filled the room at her arrival.

"Y'all know you love me," she squeaked, smiling.

"Sure we do," Hudson replied sarcastically. The girl glared at him before whipping her head around to talk to someone. I rubbed my temples. I had ten minutes left to write this essay. Miraculously, an idea appeared in my mind and the rusty gears began to spin. My pencil raced against the clock and I finished the last sentence as the bell rang. With a smug expression, I handed my paper to the teacher, imagining him sitting at his desk, reading the first sentence of my story.

"I glanced around nervously, wiping my sweaty hands on my jeans…"

Zoe Garner, Grade 10
Cypress Ranch High School, TX

My Hero

Have you ever had a time in your life when you work towards something for so long, and then don't get the results you hoped for? I have had that type of experience happen to me many times, but every time I get this feeling, I just think of Kayla and how she reacts to situations like this.

I have known Kayla for many years, and knew that she always came in second best. However, she always persevered. All those years I just blew it off and never truly understood. That is, until last year, when I realized how strong she is.

During Kayla's senior year, she went to the all-area competition on clarinet with high hopes of making state. She had been practicing this music for six months and was confident that this would be her year. I had heard her practice many times and needless to say, she was a maestro. However, when I received the news that she had not reached her goal, I expected her to be completely devastated. However, what I saw was a perfectly happy eighteen year old who looked as if nothing bad had ever happened.

This is what made me realize what kind of a person it takes to overcome something terrible and devastating. She taught me that no matter what life throws at you, you have to be able to overlook it and realize that it will only make you stronger as a person. She will always be my inspiration, mentor and hero.

Megan Steere, Grade 10
Cypress Ranch High School, TX

Violence

Violence. It's something that happens in our world. We can't control, it just happens. Thousands, maybe even millions of people know or have loved ones who fight for the freedom of our nation. Who risk their lives to protect others so we are not controlled by someone who will hurt and damage this nation. Those are the people who experience violence. The men and women who fight for our nation's freedom are the freedom fighters. They are strong, willing people who don't know if they will be coming home to see the tears welling up in the eyes or the smiles that come to the face of the loved ones they know. Those are the people that we need care for. The days when the airports are full of women, men, and even children are the days when the freedom fighters come home. The days when they get breaks from fighting for the nation on which we stand. When the people who know loved ones finally get to see their beautiful faces after months or years of fighting, joy fills them and tears burst from their eyes, knowing that their son or daughter or other family members is home and away from harm. But those who don't get to see the beautiful faces of the solider they once loved and knew burst into tears, knowing that they weren't there to protect them and keep them safe like they did for us. But they know that the proud and brave solider will always and forever be remembered, that they protected us from the harsh people who try to take over, and they know that they will be in each other's heart whether they are here on earth or up in heaven. The freedom fighters will always be loved and remembered."

Shelby Schmitt, Grade 10
Cypress Ranch High School, TX

Love for Homework

I love homework. Students may gawk and educators may rejoice upon hearing this, but I do not love homework for any scholarly reason. I used to resent doing my nightly assignments. Homework has made me realize, however, that humans are given a powerful and wonderful gift: the ability to change. We can shape our thoughts, alter our actions and transcend our situation like no other species can. And so I decided to love homework — because I can.

Of course, this wasn't easy. When I sat down to read about Mesopotamia or solve logarithmic equations, I found myself thinking about music, games, or the spots on the window. To abate this procrastination, I stopped myself and made a conscious decision to put my heart and soul into finishing my work. Putting so much of myself into what I was doing fostered a deep love inside me for my homework, for giving love and feeling love are often one and the same. I realized that I can do this with anything I do: I have the power to love instead of hate.

Homework is still not something that I would choose to do over talking with friends or looking at art, but it has brought me to discover the power of change within myself. I am less subject to the vagaries of a human life because I can choose how I feel about any situation. For showing me how to put my love into everything I do, I love homework.

Allison Yuen, Grade 11
Los Altos High School, CA

July the 4th Explosions

Greg White's 18th birthday party fell on the evening of July the 4th 2011. I only watched as chicken fights took place in the pool. The boys stumbled dangerously close to the edge. The girls struggled to push each other off the other boy's shoulders. Soon, packs of glow sticks were introduced to the party. It was now completely dark outside and we decided to climb up the blowup slide. After immersing ourselves in the chilled hose water, and several crash landings later, the fun ceased. An adrenaline-rushing game of tag in the dark was next. The safety was truly impeccable. The glow sticks offered plenty of light and even though the area was entirely new to me, it seemed innocuous.

First, Greg – a varsity runner – was the tagger. It was impossible to outrun him. First, we tried an obvious spot; only barely out of sight. But the group rushed away into the darkness after reconsidering. I lagged behind, careful to avoid holes in the ground and any uneven terrain. Finally, I spotted dark figures in an open workshop space. He was approaching quickly. The group was on the move again and I was determined to escape. I glanced ahead at Lauryn and began sprinting in her direction. I took a final look over my shoulder, wondering how near he was.

Suddenly, a loud noise exploded in my ears. My forehead throbbed intensely. I tried laughing at myself, while questioning how I hadn't seen a wooden pole. I lifted my hand and a red liquid seeped onto my fingers. I gazed up at Lauryn, whose eyes filled with concern. In a moment, there was panic. Devin screamed for help. At that, I was rushed to the ER, the most careful of them all.

Erica Brown, Grade 10
Seven Lakes High School, TX

River of Change

Change is something you can always count on being there. The ability to adapt and survive is what makes us stronger; if we allow circumstance to knock us down and we don't get up and try to survive we will be consumed by the winds of chance. Just because change is always there, you never know when it is going to strike, like a snake in the grass poised and ready to deliver a fatal blow.

The day change decided to really sink its fangs into me was the day I lost my father. After he died my life was nothing but a river of change, and I laid hopelessly at the bottom watching as my life flew by. Everything was changing and I was just letting my life flow by like leaves floating downstream. Before he died everything seemed stable to me, he was my rock in life, but after he passed my whole life seemed liquid. I felt as though my very existence was fluid and everything was crashing around me like a tsunami. That one change, the loss of my father, broke me and I allowed "the fell clutch of circumstance" to control me. After his death I allowed change to come into my life unfettered without any control, and the moment you stop controlling change, allowing it to sweep you off your feet, is the moment that you begin losing control of your life.

Theron Chrane, Grade 11
New Waverly High School, TX

The Results of a Santa Experience

What happens when a little girl sits on the lap of that white haired, jolly old man for the first time? Answer: tears, kicking, and high-pitched screams.

My brunette hair dangles from the side of my head in a shoulder-length ponytail, my overalls not fully hooked and my shoelaces untied. My mommy sits there holding my one-year-old small hand, giving reassuring strokes and saying to smile big for the camera. With downcast eyes and shaky legs, my mommy walks me to the jolly old man who brings me presents. I should be nice to him, right? After all, he does bring me free presents, anything I want.

My short, stubby legs make their way to him. He picks me up, smiles at me, and asks me what I want. Lips start trembling, eyes start tearing up, whimpers escape from my throat. I look up at his face as the old jolly man's eyes begin to widen when he realizes he has a crying toddler on his lap.

I jump off his lap and run through the mall, screaming and weaving through the legs of the people. My mommy runs after me, shoving past people, trying desperately to keep her eyes on me as I run into a crowd of tall people.

They tower over me, looking down at me, that "what is this kid doing and where is her mom?" kind of look on their faces. And when my mama finally gets to me and picks me up, that scolding look comes across their face, saying "You really need to watch your child." My mommy retorted with "Just wait until you have kids," and walked away with me in her arms to Coldstone, to get me an ice cream as bribery to never run off again.

Sierra Garza, Grade 11
Seven Lakes High School, TX

Problems

People around me can affect the way I feel. Every single day people make fun of me and tease me due to the fact that I have red hair. I personally don't think it's a bad thing, but people calling and telling me "Ginger" or "You have no soul." It's not fun and I have to deal with it every day of my life. I don't find it funny or hilarious but other people do and it lowers my self esteem. These jerks around me don't care how I feel when they call me those names. The worst part is that if I ask them to stop they keep doing it. Then so I have to get used to people calling me these names, and the thing is I may seem like the nice and happy person on the outside but on the inside I'm like a WW III bomb about to go off. I'm sick and tired of people being senseless jerks.

So now I think "Is having red hair bad?" Seriously it's the color of my hair. You don't need to be making fun of me. It's the way I was born and I can't help it. Sometimes I wonder what goes through people's heads when they put me down. All I wanted was for everything to stop and I was very close to leaving this world. But you know what, I told myself that I'm stronger than all those people and luckily I have a great mom to help me with my problems. Now as you can see this is how my surroundings have affected me.

Michael Gonzalez, Grade 10
Cypress Ranch High School, TX

Power Succession in North Korea

As a South Korean international student, I have concerns about my country's relationship with North Korea. As a result, I recently examined the hereditary succession of power from the prior dictator, Kim Jung Il to his son, Kim Jung Eun. Kim Jung Eun is a prominent North Korean economist who has studied economics at the world's best universities and has witnessed with his own eyes the way in which his father governed the economy of North Korea. All North Korean officials acknowledge his credentials and agree that he is suitable to become the next leader, even though he is not the eldest son.

Despite all the explanations above, it was still unexpected for him to be selected as a successor because of how much North Korean society values primogenitary rights. Because he was the most cherished child by Kim Jung II, and his philosophical conceptions were most similar to that of his father's, Kim Jung Eun outran his two older brothers.

Therefore, his title of Supreme Commander becomes very important because it would reinforce and maintain the 'military first' policy. As a military title, it requires absolute submission to his presence. As the North Korea's political atmosphere starts to doubt the absolute authority on their leaders, they try to reorganize the demoralized spirits of citizens. Although the world has failed to see a form of insurrection arising from inside, we still have to continue with its efforts to bring down the tyrannical actions; I am apprehensive about Kim Jung Eun's future political countermeasures, but at the same time, it will be interesting to observe in political viewpoints.

Sangyeon Sean Jin, Grade 11
Whittier Christian High School, CA

Reality

Last summer, I had this little feeling every once in a while that nothing was real. It sounds silly, and it was, but I often just felt like everything was…made up or something. I am sure it had nothing to do with electronics, and I am sure it had nothing to do with fictional books or stories.

Then, one day, as I was mountain biking, I lost control and fell over the handlebars while I was going pretty fast. As I slid over the dirt/rock trail on my left forearm, right hand, knees, belly and left shoulder, I still couldn't really wrap my mind around the fact that this was happening to me; probably due to the fact that the pain hadn't quite registered yet. As I slid to a stop (with the air knocked out of me as it has never been knocked out before) I did a quick rundown of my condition. It only took me a few seconds to see that my left forearm was skinned pretty badly, as were my knees, and the rest of me was pretty fine.

But the breath being knocked out of me was an entirely different matter. Whenever I tried to breathe, what little air that was left in my lungs started to come out. It took about twenty seconds or so before I could breathe, although it felt like minutes. This combination of pain and oxygen deprivation worked very well to bring me back to reality.

Morgan Muhlestein, Grade 12
Woods Cross High School, UT

What I Call Home

I was born in New Orleans and lived there all of my life, until 2005 when Hurricane Katrina skirted the city. The constant rain topped, and then completely leveled the levees. New Orleans sits below sea level. At certain points on Lakeshore Drive, the water line rises above the street so that it seems you're riding beneath the gently lapping gray waters of Lake Pontchartrain.

My mother, Memaw, my sisters and I evacuated the city the day before the storm hit. As my mom backed out of our driveway, her rose bushes that she'd planted in honor of her dad, swayed in the stormy breeze. Even though it was over twenty-four hours before the storm would hit, the sky was gray, the clouds laden with rain. We'd have bursts of hard showers that would slow to gentle drizzles. I detected a faint scent of the night-blooming jasmine in our garden. I thought it was strange that the flowers' sweet perfume filled the wet air. But there it was, mingling with the smell of wet Earth and approaching rain. Of course, everything about that morning was strange.

I often wonder what my life would be like if the storm had never happened. Undoubtedly, she'd take me to the French Market at the end of Decatur Street near Esplanade Avenue and the Old U.S. Mint. New Orleans will always be my home. Home to me means a place you can go and feel comforted and at ease with yourself no matter what, a place where your heart longs for when you're away for too long, and most importantly, a place where you would want to spend the rest of your life and build a family. That is what home means to me and that's what New Orleans is to me.

Zoey Megahey, Grade 10
Texas Connections Academy, TX

Over It

I am infuriated. It's anger rolling through my veins. It's frustration in my head. It's what I didn't want to happen. I anticipated and waited for the news to come in, yet what I get is disappointment. Disappointment that gets transformed into anger. Anger that takes over the night of thought. Thought that takes over my life. It consumes my dreams and lives in a speck of my brain. But that speck grows and spreads. It spreads slowly, but surely. Soon it has taken over my body. My body becomes uncontrollable. It transfers me into a world I do not know. A world that I have not seen before. It's dark and unfamiliar. Now I am lost. I ask myself, "How could I, me, bring my own self, to this?" I give up. I have finished. I don't need this. I deserve better. I can get better. I am better. The speck did not have to take over It didn't have to be implanted in my brain. This was not meant to happen. The speck was not meant to grow. I was not destined for this, it was not meant for me. I come to realize that it will be okay, the world will go on rotating and life will keep coming. We speak and I come to my senses. I can now see your point of view. I breathe in, then my sight clears. The awfulness disappears as I exhale the last breath of rage. It is gone.

Bianca Galindo, Grade 10
Cypress Ranch High School, TX

Kindergarten

I wish I could go back, back to the days when the greatest gesture of trust and friendship was sharing your crayons. When no one knew how to tie their shoe, nor had any clue about how to find the square root of pi. I want to go back to the time when taking a nap was a quiz grade, and if you were bad, you spent a day in "the cave."

I miss kindergarten. Everything was so simple. No politics or worries about paying your rent on time. It was just being, a simple and pure existence, raw, uncensored, life. Nobody cared what shoes you wore, how you did your hair, who wore more makeup, or when Sally and James would break up. Life was so perfect back then, and all we wanted was to grow up. It was a waste, and now we are grown up. All we want is to be little kids again.

I remember being woken up from my nap by my dad picking me up. I loved the feeling of being in his strong arms. I felt so safe and warm. I nudged myself closer to the epicenter of his love, pounding away in his chest. Back then I had no question, whether my dad loved me, that he wouldn't drop me carrying me to the car in my sleep. Now I can't help but question the existence of his heart, he seems so cold and distant sometimes. It seems like every time I turn a corner I've done something to let him down. I haven't felt the warm pulse emanating from his torso in a long time, and I don't know if I ever will again. Not only do I miss kindergarten, but I miss my dad.

Joseph Bowman, Grade 11
Seven Lakes High School, TX

Plastic Perfection

In a world laced with magazine covers and red carpets, beauty has become warped into something unnatural, something for people to envy but not to achieve. When staring in the mirror, one easily picks out one's own flaws: a pimple here, a crooked tooth there. But when staring at another person, we find beauty instead of the imperfection we find in ourselves.

Low self-esteem is a seed that is planted in children at a very young age. Why else do little girls clumsily paint their faces with makeup, or beg to get their ears pierced? What is it about long eyelashes, or diamonds glinting from our bodies that makes us "beautiful?" The media sets the image for beauty, and anyone with uneven complexions, bushy eyebrows, or folds of fat is immediately judged by the piercing eyes of teenage girls.

Perfection is an image that the media is fond of utilizing. Instead of informing the youth about reality, the media projects the idea that, in order to become beautiful, kids must change themselves, because there is no way to look like bubbly girls on glossy magazine covers without using a computer. Without the media shoving plastic perfection in our faces, beauty is in everyone. Beauty is not what the latest celebrities are wearing, or covering our imperfections with makeup. Beauty is the ability to look in the mirror, stare that ugly zit right in the face, and smile. We are, after all, only human.

Sarah Rich, Grade 10
San Marcos Sr High School, CA

Defining Life's Little Lessons

Some experiences in life define who we are and what we stand for. I had an experience one summer that showed me that I could unprejudicely accept people for who they were.

I had the classic pit in my stomach, slumped shoulders, and an attitude at its worst. As I got out of the car and sulked toward the crowd of people, I prayed that the cement would swallow me whole. Special Olympics was a new experience for my mom, my Down-Syndrome sister, and, especially, me.

Thinking of what I was going to do, say, and act, I joined the circle of mentally-challenged individuals. As I interacted with them, I stopped worrying about what I would say and do and focused on them. That is what made all the difference.

After that first petrifying day, I looked forward to interacting with the individuals that knew so much more about life's lessons than I did. They taught me to have a love of life and people, especially those who were different than me. I became more skilled in dealing with situations that were light-years beyond my comfort zone. Special Olympics became the highlight of my week. I became so excited about what was going on, that I even brought friends with me so that they could have the same amazing experience that I was having. This was not an ordeal that could be kept quiet. If I had the power, I would have everybody volunteer at Special Olympics!

There are some experiences in life that come and go. This was not one of those. The concept of accepting people for who they are has made me a different person.

Samantha Winward, Grade 11
West Side Sr High School, ID

Oh Non-Fictions!

Now you see, I am not a really big fan of nonfiction stories. I mean, of course I could sit here and type all this stuff about how non-fictions will never incite your imagination, saying how stories that are totally based on reality and memories from the author's past can kill your creativity, since writing the truth does not leave room for making up more interesting "facts" for the story. Because, let us face it, that is exactly the reason why history and government school books are so utterly boring. Not even mentioning the economics ones.

But this is not my point. For as much as these books may be exhausting to read, they are informative and they are the ones that helps us get good grades.

And not mentioning the possible cheating.

What I don't like about nonfiction is that, even though they are supposed to be based on total truth, they will never be. You see, there is just no way an author or whomever is writing will remember every single detail about what happened in that particular moment, being in history or in an autobiography. There will always be a little or a huge something that will be made up, because it is impossible for us humans to keep so much truth information. The mind will always play tricks and fill gaps with things that were not quite the truth.

For me, non-fictions are a kind of hypocritical work, but then again, that's no one's fault.

Raya Lima, Grade 12
Vista Ridge High School, TX

No Time Like the Past

History is cyclical. The mistakes of bygone eras are unconditionally manifested in future generations, with different names and faces playing the same tune. If the successes of classical times were already discovered once, why must they be rediscovered continuously? Yet it is true, however, that the human form is one and the same across the eons, and the young shrink away from the old lessons, only to learn that the old understand too well. Yet every generation also believes the past to be more expressive than the current, even if out of spite. All the world may be a stage for Shakespeare, but if it is, it repeats its one act play every hour, in the exact sequential order.

And yet there are signs that human progress is not only stunted, but may be in headlong retreat. For we are Eliot's "Hollow Men," dancing around the "prickly pear" with no understanding of it. Tradition and experience are discarded in the name of a progress that leads only to the abyss of doubt and despair. What would the Fathers have thought of a lost posterity?

What impression will this generation leave to those to come, those to be born in the last age of man? Will we have cringed from the highest enjoyment of humanity and leave a broken discord in our wake? I pray that is not how we are remembered. Rather, by keeping the past alive, we can meld tradition and reason into the present time, so that when future generations look at us in their past, they may behave and improve likewise.

William Linz, Grade 12
Temple High School, TX

The Influence

The apprehension that you will, inevitably, be compared to someone else. It kills us. If there was no set standard for the ideal human being, what reason would we have to feel negatively about ourselves? There would be no cause to.

A larger girl only feels bad about herself because society dictates she do so. A thin, small boy does the same, *because society dictates*. The media has portrayed to us an image of the "perfect" human being, be it male or female. Even though proved completely invalid, it's still ingrained in our brains as the "ideal."

Skinny, large breasts, a small waist. Large muscles, tall, tan. The list is endless. It's the foundation of all physical insecurities. It's why we compare each other. As a result, our self-esteem is broken down little by little because of this standard.

Eating disorders, self-harm, the harming of others. These are all problems not only for women, but for men also. They're all a byproduct of our knowing that we will be compared. However, if we really think about it, who decided what's beautiful and what's not? One hundred years ago, being pale and plump was beautiful; it's changed completely. The human mind is fickle.

We are all beautiful; that's the whole and simple truth. Yet we are losing wonderful people to this plague of self-loathing and dishonesty. We must put an end to it. It's not the media who decides how beautiful you are. You do.

Ren Howard, Grade 12
Woods Cross High School, UT

My Life

Like Playdough, my life has been changed by many different experiences that have molded me. As a marching percussionist in our band, it is my responsibility to ensure that the rhythm of the band remains constant. It also requires me to be aware of all movement and actions and be able to adjust to the variables in my surroundings. When I am on the field marching, I am aware of the patterns in the rhythms of the music and the measures of adjustment in movement that it takes to keep the underlying heartbeat of the band. I remember participating in one of my first marching competitions, and I messed up to a point that I felt like I had affected the whole band. I soon realized that the other members around me had adjusted their movement to cover my mistake. That incident reminded me that with the amount of time and effort I am required to invest in band, life lessons are bound to be learned, lessons much larger than just producing a single moving, musical performance.

Awareness is key to success, not only in band, but in life, in general. We must be aware of our surroundings and circumstances, tolerant of our differences, responsible for looking forward, and staying positive with our words, thoughts and actions toward each person we encounter in life. I have had many opportunities to experience things that have touched me, and that have all helped create the person I am today.

Merrick Lucas, Grade 10
Cypress Ranch High School, TX

Major Haunts

As the metronome ticked at a speed of eighty for a four beat measure, I was still processing what I had forgotten. Tick-tick…my head only registered the mechanical but calming strikes. Suddenly she took her seat on the podium and scanned her eyes across the musical room for her next prey.

The day of a chair test is the worst day in Orchestra. Last test I was lucky enough to achieve second chair, but everything comes with a price. That price was that I had to play earlier during testing. First chair always achieved perfection. Anything less would be a shock. Sharply she nodded at him and he arrogantly placed his bow on his strings. Gliding over the woodwork with closed eyes cinched in concentration, the rosin dusted the air, creating a nostalgic feel. After the prodigy finished the class's eyes glittered with anxiety and anger.

More time passed as she wrote her markings. When that pencil stopped, my heart began to race. I said a silent prayer in hopes of keeping my chair. My legs were shaking furiously and my hands became clammy. She raised her eyebrows at me, I transformed into the professional I had always hoped to become. All eyes fell on me and my confidence plummeted and nausea swept over me. I proceeded with a shaky bow into my first measures. Then an F-sharp slide into an F-natural piece. Longing for my missed chair follows me, with an F-sharp haunting my days.

Krystyn Malveaux, Grade 10
Cypress Ranch High School, TX

Perfunctory Machines

At school, she tosses her long, glossy, black mane while smiling at her classmates, patiently explaining to them what is simple knowledge to her. Questions hurl at her with the speed of light, sometimes probing her for her knowledge, sometimes venturing deeper in search of the secrets tucked deep within her mind. Nevertheless, these endeavors cannot peel off the layer of plastic outside to reveal the misguided, tainted creature inside. Despite her sweet smile and patient demeanor, a sinister voice, implanted by ambitious desires, lingers in the depths of her mind, reminding her of the cruelty of the world. She must be the best, thus she must conquer all her schoolmates. Nothing less than an 'A' can be printed on the piece of snow-white parchment. She must be the president, the editor, the captain, and the drum major in her various activities; she must command the forces. Her slender fingers must grace the ivory keys of the piano and produce sounds that the heavens would deem angelic. The voice whispers and taunts, its expectations molding her, pushing her, and devouring her, until a pure, innocent child becomes a cold, majestic statue, churning out knowledge mechanically. Though she listens to the voice and is successful in carrying out the burden of dreams and hopes, inside her chest, suffering from neglect, a cold, icy cavern exists. She is an emotionally barren girl, a depraved angel, that could not create her own identity. Don't be like her, for she is a robot of lost dreams, one of the many perfunctory machines in existence.

Lillian Kao, Grade 11
Milpitas High School, CA

A Live Bleeding Heart

My aunt is no longer a human being. As I stand next to her, I hear the constant hoarse coughing and gagging. She sits in a more upright position and places her hand on mine. She handed me two objects: a brush and a blank canvas.

"It's yours now. I won't be using that brush for a very long time," my aunt chuckles in what seems like the first. But, her laugh did not match the expression in her soft brown eyes.

Slowly, I dip the delicate brush in the crimson paint. I remember hearing the echoes of her laughter. And I remember when we used to pick dandelions and made wishes and dreams come alive. Suddenly, I launch the brush in the center of the canvas. The viscous paint drips down the canvas like blood dripping from a living heart on a leathery woven cloth.

My eyes finally bore into hers just in time to see her hastily cover sudden tears. Unexpectedly, my aunt coughs ferociously gasping for air. With the remainder of her energy, she whispers to me, "I will always l-l-love…" and her brown eyes gradually close.

Crying, I feel the texture of the damp crimson paint on the canvas, and demanded that the heart on the canvas stopped bleeding. With a waterfall of tears, I spluttered a reply that I had longed to say, "I l-l-love y-you too."

It was a reply that she never got to hear because Death had already caught up with her.

Pauline Truong, Grade 10
Gabrielino High School, CA

A Night Never Forgotten

Not many can say they have been face to face with death; however I am able to say that. A cold, hard metal object was put to my head and I heard "Get out of my apartment!" This object was a gun.

This all began with simply being invited to a party and bringing two different mixtures of guys together that shouldn't have been. I never expected anything bad, but what my friends and I received was a night of tragedy and disaster. Fights broke out between the guys, and as punches were being thrown and bloody faces began appearing, I watched in terror not knowing what to do. It happened so fast. Next thing I knew, the owner of the house pulled out a gun and pointed it at everyone in the room. This was so shocking to me; I was frozen in place like a statue. When the gun was put to my head, I thought that was going to be the end of me. I've never been so scared that I couldn't even think. I put my hands up and told him I was going to leave. I scooted my way to the front door and, as tears poured down my confused face, I ran my way down to where my other friends were. That night completely changed my whole outlook on life. I never have and never will waste another day in my life. I live every day as if something like that could have taken my life. Some could say I was lucky, but to me, it showed me it really just wasn't my time to go. I'll never know why he did what he did, but I was left alive to do something good with my life and do something that will make a difference.

Kolleen Tabasco, Grade 12
Seven Lakes High School, TX

Expressions for Thinkers

There is a cost for everything: for food, fun, and anything else; there is also a reward for the price paid. The price may not be known until later in life, but the cost is still there. Take a final exam, for example: you can choose to study efficiently and get a good grade, or you cannot and get a bad grade. The choice is completely yours. If you choose to study, then the cost for the moment is all the *Call of Duty* you didn't play. If you choose not to study, then the cost in the long run is the possible rejection of the college of your choice. The price of hardship today will be greatly preferable to the hardships awarded in the future.

If there is a price, then there must be a reward. The price paid will dictate what the reward is; whether it is a job or a house. The reward could be good or bad, based on how much of the price you are willing to pay and if the reward is a good reward. What price is paid is typically worth it, but you will never know if it is until the price and reward are paid for or received.

So is there a price paid for not heading these words, yes. But you will never know what it was. There is a price for listening to this idea; it may help you, or it may not. It could motivate you to never sleep again and study all the time, or it could not. You may not enjoy this expression of ideas, but that is OK. At the end of the day, all that matters is God and family.

David Chadwick, Grade 12
Rock Solid High School, CO

A Generation of Clones

Clones. Copies of a fake society. What happen to originality? I take a glance at my surroundings and all I see is people being a copy. Since when did "Let's all be the same" start being a trend?

I walked the hallways of a new school, and all I saw were robots. Girls with their blonde hair, fake tans, Vera Bradley backpacks, Ugg boots and a huge sign on their forehead: "I did this just to be popular." I was willing to sacrifice my individuality. I began to think, maybe I should buy those things, and then people might notice me. I wanted to blend in so people could see me. But, how can people notice me if I'm just like everyone else? I should have asked myself that question a long time ago. Instead here I am, turning plastic. How could someone so unique turn into a clone of a fake? I opened my eyes and realized I wasn't me. I was a poser, a fake. My mother told me, "Be the shining star that everyone can see. Be who you truly are, not a fake. People will love you for who you are."

Yes, I still have all my expensive brand items, but I haven't let them change me. I didn't wear what they all wore; I made the style more of my own. Now that I have learned the importance of individuality, I look around and grow sad when my own friends give into the superficial trends. They use fake originality to fuel the ego that comes with such superficial territory. I have never stopped to that level, I am me and I've learned that this is enough.

Ana Zuniga, Grade 10
Cypress Ranch High School, TX

Back to Baguio

As soon as I stepped outside of the Manila Airport, I knew I wasn't in the States anymore. The thick, humid air, shouts of vendors in the street, and the overall mass of confusion gave testament to that. Mom and I had finally arrived in her home country, the Philippines.

Once we'd adjusted to the 14-hour time difference, I had to adjust to the culture difference. During the 2 months we were there, I struggled to let go of past American luxuries and learn to live a much simpler way. The Philippines is a 3rd-world country, and while rich in beauty, most of the people there live in poverty. Public restrooms lack toilet paper, houses are built out of sheet-metal, and most people walk to wherever they're going. Instead of John Deer tractors out in the fields, I saw wooden plows pulled by caribou. Instead of skinny jeans and flashy tops, I saw worn-out hand-me-downs and stained clothes. And instead of complaining or a bitter spirit, I saw bright smiles and contentment.

My eyes were opened this summer, and I have never looked at things the same way. Living without the luxuries I've grown up with made me realize how spoiled I've been. Now, I marvel at the cleanliness of restaurants, at our cockroach-free restrooms, and how unhappy so many of us over-privileged Americans are. My summer in the Philippines left an impression on me, and I hope it's one I never forget.

Linda Greaves, Grade 12
Twin Falls Christian Academy, ID

Barriers

Before me stands an encouraging yet daunting wall, the physical manifestation of all of my fears, a trial of mental tenacity and fortitude. A puzzle not limited to numbers and letters, it agitates the inexperienced and disconcerts even those most accustomed to its challenges. And yet within it lies an inherent magnificence, the simplicity that one must only understand what it asks in order to overcome its intimidating nature. Often a challenger finds he is ill-equipped to climb the wall, and so he gathers an entourage of people to help him take on the ostensibly insurmountable task.

To some such a stronghold embodies an innate fear of the unknown, a diffidence that constantly tags alongside them as they journey through the world and that limits them in their future opportunities and ventures. To others it presents itself as a barricade that separates one's inherent personality from that which one desires, serving as a "souvenir" of past regrets and misgivings and a handicap towards progress and lifetime success. But in both of these scenarios, one can still manage to find hope in that to journey so far as to face the wall is to come close to conquering one's fears.

After I revitalize my mental and emotional disposition, I once again confront the bastion, which looms before me as a compendium of personal hardship and adversity. I hesitate for a moment and survey its exterior, noting footholds and armrests wherever they may be before I begin climbing the wall, conquering my fears, step by step.

Sujay Tadwalkar, Grade 11
Monta Vista High School, CA

Grateful

Dear Diary,

Today in my English class we each had to write down on a small piece of paper a problem we were currently dealing with or something that was bothering us. it took me a while to think of something, but I finally got it! Last week, my mom wouldn't buy me this shirt I had wanted and I was still upset with her. So, on my piece of paper I wrote, "My mom is bothering me because she won't buy me this cute shirt I really want!"

After we wrote down our problem, we all folded them and put them into a bowl. Then we picked a different problem out from the bowl. I unfolded the paper and proceeded to read the miniscule inscription. Tears rapidly began to swell up in my eyes. My eyes were full of embarrassment as the letters formed words that made me feel ashamed. On this person's paper it read, "My father has cancer, and I'm afraid."

Our teacher told us if we wanted to keep our new problem, then we could, but if not, to return it back to the bowl. More than half of the class stood up and returned their papers; I was one of them. Words cannot describe how I felt...pathetic, ungrateful, and thoughtless. I know that whoever wrote down that problem would trade anything to have mine.

So here I am to say how thankful I am. Because, my problems are insignificant compared to others. Be grateful, always.

Kylee Forbes, Grade 11
Woods Cross High School, UT

My New World

I was a naïve seven-year old girl. My home was in a small town in the barely noticeable country of Moldova. You could say that I was happy, until my mom told me that we were going to have to move to America. I didn't exactly know what to expect. To be honest, I thought that I could still keep living in my own little world–my playful, tree-climbing, cherry-eating, country world. It wasn't until after the move that I realized I was wrong.

We were moving to begin a new life with my stepdad, Tim. I liked Tim, but I had a hard time showing anyone my good side. After moving, my obedience and happiness went down the drain. Why wouldn't it have? The kids in my neighborhood spoke English, while I spoke Russian. Everything changed, and I didn't approve of "Mac-and-Cheese." The family that I clung to lived halfway around the world. No cherries, no tree-climbing, no playfulness, no open country. My only hope was my mom and Tim.

It wasn't until a year later that I started to feel at home. For school, I went to a foreign language class, where my loneliness began to deteriorate as I finally had friends to play on the swings with. I acquired a taste for McDonald's, and English grew easier for me.

After two years of living in the United States, my outlook slowly changed. The best part was how I came to love my meaningful, playground-climbing, "Easy-Mac"-eating, suburban world.

Daria Afanasieva, Grade 10
Cypress Ranch High School, TX

Is the American Dream for Immigrants Too?

For some people, the American Dream means one day owning a house, while for others, it might mean being afforded the right to succeed. As Pedro Trujillo Carrasco acknowledges in his essay entitled "When I Freed my Undocumented Mind," many families come here to teach their children to "work with their brains rather than with their hands." This is my parents' American Dream; to one day have their children work with their brain rather than their hands. This is mainly why my parents have always pushed my siblings and I in school, so we can invest effort into our education and someday rise out of poverty. They came to America to seek for different opportunities that are now gradually being restricted. Ultimately, my parents came to America so that we would never encounter those disgusting slashes in our hands, or coming home from work looking and smelling dirty, just because there are no decent jobs that allow one to work without proper documentation.

The situation that my family and I are in is stressful, yet I always remind myself that I will begin my post-secondary education in order to be successful and overcome this adversity. So is the American Dream for immigrants too? Of course it is, because my father and mother are doing just that, and teaching my brothers and I that we will be someone in life at the same time.

Elizabeth Castaneda, Grade 11
Animo Leadership Charter High School, CA

Kites

On spring days, when the wind tickled our skin and played with our pigtails, we'd go to the park. Some days, we'd lie on the dewy grass and watch the show the clouds threw just for us. We'd giggle and point out the cloud puppets and muse on how grand it would be to live in the sky.

But on the very best days, we'd fly kites. We'd throw our identical pink diamonds to the sky and run around until they caught hold. And then we'd just stand and watch them in awe, not noticing as the wind whipped out hair into our open mouths. Those little pink blobs had once been on the ground, and we had put them in the sky. It was magical.

But one spring, I ran eagerly over to your house, my kite fluttering up behind me in anticipation. You opened the door, glanced over my pigtails tied with pink bows and light-up shoes, and rolled your eyes. "I threw my kite away," you informed me. I nodded and turned to walk away, trying not to let you see. But as soon as you shut the door, I began to cry. I knew you'd grown up.

I went to the park alone that day. I tried to throw my kite to the sky, but the magic was lost. I left my precious kite tangled in a tree, my childhood dangling among the branches, and followed you.

Kym Goodsell, Grade 11
Woods Cross High School, UT

Untold Story

I remember the tears I shed, running down my face and seeing everyone staring at me like some kind of animal. The lights of the car flash red, blue, and yellow. I looked out of the window to see where my sister was standing. After I saw my sister, I opened the door and ran to my sister and asked her what happened. Through her tears, my sister said that our father had been arrested. The hardest part about seeing my father get arrested was the embarrassment. My sister and I should not have gone through what we went through, hearing the cops saying that they wanted to search me and my sister's backpacks just to make sure there was nothing bad in them. I never knew my dad was living a double life. My father seemed like a really nice guy. He went to church, but I guess you can't always go by that.

Ashley Ortega, Grade 11
Odessa High School, TX

You'll Never Change What You're Willing to Tolerate

Bad habits can take over our lives and define who we are. If we are willing to tolerate our bad habits, we will never change them. Bad habits become a way of life and begin to make us people that we do not know, people that we do not want to be and people that need to change.

In order to change we must first face what is wrong. We need to admit our problems and shortcomings and ask the Lord to help us overcome them. Then we should find a way that is easiest for us to overcome our bad habits. Wanting to change is the first step in getting there.

Cayla Chaney, Grade 11
Athens Christian Preparatory Academy, TX

My Dearly Beloved

"Pancakes!" my mom yelled from downstairs on a Saturday like any other.

I lurched up out of a deep sleep, eager to find myself in the presence of the gooey delicious breakfast. Out of the corner of my eyes I saw the ears of my sweet little cat and immediately moved towards her. Those pancakes could wait a few minutes, I thought to myself. My cat, Twizzler, instantly perked up when she saw me and ran over to rub herself on my legs. As I reached down to stroke her soft gray cheek, an earsplitting choked sound came from downstairs.

"What was that?" my dad asked sounding absolutely confused.

"I don't know. Hey Tanner, go see what it is," my mom responded and told my brother to find the noise's source.

Being upstairs, I couldn't do anything but listen and for some reason I wasn't able to move. I stood by the stairs now with Twizzler looking at me wide eyed. She was in as much shock as I was.

"Mom, Dad! It's Kit-kat!" Tanner yelled. Kit-kat was our boy tabby who was Twizzler's kitten that she had nursed from a baby.

"What do you mean?" I heard my dad say followed by his thudding footsteps. A moment of silence came over my family until my dad opened his mouth again.

"He's dead," my dad said in disbelief.

I looked down at Twizzler as the tears rolled down my face. I held her in my arms and buried my face into her fur. I lost a cat so dear and beloved that it breaks my heart to this day.

Kelsea Howe, Grade 10
Cypress Ranch High School, TX

Behind the Mask

So many people wear masks these days. Not the beautiful handmade Venetian masks from Italy, but fake ones. Ones that pretend to portray who a person is, just so they can hide behind it. There's the happy, "everything's all right" mask worn after a breakup, the "I'm beautiful, love me" mask traditionally worn with make-up, the "I'm so strong, I can beat you up" mask of the person that's been abused. What would the world be like if people put down their masks, even just for one day? What if, instead of hiding, people talked through their issues. What if, instead of judging those who hurt us, we looked at them in a new way, seeing what they were going through, looking at the whole picture before nitpicking at the details of their life. Josh Billings once said, "Love looks through a telescope, envy through a microscope." What he means is that, once you become jealous of someone, you can only look at them up close, analyzing all of their flaws, rather than stepping back to see their natural beauty and all that they are in their environment. If people stopped looking at themselves up close through a microscope and started seeing themselves through a telescope, perhaps they would lower their masks and come to appreciate their beauty, and together, as one, we could all light up the night sky.

Angela Fogle, Grade 11
Vista Ridge High School, TX

Individuality vs Conformity

Before you can have individuality, you must understand conformity.

Individuality is an idea defined only by its antonym. In the English language, we use words like self expression, going against the flow, and being different to define individuality. But in a world where everyone is an individual, no one stands out.

Lady Gaga is perhaps one of the most famous people in the world, simply because of all the outrageous things she does, from breaking out of eggshells to wearing lingerie in public. Nicki Minaj is one of today's most infamous rappers celebrating the Grammys by performing a mock exorcism in a performance that upset and shocked the world. Other artists like Ke$ha, Brittany Spears, and Lil Wayne all practice separate forms of individuality. But truly, these artists fail to stand out from each other. Each individual isn't breaking any sort of standard. Because we live in time where the expected is the unexpected, we are frequently unsurprised when people come up with outrageous acts. In the physics world, this can be compared to the explosion of a stationary object, in which the vector sum of all the parts is zero. As the object explodes, all the parts fly away from the object, and if you were to draw lines from all the broken parts, the sum of all of those lines in all of those directions would be zero. Picture each 'individual' person—that is, a person who defines himself an individual—as a broken part in the explosion. As each person tries harder and harder to become an individual and separate from the original object, they get farther and farther apart, and eventually, the individuality of all of their actions is cancelled out. If everyone is an individual, then no one is.

Jessica Spicer, Grade 11
Communications Arts High School, TX

How Music Affects People's Concentration

People can be easily affected by what is going on in their surroundings, and I think that music has a major effect on the way that people think. I have heard that a lot of people think listening to classical music will help you concentrate and focus. This may or may not be true, because I don't think any one type of music is right for everyone. When I work, I enjoy listening to music without words, but with a very fast pace and complicated arrangements. This could be very distracting to some people, but it helps me focus on whatever I am doing. Whenever I listen to music with words, I almost always end up focusing on what is being said as opposed to what I am doing. This is only what I have found, and I will not say that it is the right type of music for everybody, because everyone has their own tastes. Research has shown that fast-paced, abrasive music is detrimental to your concentration, although that is not true in my case. I think what will help you concentrate the most is the music that you know and like, as it will just be going through the back of your head instead of taking all of your attention. I think the more familiar you are with something, the less you focus on it, which is why I think your favorite music will actually help you and not hinder you.

Noah Lyndes, Grade 10
Cypress Ranch High School, TX

Reaching the Top

I gaze upon yellowing hills and soak in the scene before me. The afternoon sun casts its rays among the trees, shadows beckoning me with leafy fingers. The sky is stained with rich cobalt, and the song of a blue jay yearning for its mate reverberates through the air.

I focus on the towering hills and a thought enters my mind. Like hikers climbing a mountain, humans in search of a spiritual understanding of the world persevere to obtain their goals. I marvel at the parallel between an exhausting hike and the spiritual journey of discovering the workings of the universe.

I envision a group of hikers at the base of the hill, each determined to climb to the peak and gaze upon the Earth from a vast height. They start at sunrise, the pink glow of the blooming sun resting upon their cheerful expressions.

At noon, the golden orb of fire hangs high upon the sky and casts blinding beams of light across the hikers' sweltering faces. They are now fatigued, and their destination seems further away than expected. Waves of self-doubt wash over them, and they have lost their previous livelihood.

It is now nearly nighttime and faltering light is sparsely diffused throughout the air. As soon as the panting hikers about to give up, a shout rings out. Someone has spotted the peak nearby! Breathlessly, the whole group scrambles towards the top, and before them lies the magnificent landscape they anticipated for so long, more beautiful than they had expected.

Similarly, individuals seeking spiritual truth must work diligently in order to reach their goal. Light will falter at times, and the truth will seem too far away to reach, but they will eventually understand the truth they have been seeking, and all shall be worth it.

Ivy Kuo, Grade 11
Mission San Jose High School, CA

Smelling Pine

As a child there was nothing more entertaining than your own imagination.

We dived through the small hole in the tree branches, the small pine needles tickling our skin. After we dived into the tree dome, our world changed. At that moment the tree was our home and we became a wolf pack. Everyone was a wolf except for me; I enjoyed being the only kitten in the group who was brought in after running away from home.

The tree was a giant compared to the rest of us, folding over us like a dome. A time came when the group fell apart. The tree and the rest of us saw no more adventures, the game we once had died out. I soon moved away and for years have not seen the old tree again. Not even knowing what became of it.

It's the simplest things that make us dive straight into our imagination. As time passed, we soon moved far away from the tree. Forgetting the stories we made, some forgetting their entire imagination, saying it's immature to daydream. I beg to differ. Every once in a while we need to dive back into that tree, dive back into our imagination.

Madi Shull, Grade 11
Seven Lakes High School, TX

Not Your Typical Latina

On Thanksgiving, we serve not only my grandmother's famous tamales, but also canned yams, sweet potato pie, and cornbread smothered with butter. Every year, I look at my Thanksgiving dinner and I'm reminded of my newfound ethnic diversity. It is a reminder of how far my family has come.

Growing up in America, I have witnessed both overtly and subtly prejudiced attitudes. At the age of four I became aware of prejudice first hand. When my mom presented the idea of a boyfriend named Marco two years after her divorce, my grandmother was elated. She liked his name, "Marco," with the familiar rolling of the "r," and assumed he was Hispanic just like all of us. Reality shocked them one late November evening, as he nervously introduced himself to my grandmother on her birthday, offering her a birthday gift. He was immediately greeted by two cold words, "Eres negro" because of his dark skin.

My step-father is the man who has instilled in me a passion for education, which has intensified over the years. I have him to thank for being the support I desperately needed in my adolescent years and the fortitude I need today. It's because of my step-father, that I do not see myself as just a Latina, but instead as a multicultural individual who embraces African-American traditions. Seeing how difficult it was for him to be accepted taught me there's still more work to be done to rid the world of prejudice and ignorance from the world. Standing up for him and defending him against my family's unfounded hatred has taught me what it's like to fight for what is right. I am forever grateful for both my mother and my step-father for teaching me the greatest lesson in tolerance and love.

Lila Estrada, Grade 12
Independence High School, CA

Flying

The adrenaline pumps through your veins like water breaking from a canal. You step up and jump as the beeper sounds. It is flying in the most graceful manner. Speed like you've never felt. Your body is shaven after four months of not. This is what you've trained nine months out of a twelve month year for...don't mess up.

It is the rush and the safe thrill we all love. It is the feeling of winning, even if we're not first; the sensation of gliding and flying through a clear substance.

Swimming is not all fun and games in the end, though. It is hard work and practices that kill. It is never feeling dry and having a bald head...even if you are a girl.

We get, on average, less than two minutes in the pool total during a meet, yet we practice three hours each day to make each second of the one hundred and twenty we get, perfect. Twenty-six seconds of endurance seems so little, but is more tiring than an hour of any other sport.

With all this pain, you'd think it would scare us off. The reason we stay is simple. We all love and long for the natural high, the safe thrill, and the flying without the threat of the fall.

Avery Smith, Grade 10
Cypress Ranch High School, TX

Beyond the First Glance

Within life people can find others constantly morphing with diverse intensities. Oftentimes those alterations come from intense experiences. The moment could have seemed simple at first, but later snowballed to a more superior meaning, such as first impressions of an individual.

No one can know much by a first impression, yet many still judge others by it. I did exactly that when I entered into my seventh grade gym, a time where juvenility ran rampant through me. A girl stood out, she acted in an exotic animalistic fashion. Her literal baying towards others was startling causing much commotion. I looked down upon her with harsh eyes and mocked her. The words themselves were not that awful, but to my dismay she broke into tears from my words. Though guilt coursed through me, I still strutted about scorning her even more for her reaction.

Almost a week later in the middle of a personal dilemma she approached me and offered a solution that even a beloved friend wouldn't propose. The veil of misconception was lifted, I saw her for a brief moment with clear eyes. After that moment I was forced to notice her elsewhere, such as lunch. She sat completely and utterly alone. I approached her remembering her kind nature. Within weeks I found out her true nature. A lonely girl who's had a harder life than anyone knew about.

Now she stands as an angel who taught me many things, to not judge and forgive.

Lizzi Grawe, Grade 11
New Waverly High School, TX

My Final Days

It was not that long ago when I ascended from the year of the junior to the year of the senior. I'm here now, prepping for my next evolution of growth — I have to go to college. But as I look back on my previous years as a high school student, I begin to appreciate some of the trials and tribulations that I suffered through in order to reach where I am now. The lies, the tests, the late night cramming for those tests, the stress of dances, the drama of relationships, the pain of loss, the memory of fellow classmates, all of it had taken place for a purpose. Each and every test I took, every trial I defeated, every obstacle I climbed, they each molded and prepared me for what is yet to come. Don't get me wrong, I hated everything about high school...well, not everything. The social life was one thing that I enjoyed. Even though the majority of my friends were only seen by me during school, it was still very pleasing and rather fun to talk and laugh with them. Another thing that I enjoyed about the years I've spent here in high school had been the delicacy of lunch. Well more specifically, "Chicken Nugget Day!" The lunch in general was horrible and sometimes hard to look at. It always made me feel like prisoners were served better slop than us. But on the day that chicken nuggets were served, all hell would break loose. It would be a frenzy, but the fun resided in the chase. High school is no walk in the park, but in the end, it's what you learned and how far you've come that matters.

Anthony Williams, Grade 12
Seven Lakes High School, TX

Kids and Drugs

I believe that most drugs do hurt teenagers. I feel that if teens smoke weed it will affect their social and personal life. When they smoke this pot, they become too lazy to function a normal life. Even though it may not kill, it can lead a teen to becoming addicted.

But many teenagers this day don't only smoke weed. They drink alcohol and take methamphetamine, ecstasy and prescription pills. They might think that just because weed can't kill them that the harder drugs won't. Meth and prescription narcotics have a high rate of addiction which can lead to overdosing. Meth is said to be so addictive that after the second try there can be a 65% chance that they would become addicted. Ecstasy is usually a party drug but it also could potentially kill.

Teenagers sometimes take these drugs because of peer pressure. They think if their friends are taking drugs it couldn't hurt them. Some teenagers think that smoking pot is cool and try to impress their friends. Even though kids think they know what they are taking, dealers could sometimes give them something harmful to their bodies.

Personally I believe that many teenagers will never stop taking drugs no matter what the authorities say about the war on drugs. Even though drugs are bad for them, they don't really care as long as they get high. Will there ever be a solution to this problem?

Anthony Hernandez, Grade 11
Wilson High School, CA

The Distance

I remember those nights. I remember how happy we were together in a world where you and I, as individuals, were completely alone. I remember how warm my room felt whenever we stayed up all night long, talking about nothing at all and still enjoying every minute of it.

But we wasted so much time. Even when we slept on the phone together just to be close, or when we woke up before the sun and called each other first thing in the morning, or even when we revealed our deepest, darkest fears and secrets to one another, time seemed to dwindle from our grasp. Although we tried to spend every single moment together, the months apart always brought time; too much time. And time all alone in the dark prison I called a room always made me think about life. And doubt everything we had.

And I could tell you doubted me. The time I spent in school with other people and the thought of lies and disloyalty turned you cold sometimes — distant. There were times when our arguments over the trivial consumed us and forced phones to shut off permanently, silencing the only means of communication we shared. The thousand miles that separated us, the distance and the time and everything in between, seemed to be against us.

But I didn't care. With you there, I could close my eyes and sleep without worrying about what we had and how long something like this could last.

Rachel Phot, Grade 12
Seven Lakes High School, TX

Friendship from Flames

Few things are made stronger after they've been tested by fire, but my family's friendship with our friends, the Graubergers, is an exception. When we first moved to Brush, Colorado, we didn't have a house to stay in right away, so this family, whom we had never met before, immediately lent us their trailer to stay in without a second thought. Throughout the years, our two families have spent countless hours and days camping, spending holidays together, and watching all the various types of sports that the kids in our combined family are involved in. The beginning of our friendship has quite the story, however.

It was the first time our two families had hung out, so we decided to have a movie night in our new, yet very small living room. Judy, the matriarch of the Graubergers, was sitting in a rocking chair by our big window that had floor-length, flowing, and sheer curtains, when the cat, Blackie, jumped up on the table next to Judy. This cat had really long, black fur, and when Judy noticed that Blackie was entirely too close to the three-wick candle on the table, she reached her hand towards him to move him. When the feline's tail went up in a fleeting jet of flame, he jumped behind Judy's chair. All at once, all eleven of us in the room were up on our feet, trying to prevent our new home from going up in flames. Luckily, though, the flame went out as soon as it ignited.

After this first sizzling get-together, the Graubergers and my family have been essentially inseparable. Like gold, the friendship of the Graubergers and the McConnells has been refined by fire.

Sammi McConnell, Grade 10
Brush High School, CO

Just a Kiss

I'm standing in the faint glow of a street lamp, in my simple pants and t-shirt, blatantly avoiding the skeptical glances from the passersby. I glance up once I'm sure that I am alone, and see across the street a store, with its peeling paint and dusty windows, the faint neon lights slowly fading away into the darkness that surrounds it. I'm now alone in this faint halo of light, which slowly dims as the night goes on. As the minutes tick away, I watch as my breath comes in clouds of warm air, slowly disappearing as they drift u towards the sky. My hands become colder as I sit there waiting, my feet also becoming aware of the cold. I don't know why I've been waiting so long, aimlessly awaiting for what's to come, unsure of how I can leave. Your footsteps sending chills down my spine with every loping stride, beckoning me to stay for just a moment longer.

"Skye," you whisper, as your voice drifts aimlessly in the wind. "Come here, I have something I want to give you." I turn towards you as you stroll into the light, reflecting your smile as your face is gradually illuminated by the glow. You lean your head towards mine as your hand reaches to clasp mine. Our lips touch, some unknown animal that I've hidden for so long as finally emerged. I know that you love me, because that's why we kissed, but do you love me, for me?

Skye Nicholson, Grade 11
Woods Cross High School, UT

Living the Football Life

The smell of fresh cut grass, the chill of ice cold water running down your back on a hot summer night, and the taste of blood in your mouth after you have been hit hundreds of times in one night. That's living a football life. Football is a way of life. Once you come into the life of football, you don't want to leave. From the sweat, blood, and tears poured into the two-a-day practices, to the roar of a crowd after someone scores, it leaves memories forever.

Your family in the stands supporting you and your team have committed to the football life too. They have watched you grow up from the days in the Pee-Wee football leagues to the man you are today. They have supported you every step of the way. They poured money into you when they knew they couldn't because of rough times. They have committed their time, money, and love to not only you, but to the football life. They have given up lots of things to see you play the game that you have always loved. They put their hearts into the game that you have put your heart into as well.

Tyler Hayes, Grade 10
Ford High School, TX

My Worst Nightmare

There we were on the phone with my grandma. She had just told us that my uncle had hurt himself terribly and that he probably wouldn't survive. We were sitting there in shock from the unexpected news. So much for the Sunday afternoon nap that we now wouldn't be able to enjoy. My parents and I rushed to get ready and we ran to the car to make the trip from our home to the location of the incident. When we arrived, there were a lot of people there and I, being about six years old at the time, was still trying to process everything. My grandma was sitting in the family room, shaking and crying. She quickly motioned for me to go sit on her lap, and as I proceeded to do so, I began to cry uncontrollably. It wasn't until that moment that I realized that it was real and that my uncle was really hurt. I was taken to another family member's home nearby so that my parents and grandparents could go to the hospital to be with my injured uncle. I was so angry that I couldn't see him! There was nothing that anyone could do to cheer me up.

Breanne Williams, Grade 10
Woods Cross High School, UT

Today Is the First Day

Just like today is always yesterday's tomorrow and tomorrow's yesterday, today is always the first day of the rest of a person's life. It is what someone does in that day and makes of the rest of his life that sets it apart. If someone wakes up in the morning and lives just as he did the day before, then the rest of his life, as he is able to impact it, does not change, so to speak. However, if, during the course of a day, a person discovers beauty or depth in a way he hadn't expected, today marks the first day of a new rest of his life, a life he otherwise would not have known.

Kelsey Jones, Grade 11
Athens Christian Preparatory Academy, TX

Paper and Pen

Whenever an essay is assigned I think "Oh great here we go!", because the thing is I do not enjoy grabbing a pencil and paper and writing down what topic my teacher gives me. I am much more comfortable with just telling the story instead of writing it. I don't know why but I just cannot put my thoughts on paper and expect them to make sense, although I do have some days where writing is easy because the topic is straightforward and I can easily write about it. Other days it's like I have a great story to tell but I can't describe it and put a lot of detail like my teachers expect me to. Not only am I not able to write, but I fall behind on assignments which really affect my grades, bringing it down from a B to a C in a matter of weeks. If I feel strongly enough about a subject, then it will come to me really easily; but if I don't enjoy the topic and don't want to write about it, then I won't try as hard.

Xavier Beltran II, Grade 10
Cypress Ranch High School, TX

Performance

No one likes to come in second; everyone likes to see hard work pay off. Performance is something I couldn't live without. I've never liked being a spectator. Anytime I see a performance, I tap my foot to the beat and want to be out there with them. There's nothing like the sound of applause. It's the sound of approval, acceptance, awe and respect. It's when you know your hard work paid off. It's remembering to smile and point your feet. Practicing it so often you don't even count anymore, you're just going to the beat. It's the butterflies flying in your stomach, challenging you not to mess up and stay on count. It's that single moment of silence when you're done before the thunder of applause and cheers. What the crowd saw in two minutes took you two weeks, and knowing it's worth it. This is a performance, this is something I have to be a part of, not watch.

Stephenie Kirsten Clarke, Grade 10
Cypress Ranch High School, TX

Aidan

The day my first nephew was born was a day to remember! He was so small; I could fit him in the palm of my hand. He was the cutest kid I'd ever seen, and he had a tendency to raise on eyebrow, just like his dad. As he grew up, I felt sad, because he would never be so small again; so innocent. He grew attached to my brother, and I felt so left out, but I knew it had to do with my brother being more childish than me. That changed, though, as he grew to age three. Now, he likes to talk my ear off, and give me a good scolding if I ever get into an argument with my brother. What he said to me is, "Aunt Kitty! You be nice to my Wane!" He says this with his left hand on his hip and his right pointer finger pointed at me. It makes me laugh at how grown up he's trying to be. He will always make me laugh, and I'll always be his very own "Aunt Kitty."

Caitlin Lee, Grade 12
Woods Cross High School, UT

Respect

Respect to me is very important. I believe that all people are worthy of respect, no matter what part of your life they are in. Self-respect leads to self-discipline. In the Bible it says "submit yourselves to your masters with all respect, not only those who are good and considerate, but to those who are harsh." This is what I strongly believe in and feel!

School. One of the many places that the meaning of respecting one another gets thrown around. Every day I see hundreds of students judging one another, saying the worst forms of disrespect without realizing or even noticing it.

Sports. Every team has its own rules, inspiring mottos, and lessons of teamwork to try to live up to, to make them as successful as possible. Each moment on the field, court, or arena that we all play in is for respect of that game. Isn't it? I've seen lots of great athletes falling into defeat because they feel ashamed, but if they just would remember to respect the game, for all of its glory, and the gift of getting to play it at all, they might take a second look at the decision they are about to make.

Every day in our society, the decision to respect one another is never-ending. In each situation, not just at school, or in sports, but in our everyday life, we have to choose. Go one way or the other, but, just as a fallback, if you do respect whatever person you're with or the situation your in, in the end, YOU, I can count on, won't have any regrets on the way you handled it!

Megan Morrow, Grade 10
Cypress Ranch High School, TX

The Problem with Learning

Students with attention deficit hyperactivity disorder are often blown off by the teachers and school administration. Not much is known about this disorder even now. So, the teachers don't bother to give extra attention to those who need it. Instead, they brush them off and sign them off as a slacker who doesn't care about school.

Do all teachers take into consideration the effects of ADHD? Some teachers don't even believe that such a disorder exists, even with the mass of evidence proving it does. It can cause depression and anxiety along with the inability to concentrate.

Many students in their teens by now are aware of what this disorder leaves them with. As if high school wasn't cruel enough. Most students are labeled as "slow" intellectually, because it takes them longer to do their work or understand the material. This does not mean that they are unintelligent. Students with this disorder, in fact, are often very creative. Presently, that is considered to be one form of intelligence.

So why should these students have to suffer, because they take a little longer to comprehend the information given to them? It doesn't mean that they are not bright or not willing to learn. Therefore, why should students who have ADHD have to sit in class and try to learn the material given to them if their teachers are not even going to try and help them to succeed?

Caroline Pagette, Grade 12
Vista Ridge High School, TX

Controversy Over the 5.0 Scale GPA System

Learning in high school is intermixed with competition to be in the top ranks of the class. The Grade Point Average in my school, as well as many other Texas public schools, is based on a 5.0 scale, which drives many students to take advanced classes which are weighted with 6.0 GPA. One major issue with this system is that students tend to take as many AP courses as possible to be in the top ranks, which not only stresses them, but also leans them towards taking undesired classes. However much it motivates students to pursue more rigorous courses, this does not accurately reflect the students' interest or capability to challenge themselves. Another problem is that students abuse the GPA system by taking not only many, but also easy Advanced Placement courses. Students tend to take summer classes. They quit sports, band or art courses which are only 4.0 classes to replace them with advanced classes into their schedule. This takes away their time for leisure and entertainment outside of studies.

On the other hand, most high schools in the U.S., particularly in the northeast, follow a 4.0 GPA scale system, in which all classes are weighted evenly. This system more appropriately represents students' academic potential. Students enroll in tougher courses only if they are interested.

Overall, the 5.0 scale GPA system does not create a fair learning environment in school. Instead of placing learning as a priority and joy, students are burdened with competition among their peers. This essentially will not prepare them well academically for college. Additionally, the workload of many advanced classes limits high school kids from having a social life, participating in extracurricular activities and serving their community. This hurts our generation of students as their value for education is misled by a competitive mindset.

Amulya Sajja, Grade 12
The Woodlands College Park High School, TX

Lots of Work, But Little Motivation

The United States has seen drastic declines in public education. Although people blame the problem on low test scores, that is not the true issue. The workings inside a classroom change every year, and adults now think that harder material in school will solve the problem.

Nothing is wrong with the school supplies or equipment. Students and their lack of motivation to learn is the issue. Technology has advanced so much and many students are at fault; they abuse their social networks, and lose track of time, and become lazy while using the latest and greatest gadgets. If students were actually motivated to learn, then the quality of their work and test scores would be phenomenal. A school can have the oldest equipment, but it is the student who makes things work with them to progress and succeed.

Teachers are also guilty of favoritism. Some teachers will give up on the students that they see are uninterested in the school material and will only work with students who are excelling. We all have equal capacity, but when only a portion of students are learning, the rest feel excluded and unmotivated to learn.

While there are many issues concerning the decline in public education in the United States, I think the main issue is the lack of family support and encouragement. School and teachers are not sufficient enough for students to reach their highest potential. Most parents no longer sit down to help their student with homework or projects; everything relies on the Internet or some other easy way out. A student needs the support from not only teachers or peers, but also the support and encouragement from those at home. When a student is motivated by everyone around them, that student will be successful.

Bella Escot, Grade 11
Alief Early College High School, TX

Gotta Have My Games

Every high schooler will tell you they've been stressed out at one point. That's one thing all students have in common. Not every student deals with it the same way, though. Some like to run, some like to watch TV. Others even eat. I however, play video games. Video games help me get through my nights and relieve stress for me. It's like a sport to me.

Some people don't understand why I love video games so much, and others criticize me for it, but I don't mind. To me it's the same as any other stress relief activity. I love video games simply because they're fun. When I'm playing games, I'm not doing chores, I'm not working, and I'm not getting talked to about my grades. I'm just having fun. So to me, video games are just the same as running outside while I listen to my iPod. It just makes sense to me that I'd do something I enjoy to relieve my stress. So when people question or mock the fact that I'm a gamer. I just ignore it. Because to me, I'm just a high schooler trying to get away from the stressful school day and escape to a world of my own.

Jake Chavez, Grade 11
Vista Ridge High School, TX

Grandpa

When I think about him I can see everything we have ever done together, and I don't know what I would do without him.

I can remember about 5 years ago I went hunting with my grandpa. He would wake me up about three, or he would try to, but every day I would get up and go eat. Once I started to become more awake, I would start to get excited and nervous, so I would help him with loading the truck, and then we were off. Once we started moving, he would start to go over basic safety rules, like don't shoot yourself…and don't shoot other people.

I can remember sitting right next to him, waiting for something to fly over, and when something did, he would name it before it even came into view. My grandpa is someone who I am extremely close to, and I like spending time with him. Even if I'm not hunting with him, he helps me with my life and other things.

And he always helps to bring a sense of peace and calmness to me which helps balance out all the stress in my life.

Reese Bowman, Grade 10
Cypress Ranch High School, TX

A Life

I was born October 25, 1994. A loving mom, a loving dad in Utah. New brother three years later. We fell into the rosebushes, jumped on the trampoline, drove in our Barbie Jeep. My best friend Kate lived next door. No cell phones, iPods, video games, distractions. We lived outside, school was easy, there was nothing hard. Dance classes and Sunday School. Sleepovers with stories of the Boogeyman.

Move to Virginia; grandpa dies; Washington D.C. in the rain. Seven years old. Kate visits and then another move back home. School, high grades, expectations for scholarships. More ballet, new friends, Kate, old friends. Used to be just me and Porter. Now it's me, Porter, Kennedy, Cooper, Dillon, Cambelle. Hours of ballet. Sweet sixteen, new cousins, trips cross-country, Grandma baby-sitting.

Survived junior high, now high school, dating, driving. Really hard classes. Ballet, parties, choices. Building personality and character. More decisions, responsibility, growing up too fast. So much to do, can we stop and lay on the grass? No. Religion, school, ballet, friends, family. Laughing, fighting, crying, crying, fighting, laughing. The story of my life accelerating. It will keep going and going until…

That's life, isn't it? It starts simple, easy to explain, and just *good*. We grow up and it gets more complicated. Stories and words jumble, it gets hard to do anything right. All for what? Why are these things important? Life gets faster, the world speeds up, we keep going and going and then die. It is imperative to make the decision now: what we will leave behind when our time comes? The world will not remember our decisions, our actions, our words; but they *will* remember how we made them feel. And that is how we leave behind our life.

Savanna Johnson, Grade 11
Lone Peak High School, UT

Music

Music is probably the most influential thing in the world. Practically everything is touched by music in some way or form, from what we wear to what we say and do. You may not notice it, but it happens, has happened, and will happen.

The influence of music is so strong because of how fast it can make things spread. Most of the biggest fads are because of music and the artists that make it. With the way they act and dress, kids that listen to it try to be like them by imitating them. Many music artists inspire future artists to follow their dreams and eventually make it and become famous. Since music artists are probably the most idolized people in the world, right next to sports and movie stars, kids look up to them and thus try to be like them by dressing like them, saying what they say, and acting the way they do.

Music has such an influence on the world that it can cause world change. Music's influence closes the gaps in society and can stop hate around the world. There is no other force on earth that can do what music can.

Casey McCray, Grade 10
Cypress Ranch High School, TX

United as One, Divided as Strangers

Separate but equal is not equal.

Why do we continuously try to convince ourselves of otherwise? We allow laws to be passed that tell people "the way you are living is wrong." We strive to be accepting of all, yet we live with prejudice inside us. Being human is supposed to be something that unites us and strengthens us, yet many judge others based solely on superficial attributes. Our gender, our sexuality, our backgrounds—they make up who we are, but they're also the tools other use to tear us down. We are classified into groups and slowly the strong bond holding us together falters. We don't see ourselves as a family, but as strangers.

Until we reject stereotypes, open our minds, and see each other as true equals, we are going to fall and be nothing but nameless faces, drifting through the darkness of inequality, never realizing the full potential of the life that lies before us.

Sharon Munoz-Saldana, Grade 11
Washington High School, CA

The Corn Fields

I remember thinking to myself on that warm summer evening, why are they so tall? They were big, bigger than me, and they were scary. I remember sitting there on the play area we had out there, right by them, and always being afraid of being taken like the kids on TV. The swings were across from the bench I was sitting on, with the slide next to me. My older brother walked up to me and asked me why I was just sitting there, and I didn't want to reply for fear of being called a baby, I was only five after all, but he insisted, so I told him. When I did, he paused for a minute, stopped swinging and looked at me. He said, "That would never happen, Bear, you've got me and Daddy here to protect you." My brother's only a year older than me, but at the time it was one of the best memories I had, knowing that no matter what my older brother said to me, how much he teased me and picked on me, he was there to protect me, no matter what.

Ashley Dammeyer, Grade 12
Woods Cross High School, UT

Choices

Choices. In life we all have them. We choose every day to do good or evil, promote or put down, and to do or not do. These same choices can take our lives down spiraling roads that eventually lead to misery and hatred, or they can take us down the marvelous path that leads to happiness and fulfillment in life. Since most people strive to travel the second of the two, we must do our best to make the choices that will lead us down the best path. These good choices will follow us in life and will encourage us to make even better choices to ensure a bright future. Poor choices will only lead to even worse choices, which will ensure a miserable future. In life, we all have choices, so we must choose with our futures in our mind each and every time.

Matthew Pham, Grade 10
Cypress Ranch High School, TX

An Unforgettable Experience

In my AP Spanish class, a jolt of insight hit me. We had just finished watching a movie that revealed socioeconomic issues in Peru. Not only did the movie bring tears to my eyes, but it also reinvigorated my passion to serve my community.

Every night I researched internship programs for which I could provide beneficial service and experience personal growth. After months of searching, I encountered a medical program in Peru that allowed me to contribute service through leadership and personal initiative: something beyond myself!

After my application had been accepted, the day I had been awaiting arrived; I landed in Cusco, and immediately attended my first day of work. During my eleven week stay, I worked at two different health centers. In the mornings, I worked at Centro de Salud de Ttio, a government-funded clinic for the impoverished. I administered ultrasound to injured patients and to pregnant women, conducted urine tests, and cleaned stitches in the emergency room. In the evenings, I worked at San Juan de Dios, a rehabilitation facility with an orphanage for mentally and physically disabled children. Here, I spoon-fed them lunch, assisted them in the bathroom, played with them, and ultimately "mothered" them.

My affection for them amplified, even after returning to the United States. I developed a project dedicated to the children at the orphanage, which eventually became my Girl Scout Gold Project. With my troop, I made blankets, pillows, and other essentials using pastel-colored fabrics. The triumph of my accomplishments helped me realize that young people are capable of changing some of their world and can continue thereafter to improve their communities and others. Although I may be unsure of my future after college, I have experienced hands-on humanitarianism and am sure of its place in my life.

Sarah Ko, Grade 12
Gretchen Whitney High School, CA

My Hero

I softly open my parents' bedroom door. There, in the bed, lies my hero. He chased monsters from the dark. Still checks underneath my bed. He can lift me with one arm up over the top of his head. He can loosen rusty bolts with one turn of his wrench. He can pull splinters from his hand and not even flinch. He taught me to walk and talk. To ride a bike without training wheels. He's always right. In my eyes he can do no wrong. He lies there looking so fragile and small. The same man that can fix anything with WD40 and a Craftsman wrench. The same man whose hands are rough and worn from years and years of work. From always doing something for someone else. The same man who waits up for his daughters when they go on dates. The same man who has a battle between chemo and Leukemia inside his body. His whole family praying that the chemo will win. That he will be there to wait up on more dates. To go to all six graduations. To be there to walk all his daughters down the aisle. To be there for at least one more day.

Alicia Chase, Grade 10
Woods Cross High School, UT

Words on a Page

Some people think it's silly that I still write notes to people, or that I keep a journal. Why would that be bad, though? All people need some way to express how they feel. I use words. I paint a picture of emotions and scenery through the medium of words on paper. My every nagging thought, that won't stop tormenting me until it's released, needs to be written. I was never an athletic kid, so running my anger away isn't really an option. I feel like I'm well spoken, but who would want to listen to my problems? I write. I read. Over and over, I read what feelings I've poured onto any scrap of paper I can find. Each time I become a little more numb. Eventually, all I see are random characters on a page that I happened to put there not so long ago. They aren't my tormenters anymore. Just like a tree that finally dropped its dead leaves to the ground, the hurtful feelings on insignificant pieces of paper, like the leaves, blow away to be forgotten about.

Taylor Carter, Grade 10
Cypress Ranch High School, TX

Risk

Erica Jong has said: "To risk nothing, is to risk everything." Risk is fundamental to life and to growth. To not risk anything means that you deprive yourself of growth. You cannot experience excitement without risk. You risk living a life of stagnation, one that is void of experience. Risks are part of a complete life, to avoid risk is to avoid life. I would hate to grow old with regret for all I could have done. I have never met someone who said they regretted experiences or wished they had lived a less interesting life, but I have met individuals who have expressed a desire to have their youth back so they could try all those things they were afraid to experience. They risk nothing and in the end risk everything. So, I have taken risks, possibly too many, but as long as I learn from the mistakes made because of the risks I have taken, then I have nothing to regret. So I chose to take risks because I am unwilling to risk everything.

Christopher Bradford, Grade 11
Ridge View Academy, CO

Nothing Is Impossible

In this world there are challenges that everybody faces. Some people think that just because there is this obstacle in the way, that it is just plain impossible. With our Lord and Savior nothing is impossible. There is a fear that people face, but Satan is the one who places that fear in your heart; telling you that what you're about to go through is going to be tough and you just need to quit all together. When you face these obstacles you are doing the impossible by making it possible. Sure, it may hurt or be tiring but what's the point in starting something if you're not going to finish. With God any and all things are possible. We flew for goodness sake, we went to the moon, we survived wars. All this was possible because God was right there with us guiding us the whole way.

Christian Adams, Grade 10
Athens Christian Preparatory Academy, TX

I Can Make a Difference

I can make a difference by showing kindness and watching for opportunities to help. Once, I was in Disneyland with my family in January; we were deciding what ride we would go on next. I saw a family with a toddler being pushed in a stroller. The family looked so exhausted from all the fun and excitement that they hadn't noticed that the little girl had dropped her toy, but I had. I ran to pick up the lost toy. When I finally reached them, the mother looked so surprised to see me with the toy, but was also grateful. I know the little girl would have been sad without her toy. When I see a chance to help someone, I take it, this is how I can make a difference.

I also show kindness to an old widow who doesn't get out much anymore. She doesn't have many family members nearby. The first time I met her she was very nice, and it was obvious that she didn't get a lot of visitors. She told me many adventures she had as a child, and then she would give me advice on how to live my life. Since then I have become very close to her. She is another grandmother to me. I don't bring her any gifts other than my company. I show kindness by going to visit her, and I really like visiting her. By listening and trying to put myself in others' places, I understand feelings. I can make a difference by listening.

I admire the people who do really big things for people in other countries; however, I can do little things to make a difference. By watching for opportunities to give kindness, I can make a difference to everyone around me.

Carly Cheney, Grade 10
Syracuse High School, UT

Turning Over a New Leaf

Everyday life hands people a chance to change their life. These small glimpses at the opposite side of the fork in the road can be life changing in such a way that one wishes it will never end. Or it can be so dark and disheartening that it smothers out their will to live after only a few steps down the road.

Unfortunately, I landed on a road glossy with treachery that a false friend poured down. Even though I became her shoulder to cry on at all times of the day and night and never asked for anything in return, she used me. I would go to speak and she would rip the words from my mouth, crush them under her foot, and ground them down until she found something she liked. After years of being her dog, I realized this wasn't healthy so I left.

Then, I heard that she was cutting herself. I went back to her with my tail between my legs and once again, my life became hers. I loathed myself for it, but I felt like it was my fault for not steadying her. I couldn't permanently leave until freshman year.

As I look back, I realize that I am more mature now. Even though I still put other people's lives before mine, I cannot allow myself to become their prop. People should be able to soar on their own wings and live their lives how God wants them to.

Kayla Hurley, Grade 11
New Waverly High School, TX

On Writing and the Written Word

Words are powerful. Words create change. Words create progress. Words create meaning in a blind world.

My pen is mighty. My writing is mighty. The ideas I share through my words are mighty. An atomic bomb could not stop this power. The power to write, to dream, to express. With my pen, I am invincible. With my words, I can live forever.

In a reality inhibited by facts of life, writing becomes the bridge to a world where everything makes sense and anyone can do anything. There is no anchor, no leash, no laws of science that can keep a reader or a writer back. We are completely free. Completely surrounded in beauty, progress, and revolution.

Without words, we would not have the lyrics that tell our stories, the poems that capture our emotion, the fiction that pulls us away from the horrors of the real world. Without words, life would be as drab as it appears before us. Without words, life would be empty.

I believe in the power of the written word. Stephen King once said, "Fiction is the truth inside the lie," and nothing has ever rang as true in my ears. With words alone, we have the power to change the world and destroy the lies that society has created. We can open a book of fiction, wonder why the world isn't the way it is on those pages, and decide to create the change we wish to see. Nothing — not guns, not grenades, not swords — nothing is mightier than the written word.

This I believe.

Ashleigh Angell, Grade 12
River City Sr High School, CA

Tears of a Friend

In silence I sat on the bus ride home, taking in the heat from the sun shining through the window, my head rested against the glass. I was going through the day in my mind, over and over again everything played out. Where did I go wrong? The bus jerked to a stop three blocks from my house and I got off.

Walking home with a pace as slow as possible, I stared straight down at my feet, not paying attention to my surroundings at all. I watched a drop of crystal clear water hit the pavement, so I looked up at the sky.

"Rain?" I thought. "No."

So I kept walking, but another drop of water hit the pavement, I realized I was crying and without thinking about it, I ran straight home.

Bursting through my front door and locking myself in my bedroom, I slid down to the floor, my back against the wall, my face dropped into my hands and the tears wouldn't stop coming. Hours later, my eyes opened and I was lying on my bedroom floor, I had cried myself to sleep. I sat up and crawled in front of my full body mirror, wiping off the mascara and eyeliner on my face. I said aloud to my mirror, with my hand pressed against the glass, leaving a print of black makeup: "Today I lost my best friend to the reaper, what do I do now?"

Adriana Carney, Grade 12
Woods Cross High School, UT

Tolerate or Change?

It's easy to accept second rate, because we often see first rate as being too hard to achieve. If we are not willing to try hard to achieve, second best may be tolerated. It's easy to be second best, but it takes hard work and determination to be able to change things. Bad habits are easy to maintain, because the world usually accepts them. It's when we try to break those bad habits and turn them into good habits that the world turns away from us and it makes things harder.

Without the support of family and friends, a bad habit can be hard to break. But only with God will a habit truly be broken.

Trino Robles, Grade 11
Athens Christian Preparatory Academy, TX

Gay Rights

I'm the quiet girl in school, the one who doesn't talk much, the one who wears all black and keeps her head down. I normally won't stand up to people about what I believe in, but there is one thing I will never back down from: gay rights. I don't care what anyone says to me it will never be okay to discriminate against love. No one has the right to tell me who I can and can't love. I don't remember anyone voting for straight marriage, so why do people get to vote on mine? Isn't that why "and the pursuit of happiness" is in our constitution? I have the right to be happy with whomever I choose. I for one am proud of who I am, and nothing you say will change that.

Rachel Tharp, Grade 10
Cypress Ranch High School, TX

Calling

I'm trying to tell You, God, that this world's too much for me. I'm calling for You now so, Father why won't You answer me when I know that You care for me and I know You have plans for me? Without You there's no chance of me living in eternity.

So, do what You can for me. I might not reach the family tree, but You reached me when You died up on a tree up there on Calvary: for love to save me, not to forsake me. And I don't want to forsake You; but love down here is cheap.

Tyrell Hall, Grade 11
Athens Christian Preparatory Academy, TX

Nothing Is Impossible

To God nothing is impossible. If you put your mind to something and work hard for it, and if it is God's will that it works out in your favor, it will happen. Obeying God and following your dreams will pay off in the end. The goals and achievements that you would like to get in your life matter; they are not just fantasies or fake dreams. If you really want it, talk to God and ask if that is what He wants for you and your future. If so then do not give up until you have it. Nothing is impossible.

Alec Koehler, Grade 10
Athens Christian Preparatory Academy, TX

Colors

I tap the coarse surface of the white canvas and watch it bounce back. White is my favorite color. It's the color of beginning, of potential; the color before true color begins. I stare at the empty face before me, flicking the soft bristles of the tapered brush thoughtfully against my wrist. Little tubes of vivid paint lay on a small table next to me. Jammed inside containers, the tiny pieces of rainbow beg to be released in a flourish of dazzling creation. I find myself staring ever longer at a silvery blue paint that glistens invitingly when I turn my head.

The painting comes in a bright whirl, one single inhalation of images. There are strong dark clouds in the sky over gentle cobalt mountains, indigo and violet flowers dancing in a field of silver grass. A wild garden in azure twilight stretches as far as the frame displays. In that instant I can see every stormy cloud stroke, every delicate petal on each of the millions of flowers. I can smell the clean evening air. Even as I see the vision, it fades, but the colors are already on the pallet in my hands, bits of sky flowing happily free from their cramped tubes and mixing with others until there is a cacophony of cool hue at my fingertips. I pause to breathe in, holding poised blue bristles. I can smell the flowers. I gently put the brush to the canvas and end the white beginning.

Allyson Myers, Grade 11
Woods Cross High School, UT

Fear

It's funny how what we fear are the same as things we don't really understand. Most of the things that scare us are more imagined terrors than anything else. Like the monster in the closet that, we realize in our teens, never existed. Our imagination creates terrors much worse than reality ever could.

I was always a little afraid of my uncle. He was born with a mental illness, and that is what scared me the most. I never knew what he was thinking or what he would do. I was so ashamed of my fear and I spent a lot of time trying to hide it. Being scared, I had never taken the time to get to know him.

Christmas Day, two years ago, we were at my grandparent's house. I remember sitting across the room from my uncle. What I saw, I will never forget. He had the biggest smile on his face; he was clapping his hands and calling for hot cakes. That day, I finally learned that my uncle was a sweet innocent guy. That night, he went to the hospital, and after a three month stay, he died.

That's the sad truth. We spend so much time avoiding our fears that we never dare try to understand them until it is too late. When I look back now, I don't see the scary man of my imagination, but the happy, smiling man who just wanted hot cakes.

Tiffany Cohen, Grade 12
Woods Cross High School, UT

Slang

Have you ever tried to communicate with a teenager? Are you met with rolled eyes, bored comments and generally annoyed faces? Talking to a teenager is not as easy as one would assume. There is a delicate flow, the vital tone of voice and, perhaps most important, the "cool" factor. Each becomes a necessary piece in communicating successfully with today's adolescents. Take into consideration, however, that age greatly diminishes the effectiveness and overall understanding of the teen. Scientists has found that the gap between the teen's and communicator's ages offsets the balance between "Yo, Mr. H is da bomb," and "Mr. H is lame, bro." By utilizing this knowledge, we have now developed a simple equation to project the potential success of an adult in a one-on-one situation with a snotty-nosed teen. The larger the gap between ages, the "cooler" the factor must become. To do so, add one third "cool" to each year between the communicators. Many variables change this basic equation, however. By signing up for our six-week course, you will learn how to apply this equation to every conversation, respond effectively in a "sick" manner and interpret even the most foreign of slang. You will be sure to succeed every time. Our course is the number one parent and teacher recommended program in the nation. Even teens agree, "It's cool, I guess."

Madeleine Mordue, Grade 12
Woods Cross High School, UT

Beachhead

Sitting on a beach, I forget my worries. I then rest my back on the smooth white sand around myself as I stare at what's left of the night. There is no sound. No cars, no people, nothing, just the waves crashing against the sand swaying back and forth, slower as they go signaling that dawn will be here soon. The palm trees behind me begin to stir with the new morning wind, sending flocks of birds soaring overhead. She will be here soon.

It's five a.m. now, and the sky has grown considerably lighter now, and everything begins to stir. The adults wake, the motorcars pass by on a nearby road, and a rooster in the distance waits for the sun to rise just inches higher so he can call the world awake. I sit now against a tree, looking towards the east, knowing she will be running here soon and she will see me smile as she usually does. A smile, that's all I need to get through the day. Just one, that's all.

The rooster calls now for the world to wake. The peace is gone. The people talk, the children begin to cry and the motorcars rush by, scurrying to where their owners need to be. It's six a.m. now, and she slowly comes down the east side, slowly walking, staring at the sunrise. Then she draws closer and I stare and watch. She stops in front of me and smiles. There it is.

Zachary Christensen, Grade 11
Woods Cross High School, UT

Receiving from God

God sees the big picture, whether we know it, or we don't know. God is putting you in a path. He has a plan; these plans can change your life from living on the streets to living in a nice home with a great family. But it matters if you listen to Him or not and do what He tells you what to do.

Are you obedient to what He says? Do you do it when He tells you to? There's a story about a man who didn't want to do what God wanted him to do so he ran and hid. But God always knew where he was; so, God made it harder for him. He finally gave up and did what God said, and God gave him a great life. So, are you going to do what He says? Because if you don't, you are just making it hard on yourself.

Michael Allen, Grade 11
Athens Christian Preparatory Academy, TX

Nothing Is Impossible

Nothing is impossible with God. He said that if we have faith as a grain of mustard seed we can move mountains. Most of the time, the impossible is difficult to believe in. That is why true faith is difficult for a lot of people. Isn't God bigger than our issue? Do you think He loves us enough to take care of us? If so, faith really shouldn't be an issue for you. God has given us many tools to be able to do great things. We have capable minds, strong hands, functioning bodies, and a strong heart. There is little we cannot do with all the blessings He has given to us, and anything left over God can do with ease if we only have faith.

Rachel Taylor, Grade 10
Athens Christian Preparatory Academy, TX

What Makes a Great Friend?

There are many great qualities that a friend should possess, but there are two that dominate all the rest. The first quality that a friend should have is being reliable. If a friend is reliable, you can trust them to complete important tasks such as school projects. If they are reliable, you can also trust them with invaluable secrets and thoughts. A friend must also be lighthearted. If a friend is lighthearted, you will always have a good time, no matter the situation. Also, the ability to make a joke and make someone laugh is always important. Although there are many characteristics that a great friend must have, being reliable and lighthearted, triumph over all.

Cole Baldecchi, Grade 10
Foothills Academy, AZ

Grades 7-8-9 Top Ten Winners

List of Top Ten Winners for Grades 7-9; listed alphabetically

Mariah Beikman, Grade 9
St Francis High School, KS

Anders Chelgren, Grade 9
Minnehaha Academy - North Campus, MN

Alex Chen, Grade 8
J R Fugett Middle School, PA

Herminia Chow, Grade 9
Middlefield Collegiate Institute, ON

Anna Dornan, Grade 9
Rockford High School Freshman Center, MI

Faith Harron, Grade 7
Horizon Middle School, ND

Carmen Li, Grade 8
Central Park Public School, ON

Sharon Lin, Grade 7
William R Satz Middle School, NJ

Sarah Rodriguez-Soto, Grade 7
North Star Academy, CA

Zane Schechterle, Grade 8
St Gregorys Catholic School, AZ

All Top Ten Essays can be read at www.poeticpower.com

Note: The Top Ten essays were finalized through an online voting system. Creative Communication's judges first picked out the top essays. These essays were then posted online. The final step involved thousands of students and teachers who registered as the online judges and voted for the Top Ten essays. We hope you enjoy these selections.

Using the Internet as a Tool

The internet. Could you imagine where we would be without it? Many of the things we have today came because of the internet. The internet has many different tools that we can use to our benefit. Some reasons the internet is good are that it is fast, you can keep in touch with people, and it can teach you some very important life skills. The internet is a very useful tool in learning and communication in our day. In the following paragraphs I will give proof and show why the internet is a very useful tool that we should take advantage of.

Some people might say that the internet is not always reliable. And they would be correct. Although, it is true that it is not all reliable a lot of it is. You just need to search a little harder to find a reliable source. Looking for a good source is very important. You need to make sure that you use good sources and not fake ones.

The internet can do many things for you. It can teach you life lessons, it is much faster, and you can keep in touch with friends. It is a good tool that everyone should take advantage of.

Taylor Robinson, Grade 9
South Jordan Middle School, UT

Music in My Ears

Is music a liar, a betrayer, a trouble maker? No, music is my friend. Music controls what I do and what I say. It is the pilot of my life. As for my brain, it is the copilot. It takes in what is heard, preparing for its turn to take the music in through my ears and out my mouth. When it speaks its words, hopefully it will bring joy to others. I put the headphone up to my ear, and it automatically pushes peaceful words into my head that speak my life. You may not understand the rhythm and the rhymes that the singer blurts out, but I do. It helps my brain learn unknown words. Music controls my anger. In my brain, the beats and the long-known lyrics form a song. The lyrics steam in my head. I will tell the story of my life one day, not by writing it down on a piece of paper, but by blurting out in a rhythmic form. The words I once knew are the music in my ears.

Kristen Scanga, Grade 7
Salida Middle School, CO

My True Love

Music is an internationally loved-pastime that has been and will be around for a long time. Music is more than lyrics and instruments; it can also be an escape from life's stresses and creates needed relaxation. Music puts me in a relaxed state of mind which I hate to leave! Music never fails to melt the stress away and make me headache-free! The genre of music you listen to can be a common ground to start new friendships. When people listen to the same music, they can discuss new songs, new artists and even new genres. By listening to music with friends, you can create bonds. Music is timeless pieces of art that can help you relax and leads to new friendships, which is why I always love music.

Peter Ghassan Ishak, Grade 9
Foothills Academy, AZ

The Sting

The cold water pushing water higher on our waists the farther we went out, we eventually came to a stop and decided not to go out any more; Christopher would get lost in the great waves crashing into us. We decided to come up with games, like who could stand on one foot the longest without taking a step with the other foot, and who could stay in one spot without drifting away. While laughing and having a good time with our feet buried in the sand, that is when it happened.

It was between Christopher and me; my dad lost his footing, so he watched us, making sure neither of us cheated. We gave each other a glare, a look of determination and unwillingness to lose. At that moment, the largest wave we had seen that day collided into us and all of us were swept off our feet and landed in the harsh ocean. My dad and brother had come up from the impact, but I was underneath a little while longer, swimming through the water around me. I felt an unforgiving stinging sensation on precisely my lower calf and approached the surface of the water, screaming, not aware of what I had just felt.

Kaitlyn Eckart, Grade 9
Saint Mary's Hall, TX

The Storm

I know that most people have been through storms that are a lot worse than this. I also know that most of those people will just laugh when they read this. I'm here to say that it rarely ever hails in Arizona, and most people were not ready for this.

When it started to hail, I was at home, outside, and believe me that wasn't fun. The hail was the size of golf balls and they hurt! It was like having rocks thrown at you. I hurried inside just in time to see my nana trying to calm down my one-year-old cousin, Gracie. I watched the entire hailstorm from inside. I was terrified when a gigantic branch, the size of a car, fell and almost hit my neighbor's house.

After the storm ended, my neighbors and I started taking pictures of the huge branch that had fallen. We also took a walk around the block to see all the damage that had happened.

Amanda Marvel, Grade 8
St Gregorys Catholic School, AZ

New York

Flash! Broadway lights are gleaming everywhere in the city that never sleeps, New York. The crowds, entertainment, and beautiful lights make you want to stay up and see everything. There are street dancers showing off their amazing moves. Also, there are very talented musicians playing their catchy tunes. While you're in New York, you will realize how ridiculous the crowds are. Everyone shoves and pushes their way through the city. Thousands of people ride the subways every day to make their way around the city; it really shows the humongous population of New York, a place where you can move around in a limited space. New York is known as the great big city where everyone stays up and sees the sites.

Natalie Curatola, Grade 8
Foothills Academy, AZ

School Vouchers ~ Positive Option

Parents should have the option to use tax money to send their children to private or religious schools because it will allow private schools to expand, increase the academic opportunities of students, and give low-income families more options. Vouchers will allow people to place their children in better schools and increase competition among the schools to vie for students.

Some private schools are withering, but with the aid of vouchers, they can remain functioning. According to New York City School Choice Scholarship Program, children in private schools have higher satisfaction rates regarding their education. Large private schools have created a sense of academic competition, resulting in students performing at above-average school standards, resulting in more academic opportunities. Studies show that the percentage of students that have graduated from public school and are attending college ranges between 61% and 63%. The percentage of students that have attended private school and are now in college ranges between 93% and 96%.

Low-income families do not have a choice in the type of education their children receive. Vouchers in some states give low-income families a budget of $4,500 towards school tuition for their children. With that money, children can attend schools better suited to their needs. An evaluation of the New York City School Choice Scholarship Program found that African-American participants who used the vouchers to attend private school reported more diverse classrooms. Studies show that students who have been placed in better schools have received test scores that are 107% higher than their peers in public schools. Low-income families have changed their children's futures due to school vouchers. School vouchers have many benefits, especially to those poorly served by the current educational system.

Kaylah Rose Mitchell, Grade 8
Vacaville Christian Schools, CA

Prevent Cyber-bullying

Cyber-bullying should be illegal because cyber-bullying can lead to suicide, ruin a reputation, and cause lasting emotional harm. According to kidshealth.com, in some rare but highly publicized cases, some teens have turned to suicide because of bullying. A study in Britain says that half of suicides among young people are because of cyber-bullying. In addition, cyber-bullying can ruin one's reputation very quickly. If someone is bullied on Facebook and they have 100+ friends who all see the rumors or harsh comments, it will spread quickly from there. www.reputationroulette.com reported that reputation damage stemming from bullying, gossip, and lies is particularly difficult to shake off and can cause lasting psychological, social, and physical damage for teens, and victims of cyber-bullying will sometimes resort to cyber-bullying themselves.

Cyber-bullying may cause lasting harm to a young person not mature enough to handle it. According to www.kidshealth.org, frequent headaches and feeling unsafe at school have been reported by both victims and cyber-bullies. According to www.webmd.com, cyber-bullies also reported emotional difficulties, concentration, and behavior issues and difficulties getting along with peers and were more likely to be hyperactive, have drug problems, abuse alcohol, and smoke cigarettes. Reported by www.kidshealth.org, severe or chronic cyber-bullying can leave victims at greater risk for anxiety, depression, and other stress-related disorders. Bullies and the victim are more likely to suffer from depression as an adult than the adults who were not bullied as a child, indicating a permanent scar left on a person's life.

Cyber-bullying should be made illegal by the federal government because of the harm it can do to young people today. Although the Constitution guarantees freedom of speech, cyber-bullying is harmful to everyone and should be eliminated.

Kayla Burnett, Grade 8
Vacaville Christian Schools, CA

Influence

Click, the handcuffs locked, he shut the door, and locked me in the cop car, and turned the sirens on. I felt like I was getting arrested. This wasn't cool because it felt like I was a criminal or I was in trouble. This made me think I wanted to do something with the government like the FBI or the CIA.

My Uncle was a police officer for thirty one years. He got offered a job to be a Texas Ranger two times. My Uncle didn't take the job because he would have had to move his family all the way to San Antonio or Austin. He was in DPS for twenty five years, and the initials DPS stands for Department of Public Safety. He also was a Sergeant Investigator for 5 years.

In 2010, he retired. He is married to my Aunt Martha, and has a son named Zach in college. My Uncle inspired me so much that day when he locked me in the car, that now I want to be a police officer. Ever since then, I've watched cop shows like CSI and NCIS. I hope I'm as good as he was when he was a police officer.

Cody Adams, Grade 7
League City Intermediate School, TX

Heroes

As we go through life we meet that group of people that are a big part of our lives. In my life there is my older brother named Curtiss. He has taught me how to be a man and not a boy. He was there and taught me some things that my parents couldn't. When I was about to do the wrong thing, all I had to do was think of what he would think of me if I did that. If I needed to talk to somebody he would always be there for me. He had taught me to persevere through the hard times and keep family a close part of my life. He has taught me mostly by his example, sometimes he didn't know I was watching him, but I was there. He mostly showed me how to treat girls with respect and how to be a good husband and father. But the biggest thing he has taught me is kindness, there was never a time in my life where he was not kind to me. He is truly my hero. If it were not for him I do not know where I would be in life, but I would definitely not be in the same spot as I am today.

Cameron Smith, Grade 9
South Jordan Middle School, UT

Truth in Advertising

Magazine companies should have to keep their photos original and unedited to eliminate problems with false advertising that presents women with a false image of the perfect body, and hold accountable companies who Photoshop their advertisements. Under the Federal Trade Commission, false advertising is illegal. Photoshopping images can manipulate perception of the perfect body image and companies who Photoshop advertisements should be held accountable.

The FTC rules state that all advertising needs to be backed by evidence, meaning a company cannot put a product on the market without testing it. Under the FTC, the company is responsible for what the ad does or does not say. Ads cannot be deceptive or misleading to consumers, just to prevent the failure of the product to flourish in sales. Statistics show that every year women spend too much unnecessary money on products that will help them look like women from magazines: fake. Studies also show many teens have been hospitalized due to eating disorders because they were trying to look as skinny as magazine models. Photoshopping decreases self-esteem when girls and women are compared to images that have been abused by technology.

Companies should be held fully accountable if their ad is falsely edited. In a recent Cover girl mascara ad featuring Taylor Swift, her eyelashes were filled in and volumized using technological enhancement. Abuse of technology in this case led to the removal of the ad. The FTC provides many reasonable restrictions and guidelines to protect consumers from false advertisement incidents. Photoshopping can be degrading, affecting the health and self-esteem of women to whom the ad is directed. Although Photoshopping might make an image more appealing, it is wrong, misleading, and demoralizing in the eyes of the public.

Hailey Kenyon, Grade 8
Vacaville Christian Schools, CA

Nature

Nature is beautiful in every way to me. Although it has beautiful scenery, and amazing sounds, the best part of all the time I spend in nature is the time I spend with my family. I love the amazing experience you get when you're hiking up a remote mountain trail where everything is larger than life. Nature is the only place where you can get that kind of view. Pictures do no justice compared to what it's like to be in the moment. To me there are a million things that you could do in nature. I don't see how people take it for granted when it's just too amazing too pass up. So just go out and take advantage of all the sights and sounds that nature has to offer, like the sound of raindrops pattering on the gentle ground. Or the sound of the ocean inside a seashell appearing to be far away when it is really so close. I hope nature means as much to you as it does to me. It is perhaps the greatest feature on Earth. It has forever changed my life and I hope it will do the same to yours.

Elias Pergande, Grade 7
Salida Middle School, CO

Skateboarding

According to Webster's dictionary, skateboarding means to ride or perform stunts on a skateboard. To me skateboarding means a fun, thrilling experience that is enjoyed by all different types of people all over the world. Skateboarding is an extreme sport that gets people moving and active. There are an endless amount of tricks that are performable on a skateboard and each one is unique. Most people think that skateboarding is not a sport and is not a skill or talent. As a skateboarder who plays other sports, I know that skateboarding requires more practice and skill than almost any other sport. To be able to pop a skateboard off the ground, get it to spin in the exact way you want it to, and then land back on it is one of the most challenging things I can do.

Skateboarding was started in the 1950's in California. Surfers wanted a way to surf when they couldn't. The anxious surfers got the idea to strap their roller-skates to a block of wood and ride in the street. Nobody knows who first started doing this, and it is likely that nobody will ever know. From then on, skateboarders evolved the skateboard into what it is today. At first skateboards were only to ride, but then one skater named Rodney Mullen changed everything. People had done tricks before, but never like he did. He has created many tricks that are performed by skateboarders every day, but the most important trick he created was the most fundamental trick of them all, the "Ollie." This trick makes the skater and the board spring up into the air. So next time you think about yelling at a skateboarder, remember that they are only doing what they love.

Matthew Aijala, Grade 8
Aviara Oaks Middle School, CA

Dogs vs Cats

If you're a cat person, then pay close attention, because I'm going to tell you why a dog makes a much better companion than a cat. First off, a dog is loyal. It cares deeply about its owners and is sad when they leave. A cat, on the other hand, doesn't care who is there. A dog is obedient. He will listen and love you. A cat is independent and will do its own thing without a care in the world about what you want it to do. A dog has a conscience. If it does something it knows was wrong, it feels bad about it. He deeply wants you to forgive him, because he has feelings. Have you ever seen a cat give you puppy-dog eyes? No. That is because cats have no sense of what is right and wrong. Another reason a dog is a better pet than a cat is that a dog will protect you and your home from intruders. There are no guard cats. If your home is being robbed, a dog will bark and bite its way to victory. Your cat on the other hand will probably be asleep. A dog, for many reasons is better is because when you're sad, it's also sad. A cat doesn't care how you feel. Is it a cat or a dog that has the rightly earned title, "man's best friend?" A dog. For many reasons. In fact, a cat doesn't even have a nickname. Due to loyalty, obedience, conscience, compassion, and protection, a dog makes a much better pet than a cat.

Nicole Tilford, Grade 8
White Pine Charter School, ID

Stereotypes and Misconceptions

People often associate the word Arab with Muslim or terrorist, but there has always been an Arab Christian community struggling to find their place in the Arab world, facing violence and persecution, while trying to live in peace. In reality, Arabs were around before Islam, and Christian kingdoms from the third to the eighth century shared the Arabic language.

During the Crusades, Arab Christians faced violence from their fellow Christians and were "slaughtered along with Muslims by the Crusaders and caught in the crossfire between Islam and the Christian West, [which caused their] long steady retreat into the minority."* Evidence of Palestinian and Israeli Arab Christians' decline is staggering. The number of Israeli Arab Christians has dropped from 13 percent of the population in 1894 to less than 2 percent today. Once these Christians immigrate to other places they continue to face discrimination. When Mark was living in the United States post 9/11 he said, "They've never heard of Arab Christians. They assume all Arabs are Muslim — terrorists, that is — and that Christianity was invented in Italy or something." Despite hardships and struggles, Arab Christians still hold on to their faith and yearn for peace. Not too long ago, during a Good Friday Service near the Garden of Gethsemane, in Israel, Lisa, a tiny Arab Christian woman moving through a crowd, was pushed around by a mob of Christian pilgrims from all over the world as if she did not exist. She told a reporter: "Do you see how it is...this is our home. And it's like we're not even here!" The Arab Christians of the Holy Land are still there, ignored and neglected.

Vincenzo Vecchiola, Grade 8
Vacaville Christian Schools, CA

Growing as a Person

Many people have inspired me to grow. One person in particular has inspired me more than others. He is always available to me and always reminds me of my potential. He is the most humble person I know and is especially radiant.

My father inspires me to grow since he is incredibly self-disciplined. He is always prepared to assist my sister and me with our latest "catastrophe." He is very unique in the way that he always comes home with a smile, ready to cater to my needs, even if he had a rough day. Above all, the thing that most inspires me is his great job. His job to help other inspires me to be successful.

From this day forward, my goal is to be as spirited as him. Without flaw, he makes me want to find a great job and help others. I want to be just as accepting and caring. He also inspires me to be the best I can be. If I can achieve it, I'd like to be as understanding as he is.

I love my father with all of my heart. Most of the time I forget to appreciate the things he does for me. He is truly the ultimate father, not just a motivator, but a role model. I take from him a life ahead full of support. He always tells me I inspire him to do better. I can't wait to tell him that the feeling is mutual.

Sierra Rivera, Grade 7
St Matthew Catholic School, TX

Being Blessed

Planting seeds of faith is a line that speaks to me. God has sent me many inspirational people in my life to guide me through my life on Earth. Some left a more retentive memory than others. My great grandmother and granddaddy were and will always be the two people who cross my mind a different way than most people.

My granddaddy, Rafael Lopez is my role model. He was always there for me. My granddaddy, unfortunately, passed away when I was of the age eight, on December 6, 2006. I was anguished but I knew I had to be very stoical because he always taught me to never feel bad for myself.

"You can always do better, kiddo." Every time I evolve in any way, I always imagine him telling me that. He helped me understand the fact that there will always be someone smarter than me, nicer than me, prettier than me, but that there will never ever be someone just like me.

My great grandmother, Rebecca Lona is a whole other inspiration for me. My great grandmother had a bad case of arthritis in her hands. She made a commitment to drink St. Therese's tea. She no longer suffers from arthritis and was also blessed to grow back her black hair. I have never seen someone be so dedicated to something and not only that but to be rewarded with a miracle like that.

I am so very lucky to have the role models I do. I can with no doubt in my mind say that they have not only planted seeds in my life but have managed to grow two beautiful flowers in my heart. I do not know where I would be without them.

Alyssa Lona, Grade 8
St Matthew Catholic School, TX

How to Feed Cows

Have you ever had the exciting chance to feed hungry cows? If you have, did you know how to do it, or did someone have to help you? If you follow these simple steps, you can feed cows as easily as can be!

Before you begin, you will need a sack of cow feed, a forty to fifty pound bucket, a knife, a heavy duty feeding trough, and if desired, some heavy duty gloves. First, you will carefully cut open the sack of feed with your knife. Then, pour the sack of feed into the bucket. (Be careful when you pour the feed into the bucket, or you might get covered in dust.) Next, start walking toward the cow pen or cow pasture to pour the feed into the trough. If the cows are not where you can see them, then call them by saying, "Brough C'mon!" (Be ready for them when they do come, because if you're not careful, they will trample you to the ground trying to get the feed.) Now, push your way through the monstrous cows, and pour the feed into the heavy duty feeding trough. Finally, work your way out of the herd of hungry cows, and do the challenging, but fun process again tomorrow!

Now that you know how to feed a herd of hungry cows, you can feed almost anything! It is always very exciting to watch the cows trample over each other to get to the tasty feed! I love to feed cows, and hope to do it again and again! Cows are great!

Brady Weaver, Grade 7
Lindale Jr High School, TX

The Question That Matters

A million tin drums pounded violently in my head. My heart was going to burst along with my sanity. My blood ran cold, and my fists clenched the metal frame of my bed.

"Your grandma passed away this morning." All the things my dad mumbled after that blurred together.

Those seemingly simple six words changed me. My face turned into a waterfall of emotions. Tears pooled in my eyes and rolled down the side of my reddening cheek. Then my expression became scrunched up, and I started bawling.

"You weren't supposed to take her!" I glared at the ceiling. "Cancer wasn't supposed to win! She was meant to defeat it and be my miracle," I screamed in my head. I laid there, depressed, outraged, and confused.

I still felt that way when I arrived at her funeral. The small town Baptist church was saturated with anguish.

I managed to hold my fragile composure together until they played the video tribute for my grandma. A picture of her cradling me as a baby flashed across the screen. I wanted to get up, storm out, curl up in bed and stain my pillows with more tears of grief.

But then my grandfather ended her funeral by reading from the Linda Ellis poem called "The Dash." He said that it didn't matter what time she died — what mattered was how she had spent her life. He asked us, "How do you live your dash?"

I decided, at that moment, to live my life like my grandma, Elsie Mae Lewis. She was a person who had put God and others above herself and who had lived her dash as an angel.

Gabrielle Lewis, Grade 7
Meridian School, TX

The World of My Books

Reading makes it possible for me to travel to the farthest reaches of the universe. Flying through magical lands, or traveling through space and time, reading takes me to places I have only dreamed of. When I dive into a book, I am there, observing the action firsthand. I am gone, lost in a world of mystery, never knowing what to expect. The words play through my head in a movie, bringing the images of my imagination to life. I get to know the characters, what they like, who they are, and what their personality is. When I read, the places and characters are what I want them to be, not what others make them. No matter what mood I'm in, reading brightens my day. Reading can take me to happy places, where hopes and dreams come true, but it can also take me to places of sorrow, regret, and lost dreams. I can choose where I want to be, not where I am supposed to be. Within a page, I have made my way to places never explored, except in my imagination. I welcome unknown stories, ready to experience new thoughts and places, new characters and tales. I relish in the thoughts of another who loves to travel to these unknown places, just like me. I know that when I am in a book, I am locked inside my imagination, unmoving, only reading. No matter where I happen to be, I can always escape to the unknown places that only a book has to offer.

Hallie Whittington, Grade 7
Salida Middle School, CO

Gun Rights

The rights of gun owners need to be protected because it states in the second amendment that all free citizens have the right to own and bear arms. Stricter gun laws do not result in a safer community. Most people use guns for hunting or personal collections.

First, many people think that we can make the world safer by banning guns completely. The data shows that this is not accurate. Great Britain banned guns 20 years ago. According to the Daily Mail, a leading newspaper, the crime rate increased 89% during this time.

The proponents of stricter gun laws believe that guns are very powerful and there is no need to own an automatic rifle. I don't believe the government of a free society should have the power to tell us what we can and can't buy. Guns don't kill people; people kill people. This is like the government telling us that we can't buy sports cars because they go too fast and will result in more accidents. Cars don't kill people; people kill people.

Lastly, the majority of people have guns for hunting and personal collections. The NRA estimates that half of all American households have at least one gun owner. Also the gun laws are already strict enough. To buy a gun you have to have a background check. If you have any crimes whatsoever, you will not be allowed to purchase a gun.

In conclusion, we should not ban or change gun laws. Our Constitution gives us the right to bear arms. Gun laws are strict enough. Other countries that have banned guns have not seen a decline in crime.

Carl Composanto, Grade 7
Beacon Country Day School, CO

My Grandma <3

My grandma is a very important person in my life. She is a very inspirational person and one of the people I admire the most. She has always been there for me no matter how busy she is or what time of day it may be. She always goes to daily mass and is a very spiritual person.

All my life she has raised me to be the best person I can be. She has always baby-sat my brother and me since we were little and always loves helping us with our homework. She's very unflagging, always on the move and ready to support us. She has a strong perspective on life and would never let us capitulate in life and helps hold our ground. Every time I see her she always loves telling me stories about her life in Spain, and when my dad was a child who lived there too. She always bolsters my spirit by telling me funny stories. She always starts to get off topic telling me other stories that are not pertinent to the conversation.

She always has a disarming smile on her face and endows us with her love. When we are sick, she always wants to be the one to take care of us. I love her so much because she loves teaching and asserting us with new knowledge. Her personality is very jaunty and audacious. She helps build my character and helps me grow inspirationally closer to God.

Victoria Smelser, Grade 8
St Matthew Catholic School, TX

The True Meaning of Friendship

"Don't walk behind me; I may not lead. Don't walk in front of me; I may not follow. Just walk beside me and be my friend." — Albert Camus. Have you ever had a friend that was the best person you knew? When looking for a friend, choose someone who likes the same stuff as you, is a good example, and has a great personality.

When meeting new friends, look for someone who has the same interests. My friend, Ellie, and I both love soccer. Even though we are not on the same team, we still bond over soccer. We encourage each other to try our hardest and because of that I feel like I am a better soccer player.

"A true friend never gets in your way unless you happen to be going down." — Arnold H. Glasgow. Your friends should support you in whatever you are doing but a good friend should also look out for you. True friends are the kind of people who know what to do in any kind of situation or problem.

Your friends should be good examples to you and others. If your friends are pressuring you to do something you are not comfortable with, don't do it! True friends understand and share your values. I have friends who I know I will be friends with for life because they are the kind of people that lift you up, not down.

When you are surrounded by great friends, you will turn into a great friend. If you choose the right friends, you will achieve greatness. I know that because of my great friends, I am a better sister, daughter, student, cousin, and friend. Friends are big factors in shaping your character so don't settle for second best.

Hadley Cowan, Grade 7
Sunrise Ridge Intermediate School, UT

Just a Dream...

I get home from school and sit down at the kitchen table, pulling out my homework I start working, oblivious to the time.

My mom calls my name and I look up from my homework. "Someone is here to see you" she says, smiling sweetly.

I hear heavy footsteps coming down the hall. I look over and my heart stops, then starts to thud quickly in my chest. I jump out of my chair and rush to him. I haven't seen him since that long ago summer night when we had to say goodbye. Less than two days together and then we had to part. I wrapped my arms around his neck, and he put his around my waist. I never want him to leave me again. With all the joy I'm feeling a single tear escapes my eye and slowly makes its way down my cheek, it is a tear of happiness. I turn my head and gently kiss his collar bone, it is a tender kiss, one full of passion and longing. I keep hugging him, I love and have missed his warm embrace, I am about to tell him when soft music starts and everything fades to darkness. I open my eyes and I'm in my bedroom. It was just a dream. A tear falls down my cheek, replacing the track of the happy tear that I had shed in my dream. I bring a finger to my lips, I can feel his skin lingering there...

Eleanor Horrocks, Grade 9
South Jordan Middle School, UT

Food Irradiation

Irradiating food is safe, so we need to irradiate all of our food. Irradiated food is still nutritious, reduces bacteria that leads to illness, and it has been used for decades.

Firstly, irradiation on food increases food safety and can lengthen shelf life. Irradiated food is food exposed to radiant energy like gamma rays, electron beams, and x-rays. The radiant energy destroys bacteria that could harm or even kill people or animals. The same radiant energy also destroys microorganisms that cause food spoilage, causing irradiated food to have a longer shelf life.

On the other hand, no long-term studies have been made on food irradiation to prove its safety. However, food irradiation has been used for decades in 37 countries. Many groups have approved irradiation of food, like the USDA (United States Department of Agriculture) and the United Nations World Health Organization.

Although irradiated food does lose some of its nutrition, so does any other food after any method of food processing. According to the USDA, scientific studies show irradiated food doesn't lose its flavor, texture, or its nutritious value. Irradiation is similar to heat pasteurization of milk. When milk is pasteurized, it is heated up and cooled down simultaneously to get rid of bacteria. The milk isn't harmed nor is food when irradiated.

If we use irradiated food, it will last longer, and have less bacteria. It has been used for decades and has been approved by food organizations. Irradiated food has the same nutrition as other processed food. Irradiate food, it won't kill you!

Katie Lennon, Grade 7
Beacon Country Day School, CO

The World of Space

I'm holding a star pillow then I imagine that I have star power and blast off to space. I'm flying to other planets like Mars. Space is cool and when I think about it I black out everything but space. I pretend like I'm in a spaceship that takes me away from home and I catch a star for my friends to see. When I'm in space I feel like I can breathe, and walk on water. Sometimes I can go to other galaxies, and universes in under a minute. I will go to the moon and find some universal rocks and take them to scientists when I get home. Then I will go see the blue aura on the earth from a space station nearby. I will go sit on Saturn's ring and fall asleep for a while.

I will come back home and tell everyone all about my adventure up there where I went. Then I will say bye and blast off again. Then I will race a comet then land on a meteor. I will go to Pluto to see how small it is. Maybe I could watch the stars and find the Little and Big Dipper and many more constellations. I will go to Mars and bring back some red rocks. I will go to earth and stay far away from the atmosphere, and when the time is right I will blast down and land on Australia. Then I will blast off one last time and go to a meteor and sit on it a while and then go back down then tell my family about my trip. If there was no space there would be no Earth.

Skyler Sheesley, Grade 7
Salida Middle School, CO

Need for ADHD Counselors in School

There should be more counseling at schools for ADHD students, families, and staff, to help everyone understand more about ADHD. Counseling can help an ADHD student build a positive self-image. Regularly discussing their progress and being acknowledged for small successes can be a great incentive for kids with ADHD. Group counseling, where ADHD students can discuss life management skills with other students, helps the students realize that they are not the worst kid ever, not weird or strange, and in doing so sets goals on how they can form better relationships with other students.

There is a need for specialized ADHD counselors in the school setting to provide education and support for school staff, parents, and medical professionals. Teachers need to be informed that these students may have trouble paying attention or sitting still in class, may act and talk without thinking, and interrupt or show poor judgment. Most teachers do not even know that it takes them longer to think and they should not put time limits on test and quizzes for ADHD students. The parents of children with ADHD need to know that their kid is not trying to behave badly, but they cannot help it. Doctors need to cooperate with the counselors because the doctor is not at school with the student, but the counselor takes notes and then consults with the doctor. The counselor can help the student understand ADHD and how he can improve his circumstances, including the side affects of the medicine he/she is taking and how to deal with bullying issues, facts that clearly show that more counseling is needed in schools for ADHD.

Aaron Aiken, Grade 8
Vacaville Christian Schools, CA

Painting America in Diversity

Nobody around you is exactly the same as you. No matter how diverse one is, everyone is important and in order to make our country stronger, we have to recognize it.

As Americans, we need to take the time to include the different people around us. We need to realize that everyone is special and can do amazing things. I have a friend who is mentally handicapped. He can't do what most people can, but he is the nicest person I know. He loves everyone and is friends to everybody he meets. He tries to "protect" people who are made fun of by standing in front of them and simply saying, "No." If he and other people similar to him weren't alive today, I know some people would still be made fun of today.

Everybody has the tendency to judge people. At school I know a kid who is often picked on by the "cooler kids." One day, I got the courage to stand up for him. Ever since then, nobody's picked on him. If everyone would stand up for those people who are made fun of, no one person would become the oddball or feel worthless.

Think of others around you and make a special effort to include them in everything you do. By doing this our country will be painted with diversity and opinion. Recognize others' differences and make America a better place for everyone.

Rachel Vance, Grade 7
White Pine Charter School, ID

Physical Education Should Not Be Required

Physical education should not be required in school because it unfairly lowers some students' GPAs, school is for study, not play, and PE can be dangerous. For some students, PE will decrease their GPA regardless of their efforts. For example, in some schools where PE is graded on ability rather than participation, the student who is athletically weaker receives a bad grade. At other schools where gym class is graded on participation rather than ability, students with health problems such as asthma cannot participate fully which leads to a drop in grades as well. Not only is PE sometimes unfairly graded, it creates less time for actual academic learning.

School's purpose is to teach academic skills that students will use in the future. Instead of PE, students could have an extra academic course or a study hall to increase academic success. Studies show that the average high school PE class only equates to about 16 minutes of exercise a day, and the chosen activities are more sedentary than active. In addition, gym class is a place where students have injuries that cause them to miss school, and some teachers make them run in the heat causing heatstroke, fainting, and heart palpitations, or push some students too far causing them to get hurt. Gym class is not always safe, which is why it should be eliminated.

Gym class should not be mandatory when it affects students' grades, and a study hall or extra academic class would be beneficial because it would not be wasting time but improving knowledge. Despite some of the benefits of physical education, its negative attributes override those benefits for the serious student.

Katarina Stashyn, Grade 8
Vacaville Christian Schools, CA

Who Influences Me the Most

Just before Thanksgiving break, I found out what my grades looked like. I came home with a copy of my grades in my hand, as did my brother. I saw my brother's grades and then I thought, why not, why can't I do that? He had all A's when I just had two. My very wise grandfather was not mad because he knew my brother's grades would have an impact on mine.

Over the break, I found myself studying every chance I got. The most studied subject at the time was math, in which I had a 41. The next most studied subject was social studies, in which at the time I had a 54.

I knew we had tests when we got back, so I continued to study throughout the week. When the tests came around I was nervous, excited, and confident all at the same time. Yeah!

Days later, the week after, I got my grades back, and I was astonished; an 85 or higher on each test! Nice. I was extremely happy on the way home on the bus. I sprinted home from the stop pretty quickly; I consider myself fast, so don't judge.

I busted through the front door, ran to my grandparents' room, and in between breaths, told him my grades. As usual, when I do well, my grandpa gave me an aggressive head rub. I walked back to my brother's room, still panting, and thanked him. He didn't know what for, but I still thanked him.

Donavan Menard, Grade 7
League City Intermediate School, TX

SOPA and PIPA

SOPA and PIPA: two bills that have met high resistance from the public and were temporarily put on hold after a massive Wednesday protest on January 18, 2012. Websites of all popularity participated in this protest, excluding its supporters. Opponents of the bill include Wikipedia, Yahoo, Google, Reddit, GoDaddy, and Mozilla.

Why have these bills attracted so much attention? First, let's explain what they are. SOPA stands for Stop Online Piracy Act. PIPA stands for Protect IP (Intellectual Property) Act. Their purpose is to help stop the selling of pirated or counterfeit goods like music, videos, and medicine that can be found on the Internet.

The bills allow the Attorney General to shut down any suspected website until it has finished its search. It completely affects the website, not just the one violating user. The General could shut down the sites, and companies would not be able to transmit funds or information until it is freed. Opponents say it's like "using a hand grenade to take care of a gopher problem." Most are concerned about a restriction of free speech, protected by the First Amendment.

Proponents argue that these bills will protect industries and children. Online piracy, causes loss of millions of dollars for industries. With the bill, industries like the music and entertainment industries will be saved form online piracy. Many proponents of them accuse opponents of exaggerating consequences, which is also true.

Many people protest these bills. Others support it. Think carefully about your response.

Caroline Luong, Grade 7
Stratford Elementary/Middle School, CA

Fear

Fear, the one thing that controls our lives! Why? That's a question only you can answer yourself. It's your choice if you let fear control your life. Fear is one thing we can never get rid of, and we can never get away from it either. Without fear we have nothing to overcome in life. Then what would we do, who would we become? Everyone's afraid of something, and sometimes we get so lost or frustrated by an obstacle we can't seem to overcome, then we give up. It's never going to stop, one after another. After you conquer one fear, another fear will jump out and scare you.

In life we can never stop, we can never give up. If we do our fears will get worse. My own fear is…never achieving my dreams and goals. I want to be famous, rich, or be a role model. Fear used to scare me from thinking that achieving my dreams was possible. Fear is like a bully, it never stops picking on you until you stand up to it. Once I stood up to fear, I realized doing the impossible is easy. I still have fears and challenges in life, but that doesn't mean I'll ever stop reaching to success.

I used to be afraid of failure, but I learned, don't be afraid from failure, because from failure you learn, from success, not so much. Fear has brought me to a conclusion I will never stop overcoming my fears!

Jordynn Fisher, Grade 7
White Pine Charter School, ID

The Internet: Harmful or Useful?

The internet, a tool used for learning and communication all over. Some people spend so much time on the internet that they have a second life on it. Almost every home has a laptop or computer with internet access, but is the internet harmful, or useful?

The answer is: useful. First of all, the internet is used for almost everything. A person does a quick search on Google and gets millions of results! The internet is full of endless possibilities that shouldn't be missed.

Second, education. There is plenty of accurate information found on the internet. The learning opportunities on the internet are endless. The internet surely couldn't be called harmful if it makes a person more knowledgeable!

Lastly, the internet is full of ways to communicate. Facebook, MySpace, and Twitter, those are just the tips of the iceberg of numerous social networks found. People are able to stay in touch with old friends and classmates, and meet new people.

Then again, some people may not believe that the internet is safe. Unwanted attention by predators could render a website dangerous. Internet viruses could infect computers. These reasons shouldn't make people think the internet is unsafe. It's the way to go for just about everything.

In conclusion, the internet is a useful tool for learning and communication. It's versatile and can be very fun. It helps in almost every way. Think of it as a giant encyclopedia, except more vast. The internet is truly a spectacular tool.

Kendra Nuttall, Grade 9
South Jordan Middle School, UT

The Time I Stood Up for My Friend

There are some times in a person's life when they must be brave and stand up for something they believe in. I was being fearless when I stood up for my friend.

It was a sweltering mid-May school lunch, and all of the other kids were running around and talking. I was walking toward my friend to have some lunch with him, but then, when I turned the corner to our habitual meeting spot, I heard a bunch of commotion going on. I glanced over and saw my friend being pushed around by gigantic 8th graders. They were calling my friend insolent names and they were beating him up. I didn't know what to do, so I just waited for the bullies to leave. I figured that they wouldn't go away, so I decided to get rid of them myself.

I asked them what they were doing, and they said they were playing around with my friend. I told them that I was watching them the whole time and if they didn't leave my friend alone, I would tell on them. They walked away grumpily and muttering. My friend thanked me so many times, but I was just delighted that my friend was okay. When I was helping my friend, I felt really nervous. I couldn't let my friend down so I just stood up and did a courageous thing to help my friend. I learned after this experience that I should always be bold and stand up for what I believe in any difficult situation.

Justin Yung, Grade 7
Carmel Valley Middle School, CA

The Reality of My English Class

Making exceptional grades in English class has always proven to be a struggle for me. I like being able to write what I desire and create stories about fairy tales and dreams. I love doing grammar and making phrases and clauses that make no sense whatsoever. However, the reality of English class is that half of the work we do is analyzing other stories that we read.

Now, I don't have a problem with reading other stories by other authors. My problem is that teachers command us to analyze them. I do not believe it is right when a teacher gives you a text and inquires of you what tone the author is portraying with one word, because the teacher never knew the author. For example, if the author wrote, "The car is yellow" and the teacher requires you to think about what the author's meaning was by using "yellow" in that sentence. Well, according to the teacher the author meant to portray a feeling of happiness; whereas, according to the author he or she might have really meant that the car was actually the color yellow. The author could have no meaning beneath that word whatsoever. It could be as clear as the blue sky.

English teachers intend for one to dig beneath the words and find meaning, but I object to this nonsense. The teachers never knew the author and have no clue what the author really meant. Why is it fair to our schools when the teachers test us on what they think the author meant? I do not think this is a reliable way of learning or analyzing texts. The student and the teacher could both be correct in their analyzing; however, they do not know it because neither of them knew the author.

Cathy Leavitt, Grade 9
Saint Mary's Hall, TX

Celebration of Life

Aunt Diane was a spontaneous and energetic person. Nothing ever hurt her spirit. She was simply optimistic about any situation. When she was diagnosed with breast cancer in 1983, she still kept that pearly white smile of hers. Her heart never quit, and her spirit never really died. In 2005 her body gave up, she simply had no energy left within her. In 2008, we were finally able to gather for her celebration of life.

My family expected a depressing funeral. After awhile, we noticed it really was a celebration of life. During the whole gathering, I personally realized we were thanking God for such a wonderful person. She fought until her death. She is a hero to my family for bringing such a bright light into our lives. At the end of the gathering, I realized how amazing that night really was. I knew it was a night that I would never forget. She always showed her passion and taught us how to dance in the POURING rain.

Aunt Diane, you were truly a hero to me! You taught me many useful lessons that I promise to live by. I promise to live life to the fullest, live strong, and to keep my faith and hope. Talking about Aunt Diane is still a touchy subject in my family. R.I.P. Aunt Diane. We love and miss you more than I could possibly write down on this piece of paper. You will never be forgotten.

Morgan Sims, Grade 7
St Gregorys Catholic School, AZ

College Students Shouldn't Go to Mexico for Spring Break

Spring break is a dangerous time for college students. It is especially dangerous to go to Mexico during spring break. Students should be wise and not go.

First, college students are oblivious to a lot of things when they sign up for tour packages. The travel companies market alcohol because the drinking age in Mexico is 18. This law is not very enforced in Mexico. Even college students, who don't normally drink, end up drinking until they pass out. According to Mayday360.com, spring-breakers act like they are in the U.S., so they think that the U.S. laws will protect them.

On the other hand, college students think that spring break is a great time to blow off steam. Students are warned with websites to be cautious. According to US-based tour operations, trips are cheap. According to USA Today, beer and liquor companies think they are doing nothing wrong.

Lastly, college student's actions are not taken into much consideration. Students — mostly girls — participate in wet T-shirt contests, without thinking about the long-term consequences. Some of those consequences are unauthorized pictures of them and unauthorized videos of them on MTV. According to Mexico Vacation Awareness, 12,000 people died of drug violence in 2011. Also according to familes.com, most parents are unaware of what their kids do during spring break.

In conclusion, spring break in Mexico is dangerous for college students. Many consequences are involved in just one week. Parents should lay down the law and make sure that their kids don't do stupid things over spring break. Students should be wise and not go to Mexico.

Abigail Bronchick, Grade 8
Beacon Country Day School, CO

The Time I Learned to Ride My Bike

Whhoosshh!! Excitedly, I can feel the air as it goes through my hair. As I ride fast down the street, I can barely see the houses.

When I was five years old, I learned how to ride my bike. As I look back, I can still remember when my dad was helping me learn. It was hard, but I eventually learned. I can still remember that day like as if it was yesterday. At first, I was worried I would fall and hurt myself, but my dad told me that if I did, just to get back up and try again. My dad held me up most of the time, but at one point he let me go and I was riding well until…BANG!!! I crashed into my neighbor's mailbox and hit my face hard. It really hurt, but in my head I could hear my dad's voice telling me to get back up, so that's what I did. When I got back up, I started riding down the street by myself. At that point I realized I was doing it. As I was riding, I could hear my dad cheering behind me. I was doing it; I was finally riding my bike.

After I realized that I could ride my bike, I was relieved. I was proud of myself because if I didn't learn, I would not have been able to ride my bike.

Ashley Flores, Grade 7
Lindale Jr High School, TX

Evolution: Theory Not Fact

Acceptance of evolution as theory rather than scientific fact is supported because scientists cannot prove this is how life originated, even the simplest cell is complex beyond belief, and evolutionary theories are not supported by evidence.

Scientists cannot prove that evolution brought about life. Dr. Gerald Joyce, in a New York Times article, states, "Details remain obscure and are not likely to be found in the near future…" All breakthroughs that have been made have been under strict supervision, under some of the most brilliant scientific minds, with the most advanced technology, yet Dr. Shapiro in Dr. Overbye's article states, "The concept that the scientists are actually illustrating is the one of Intelligent Design." To put this in other terms, scientists have made it undeniably clear that these steps have to be taken with direct involvement of a highly intelligent life force. Even the tiniest cell is so intricately created that it is beyond comprehension. Dr. Paul Davis says, "Bacteria have a fine tuning and complexity as yet unmatched by human."

In contrast, the "facts" of evolution are hotly debated between researchers. Theorist H.P. Yockey said, "A scenario describing the genesis of life on Earth by chance and natural causes which can be accepted on the basis of fact and faith has not yet been written…" Evolution should only be considered a theory because there is no possible way the whole Earth, creatures, and the tiniest cell could be made by a large explosion with nothing to support the life. The millions of galaxies and bacteria could not have been made by random nature but only by intelligent design. Scientists themselves have proved, without intent, that it is not possible to have life without intelligent design.

Courtney Chandler, Grade 8
Vacaville Christian Schools, CA

Art and the Arts

Art is one of the best subjects. Why? Because there are so many different kinds of art. There's literature, choreography, painting, drawing, pottery, and so many more! Literature is my personal favorite because poetry and stories are branches of literature. My dream has to do with art since I want to be an author. I hope to at least publish one book. I want to share my unique world with others using captivating words that encourage my readers to keep turning the pages. My sister's dream also has to do with art. She wants to become an artist. Her favorite pastime is drawing. Her favorite subject to draw is fantasy creatures. Dragons, unicorns, Pegasus, you name it. She can draw almost anything if she puts enough effort into it.

When most people think about art, they think about famous paintings and the famous artists that painted them, but for me, art reminds me of my dream, what I want to achieve in life. Art means so many things to me; my sister's drawings, my younger sister's dance class, and our dreams. I think that most of us have a dream that we want to accomplish in our lives that has something to do with the arts. Whatever the reason, arts-related or not, GO FOR IT!!!

Caitlynn Hendricks, Grade 7
Excelsior Academy, UT

Summer Vacation

What's your typical summer vacation? Is it the beach, Hawaii, Florida, whatever! Well mine was Yellowstone, and in my opinion it is one of the most beautiful places on Earth. When my family and I started out we drove into what seemed like the middle of nowhere, close to our destination. When we finally arrived in Yellowstone, it was dusk and the sun slowly sank behind the immense mountains. The sunset reflected off the water of the lake as if to give a mirror-like image. The majestic mountains seemed to create a room whose walls stretched all the way up to the bright sky that was slowly fading to black. The next day came faster than expected, we all woke up early and headed out, eager to get started. The first animal that met our eyes was a grizzly bear, large and ferocious. It walked slowly into the trees and vanished from sight. My dad, who had gone to Yellowstone when he was a kid, was eager to show us Old Faithful. When we arrived I could already feel the excitement boiling within me and many people were already lined up waiting to see the geyser erupt. We waited maybe a total of twenty-five minutes until finally just a few seconds remained. In 5 4 3 2…

Ashley Berry, Grade 7
St Joseph Catholic School, CA

Deep Affection

Love, love — so much can be written about love. True love is sought after by the noblest of men, the bravest of the brave, and the meager peasant. Love can reduce the barbarian to a docile soldier. Love does not boast. Stories have been told and written about love as far back as records have been kept.

Lots of people have problems with their loved ones, whether it be family, husbands, friends, and others. Do you really love your family? Do you listen carefully to what they say? Do you care about what they say? All people, big and small, get in fights. If they love you, they will not lie to you. Love is different in everyone's eyes. If someone was to say that they loved you but really didn't show it, don't let that tear you down. These are the things we learn in life as we age. The longer you are with someone you love, the more you love them. Everyone in the world has a special connection between themselves and their mother; the sound of a mother's voice that calms them.

Holly Wayman, Grade 7
Excelsior Academy, UT

The Different Qualities in a Friend

There are a couple of qualities a real friend needs. One is loyalty. Loyalty is important because they will not leave you alone when you need them most. Another reason is that you can share things that you normally would not talk to most people about. The second quality would be strength, so that they can encourage you. A strong friend is one that you can depend on. Also a strong friend is one that will protect your back no matter what happens. There are many more qualities that a good friend needs but I count on loyalty and strength of conviction.

Nathan Bognar, Grade 9
Foothills Academy, AZ

The Dancer's Dream

Her heart was pounding as she returned to the stage, barely catching her breath. The audience's applause pierced through the frenzied thud of her heartbeat throbbing in her temple. She took a bow and smiled at the reward of her efforts. Yes, she felt that her struggles for the previous months had been worth it. After all, she was a dancer.

One hour before, nervously chattering her teeth, the performer left the dressing room's comfort; nonetheless, she had been looking foreword to this night for a long time. She was going to give it her all, no matter what happened. A few days before, the nimble artist had tripped and had hurt her ankle. When she plummeted to the ground, clutching her injured ankle, tears flooded her eyes, streaming down her face. She had been anticipating this show for eight years. Nights when her calves cried out in pain, she would dream of her senior year dance, when everything would be perfect, including her. When she crouched down to nurse her swollen ankle, she realized her dream might not come true. As she continued to her car, she felt her ankle protest for putting weight on it as if nothing were wrong. But something was wrong. Her ankle, so fragile yet strong, had betrayed her, but she decided she would not allow anything to stand between her and her goal. She was determined to make her dance flawless.

With this flashback running through her mind, she looked over the crowd as if she were a princess looking over her realm. She regally bowed again, knowing that no matter what, where there is a will, there is a way, though sometimes filled with obstacles, but worthwhile in the end. She was, after all, the girl with a dream, the dancer.

Veena Agusala, Grade 9
Trinity School of Midland, TX

You Say Football, I Say Soccer

Soccer, also known as football, is the most famous sport in the world and is played in almost every country. In soccer, there are four positions. There is goalie, defense, midfield, and forwards. All are also known as different names. Goalie is also known as keeper, defense is also known as defenders, midfield is also known as halfbacks, and forwards are also known as strikers.

All of the positions have different jobs they have to play. Goalie is the player that stands in front of the goal and tries to block every ball that comes at them. Unlike all of the other positions, the goalie can use their hands. Defense is the players that protect the goal, help the goalie out. Midfield is the most intense position. Midfielders protect the middle and run most of the game. The midfield doesn't have a designated spot where they are supposed to be, that's why they end up running most of the game. As for forwards, they score almost all of the goals. Forwards are supposed to stay at the top of the field, by the other team's goal, so they can have a better opportunity to score. The different positions have a certain amount of players that play the position at one time. One player plays the goalie. Defense is played by three or four players. Three or four players play midfield. Two to four players play as a forward. The amount of players varies according to how the team wants to play.

If you're playing the most famous sport in the world, you don't want to be caught not knowing what you're doing. That's why knowing the positions is essential to the game. "I eat football, I sleep football. I breathe football. I'm not mad, I'm just passionate" — Thierry Henry.

Brenna Owen, Grade 7
Sunrise Ridge Intermediate School, UT

The Passion I Have for Music

Music…the overwhelming feeling of joy. When I listen to music, it makes me feel free. It can make a person feel like they are in their own world, nobody else's. I know that a lot people listen to a certain kind of music because maybe it's the new trend at school of that's what all their friends are listening to. When I listen to music, I listen to it because it makes me feel happy and kind of relieved. Maybe you had a bad day at school, and you listen to music, it just makes your day better. Music makes everybody want to dance; every time you listen to it you feel like dancing and being yourself. Music can make you happy, excited, and help you be in a better mood. Many people, including myself, listen to music to help them sleep or do homework and even cool stress. We all have different tastes in music; I like techno and screamo, and there are plenty of different varieties of music in the world, like country, rock, rap, R&B, and so many more. Listening to music strengthens your attitude in a good way and it will even bring you to do more things that you might not have done before. Be daring and listen to a variety of music and find the music that you truly love; not the music your friends love, listen to the music that you love and that makes you…you.

Kayla Iohmeyer, Grade 7
Excelsior Academy, UT

Learning to Rake

Have you ever needed to rake your yard because you were having people over? If you follow these simple steps your yard will be leaf free in no time.

When you pick up leaves you will needed a pair of heavy duty gloves, a trash bag, (any size), and a strong rake. Gloves would help to prevent thorns, but you don't have to have them. You wouldn't want to rake on a rainy, windy, or a cloudy day because that means it might rain. First, you get all your supplies ready to go. Then, you start raking the leaves. In my opinion it helps if you rake them into one or more piles. When you are raking the leaves you will hear the leaves crumble as they get pushed together. When you are raking be careful not to get any dirt in your mouth. Just keep repeating until completed. Once you complete it, you should get someone else to hold the trash bag, but if you don't it is going to be a little harder. You could also set it on something or hang it from something. Open the trash bag nice and wide and grab many leaves with your hands, repeat until completed. Once, you finish the job you will see a leaf free place.

Now that you have finished the task raking leaves, you are ready to show off your yard. Just don't rake up your flowers.

Megan McClellan, Grade 7
Lindale Jr High School, TX

The Costume

Seven years ago, when I was very little, I learned how to appreciate a gift given to me and show it off with pride.

I bounded down the stairs to greet my mother as she pulled into the driveway from her day of running errands. When she walked in the house and set her bags down, I leaped up onto the kitchen counter and started to dig through the plastic bags. Soon enough, I encountered what I was looking for and ripped it out of the bag, spilling the other contents onto the tile floor in the process. My mother had so gratefully gone to the store to pick out a costume for me to wear for the Halloween carnival that night at my school. I stopped short at what I saw inside the clear bag, a bright orange costume that looked cheap and hideous because of its fabric. It swallowed up the clear bag that I was holding at arms' length.

I stared at the blow up pumpkin costume blankly. I was at a loss for words. Right then and there I decided I hated it but instead the words that came out of my mouth were, "I think it's the best costume ever." When I said that, I immediately regretted it because it was not true.

At the party, I waddled around in it like a penguin. I slipped into the bathroom before any of my friends could see me. When I was washing my face, two of my friends came through the door.

One of my friends Maggie mentioned, "Hey, you have a nice costume on. No joke. Where did you get it?"

Right then, I was suddenly very thankful that my mom had gone through the trouble of buying me the costume. "Ya," I answered, "It is a cool costume; I just never realized it until now."

Sophia Sanchez, Grade 9
Saint Mary's Hall, TX

The Legendary Coach

My coach, Coach Rivera, has been my basketball coach for the last three years. He taught me how sustain and undergo a lot of tough things in my life. We had a lot of tough practices but he would always help me through a lot of things. I reminisce one practice when we did the Chinese fire drill, where you run up and down the steps for one minute. He was always enterprising to start new things.

Even though he didn't coach me in seventh grade, he is still is a great coach. I like motivational speeches before and after basketball games. I will always look up to him as a coach. He liked to collaborate.

This year I made A-team for basketball. Our team is really good and we had a lot of fun this year. This year our team only lost four games; this tells you how good of a team we were. Our team won city this year so our team was really abashed. It made our team feel elite.

He was the best coach I have had for the past three years. He has always wanted me to do my best in basketball. He was sometimes volatile with me but always forthright and direct in telling me what I did wrong. He instilled his faith in me to get the job done. I will miss him next year.

Justin Dylla, Grade 8
St Matthew Catholic School, TX

More Than a Game

"Eli Manning passes to Victor Cruz for a 99-yard touchdown!" Those words changed the course of what had been a normal Saturday afternoon. The sofa that my body had been sprawled on just a few moments ago is now empty as I am on my feet, cheering and staring in disbelief. Nothing is more satisfying to me than watching football. Football has the ability to transport me to another world and experience intense feelings of victory and adrenaline I could not experience otherwise.

While watching football I experience the feeling of physically being on the field with my favorite team. A victory over a rival brightens up my whole week; a loss makes me wonder what I should have done differently to ensure a victory. When referring to my favorite team, I find myself using "we" instead of the actual name of the team.

Football feeds my inner need for unpredictability. The structure of the NFL promotes volatility. With only sixteen regular season games, every game makes an enormous difference in the outcome of the season. The NFL playoff structure also promotes insanity. With single game elimination, any one of the twelve playoff teams has a chance at winning the championship.

I am a coward. I have only played tackle football a handful of times in my life, and I admit that I am not very good at it. This concession brings us to the greatest appeal of watching football. Football invites me to be the hero of the game. As Drew Brees drops back and releases the ball, I am Marques Colston sprinting down the sideline. I dive and watch as the ball trickles into my hands as I cross the goal line. Ah, victory is sweet.

Amaan Virani, Grade 9
Saint Mary's Hall, TX

Everyday Fairness in Everyday Life

Can you imagine what the world would be like if everyone was fair? It seems too good to be true, right? Well, if everyone in the world was fair there would be no need for rebellions or debates because everyone would know what would be right and what would be wrong easily. There would be no need for court or even jails because no one would commit crimes because everyone would know what fair is and how to be fair. Everyone would know right from wrong, everyone would be happy, and there would be no worries in the world or maybe even no homeless. Well, sadly, as we all know, the world is not like this, it is actually almost the exact opposite if you look at it from a certain angle. You might be wondering what fairness means to me. I would tell you that being fair is knowing what is right and doing it no matter what or who you have to face for your choice. Fairness is the first step to justice and you must always remember that there are not unimportant acts of justice, making it also no unimportant acts of fairness. Even though the world is not like this does not mean that you should be discouraged from being fair. If you want the world to be fair you have to start with yourself because it would make you a hypocrite if you say one thing then do another.

Alyssa Anguiano, Grade 7
St Ferdinand Catholic School, CA

Act Now

Every day on our way to school, or work, it's hard not to notice individuals at street corners with a sign saying "HUNGRY, HELP." What a way to start a day for the poor! It is very sad to say that this is not an uncommon scene. The world population has reached 7 billion. The fact is that our planet has enough food for everyone. But there is a big gap between the available food and the needy. Why is this?

News media talk about national security, but do they talk enough about food security? History has taught us that hunger is the worst enemy of peace. Global security cannot be achieved without addressing food insecurity and poverty. Here are some numbers which will show the gravity of this matter: the official poverty rate in 2010 (USA) was 15.1 percent. As of 2008, the World Bank has estimated that 1.3 billion poor people in developing countries live on $1.25 a day or less. There are 925 million hungry people in the world. 925 million people is 13.6 percent of the world population. In other words, one in seven are hungry.

Knowing the facts about hunger is important, but that in itself accomplishes little. Bill Vaughan (American columnist and author) said, "It would be nice if the poor were to get half of what is spent in studying them." Ending hunger will not come about by us talking about the poor and hungry. We will end hunger only when we realize that we have to act. Do something real and active. There are literally thousands of ways we can help stop hunger (e.g. donating to a local food bank, and participating in a food run/walk). Mother Teresa said "If you cannot feed a hundred people, then feed just one." This one line says it all.

Akilan Murugesan, Grade 8
Sacramento Country Day School, CA

Water Conservation

The average American uses 140-170 gallons of water every day. An average bath requires 37 gallons of water, a single flush of the toilet uses 6 1/2 gallons, and if the faucet is left running while brushing teeth, five gallons can be wasted. Water is part of our everyday lives so it is important to help conserve it.

Water is a critical resource needed for human survival; however, only one percent of the Earth's water is available for drinking. As the world's population continues to grow, so does the demand for water, so it is important to ensure that a healthy water supply will still be available.

Some of the ways I have conserved water are taking shorter showers and running the dishwasher and washing machine only when they are full. When gardening, I water lawns during the early morning or evening when temperatures are the lowest to reduce losses from evaporation, and water plants heavily, but less often to build stronger roots and save water. Small steps like these can made a big difference.

Another way I have conserved water is by checking for leaks in pipes, hoses, faucets, and couplings. Some leak signs around the home are low water pressure, high water bills, damp patches on floors and walls, hissing water sounds, and unusual plant growth. Having unidentified leaks in the home can lead to silent water waste, and a leaky faucet can waste one hundred gallons a day, so to conserve water, it is important to stop water leaks.

The demand for water will increase over time, so we need to conserve water. When we are educated on water conservation, we can conserve water, and have a brighter, greener future.

Kevin Braza, Grade 8
Santa Clara Elementary School, CA

An Interesting Trip

One of the coolest trips I've ever been on would have to be the time I visited New York City. Half of the trip I was actually in New Jersey visiting some friends. We have friends that live in Cranford and Atlantic Highlands, near the Jersey Shore. Everything started at a New Jersey dock. My mom and brother Alex went on the trip, too. We rode a ferry from Highlands, New Jersey to New York. During the ride, I got to see the Statue of Liberty with my own eyes. When we left the boat, we walked into the city. It's amazing how many "yellow cabs" there are! They are on literally every street. It took almost no time to get one. We were riding to the American Museum of Natural History. People know it best because of the "Night at the Museum" movies. In front of the museum is a giant statue of Teddy Roosevelt. It's about 30 to 50 feet tall. It was amazing inside the museum! The displays were even better than in the movie. One of my favorite exhibits was the cavemen. Another was the Easter Island head. One of the coolest secrets of the museum was that there is a subway under the museum. The one thing that gets sometimes annoying about New York and New Jersey, is that it gets so cold. But other than the coldness, it was the best trip I've been on yet.

Nick Wille, Grade 7
St Gregorys Catholic School, AZ

The Future Comes Each Day

Everyone has dreams. They vary depending on the person, but we all have them and we all want them to come true. We want that Prince Charming or the perfect girl, that house on the hill or a trip around the world. We want the pot of gold at the end of the rainbow.

Everyone loves to dream, but many of us miss an important point that is crucial to our happiness. Since we are so often longing for things we see in other people's lives, we tend to pay little attention to the dreams which are coming true in our own lives. We live our lives each day, looking to the future and what it holds, its chances and possibilities. The world doesn't seem to hold enough for us, so we dream on. We dream about our first car or of going to college. After we have those things, we dream further — of our ideal house, job, children and more. We scarcely stop to notice when we get our dreams, and every time one is fulfilled, we dream of the next. We must be able to dream, but when our dreams are fulfilled, let's remember to take a moment to be grateful before dreaming on. Our lives are filled with countless, wonderful memories. True happiness will come from being satisfied with our lives today.

Abigail Johnson, Grade 8
Home School, TX

Something I Live For

Soccer is the most popular sport in the world and soccer has been around for hundreds of years. Soccer is also the most active sport in the world. What is there not to love?

Soccer has been a part of my life since I was five years old. Soccer is my life. I came a long way since my first day. I have always played AYSO every season because that is what built me as an athlete. After a few years of AYSO, I played or a club team called San Miguel. That season gave me confidence and no one or team scares me or stops me from pushing on. I always play until I faint on the field because I take pride in what I do and love. The only thing that gets me off the field is an injury like a bloody foot, which I have experienced.

When I play soccer, I feel at home with my ancestors from when they played the game. I feel calm and it relaxes me. This is a sport where I can show my perseverance. It also shows how self-disciplined I am. This is a conditioning sport that needs lot of preparation. I, especially, had to work on my form on my shot. Now, I can pull off any shot, any angle, any situation with full power because I do not take any shortcuts. It is unexpected to people who try and shut me down.

From lightning speed to excessive power, discipline, strength, and perseverance makes me successful. That can get you somewhere too, because you have the power to make yourself successful in anything. This is something that my ancestors did and I feel like that I should continue the streak.

John Heath, Grade 8
Santa Clara Elementary School, CA

Wax Museums

Wax museums are one of the most popular things people visit. All year long people come to see celebrities, creatures, and animals in wax form. A wax sculpture is a very difficult form of art. Not many people are known for making wax art.

My favorite places to visit are wax museums. They give me exotic feelings when I see them. It is just so fascinating because of the detail and time that is put into them. Someday I would like to become a wax artist. One of my favorite parts I like about a wax museum is the animals. It always looks like they have realistic fur. I probably would not be as happy without wax museums.

At the wax museum I went to go see the aliens. Aliens are one of my favorite creatures. They are one of the Earth's mysteries. Aliens are made to the best detail with wax.

In the wax museums there are different parts of sections. One section that I do not really understand is the car section. There are cars that I did not know existed. The planes were awesome. They had a wax model of the Wright brother's first plane.

The animals were very scary looking. They would play sound effects next to the wax models. In one of the sections they had a background of Africa and the water that looked like ocean was beautiful.

I wish more people could get to experience what I have experienced.

Samuel Camacho, Grade 8
Santa Clara Elementary School, CA

Welcome to the Circus

Have you ever heard the saying "My family is like fudge; sweet, with a few nuts?" That saying describes my family so well! Even though they tend to get on my nerves sometimes, I love them! We are a very close family, and I feel very blessed to be close to my family!

Does your family like to spend time together? My family does! We are very passionate about hockey! We love watching it, going to the games, and most importantly, playing it together! I would say that my 2 year old nephew is my family's biggest hockey fan! We love spending time together, but, as I mentioned above, since my family is so big it is hard to get all of us together, especially because some of them live in Texas and Georgia!

My family is very special to me! We don't always get along, but no family gets along all of the time. We will always be there for each other, through thick and thin! We have been through many things together, including trials, and those trials make my family closer. They allow us to have a closer bond with each other.

In closing, I would like to say that I love my family! I would do anything for them and I know that they would do anything for me as well. Without my family, I wouldn't have been able to make it this far in life! I have always put my family first and that is the way it will always be, no matter what we go through! My family is forever!

Madison Beckham, Grade 8
Excelsior Academy, UT

Music Is an Inspiration

Music has united people for ages. Music is a universal language; everyone speaks it. It unites people, like how the African Americans were united by the song "We Shall Overcome." Songs have even become a sign to people. Our country has an anthem that unites our people.

People have been using music for a long time. For instance, Green Sleeves has been sung all throughout history. There have been famous songs throughout history as well as famous composers, such as Beethoven. He wrote and composed some of the most famous songs in history. Almost everyone knows his music. This is another thing that makes music an international language.

All cultures have music in them. Music might be part of one of their rituals, or just something that brings joy to the people of the culture, or the music could just be there to unite a people. This has happened all throughout history. Native Americans used music as a sort of war cry. Music has certainly affected history, in mostly a good way.

I play the trumpet and enjoy doing so. By itself it can sound good, but when a whole band is playing a song, that is when it becomes a masterpiece. Most everyone enjoys creating or listening to music. Ever since I was a little kid I have heard and enjoyed music, and I want everyone to enjoy music also, or even trying to play an instrument. If music has inspired people for such a long time, it should always inspire people.

Spencer Bohman, Grade 8
Excelsior Academy, UT

Art Is Important to Me

The most important thing to me is art. It is the way I express myself and it is what I hope to do when I graduate college. Art is important to me.

Most artists express their emotions through creativity. When I feel happy, I draw something which conveys it. But drawing is not the only form of art. Music is also how I express myself. Although the gift of creating music is not my strong point, listening to music is a great way to let friends know what interests me.

No limit can be found to where I can use my artistic ability. In an expanding society, architects design stupendous buildings. To honor an important leader, we create memorials. The many memorials we see in our great country have all been designed by an artist. In a world ruled by celebrities, fashion is a major influence. Whatever celebrities wear, their attire is a work of art, much of which they pay for at the highest price, especially when imbedded with precious stones. Another job opportunity is through movies. Directors always require someone to design costumes or make props. When it comes to designing buildings, memorials, clothing, props, or even simply adding a special touch to someone's living room, art is how I hope to make a living, even if I have not yet decided what exactly it is I want to do.

Art is my passion, whether I am creating a "Picasso" or simply doodling.

Crystal Stolze, Grade 9
First Baptist Academy, TX

The Dichotomy of a Decision

The decision of whether juveniles who commit violent crimes should be tried as adults relies on many factors including cognizance of the crime, protecting society, and the desired outcome. Some say that juveniles who commit violent crimes are not capable of understanding their decisions because they lack life experience, while others say that children know right from wrong at a young age. Gina Savini, who prosecutes cases in Cook County's juvenile court states, "If they are old enough to pick up a gun and shoot it, they're old enough to take responsibility for their actions." The adult criminal system should protect society from violent delinquents.

The argument continues as to whether trying kids as adults is fair to the juvenile. Trying them as adults provides more representation than in the juvenile court system, but a longer sentence makes the juvenile feel hopeless. The system must balance protecting both the public and the rights of the juvenile.

If a juvenile is tried as an adult offender, their mind, rights, and life are at stake, but one must consider the rights of the victim and the community. Age should not matter in these situations, only the ramifications of the crime because there is always a victim and they deserve justice. The victim's justice should come first and the violent juvenile should be held accountable for his actions regardless of his age.

Katelynn McClellin, Grade 8
Vacaville Christian Schools, CA

My New Cousins

I was eight years old when my mom told me about my cousin Emily. Emily and her brother, mom and dad live in a small town in England. They are my second cousins. I found out that Emily was also eight years old just like me! A couple months later my mom told me the greatest news an eight year old could ever get!

Emily and her family were coming to America next summer! I was ecstatic and I couldn't wait to meet them! From then until that summer we wrote each other and called each other every weekend and whenever we could. Emily sent us some pictures so when they met us in San Francisco we could recognize them.

Before I knew it, it was summer of 2009. When my family and I were on our way to meet our cousins I was so nervous and overjoyed to meet them. It was my birthday too, so when we met up with them they gave me a present. It was a teddy bear that smelled like berries and it was super cute. I still have it to this day. Then we all went to lunch on Fisherman's Wharf, it was a good day!

My mom surprised me the next day. She, I, and our cousins were going to go to Disney Land! Can you believe they have never been there? We were having so much fun that I didn't even think about when they had to leave! We were all devastated when it was time for everyone to go home and we had to leave each other. They did promise that they would be coming back. I held them to that promise!

The next summer they came overseas again to America and we went to Lake Tahoe! I can't believe it's been three years since I've seen them. They might be coming back this summer. I'm so glad that they made time to see us. Maybe next time I can go to England to visit them?

Amanda Ebert, Grade 7
Thornton Jr High School, CA

True Healing

What is true healing? Some say healing is getting medicine from a doctor and whatever problem you had will go away. Yes, that may heal the body, but that is not true healing. True healing heals the soul. True healing is knowing when to relax and let go of the pain. True healing is forgiving when forgiving isn't easy. True healing is praying to God that the trouble has been knocked out. True healing is looking at past mistakes, heartaches, and pains and telling them, "I will not allow you to damage my future." For me true healing is being held in my mother's arms and just knowing that she cares. Even if I don't need the healing, that hug means she is adding on an extra layer of armor for me to get through another day. That armor is my mother's love, because no matter how far you go out in your life nothing can break that love. Healing your heart is what you need. Don't let anyone or anything hold you down. There may be days that are so bad that you may want to cry. That's OK, but let your burdens fall along with your tears and you shall have true healing. "I love you Mommy. I am such a child."

Mia Glenn, Grade 9
Florence High School, AZ

PE — Not an Academic Grade

Physical education should not affect the overall grade point average because academic school performance should not also measure physical performance, PE should be separate from academics, and a lower grade point average penalizes academic standings and opportunities. The purpose of a GPA is to measure academic standings in school, not physical standings. Some students may not be gifted in sports or running, resulting in a decreasing GPA. According to www.onlineuniversities.com, "A student's GPA is important while they are in school because it can greatly affect future academic circumstances." The GPA analyzes how a person does in school academically. According to www.nassp.org, "The purpose of a grade point average is to measure and compare students' academic achievements, and promote fairness and equity in college admission procedures." The disadvantage of physical education being included in the GPA is that if a student gets a lower grade in PE, their overall grade decreases. This affects students who are academically competent, but may struggle in the physical environment.

Although, a student may be intelligent, their overall grade could decrease due to lack of skill in physical education. A student's future depends on how they do in school. According to www.thefischbowl.com, "The purpose of education is to appropriately prepare our children for their future." It is imperative to get decent grades in school to be successful in life, but when students are incompetent in PE, it can jeopardize future situations such as college and job opportunities. The grade a student gets in physical education should be inconsequential to the overall grade point average because a GPA measures how a student does in school academically, not physically. This would base academic achievements on intelligence, not physical ability.

Shelbie Petersen, Grade 8
Vacaville Christian Schools, CA

Not Far Enough

Although women's status is challenging traditional norms academically, women have yet to surpass men economically and politically. There is compelling evidence to show that women are overtaking the field of academics. Christina Hoff Somers, resident scholar at the American Enterprise Institute, finds in a study that 3/5 of all prodigies are girls. Christina Hoff Somers and others conclude that while women lead academically, men continue to lead in the workplace.

Leaders of top corporations are largely led by men, dispelling any argument that women have taken over the workplace. The article "Decline of the Working Man" by Philadelphia says that there are more unemployed men than women, but this article fails to recognize that more men work than women. Many studies have shown that men are more successful. On average a man earns $431,000 more than an average working woman. In addition to economics, another area where women are not on top is politics.

Similar to corporate America, women are not taking over the role of elected offices. The U.S. has overcome the racial barrier by electing an African-American President before electing a female President. Roughly 50% of America's population is female. Significantly less than that is African American. There are currently 362 seats in the U.S. House of Representatives, but only 76 are women. In the Senate there are only 17 women, and in all state legislatures only 23.6% are women, indicating that women are far from taking over male roles in our government.

Statistics support the fact that women in society have not reached equal status with men, either politically or economically, in spite of academic indications of equal abilities.

Blake Sprunk, Grade 8
Vacaville Christian Schools, CA

Snowboarding Is Life

Snowboarding is my favorite thing to do in the world. I love to snowboard because when I get going fast down the slopes, it feels like I'm flying. I love to have the wind blowing in my face. When you are going through the powder, it flies up at you and splashes in your face. It makes me feel like I'm on top of the world. It feels like I can do anything.

What first got me to like snowboarding was, for my birthday, my dad took me to take a snowboarding lesson. My teacher said I was a natural. My parents have taken me every year since then for Christmas. Over the years I keep getting better. I want to join a team instead of just going for fun.

One of my heroes is Shaun White because he is the greatest snowboarder in the world. He competes in the Olympics every year and each year he makes up a cooler, harder trick. When I get older I want to be in the Olympics just like him.

My dad is also one of my role models because he tries to come with me whenever I go. When I get older, I want to take my kids snowboarding and teach them how to snowboard. Snowboarding is my life!

Mason Curtis, Grade 8
Excelsior Academy, UT

A Dog's Influence

Whenever I'm feeling down, I can count on my dog Tundra to cheer me up. Once, after a stressful day at school, I came home and went upstairs to sulk. Tundra followed me up, then placed her head on my lap and whistled a jaunty tune through her nose. Tundra can reliably be counted on to help, whether as a pillow or a playmate. Tundra seems to understand all my struggles and pains, and always knows the perfect way to lighten up my day. After a particularly stressful test, playing ball with Tundra is a great way to relieve additional stress, between kicking or throwing a ball and her hilarious antics with the ball, playing with Tundra is relieving. Even her hilarious growls and moans manage to add a little sparkle to an otherwise dreary day. Tundra understands that humor is a great way to inspire joy, and she can be counted on to help whenever I need a little happiness. Tundra radiates joy around her and takes advantage of that to entertain everyone around her. Even on walks, the nearby wildlife is friendly towards her, when normally they would run in fear. Tundra cheers me up even if the rest of my day was putrid!

Stelth Taylor, Grade 7
Salida Middle School, CO

Gum-chewing Benefits Students

Students should be allowed to chew gum in school because it helps students concentrate, reduces stress, and increases cognition. Chewing gum prevents students from talking, while chewing mint gum has been shown to help students in the classroom by decreasing sleepiness, which increases the chances of studying effectively.

Chewing gum relieves anxiety, leading students to stay calm while studying or taking tests. Studies of chewing gum have found that it decreases hunger that bothers students while trying to concentrate. Chewing gum has an impact on levels of mood-altering hormones, such as reducing cortisol. Cortisol causes feelings of stress, therefore gum helps students to stay peaceful. To prove this, researchers measured students' heart rates and cortisol levels after testing while playing a screeching noise to build stress. Those who chewed gum during the stressful noise were less annoyed by the noise.

Recent studies have demonstrated chewing gum is an effective booster while performing cognitive tasks. Students who chewed gum did 26% to 36% better, because it caused their hearts to pump more blood to the brain. Blood carries brain-nourishing oxygen that helps brain to function better than usual; therefore, those who chewed gum significantly outscored students in normal conditions.

Chewing gum improves the behavior and performance of the students by enabling them to concentrate by keeping them silent, and mint gum helps to focus. Just like some people shake their legs while studying, chewing gum relieves nervousness by lowering cortisol. Although students might not dispose of gum correctly through carelessness, by thinking before the action and establishing strict rules about it, students should be allowed to chew gum in school for academic reasons.

Min-Jun Song, Grade 8
Vacaville Christian Schools, CA

Protecting Exotic Animals

People should retain exotic animals in their natural habitat because owning them as pets creates a hazard to society, harms the animal, and return to their natural environment disrupts the ecosystem. Exotic animals can infect humans with diseases such as hepatitis, rabies, and tuberculosis. Malnutrition, stress, trauma, and behavioral disorders are common factors for exotic animal pets. When exotic pets are released after captivity, they spread diseases to native species or kill native animals and free-roaming pets. Exotic animals kept as pets greatly impact the native society with high-risk health and safety conditions.

U.S. Fish and Wildlife Services say that 90% of imported green iguanas most likely carry some strain of intestinal bacteria, and up to 25% of both imported and domestically bred macaque monkeys carry the herpes B virus. Studies show that pet raccoons have killed children; lions and tigers have mauled their owners. One particularly notorious act involved a wrestling bear that, though muzzled and declawed, managed to bite off fingers and break the bones of his handler.

The needs essential to the survival of exotic animals in captivity are enormous and specialized. If their needs are not satisfactorily met, many problems can arise, for example, malnutrition, stress, trauma, and behavioral disorders. In addition, the release of exotic animals greatly impacts the ecosystem, and usually spells the ultimate demise of the animal by starvation, disease, or a run-in with law enforcement. When set loose, exotic animals are not adapted to the natural habitat can propagate diseases to aboriginal species: rabies, measles, ringworm, and tuberculosis are some of the transmitted diseases. Although some people may argue that owning an exotic animal would be fascinating, taking care of an exotic animal negatively affects both the animal and society.

Lindsey Munar, Grade 8
Vacaville Christian Schools, CA

Monsters

Let me ask a question. Does anyone know how to write a good essay? I need to have something, between 100 and 250 words. It's quite compelling; I've thought of countless ideas, but all of them are either too long, to boring, or not any type of nonfiction. It drives you insane staring at a blank piece of paper trying to make words come right on to it; but the paper just sits, without response. No matter how mighty the pen, the one who holds the thing has to have the equal amount of brains that the pen does to make a good essay.

However, the most nerve-racking perplexing situation in all of the entire world is when you end up making a masterpiece, and then it amazingly disappears. They can be known right now as siblings. They turn everything you ever worked at upside down and flip you inside-out. If there is a monster worse than these, I have yet to hear about it. Still it is a great feeling when you get the paper done until of course, LKASklayu--)9lkllk CTRL-ALT-DLT,'; this is a great example of what I was trying to explain earlier: siblings are craz-(CONNECTION LOST).

Kayson Reardon, Grade 7
Sunrise Ridge Intermediate School, UT

My Coach

I once had a coach and his name is Jorge Collazo. We called him Coach Jorge. I first started playing for him about two years ago on the San Antonio Shox organization. He was always very laid back and nice. He never got mad at our team if we made a mistake. The only time he would get mad is if we did not try one hundred percent. I remember he always used to tell us that it didn't matter if we made an error, what did matter was how we reacted to it and how our attitude was after the play.

He is a very good man, never got after anyone, and always made sure everyone was having fun. I see him as a role model in my life because he never mistreats anyone and does everything to the best of his ability. I remember that after some tournaments some of the players would go over to coach's house because he has a son, J, that also played on the team.

I will never forget the great memories I have had with my coach Jorge, not only on the field but everywhere else I got to spend time with him and his family. He not only inspired me athletically but also spiritually. There will always be a place in my heart for him and I will remember him always.

Eric Cantu, Grade 8
St Matthew Catholic School, TX

Quality Traits of a Friend

A quality friend needs to have certain characteristics. The characteristics a quality friend needs to have is humor, kindness, trustworthiness, honesty and understanding.

A friend needs to be funny because you need someone to make you laugh. You also need a funny friend so when you're sad they're there to make you laugh. Being funny is a quality trait a friend should have.

Your friend should be trustworthy as well. Your friend needs to have trustworthiness because you need to be able to trust one another. You also need to have a trustworthy friend because if you need to tell them something classified they need to keep it a secret.

Honesty is another trait. Your friend needs to be honest because even if sometimes the truth hurts it is good to know. Your friend needs to be honest with you because if they have something bugging them you could possibly help.

Understanding is another quality. Your friends should understand because they need to understand you. They also need to be understanding because they need to get you in the sense they'd know what makes you hurt and what makes you happy. They should also understand that way they know what you're going through. When your friend understands they need to know your strengths and weaknesses.

Your friend should be kind too. If your friend is kind to you and others then you know they truly care. If your friend cares then you know they're there for you. Also when your friend has kindness then you know they want to help and they want to be there for you.

Kindness, trustworthiness, understanding, honesty and humor are all quality traits an amazing friend should have. The perfect friend needs to have these ideal characteristics.

Vanessa Harvey, Grade 8
St Elizabeth Ann Seton Catholic School, AZ

My Influence

As I pressed play, the most beautiful sound came out of my stereo system; it was opera. I listen to opera in Italian most of the time, but I have never heard opera in English. So I went on YouTube and looked it up. The one that stuck out the most was a little girl around the age of eight. She sings opera and gospel music. Then I saw that she was interviewed on CNN, so I watched that when I got done with the other videos, and they talked about why she loved opera and gospel music. I was right. She is an eight-year-old, and her name is Rhema.

Closer to the end of the interview, she talked about her mom dying. She died of ovarian cancer at a very young age. That is a cancer that cannot be cured. There are videos of her holding her mom's hand while she was getting her chemotherapy. One thing that her parents did is not hide the fact that Rhema's mom had cancer.

A week after she had turned four, her mom died. She was there for her last breath. When I saw those videos I almost started to cry. Rhema has influenced me to stay positive through rough times.

Alexandra Foreman, Grade 7
League City Intermediate School, TX

Refugee

My grandmother Phillis's art is a tool to end all my problems. It portrays nature in perfection. She cared for me with an open heart in life, and in death she left me with paintings to calm the turbulence of life. Her pieces show not pompous glamour, but the truth and flawless soul of the world. The art can change your life over a period of time. It consists of miniscule marks and details to bring out an object as if you had seen it with your own eyes. To watch one work with such focus is a cherished memory I am lucky enough to hold. Anger penetrates the fortress walls of my everyday life, but to look at the art is to toss my troubles away. It evokes a gentle feeling of harmony. Death has injured my spirit a few times, but when it does, I know I can find hope in her paintings and sculptures. Pain is a veil that blocks out the beauty in life, but the countless infinitesimal marks of paint lift it. Phillis's paintings are sentries that watch over me. My lackadaisical feelings are banished with a mere glimpse of the sight portrayed in her sculptures. The graceful paint marks beckon to me, not as a pretty house decoration, but as a refuge from the hurtful world, and I…am a refugee.

Evan Coit, Grade 7
Salida Middle School, CO

Goalie

Being goalie is a large responsibility; however, it is my favorite position. I'm standing in the vast field of wavy grass, anticipating the time when the ball is coming and where it's going, so I know what body part to throw in front of it so the opponent does not score. Every time the opponent comes into the goalie box my heart jumps, because I know that I'm the only one standing in front of the team's goal. Nevertheless, when that dreadful time comes that the opponent puts the ball by me, I suddenly get a sinking feeling in my gut. On the contrary, when the ball ricochets off my body, I relax and take a deep breath. Furthermore, when I catch the ball and play it back to my team, I feel as if a huge burden has been lifted from me. At the end of the first half, considering that I did a good job, I feel as if I don't want to leave the big responsibility. Goalie is the best position in my opinion. Standing in the vast field of wavy grass is where I love to be.

Hunter Beem, Grade 7
Salida Middle School, CO

My Father

In my life, my father is an important person. He helps me study for my teachers' evil tests and almost always joins me outside when I am shooting hoops. When my father and I have a disagreement, I know that he continues arguing for my own good. My father and I like lots of the same activities, such as television shows and sports. These similarities only strengthen our bonds of friendship and fun. He also drives me to my after-school activities whenever I have them. If my father was never there for me, then my life would be duller and harder. Without my father, I don't know what I would do!

Andrew Goddard, Grade 7
North Star Academy, CA

My True Friend

I don't understand how some people make it through life without a sister by their side. When it's her and I against the world we fight it together. She is my defender, my listener, and my friend. She has always been there for me, through the ups and downs, through the good times and a bad times, no matter what happens.

For that I love my sister so much, but there are many reasons why I love her. She is there to lean on and there to count on. Sometimes sisters don't forgive each other for something that happened in the past, and never will. My sister is different because she will forgive me. That's why I look up to her, and she means the world to me because when Mom and Dad don't understand, my sister always will. She's my witness; she sees me at my worst and best and still loves me. Even when it seems I'm happy she knows when I'm in pain and knows when I'm smiling even in the dark. She's a good example, and courageous to do good things. She is more than any kind of sister to me; she is my forever friend. She will always have a piece in my heart and forever it will stay.

Adriana Flores, Grade 7
Salida Middle School, CO

My Inspiration

Many things are important to me, but one out of hundreds always seems to stick out. Sports. They are all inspiring and wonderful. They will always intertwine with my life. It is an inspiration to me, like pilots inspired by Wilbur and Orville's planes. Sports inspire me to advance in new challenges such as trying to become as good as my favorite athletes.

Sports are wonderful to me in many ways. It gives me a healthy physical body and strengthens both mental and physical traits. Each time I play a sport, I think to myself how privileged I am to do something so wonderful. Whenever I play a sport, I feel enlightened to accomplish new challenges. Though I don't accomplish my goals the first time, I will always try because of my enormous inspiration. When I watch a sport I have a wonderful sensation that makes me imagine a movie of me doing what an athlete just did. Without the inspiration of sports I would never be the person I am today.

Owen Shin, Grade 7
Salida Middle School, CO

First Day

Today is the first day of the rest of my life. I have a full life to live and it's all ahead of me. I wouldn't say necessarily today is a new beginning or huge change for me, but it is a little change. In life you can either be positive or negative about things, and the way you approach situations. You can say, "I am going to make the best of life and put all the negative stuff behind me," or you could say, "What's so special about today? It is just a regular day." Every day is a blessing from God and we should be thankful for it. He gives us the blessing of being able to wake up to a new day. So, I guess today is the first day of the rest of my life.

Olivia Whatley, Grade 7
Athens Christian Preparatory Academy, TX

Dance

Ever since I was 3 years old, dance has been my favorite sport. Dance is physically challenging and requires a lot of hard work. Dance is a form of expression, and I have learned important life skills.

Dancers have to have a lot of stamina. They have to be in good shape to avoid getting injured or passing out. If you want to become a great dancer, you have to work hard and must be able to take constructive criticism.

Dancing is not only a sport, it is an art. Dance is a form of expressing who you are and showing your emotions. One of my favorite quotes is "It takes an athlete to dance, but an artist to be a dancer." This means anybody can do the movements and motions, but the flawless dancers are the ones who tell a story through their body language and facial expression.

Dance has taught me very valuable life lessons. I have learned how to be passionate, inspiring, and confident. I have been blessed with many opportunities, and I have learned if I don't get something right the first time, I am not a failure, rather more determined to succeed. I have also learned to never give up. Most people who give up don't realize how close they were to success before they quit.

People say dance isn't a sport, but most dancers are physically fit and active. When I walk into my dance studio, I feel like I am part of something special. Nobody judges or treats you unfairly; they are just there to dance. There are many incredible dancers in the world, but you have to set yourself apart and have your own pizzazz in order to be a star. Many people are trained to dance, but I was born to.

Zoe Stinson, Grade 8
St Elizabeth Ann Seton Catholic School, AZ

My Hero

Thirteen years ago she was diagnosed with the dreadful disease we know as breast cancer. Ever since, she has been fighting her entire life to be with her children. She once spoke, "God, let me be here with my daughter until she turns eighteen, then I can leave this world to go with you." Her goal is months away from being accomplished.

In January she was given the worst news yet. She got her scan: six tumors throughout the lungs and the brain, her entire back covered with black spots like a Dalmatian and her leg was bone and full of blood blobs. The doctor told her "You have three months to live." She didn't listen; she had hope in the possibilities. When those wishes started coming true twenty days later she went in for her chemotherapy. The doctor said she was the luckiest person in the world getting the last of this chemotherapy just before it went out of stock throughout the entire world. Days later, the scan was a miracle; to this day no one knows how it happened. From six tumors, she only had half of one left, and her back having only three black spots. It is March and she is better than ever. My aunt — Marithere is the biggest fighter I know in the world, having suffered breast, lung, brain and back cancer. She is still here with us now. Knowing her story you will know why I call her my hero.

Sofia Ancira, Grade 9
Saint Mary's Hall, TX

Duke Ellington

Duke Ellington was a famous composer from the 1900s whose actual name is Edward Kennedy Ellington. He got the name "Duke" for his love of fancy clothes. He was an African-American who led and composed an orchestra, the Washingtonians, and traveled around the world performing. He wrote mostly jazz and "the blues" songs that he performed all around the world to an estimated twenty thousand different places. Astoundingly, he never learned to read music. He would compose his pieces by ear. His work was influenced by the piano technique "ragtime," a technique with syncopated rhythms.

In the 1920s, Duke and his band started playing in New York. They played at a place called "The Cotton Club." It was famous for its African-American performers. They regularly played there for three years. Although they entertained at "The Cotton Club," Duke's band wasn't allowed as guests.

Duke's band consisted of Cootie Williams, Ben Webster, Juan Tizol, and Barney Bigard. Duke would compose the music specific for each player to try to bring out as much talent as he could. Duke continued to have an amazing musical career traveling the world. Duke's band also played in one of the most important Jazz festivals of the 20th century, almost every year.

Duke married his high school sweetheart, Edna Thompson, in 1918. Some of his most popular compositions include "Sophisticated Ladies," and "Take The 'A' Train." Duke wrote more than 2,000 songs in his music career.

On May 24, 1974, Duke died from lung cancer. He was a memorable composer who will live throughout the Jazz era for many generations to come.

Conner McArthur, Grade 7
Sunrise Ridge Intermediate School, UT

Father White: Inspiration and Life Changer

Many people have planted the seeds of faith and inspired me. But, there is one person in particular. His name is Father Stephen White. I have known him since I was very little. He's a very inspiring person. He has devoted his life to the priesthood. He enjoys children and teaching us about his journeys, about religion and the church. He served as a priest in Ireland, New Guinea, California and here in San Antonio. He served in the St. Matthew Parish since 1995 and made visits to the school and went out of his way to teach us and make us learn.

There was one point in his life where he thought he was going to die, but somehow he made it. He suffered some disease at that point. God wanted him to live and serve the community just a little longer. He always liked to give us a quiz on what he taught us and if we got the answer correct he gave us a prayer card. One time he said that on the card it had Mother Teresa and said that it was his girlfriend and joked about it. He taught me to care about people and to serve the community. He cared about others before himself. He always did good homilies that you enjoyed hearing and wouldn't put you to sleep. He died on February 6, 2012. He will always be remembered for the good he did. He was a good and honest person, and he will be missed. He will always be my inspiration to continue my faith journey.

Francisco Garcia, Grade 8
St Matthew Catholic School, TX

Television

Television has been commercially available since the late 1920's. Families have been gathered around the television set ever since then. The use of television can be beneficial, or harmful.

Television is a very popular way to advertise a company's products. During a thirty-minute television show there are nine minutes of commercials. Each commercial break is three minutes long, giving an average of six commercials. Companies usually program their commercials to be on when their general audience is home. If a toy company is advertising a new remote controlled helicopter, it will come on around the end of school. If a commercial for a Kobalt wrench comes on, it will be around six o' clock. This is normally the time your dad would be home watching television.

Television is used too much. In fact, most teenagers watch about twenty-eight hours in one week. In a sixty-five year life, the average person will have watched television a total of nine years. Ninety-nine percent of all households in the United States have a TV. Television is becoming addictive to people.

The things our youth watch are bad for them. The average amount of murders seen on television by the time a kid finishes Elementary School is about eight-thousand. The number of violent acts seen on TV by age eighteen is around 200,000. This kind of violence is ruining the minds of our kids.

Television can be beneficial if you limit the hours you watch and avoid bad content. By limiting the hours of television watched you could spend time doing better things, like playing with friends outside, or studying for that big test.

Nicolo Monson, Grade 8
Holliday Middle School, TX

Diversity Is an Open Doorway

Diversity is a constant factor in everyone's lives. We live and breathe it every second of every day. It shapes who we are and who we will become. The way we react to diverse situations affects us and everyone around us. When we combine others' experiences with our own, we can learn to look at these differences in a positive way. Being willing to have diversity in our lives will cause significant results to be accomplished.

Someone that has helped me appreciate diversity is a person I met at dance. He's male; because of that he suffered through a lot of teasing and put-downs. However, he ignored that and worked even harder to become the best he could be. Now, he has made it through several elimination rounds of the television show So You Think You Can Dance? He has taught his students to always try and to work their hardest, no matter what obstacles get in their way. He's an example to me of how ignoring others' negative views about being different can cause us to become great at something unique.

My experiences have taught me to stick up for the things I believe in, even if those things contrast most other people's beliefs. No matter what, we should never decide against doing something in fear of being in the minority. I see being different as an open doorway to the things we can accomplish.

Bailee Anderson, Grade 8
White Pine Charter School, ID

Diversity

Diversity is the condition of being different from others. Our differences are what make us unique. If we weren't different, we wouldn't be diverse.

Some people have differences that other people think are funny or stupid. My brother is partly deaf in his left ear. This hearing loss is permanent and causes him to have problems with his speech. We were at my grandparents' house one day and my brother said something that didn't sound right. My grandpa's friend started mocking him. This example shows how some people aren't always kind to others who are different from them.

Some people's differences are rewarding to them and some aren't. People make fun of other people, not even realizing what might be different about them. What's different about you is what makes you who you are. If we weren't different and didn't have different goals in life, the community would be going nowhere.

Some people may be similar or have similar talents, but they aren't the same; in fact, they are very different. Say two people are good at something, like drawing. They both could become artists later on in life, but maybe one wants to be something else, like a dancer. Different people have different dreams and goals.

Several people have different opinions, too. One person could like basketball, another might like volleyball. Opinions do matter! We can't all be the same, not because it would be boring, but because if we were, the world would be so much different than it is now.

Kira Croft, Grade 8
White Pine Charter School, ID

The Misconceptions of Birders

For the greater part of American history, birding was a respected hobby that was portrayed as being intellectual and down-to-earth. John James Audubon made a living from his vivid paintings of birds and his unique observations on bird behavior. Theodore Roosevelt was revered for not only being a great president, but also having a strong interest in bird watching. Even the Native Americans hung up hollowed out gourds for breeding purple martins because they admired their beauty and gracefulness in flight. In short, birders were not only respected but admired. Recently, however, birders have acquired a negative stereotype of being very "nerdy" and lacking any social life. This comes from the misconception that all birders care about are birds. While there are a handful of extremists who do fit this stereotype, most birders have a variety of interests. Personally, my weekends are composed of birding, sports, and social life, a common set of activities that most birders participate in. Most birders only bird in the morning, when the birds are most active. Throughout the rest of the day, birders often do physical activities such as basketball, running, and baseball. Although many people would perceive them as being bad at such past times, birders actually make excellent athletes. I attribute this partially to the fact that birders must do strenuous physical activities such as climb trees or go on long hikes up mountains in order to find the birds they desire. As for social life, birders often bird watch in groups and for most of the time when no birds are present, the birders carry on everyday conversations, just like any other person would.

Danny Kelleher, Grade 9
Saint Mary's Hall, TX

The Stories

Living in the modern world today, it is difficult to take the time to stop and think of the hard work and dedication it took to survive in this unforgiving world. Hard work and dedication, that is exactly what my dad offered the world, and the world repaid him, but it wasn't a walk in the park.

My dad is an extraordinary person who is loving and a hard worker, but as a child the money needed wasn't always there. My dad grew up in Laredo, Texas, a city near the Mexican border. He was dedicated to the church and he excelled in school, even though his surroundings pushed him back. He pushed himself to work harder so he could make his mark on the world, and he did.

The stories are what really influenced me. The stories of how him and his siblings used to play outside all day and make their own toys out of cardboard and whatever else they could find. These stories influenced me in a way that no other person could; only memories could convince me to appreciate my blessings.

Those stories really spoke to me and convinced me to appreciate my blessings, like having a hard working dad and how good I have it compared to him. It pushes me every day to work even harder to also have some stories to tell my kids.

Samantha Salazar, Grade 8
League City Intermediate School, TX

The Internet

The internet is filled with billions of information that is useful to anyone searching any subject. It is obvious that the internet is helpful with learning and communication. Many get thousands of answers to questions with a matter of a click. Many have electronic messaging, instant messaging, Facebook, Twitter, etc.; therefore, it is very easy to communicate. Many get help with health problems, directions, and other things, from the internet. People should know that the internet is the greatest tool anyone could have imagined.

Many get thousands of answers to any question with a matter of a click. It helps others with research papers, essays, or just simple information that we need to know in a spur of the moment situation. Others find information on politics, sports, etc. that could easily help them with situations. For example, someone could find a video on a presidential debate and find the one he wants to vote for. Coaches can find techniques that professionals do so that they can make the kids on their team better. Many have electronic messaging, instant messaging, etc.; therefore, it is very easy to communicate. Emails are the most used communication systems because it is very easy to use and is easy to send a quick little message to someone. The internet is the greatest tool of all time.

Jordan Matthews, Grade 9
South Jordan Middle School, UT

Working with Food

Can you smell something delicious in the kitchen? You would probably find me in the kitchen because I love to bake and cook. Making food is one of the many things that interest me.

I first started enjoying working with food when I was very young. I always used to watch food television shows because I loved food. I also used to cook and bake with my parents all the time. When I was in the kitchen, I would always play around with the food trying to make original recipes. One day when I made my first batch of cupcakes, I realized that I loved working in the kitchen.

I love baking and cooking because food is fun to work with. You can be creative with it. It is especially fun when the food looks and tastes good. Sometimes food does not look or taste so good, so I want to change that when I bake and cook. Knowing how to cook will also help me in the future because I will know how to cook when I am on my own.

Now, I cook and bake with friends when we get together. I also try out many new recipes. Some of the new recipes I have tried were a recipe on how to make peanut butter frosting and a recipe for cake pops. I am also trying to learn some family recipes.

I love working in the kitchen. It is a great way to make your food the way you want it. Baking and cooking are some of my favorite things to do!

Athena Giron, Grade 8
Santa Clara Elementary School, CA

Hunting: Good or Bad?

Hunting, in most eyes, is a dreadful thing. I, on the other hand, see hunting as a great way to obtain food without expense and keep animal overpopulation under control, while having fun all at the same time.

Hunting provides an opportunity to deal with the animal as wished. If the consumer is on a strict diet, they may desire thoroughly trimmed meat. If the consumer is not troubled by the fat, they may leave the meat as it is and not waste time on trimming it.

Overpopulation, when a group of living things take over an area, is a growing threat in most regions. Hunting not only provides for families, but keeps overpopulation under control. Overpopulation can be so drastic that animals may approach patio decoration in search of food. Most animals reproduce quickly allowing hunting to have an expanding purpose.

Although useful, hunting does have a few downsides. People who desire to hunt must keep in mind the amount of work ahead. A hunter must clear a region for a blind and an area for the animal to stop and eat the food prepared for it. Also, anyone who hunts for sport or the hide is trashing a perfectly useful animal. Wasting an animal is what most people frown upon because in their eyes, a helpless animal has just been slain.

I believe hunting is a good thing because of its many uses. Anyone who believes hunting is a terrible thing should consider the good it brings.

Jordan Zaruba, Grade 9
First Baptist Academy, TX

Reading: The Gateway to Power

Reading is one of the most important things in this world. Some books may be entertaining, but there is so much more to them than just that. Textbooks, biographies, newspapers, even a few entertainment books; they teach morals, state facts, describe happenings in the world and the government, and give people the ability to think for themselves. But most people don't read these or any kind of books. The reason why kings and dictators have existed for millennia is that their subjects are uneducated.

An old Chinese emperor had his soldiers go out to his kingdom to destroy all of the scrolls. If you were caught with any kind of reading material, you could be executed. And why? Because the emperor wanted to stay on the throne! Similar events have occurred throughout history. People have been oppressed for one reason. They can't read or write and they can't do anything about it.

If you know how to read well, you could be so much more powerful. Knowledge is power. Yet, most people take it for granted. Most of the people in the world simply do not understand the value of books. The forefathers of this great country founded the United States because they were learned. If they weren't, we might still be ruled by England, forced to pay taxes and grovel to the king or queen. So if you don't think reading is worth the trouble, then you should just take one good look at any history book.

Eric Carlson, Grade 7
Excelsior Academy, UT

Going to Sea World

Someone once said: "You must do the thing you think you cannot do." That's exactly what I did on my awesome day in San Antonio.

It was summer, late in July, when we went to Sea World. We got in the car and headed out on our long adventure. It was a long six hours away, so I occupied myself the entire six hours by watching videos and playing games until we got to LaQuinta hotel. It was a nice hotel, but bad at the same time; it was very pretty, but they needed to do a lot of cleaning. There was sticky makeup stains on the bed and gooey green mold on the shower curtain, but I didn't let that get in the way of our awesome fun the next day. A few hours later we ate a scrumptious dinner and went to bed. The next morning we woke up and went to Sea World. The sky was as blue as the ocean when we walked out of the delightful hotel.

When we walked through the Sea World entrance, I saw all the spectacular rides! As we walked more, I caught a glimpse of the Great White, an upside-down roller coaster! My heart was racing as fast as a rabbit getting hunted by men, as I stepped on the roller coaster.

I feel very grateful this happened, because I became closer to my loving family, but I was also sad we had to leave. This exciting event changed my life forever, so I think everyone should experience this wonderful event, even if it was one thousand degrees!

Olivia Smith, Grade 7
Lindale Jr High School, TX

Courage

The dictionary definition of courageous is the ability to do something that frightens someone. When most people think about courage, however, they imagine super heroes, soldiers, perhaps even Disney characters. They never think about themselves being courageous. People don't realize they have courage every day.

Many people struggle with bullies teasing and abusing them. For those people just going to school can require all the courage one has. People who have depression and self-confidence issues often have a hard time just getting out of bed and into the crazy world. They often need help from others to rise above their depression and other problems to get by. Along with those, many people need courage just to talk to people. They are constantly worrying about what others are thinking or someone's popularity status. It takes plenty of courage just to get up and say, "Hi." Not only do people struggle with self confidence in speaking to others, but big crowds of people may intimidate them. When someone talks to a crowd of people for the first time, they want to sound professional and speak loud and clear. They stress themselves out over things they are not used to.

In conclusion, people use courage all the time. Every day, we have something that scares us or puts us in danger. We use courage to get through our problems. Courage is hard to find when you are scared or stressed. If you just relax and think, life will be easier.

Maddie Pack, Grade 9
South Jordan Middle School, UT

The One Who Inspired Me

I once had a coach named Louis Alvarado; we all called him Coach Louis. He would always make us laugh because he always had the funniest things to say. Every time we either lost a game or someone was down he would always pick us up with his jokes. Coach Louis has three boys: one who just got out of college, one in college and one in eighth grade. All the boys in the family went to Central Catholic High School. Coach Louis sent his two oldest sons to Central Catholic and is planning on sending his youngest son there.

When I was younger Coach Louis would always tell my mom that she should send me to Central with his youngest son. At that time I was attending a public school; once I was in fifth grade my mom moved me to St. Matthew Catholic School. Ever since I changed from public to Catholic School Coach Louis really started pushing for me to go to Central. Every practice he would ask me, "So are you ready for Central?"

He would also always bug my mom about letting me attend Central with his son. Coach Louis' middle son was on the Central football team so Coach Louis would always ask me to go with them to go watch his son play. The games were very exciting and really fun. This year I am an eighth grader so we got to tour Central for the day. I had to take a test to get into Central and I surprisingly scored either average or over average on my test. A few weeks later my mom got a call and it was Central calling to inform my mom that I had gotten into Central. I was so excited and so was Coach Louis.

Gabriel E. Gonzalez, Grade 8
St Matthew Catholic School, TX

Baking Is a Piece of Cake

Does your mom's baking aroma ever reach you? Does it make you want to bake too? Well, baking is challenging, but once you get the hang of it, it is simple. Baking is a piece of cake.

To me, baking is time consuming, fun, and easy to learn. I can put my own original spin on a recipe making it homemade. When it comes to decorating, I like to be creative and think outside the box.

To bake, there are different instructions in each recipe. In general, I first gather all ingredients and supplies, preheat the oven, and start my creation. While it is baking, I go over my design, then decorate. After that, I clean up and dig into my creation. Baking instructions can be tricky, so I try to read it carefully.

There are a lot of different things you can bake. My favorite things to bake are mostly cupcakes, cake pops, cake, and cookie cakes because they are delicious and I bake them very often. I also like to bake brownies, pie, and fresh French bread. My favorite part is when it is fresh out of the oven, the most delicious time to eat it!

Baking has been a big influence on my life and I learn different things every time I do. Now every time you bake, remember to check your supplies, read the instructions and have a lot of creativity!

Margaux Ugalino, Grade 8
Santa Clara Elementary School, CA

Basketball Is Life

Basketball is life. I love basketball. Basketball is my favorite sport. I have been playing this sport for four years and love it ever since I started playing.

I started playing basketball when I was in fourth grade. I started playing on my school's third and fourth grade coed basketball team. My team was not too good, but we ended up winning two games.

I have played on many teams. Right now, I am currently playing on two teams. I am playing for my school team and 805. I have also played on five other teams called Jagz, Fusion, Swoosh, Athletics, and a basketball league named Ventura Wildcats. All of these teams have helped me a lot. I enjoy playing on teams because I meet new people and learn new skills.

I have been very successful in basketball. On my school team I am the team captain and top rebounder. I get about eight rebounds a game. Last summer, I was the MVP for my summer team. In the summer I had a game where I scored sixteen points in under four minutes. I was also on the All-Star Wildcat Team for my summer league.

I am very proud of my achievements. I still have a lot I want to accomplish. I love basketball. I do not know who I would be today if I did not play basketball. I hope to go far in my basketball career and be very successful.

Crystal Altman, Grade 8
Santa Clara Elementary School, CA

Silence Is Golden

One Easter, my family and I were at a party on a ranch. On the dirt road to the ranch, we saw dead coyotes, dressed in clothes, hanging on the fences. The dirt road was treacherous, with deep creek beds.

When I arrived at the ranch, I shot off some rockets with my Dad, my brothers, and our friends. My favorite rocket was the multiple stage F engine. It was so heavy that the bottom stage was only to get it off the ground. When it finally did launch, it went supersonic, and we heard a sonic boom.

The fun was about to end, though, as I did a stupid stunt and built a rocket with mixed pieces. This rocket would not launch, so I walked over and picked it up without disconnecting the igniter. Cameron, my six-year-old brother, pushed the launch button and surprisingly, the rocket went off in my hand. I was stunned and watched the smoke rise from my hand.

Once I realized my fingers were burned, I began to freak out and scream some extremely mean words to Cameron. My parents put ice on my hand, and we drove quickly to the hospital. The whole time we were driving, I was whimpering, calling my brother names, and saying means things to him. My parents told me to stop, but I would not listen.

Once I had my fingers and hand bandaged, I felt better and calmed down. Even though I apologized to Cameron for saying mean things to him, I still feel guilty for doing so and am learning to hold my tongue when I am hurt or upset.

Andrew Meline, Grade 9
University Preparatory School, CA

Do Good and Make a Change

How does it feel when you help others while doing a good deed? Doing good helps the world. We have enough bad, so make a change. Be different and help out others.

A reason why I like to help others is because it makes me feel very good. I really enjoy helping others in need. I always feel like helping others out is the right thing to do. It is better to give than to receive, someone is always in need of what we take for granted. Helping is really exciting, you feel like you made a big impact, and helped others out a lot.

Some feelings you receive when helping out people in need are happiness. You feel warm inside, like what you did had occupied your heart. You feel joyous, you get the "again, again" feeling because you truly know that the person is thankful. It may not always seem rewarding, but, it is not about money, knowing you did the right thing, for me, is a huge reward.

You may not always receive a reward, but the experience is rewarding. The new friend you have made. The "thank you" that you have received. Even the smiles on the person's face. The way you feel is also a reward. Also, the knowledge of the good that you did.

Doing good, the most unexplainable feeling. You need to experience the feeling to know it. Doing good is good, even without rewards.

Alexiss Rakestraw, Grade 8
Santa Clara Elementary School, CA

Epic Hero

The quality an epic hero resembles or possesses is a character that resembles courage, strength, and a desire to achieve immortality through heroic actions. In the book *The Odyssey*, by Homer, Odysseus exemplifies the qualities of an epic hero. The main qualities Odysseus deals with are being brave, being strong, and showing courage.

The first quality Odysseus resembles is a hero of bravery. Odysseus does many thrilling and dangerous deeds or actions to get back home, since he has been in the Trojan War for a very long time period. As Odysseus tries to journey home, he and his crewmen face many monsters and gods out to get them. However, Odysseus does everything in his will to save his men.

Odysseus is a character of mighty strength and courage. This quality is very important when it comes to Odysseus' desire to return home to his love, Penelope. Had Odysseus had no wife, he would most likely not have shown his incredible strength or courage that he did show. Odysseus fights many monsters traveling over the seas. Therefore, Odysseus was in the right doing all he did to get home to Penelope.

In conclusion, Odysseus is an epic hero in the book *The Odyssey*. As mentioned before, epic heroes most likely resemble or deal with many trials or obstacles such as bravery and having strength and courage. Therefore, many characters must need to have some of the qualities mentioned to be an epic hero.

Brooklynne Brown, Grade 9
South Jordan Middle School, UT

The World Within Me

When I step on the waxed wooden floor of the basketball court, all of the world's problems suddenly disappear, and I show what is really within me. Once the basketball is in my hands, happy is the only emotion that is not in my pocket. Though it may seem stressful to you, I have no worry or stress when I'm on the court. When I was young, basketball was not at all important to me, but now it's something I can't live without. I feel like I'm important when I'm on this court, whether it's my team and me, or just me. After school I race home and get ready, trying not to hurry too much and be way too early for practice. Everybody thinks that Saturday is a day for messing around with your friends, but not me. I think Saturday is game day, a day that you get together with your friends and other teams to play serious basketball. Then coach never schedules practice on Sunday even though I think she should. So even if we don't have practice as a team, I have my own practice, on my own court, with my own basket, and with my own basketball. "You win some and you lose some," is what people say, but it's not what I think. If I lose a game, it's not okay, unless there was no way to beat the team that we were playing. So even if my team is losing, I don't be impudent and fight, I just play my game. My brain tells my heart to beat and keep me alive, but my heart tells my brain to love the sport of basketball.

Jesse Schoenfeld, Grade 7
Salida Middle School, CO

A Later Start Isn't All Bad

Starting middle school and high school classes later in the morning will benefit student academic performance in terms of classroom attentiveness, reduce depression, and promote better sleeping habits that are more consistent with teenagers' lifestyles. Encouraging sleep patterns more in tune with teenagers' late-to-bed, late-to-rise sleep cycles will give students a longer period to wake up, leading to more alertness and observance throughout the day, improving students' grades and enhancing academic performance.

Teens' sleep patterns differ from those of younger children and adults. According to the College of Education and Human Development, "Typical youth are not able to fall asleep much before 11 p.m., and their brains will remain in sleep mode until about 8 a.m., regardless of what time they go to bed." Therefore, students are not able to fully function until sometime during first period, depending on the school, hindering their ability to receive and retain teaching. With later start times, students are more attentive, resulting in improved academic performance. Also, studies show that schools who have adapted the later start times have seen decreased depression rates in students due to their motivation to attend and excel in school. Students who begin classes later in the morning are able to go to sleep later and wake up later, a pattern which teenage bodies prefer. Although some may view shifting school start times as an inconvenience, it is all in the interest and benefit of the students.

Logan Bradeson, Grade 8
Vacaville Christian Schools, CA

Me and Dad

When my Dad asked me if I wanted to run a 16-mile race, I was up and excited to say yes. Now that I think about it, I just can't believe I said yes to this event all those years ago.

Sweat dripped from my head like raindrops. I almost couldn't breathe. I was in the biggest race of my life. I was in 6th place out of about 200 other people. I had a water bottle clanking at my side, and my dad there, too. I was 9 miles into the race and super exhausted. My dad told me to move up. As my dad held 6th, I moved up to 4th. We had practiced this routine where one of us would move up to another place and then that person would give a thumbs up, and the other person would come up with them. I gave my dad thumbs up and he came to 4th. We passed the 10-mile mark, the 12-mile mark, and I was about to puke. We were still in 4th place. Finally we passed the 15-mile mark. This time my dad went up to 2nd and gave the go. I went up to him. We were halfway through the 15-mile mark when I just couldn't take it anymore! I fell back to 3rd and stayed there. The race had started with 211 people and ended with 45.

After the race, of course, we slept for hours. My father and I took home an amazing trophy and $400. Also, we enjoyed the party held for our good work. But most of all, I loved having a great time with my dad. In truth, I never could've done it without him.

Lane Young, Grade 7
Lindale Jr High School, TX

The Internet Is Very Useful

The internet is essential to modern-day technology. The internet has many amazing uses that help people every day. These uses include: helping people learn, providing hours of entertainment, and helping people communicate with others. The internet is a very useful tool.

When doing research, one of the most effective ways of finding information is online. It has an unlimited amount of knowledge that can be accessed instantly. For people who want to go to college, the fastest way to get an education would be by taking online classes.

The internet can provide endless entertainment. For example, at hulu.com people can watch hours of movies. There is also the option of watching television shows, videos, and music videos. People who also have the internet have access to thousands of free, online games.

Email is a valuable internet service. Email is an online tool that lets you send digital letters to other people. Email is fast, compared to waiting days for a response by normal postage services. People may also communicate face to face, even when they're thousands of miles apart! They can do this by using an online tool, Skype.

In conclusion, the internet can be useful in many different ways. The internet can help people learn about many different things. It provides people with hours of entertainment. Lastly, it helps us communicate with others. The internet is a very useful tool.

Cody Crossley, Grade 9
South Jordan Middle School, UT

Grandma's Cloth

She was my grandma. She made a huge impact on me and other people; many still affected today, even since she died. My Kente cloth for her has three colors. Blue is for how peaceful she was. She did not say much, but she loved much. Red is for the struggles my family, others who knew her, and I went through in losing her. Pink is for her being an important female figure in my life, with diamonds for her beauty.

There are triangles for three traits that describe her: funny, loving, beautiful. Dots are for her bubbly personality, while the solid stripes are for her never ending, never changing love. The boxes are for the many gifts she provided for everyone. They are solid colors for how she was always there for me. My dad doesn't show his emotion, but when my grandma died, I saw him cry for the first time.

I remember when my brothers and I were little; our mom told my grandma, "Don't let the kids have Oreos," and my grandma said, "OK." When my mom picked us up she asked us if we had Oreos. We said no, even though there were Oreo cookie crumbs on our faces.

I also remember when she started living at the convalescent home. She had her nurse do her hair in pigtails; and when she started losing weight her roommate called her Dollypop.

I know she is watching over me now. My Kente cloth tells the story of Dolores Lachica Hood. May she rest in peace.

Magdalena Hood, Grade 7
Vacaville Christian Schools, CA

My Highest Goal

When I think about playing basketball in college it gives me a nervous feeling in the pit of my stomach. Thoughts start to quickly pass through my head. Am I working hard enough? Is it in my reach? Will I even get recruited? Playing on a division one court is my dream. Stanford is my first choice. I want to wear the maroon and white proudly. Listen to everything Coach Vandaveer has to say. And hear the crowd cheer.

Basketball is my life, it means everything to me. Waiting for college is agonizing. Hoping is the only thing that gets me through. My parents both support me, which helps my doubt slip away. Their support enables me to believe that I can do anything. In the past year I saw the verse Philippians 4:13 on the back shirts of many of the athletes at my school. The verse really made me realize that I am capable of anything, and everything. It's just up to which path I choose. I've chosen basketball. Where it will take me, I don't know. The anxiousness of what the future holds is part of what makes basketball so great.

If I keep working hard, eventually it will all pay off. I sometimes wish I could see what my future entails. But, I quickly change my mind because the curiosity is what keeps me going. When it is all said and done, I want to look back and be proud of myself, or my basketball career, and most of all, the impact basketball has helped me have on others. The future might seem scary to me now, but it's going to be great when it finally comes.

Avery Keathley, Grade 8
Monte Vista Christian School, CA

The Odyssey

What classifies the story of "The Odyssey" as an epic poem? An epic is a long journey that usually has a super hero in it. The story "The Odyssey" is an epic because it includes a super being, and he is helped by the supernatural.

Odysseus is stranded on an island with a nymph, Calypso. Calypso is in love with Odysseus and never wants him to leave. Odysseus wants to return back to his home town. Athena orders Calypso to free Odysseus. Poseidon sees Odysseus on the water and attempts to shipwreck him, luckily Athena steps in just in time. In this case, Odysseus is helped and hurt by the gods.

Odysseus and his shipmates go to islands. The crew went to the island of the lotus eaters in search of water. The lotus eaters forget their wants and needs and just want the lotuses. Though Odysseus warned his crew about the lotus eaters, some disobeyed him and tried the lotus flower.

Some people may believe that "The Odyssey" is not an epic poem because it doesn't seem to be real in many ways. However, they are incorrect, because these stories are what the ancient Greeks and Romans used to describe the events around us and also used these stories as their religion.

In conclusion, "The Odyssey" by Homer is an epic because they get help from supernatural beings, they go on a long journey, and they also use great powers to overcome the darkness or evil.

Hailey Conder, Grade 9
South Jordan Middle School, UT

Food: Safe...Unsafe? Which One?

Okay, now we have to admit that we all have eaten food without knowing the contents of it. This unawareness can sometimes be life-threatening and very risky to those who have allergies, sensitivity to certain foods, or those already at risk of health problems. First, let us get one thing straight. We are not discussing the problems with fatty foods. Yes, that is important to watch out for, but the existing issue is regarding all the artificial food additives and preservatives.

This is my life story: As a child, I used to act up a few hours after I ate something with high sugar content. My parents thought it was just me being hyperactive after a sugar rush. Later, they noticed that after eating attractive, colorful sweets, I began to get rashes. Some research was done, and it turned out that some people (like me) are sensitive to artificial dyes. I went on a 'diet' for a few months, eating all-natural foods. I then decided that I wanted to eat healthy for the rest of my life.

Artificial food dyes, flavors, and preservatives are not only dangerous to our health, but are also very unhealthy. This isn't only for children, I would like to stress. "Leaving out foods with dyes, preservatives, and gluten have kept me out of the hospital for a long time," said adult S.F. On www.feingold.org, recent studies have showed that 75% of people on this diet have shown a significant amount of improvement, whether in school, in behavior, with peers, or with family. But if that's not good enough reason for you, do not do this for others, do it for yourself. Be good to your body.

Aashika Korrapati, Grade 7
Stratford Elementary/Middle School, CA

History, an Interesting Subject

Ever since I was little, I have been fascinated with history. I love learning about ancient empires, sunken ships.

Did you know many of the ancient empires invented some of the technology we use today? For example, during the Chinese Empire a group of people invented gun powder. Another example is people in the Roman Empire invented the roads, and the first heating system. During another empire, the Greek people designed much of the architecture for buildings we use today. During the Egyptian Empire the people invented papyrus which led to the invention of the paper we use now.

Sunken ships also interest me. The stories and sometimes the mystery behind the sinking fascinate me. Many merchant ships have sunk but one that intrigues me is the recently discovered Greek merchant ship. Its story is a mystery to people but oceanographers are finding out how the ship sunk. The Titanic is a ship that many people know about from movies and countless documentaries. Its story is tragic because of the loss of life and how many families lost members. Its story fascinates me. The Lusitania sunk in 1914 because of a German torpedo. The sinking caused outrage because it was a passenger ship not a merchant ship during W.W.I.

History, my favorite subject to learn about, has a multitude of different aspects. Each aspect is interesting and enjoyable to learn about.

Annamarie Tontz, Grade 9
First Baptist Academy, TX

Love for the Game

Softball is the one sport I can never get tired of. When I look out the window on a freezing February day and see the ground covered with a thick blanket of snow, I remember everything I love about playing softball. I remember the late night softball games, the clear sky with billions of stars, and the bright lights beating down on the freshly painted field. I remember the soft, green grass, and the sweaty gloves. I think about how great it feels to swing the bat, feel the ball collide with the metal, and run as hard as I can to the bases. I remember being nervous for games, but leaving those nerves behind as the fun began. I remember the friends I made and the fun we had. I remember the great feeling I got in my stomach when we won, and the encouragement from my teammates. I remember both the scorching summer days, and the rainy weather. I remember the sugary banana milkshakes we would always get after an away game. When it is cold outside, I miss all of this so much, but I know that soon enough, when summer comes around, I will discover all of this again, and that is all I can ask for.

Ella Potts, Grade 7
Salida Middle School, CO

The Way Things Are

Ambition is what helps you accomplish your dreams. It is your level of motivation. My life dream is to be in the Navy. I want to be a fighter pilot or a Navy SEAL. Women aren't' allowed in either of those fields because it is too dangerous, but it just as dangerous for men as it is for women. I plan on being the first woman SEAL not in intelligence and also the first woman fighter pilot, because women will fight to stay alive just as hard as men do, so women should be able to be SEALs and fighter pilots and anything else they want to be. Why shouldn't women be allowed to do the things they want an feel they need to do? They should be allowed to because they work hard to be able to do these things. Women do their homework just as much as men do; they do the best they can so they should be able to do the things they want to do.

Diana Stoddard, Grade 8
Excelsior Academy, UT

The Effect of Drugs on My Relationship with My Uncle

In my family, I have an uncle who smokes and does other drugs. This bothers me because he is my favorite uncle, too. He has tried to quit but he did not try hard enough. It also bothers me because he is a great guy and I want him to stop. When we went to a family reunion he would smoke and then the camp would start to smell weird. He was never around because he would drive down to the nearest town to buy cigarettes or he was off smoking. When we are at their house, he is usually out back smoking. He also drinks beer and does not care if people see that. This affects my life because I cannot really spend time with him. I'm concerned that smoking and drinking will cause him severe health problems. Smoking is causing millions of people to get cancer and other health problems. Don't let this happen to you.

Brendan Crump, Grade 7
Excelsior Academy, UT

Best Dog Ever!

Our dog Ginger was a Jack Russell Terrier. We would play with her. She usually spent most of her time at our grandma's house. Ginger would also get into fights with our cat named Midnight. She had many companions, including us. She was the best dog ever. She would always sleep in my older sister's room. She even went to a beach where we had lots of fun with her. Then tumors appeared, one on her belly and one on her ear. She was then on medication for her tumors. She remained loyal to us as she would normally, but then there was a time when she got lost. Someone opened the gate and Ginger got out. We were all hoping for her to come back. My sister put up posters all around the streets. I researched some pictures of her for the poster. Then one rainy night, we received word that she got ran over. After that, we buried her behind the shed. Today she's still there, warming our hearts, watching over us. We figured out we couldn't replace a loyal, loving dog. My sister Madelyn then made a scrapbook that was a Christmas gift to the person who loved Ginger the most: my sister Danielle.

David Wordelman, Grade 7
St Joseph Catholic School, CA

A Cracking Family

In this world that we live in, family plays a big part in the life of middle school teens. Many teens are under a lot of stress. They think that if they have problems at home, they are not as good as other kids who don't have problems with their families. Kids might think that their parents going through a divorce is their fault. I know that when my parents went through a divorce, I felt like it was entirely my fault. Not only is divorce a big part of what makes teens stressed, but a death in the family might as well. I know that I was very sad and stressed when my great uncle died. Teens go through a lot of stress at school. Stress can cause many problems for a teen. It can cause them to have emotional breakdowns and things like that. Teens might not always show that they are stressed about a divorce or a death in the family.

Alexia Hugelen, Grade 7
Excelsior Academy, UT

My Dog Toby

My dog is an amazing dog. He's loving and kind. I love him so much that I want to tell you about how I got him. It was maybe a couple months after my first dog Koda died. We were desperately looking for a new dog because the house was getting lonely. So then we looked online, at the lab rescue web site, and found an adorable yellow lab named Buckaroo. He was at the lab rescue place because his previous owners wouldn't let him come inside and they made him stay in a cardboard box out on the street. We went to Yuba City to meet him. He came and put his head on my lap. That was when we knew he was the right dog for us. We took him home, changed his name to Toby, and bought him a bed and food. That, my friends, is how I got my dog Toby. He is now four years old and is really sweet dog.

Nick Ursano, Grade 7
St Joseph Catholic School, CA

Friends

"It's not always what you know, but the people you know." I like that quote because it reminds me that even if you are smart, if you don't have friends, you aren't going to have any good memories to look back on. You won't know who to talk to when you have a school problem, or any problem at all. Your family, I know, is always there for you, and it's good to talk to them about your life. But there is something special about having a friend there to listen to you and be there for you.

Friendship is simply fun! It is amazing to share who you are with others that appreciate you more than you do. True friends love your good side and can accept the bad side and just like you for who you are. They don't judge you or make you change. They are always there for you and expect you'll be there for them.

I think friendship is essential to growing up. I personally will try to be a friend to everybody and accept their differences because everyone is unique. Friendship is a wonderful thing and I'm glad to have it in my life!

Emma Wasson, Grade 7
Excelsior Academy, UT

The Life of a Wolf Pup

Between the months of March and June, four to six wolf pups may be born in a den. At first, these pups will only live off their mother's milk. Twelve to fifteen days after their birth, they will open their eyes. About two weeks after birth, they will learn to walk. Only a week after they learn to walk, the pups will be able to leave the den. Also, when they are four to five weeks old, they will begin to eat meat. Throughout all of this, the pups will be playful and most likely have blue eyes. All the exciting parts of being a wolf will happen much later, though of course they have to grow up first, just like people, but much quicker. When the pups are twelve weeks old, they will begin to travel with the packs on the hunt, but they will have to wait until they are seven to eight months before they are actually able to hunt with the pack.

Alisa Bartholomew, Grade 7
Sunrise Ridge Intermediate School, UT

Ocean Royalty

A peaceful monolith glides through the ocean depths, its flukes intricately carving the salty fluid surrounding them. Melodic echoes vibrate across the seven seas, their elaborate composition bewitching any mortal being. Majestic royalty, through mother and calf, shall continue to behold the ocean's throne. Nothing compares to the breathtaking splendor the ocean lovingly shelters.

What else, besides the whale, may produce such visions, such enlightening prospects? What other creature may come to mind when reading the above? Nothing. Nothing but the whale is foreseen. This cetacean, made up of no more than chaste glory and pure sentiment, claims reign over the great blue expanse of ocean water. After all, royalty deserves to be honored the Laurels of the Heavens.

Ysabel-Rose Vargas Lew, Grade 9
Saint Mary's Hall, TX

Video Games Benefit Teens

Video games should be rated "T" for teen because of violence, eliminating the "M" for mature, because violent video games do not create violent teens and violent video games help teens relieve stress and release their anger. Studies from a variety of sources have shown little to no link between thoughts of aggression and violent video games, and actually have been shown to be beneficial to teens by lowering rates of depression and helping relieve stress.

A 2008 study showed that while video games sales have quadrupled, violent juvenile crimes have decreased from 72% to 49%. Another study by the Secret Service showed that only one-eighth of violent school crimes were linked to violent video games; a lower rate than any other forms of violent media. Multiple sources, including the book *Grand Theft Childhood*, have shown that teen gamers who play rated "M" games are more likely to play with another person and exhibit interactive behavior. These games, other than being great entertaining experiences for teens, have been shown to be beneficial psychologically. According to a study at Texas A&M, young adults who play violent video games handle stress better than non-players. Another study showed that 45% of boys play video games "to get out their anger" and 62% said they played because it "helped them relax."

Video games should be rated "T" for teen because of violence, eliminating the "M" for mature, because violent video games do not create violent young adults, and violent video games have positive mental benefits. Different studies from a variety of sources have shown no link between violent video games and violent actions from teens. Video games should not be rated "M" for mature for violence and should be changed to "T" for teen.

Jesse Galeano-Buggs, Grade 8
Vacaville Christian Schools, CA

Imagination: The Vivid Ability

Imagination is the ability to create a fictional image within a person's mind. This ability is very important to mankind, however it is slowly fading away. First, imagination is the fun of a child. What many see as a box, a child might see as a spaceship, a car, or maybe a house. Sadly, imagination is being replaced with video games, and the mental extent of imagination is cut short. Secondly, writers need imagination. Without it, stories would be boring and dull. But this need does not only require the imagination of the writer, but the imagination of the reader. As a result, reading broadens the scope of people's imagination. Thirdly, imagination is how humans set goals or create ideas. Little kids set goals by imagining what they want to be. And humankind would have never made it to the moon unless some person had imagined it possible.

In all this, I think imagination is one of the most important attributes of mankind. And we need to keep it going. Making up stuff is a much better alternative than sitting in front of a TV. So go write a story. Go imagine.

Nathanael Vickery, Grade 9
First Baptist Academy, TX

Science Fair

Nearly a hundred students filed into the auditorium accompanied by their parents. The students quickly stood next to their respective decorated science fair presentation boards. Next to each board, they found an unopened bottle of water. Soon after they had set up their materials, a myriad number of parents swarmed the narrow aisles, asking questions to the students. The students happily answered the parent's questions and left their boards to see their friends' boards. After the one and a half hours of Science Fair, the students start packing up their materials to go back home.

Science Fair is a great opportunity for students to learn. Even though Science Fair takes a lot of time and effort, it teaches students the skills of writing, presenting, experimenting, and art. Most of the projects have subjects that affect people's daily routines, so students can apply their studies to real life. Plus, Science Fair makes up a lot of a student's grade, so it mostly can pull one's grades up.

Science Fair can also be fun. At the end of Science Fair, students go to a large room with many other projects. There they will have a fun time by explaining their projects and looking at their friends' projects. Also, the procedure of the project is sometimes fun. Experimenting with chemicals is fun for many people.

Science Fair is a great experience for students to have fun and learn many skills that can be applied to real life, so ask your teacher to give you a science project today.

Austin Bi, Grade 7
Stratford Elementary/Middle School, CA

For the Love of Cooking

My mother's cooking is like a snowflake: no two meals are alike. Every evening, I go home, wondering what will be for dinner. I can always expect something different from the last night's meal, because they usually have a wide variety. Every two weeks, while my mom is making her list of meals, the dreaded question always comes up, "What suggestions do you have for dinners?" I never know what to say because I love all of her meals, even so, I do have one favorite, Swedish Meatballs. I just love the distinct taste of the meatballs and fluffy mashed potatoes combined. I also like when she finds new recipes, because they usually turn out well. No one's cooking is the same as my mom's. Whenever I eat somewhere else, my taste buds crave a homemade meal, since that's what they get every night. I hope that I will get the wonderful trait of good cooking when I am older. My mother's cooking is so special to me, that I hope I can share some of her skills and recipes with my children, just as she did. Sometimes, my family and I worry about the meal that is coming up, but it usually turns out yummy. Most nights, my mom has a back-up plan, just in case her meal doesn't turn out the way that she wanted it to. I think that my mother's goal is to impress us, but no matter what, we will always love her. It is always difficult for me to not brag about her cooking too often, because I love it so much and it has a big impact on my life. I appreciate everything that my mother does for me, but her cooking is one thing that really stands out.

Lauren Gobin, Grade 7
Salida Middle School, CO

Karate

"Fake it till you make it." One of the things that is most important to me is karate.

The principles that karate teaches me are modesty, courtesy, perseverance, integrity and indomitable spirit. Without them I would not be the way I am. I would not be a leader, but a follower. I would not be listening to my parents and teachers. They teach me to be responsible. With these principles I am careful with what I say and do. These principles will help me choose to do right.

In karate I learn techniques. I learn how to punch and remember things. I also learn how to protect myself. Without techniques I would not know how to defend myself.

I learn how to teach others. If I did not teach I would not know the right way to talk to the kids. I would not know how to talk to the adults.

Karate makes me feel unique and special. I feel that I do not have to be scared of any one, and I feel happy. I can be my own person. I do not have to be someone I am not. I feel special. I feel that I belong to something big when I do karate.

Without karate I do not know where I would be today. Karate will help keep me alive. Karate is my life. I breath, live, and sleep karate. I love karate. When I do karate I feel like a new person. It is part of me. I have been doing karate for eight years. I am glad to be doing karate.

Serena Mumford, Grade 8
Santa Clara Elementary School, CA

Softball = Life

Do you have that one sport or hobby that you just love? Well I know I do. That sport is softball. Softball has been in my life for a long time. Basically softball equals my whole life. It revels around me either with baseball of softball. And I want to tell everyone how softball is important.

Softball teaches you a lot of things on and off of the field. Especially teamwork and perseverance on and off the field. Softball teaches you to work together. The sport teaches everyone to trust each other with everything they do. It's how to bond with your team in many different ways. You make new friends from different schools in different areas, especially if you play travel softball. And most importantly you have fun!

"Practice makes perfect." That saying is very true. In softball you always have to practice as a team because if you don't you fall apart. When we practice we never give up on each other. Everyone has to hold their own weight. Also we always practice as if we were in a game because you practice as if you were to play in a game.

I have always loved this sport. It teaches morals about life on the field and off the field. Hopefully everyone has a passion or sport like I do. I plan to continue playing softball in high school. I would really try to keep in touch with this sport in college. I would very much enjoy seeing softball in my future because softball equals my life.

Katelynn Hernandez, Grade 8
Santa Clara Elementary School, CA

The Heart Attack

It was the year of 2008. I was 10 years old. I was walking home from school with my brother Jesse. We got to our house and my dad was there. He told us to get changed because my sister Jeslene who went to Clark had a softball game. Once we got to the softball field we saw my Grandpa Johnny and my Uncle Gerard. The game had started and the Clark team was winning. During the game all I could remember is my dad getting up from his chair, whispering something to my grandpa and then leaving. My brother and I thought he had something for work.

When the softball game was done, Clark won the game. Jeslene, Jesse, and I drove home. As soon as we got home we didn't see Mom or Dad. Then Jeslene got a call on her cell phone. After she hung up her phone, she said that Dad just had a heart attack. Then later on in the day my mom came and took all of us to the hospital to see Dad.

Once we got to the hospital our whole family was there and they were anguished on what had happened. We waited in the waiting room until someone said we could see him. When all of this was happening my mom had to be stoical. When my dad got out of the hospital we started living healthier. My mom and dad would take a class on how to live a healthy life and they would also walk together. But also our faith grew more. Every day before we went to bed we would pray and read the Bible. If the heart attack had never happened only God will know where we would be today.

Juan Renteria, Grade 8
St Matthew Catholic School, TX

Losing Mom

You never know what you have until it's gone. When someone passes away, you see how important they are and realize that your life will change. I believe that one of the hardest people to lose is your mom. You never know what blessing a mother is until she's gone.

My aunt Catherine left my four cousins and my uncle, after her kidneys bled for nine days. This led to the discovery of kidney cancer, pneumonia, and many failing organ systems. Her death caused rapid changes in their home. One of my cousin's grades started dropping. Another cousin of mine cries more because she misses her mom. Their family decided to move in with our grandparents. They have more chores around the house that they wouldn't normally do, and their dad has to work, leaving them alone more.

My aunt had a huge impact on her family's life. In many families I know of, the father is the one who goes to work to provide for his family, and the mother is the one who stays home and cares for her children. The mother cooks, does the dishes, helps the kids with homework, does the laundry and nurtures her children. When a mother passes away, the family has more stress, and there isn't a mother to do those chores. That's why we shouldn't take things for granted. We should see the blessings we have right now because you never know when you'll lose someone who's dear to you.

Megan Reger, Grade 7
Excelsior Academy, UT

Hunting

Hunting has put happiness in my life. Though the scenes are beautiful and there are animals that are the amazing to see, the best part of all is spending time with my uncle and dad. When spending time with my uncle, I learn more about him and his lifestyle during the time hunting with him. When my uncle and I hunt, we always try to find the best spots. When we find those great spots, we find the true beauty in life by looking at breathtaking sites and scenes of the amazing grasslands and woodlands. Also, when we have the time to sit and take breaks, I try to take the time to build up conversations to talk about, things that bring my uncle and I closer as a family. As for my loving, caring, yet funny father, he is the one that I love to spend time with. My uncle likes to talk about the beautiful scenes, but my dad loves to talk about the amazing animals and birds. As my dad and I hunt, we usually come across unusual creatures. Most of them I don't know about, but my dad does. When he talks about them, it makes me feel like the best kid in the world. When my father is talking, I learn more about animals and the whole main focus of hunting in the great outdoors. Also, I love to hear him talk about how, when he was little, he used to love hunting. Hearing him talk on forever about his life and that helps me learn more about him. As for our relationship, it really makes it stronger and more effective. Though there are some ups and downs in the relationship of my dad and uncle, I am thankful to have them in my family.

Tristan Stone, Grade 7
Salida Middle School, CO

Friendship Begins with You

As I have thought about different ways that friendships are formed, and memories of my past and current friendships have flooded my mind. Some friendships have been better than others. In order to create lasting bonds of friendship, you have to unselfishly serve others.

Serve others even if they do not necessarily need it. Sometimes serving others can help them feel like others love them. In order to serve others it is very essential to pay careful attention to their needs. People generally will not ask for service but when people offer it, appreciate it. Service is a great way to deal with difficult situations.

Over the summer I was in an ATV accident with one of my best friends. She crushed her hand and I walked away without any damage done to me. I felt very guilty because of this. Her mom had told me that what they needed most at the time was freezer meals, so my mom and I made freezer meals for them. Performing this act of service allowed her and I both to deal with the difficult situation we were going through.

Serving others requires unselfishness. The needs of others must come before our own. One of the best friends I have is one who can just listen, something I wish I could do so well.

Find other people's needs, serve others, and listen to your friends when they need a friend. See how it changes your relationship with them.

Brianne Caldwell, Grade 8
White Pine Charter School, ID

Why I Love Baseball

Bottom of the 9th, two outs, and the count was two and two. We were down by one with runners at second and third. I was up to bat! I hit the next pitch foul. Then a change-up came right down the middle; I hit it into the outfield about 5 feet over the shortstop's head. The outfielders could not throw the ball in time before both runners scored. We won four to three. That's my memorable story and this is why I love baseball.

I love to bat, standing in the batter's box and watching the ball come in. I like getting good contact between the bat and the ball. You can get singles, doubles, triples, home runs, or winning hits. I like running the bases after I hit the ball and playing under the lights. Bunting is fun and easy for me. I also enjoy hitting the balls to the fence.

I also love to pitch and getting signals from the catcher, coach or infield. Throwing different pitches is fun too. Throwing strikes makes me feel good and I like it when I strike somebody out. I love it when I pick people off trying to steal a base. I am the captain on the field.

I also enjoy playing third base. The balls get hit hard toward me when I am over there. It is scary but fun. I like diving down the line and jumping for the balls. Throwing to first and getting them out is fun. I also like holding on the runners. Another thing is tagging people out and running back and calling people off.

I love baseball and that's that. I would not be myself today without baseball. Maybe you can play sometime.

Ricky Gill, Grade 8
Santa Clara Elementary School, CA

One Step at a Time

My journey has already begun as I confidently approach the toughest mountain on the trail. I take a deep breath and begin to climb this immense peak. As I cling tightly to the wavering mountainside, I think of how this situation incredibly resembles my difficult but fantastical life. In my life, I succeed in various things, but make many mistakes at the same time. I've learned that it is essential to never give up and always reach for your dreams so you can become the stronger, better person you've always tried to be.

In life, there awaits a brighter future that can only be won if we strive for it. We need to forget the doubtful past, and take one step at a time to get to this mental finish line. Although there are many obstacles, a powerful urge of hope can get us through such troublesome times. We simply need to remember our purposes in life and seek to accomplish them.

These simple thoughts surge through my mind and give me confidence to keep on climbing. Amazed at how far I've gone, I swivel around and glance behind me, looking out on the bug-like world below me. My eyes come upon the dangerous steps I took on the trail that caused me to fall and feel of no worth, but I remember that every step I take gets me closer to the end, no matter what. I turn back around and continue to climb, reminding myself that I can reach the top, for this is a journey of a lifetime.

Natalie Brower, Grade 7
White Pine Charter School, ID

One Year Ago

"If you really love someone you will let them go." I never understood what that meant, until I heard the news.

The crash was too sudden for me to realize that it was true. It was the crash that killed my cousin; his name was Junior. When my mother told me what had happened, I didn't show any expression to what she said. I'm one of those people that don't like to show somber or bitter emotions around people. My family and I rushed to the E.R. as soon as we knew which hospital they were taken to. Everyone in the E.R. was quiet and still, as if they knew what had happened. They were just staring, waiting for me to rage in fury or fall in anguish. I found a place to sit where no one could see me and where I could think everything through. For six hours I sat in that same spot, waiting for someone to come up and simply ask how I was doing. Everyone was too busy running around and panicking to realize things. The funeral was three weeks later. It was the worst thing to see men dump dirt into the hole and fill it up. The mother fell on her knees and her head touched the ground. She cried, screamed, and pounded her fist on the hollow dirt. It's hard to get over something when you've felt so many mournful feelings. Eventually I would get over it, but I figured it would take a while.

This experience shocked me; it was one of the hardest things to get over. Never had I known the feeling of losing something. I've learned to control that terrible feeling. I've learned that Junior is in a better place now; a place with no more tears.

Rajel Flores, Grade 7
Lindale Jr High School, TX

My Family

"Families are like fudge...mostly sweet with a few nuts." I think this quote can somewhat describe my family. My family is loving and kind, but we can also be very funny!

My family is always my first priority. My family is very important to me because they will always be there for me, so I should be there for them. Without my family, I do not know where I would be! We always will have each other's backs and watch out for one another. We know how to brighten each other's days and make each other happy.

My family shares many memories together. We make memories every day! We have good and bad memories to remember. A bad memory is losing a loved one. The good memories are all the laughs we shared, our smiles, and every single moment we have spent together. Memories are important to my family because they will always help us to remember each other. Most importantly, my family always tries to make the best out of everything. That has taught me to cherish every moment of my life.

As you can see, my family means a lot to me. I love my family so much and I would not be who I am today without them. Even though we have our ups and downs, we will always care and love each other. Also, we make each other laugh every day, which makes us happy! My family is united as one, and I hope it stays that way forever.

Diana Catapusan, Grade 8
Santa Clara Elementary School, CA

Friends

"A best friend is someone who knows all about you and loves you anyway." — Elbert Hubbard

My friends make my life complete. If I had never met them, I do not know what I would do. I love them like they are my family.

One of my closest friends is Sheyenne. She is really loving, caring, funny, hardworking, and shy. She likes playing softball and we met at school in first grade. I love her like she is my sister. I do not know what I would do without her.

My other closest friend is Allison. She is also loving, caring, funny, and friendly. Allison is really outgoing and unpredictable, but in a good way. She likes playing soccer, unlike Sheyenne. We all like playing volleyball, but I think I enjoy it the most. I've known Allison since first grade too and I love her a lot.

My friends and I have been through so much together. Next year, when we are in high school, I am really going to miss them. I do not know what I will do without them. We have so many amazing memories. We created a garden for the county fair, went sledding in the snow, and even worked at the farmer's market. We have been friends for so long it is going to be hard to say goodbye even though we will still see each other sometimes.

Next year I am going to have to make new friends, but I am sure we will always remain friends.

Robin Rydberg, Grade 8
Santa Clara Elementary School, CA

Music Is My Life

I am a pianist, singer, and songwriter, and hopefully, someday, through hard work, confidence, and a little support, I will be there, center stage in front of millions of people waiting to see me.

How will I get there? The most important thing to do is to practice, practice, practice, until I become a master. With the money I save, I will invest in everything I need for a home recording studio, and begin recording. Afterwards, I will keep practicing and continue to learn from other experienced musicians. Then I will land a few gigs, work my way up, and eventually, my career will take off. It is a long journey, but I am almost there.

After I make enough money, I will start a nonprofit that helps children in need everywhere, particularly those in the poverty stricken areas of Africa.

The only thing standing in my way is doubt and nervousness. If I concentrate on my music, that should not be a problem, and everyone has it, I just need to overcome it.

The thing I love most about music is that whenever I sing, play piano, or write a song, I fit in. In other words, music is an escape, and it is the one place I can be me.

If I become a musician, I hope my future grandchildren and great grandchildren will look back and think of me as one of the greatest musicians of all time. Maybe they will be inspired and become musicians too. Who knows? For right now, I think I will focus on doing well in school and mastering music.

Diego Magaña, Grade 8
Santa Clara Elementary School, CA

The Pizza

The Margarita pizza served at Da Michele Pizzeria in Naples, Italy is the jewel of all pizzas. I think Da Michele's traditional, Italian pizza embodies everything a pizza should; it contains the perfect amount of cheese complimented by fresh tomato sauce. All of the ingredients are fused together and create the famous Margarita pizza

At first glance, Da Michele appears to be very unappealing with only one pizza on the menu, but a line consisting of forty or more people is spilling out the restaurant and onto the street. On the inside, the pizzeria is adorned with pictures of famous people who have ventured down to the small city of Naples, Italy.

Upon entering, the customers are guided to a table with other customers, whom they do not know, and take their seats. The waiters zip through the tiny two room restaurant and hand the customers miniature plastic Dixie cups for water. The atmosphere is loud and overwhelming, and then a steaming margarita pizza floats through the room and silences everyone.

When the Margarita arrives at the table, it is steaming with passion from the chefs and bubbling with cheese. Once it is lifted out from the platter, a cape of fresh mozzarella cheese follows and seems to melt in your mouth. Once the whole pizza is gone, the customers have gained an experience as precious as a jewel, with new friends and a new favorite pizzeria.

Madison Trusevich, Grade 9
Saint Mary's Hall, TX

Out of Struggle Came Success

My freshman soccer season appeared to be off to a great start, until the 26th Annual Saint Mary's Hall Soccer Tournament. As a freshman, I was named a Varsity player and was starting at the defensive center-mid position. My very first Varsity tournament was rapidly approaching; I was released from school all day Friday to play soccer. What could be better? Just as all good things seem to do, the tournament concluded, but it ended with my selection to the All-Tournament Team. Just as it seemed like the field was completely level, I fell into a hole. My shins continued to bother me and I was told that a third surgery would be the necessary treatment. I was devastated; this was going to be my third surgery in less than seven months. I rationally thought through my timing options for the surgery. With the upcoming Christmas holiday, I decided this was the ideal time for a surgery. Three days after surgery, I was crutching around on the field with my teammates. Everyone on the team instantly encouraged and supported me. I spent countless hours in the all too familiar training-room, completing the necessary rehab to get me back onto the field. There were many days when I was frustrated; I just wanted to play soccer, my true passion in life; I was tired of being sidelined by injuries. About a month later, after only missing two games, I walked onto the field prepared to start at my usual position of defensive center-mid.

Alexandra Flaherty, Grade 9
Saint Mary's Hall, TX

Time-Saving Technology

Technology is a very good thing. It makes everyday tasks quicker and easier. Some examples of time-saving technology are microwave ovens, automobiles, airplanes, and computers.

First, the microwave oven allows for much faster cooking times. No longer does one have to heat up an oven to cook a meal, and then have to wait a while for the food to cook. The microwave oven allows food to be prepared in a matter of minutes.

Automobiles are a second example of time-saving technology. They have been around for over a century, and have changed the way people think about distances. For example, if someone desires to travel to another state, he could easily drive there in a few hours, rather than have to pack a wagon and travel for days.

A third example of time-saving technology is the airplane. Unlike the automobile, the airplane is not limited to the ground. It is quite the opposite, as it is only effective in the air. Nevertheless, the airplane is an excellent method of traveling to places very far away.

A fourth example of time-saving technology is the computer. The computer did not start out as the speedy piece of hardware it is today. It started as a huge machine that filled an entire room and could only perform the functions of a common calculator. But in time, the computer was improved, and eventually became that laptop that is carried everywhere or a staple on every office desk.

Douglass Hooker, Grade 9
First Baptist Academy, TX

Soul Model-Role Model

Webster's Dictionary defines role model as "a person who is unusually effective or inspiring and so serves as a model for another or others." When I read this definition and how it relates to my faith, I immediately think of my Great-Aunt Jan who has planted a seed of faith.

Her siblings and she attended Catholic school. In her spare time, she yearned to read the Bible which gave her courage and motivation. This germinated a drive to become a nun. A few years later, she left the convent to marry her true love. She has never forgotten how close she was to God and how much she loved him. She has always been so thankful for all that God has done for her, that she wants everyone else to feel his love and mercy. When I look at her, I see the fingerprints of God.

She was nurturing to my mother, while in college, by encouraging her to continue to keep her faith even though she was living the life of a student. Over the years, she and my mother have shared stories, mostly related to ACTS retreats. However, when she and I talk, she caters to my questions about my faith and verifies questions I may have, even if they are controversial. When I think about my inspiration and my faith, I have the utmost respect for her who unselfishly lives the unique life Christ wants for all of us, one filled with His abundant love. She is my role model and I only hope that I can walk in her footsteps.

Camryn Longoria, Grade 7
St Matthew Catholic School, TX

Net Trix

The movie industry and the human race are currently selecting their course to a briskly bewildering end.

I recently stumbled into a depressingly empty, blue building where humans formerly bought picture shows. We once knew our source for instant movies as Blockbuster, but our species has regressed. An antisocial being, which prefers an LED lit computer screen to daylight, the human of the 21st century has redefined the word instant in the movie business as literally instant. In a poof or, more appropriately, a tap, one can order and stream TV shows and movies from one's personal bedroom or Starbucks. A necessity has ceased to exist for such superfluous limbs as legs. Eventually, we may all explode due to lack of exercise and unhealthy eating habits, or implode from who knows what!

As for the entertainment industry, there will be one victor, who sadly is not the consumer. Netflix will continue to loot the human race of its virtual currency, while competitors, struggling to meet our progressively lazier needs, will perish like Redbox. We rise from our ceremonial futons to buy beverages from vending machines; now, we cannot perform an identical ritual for movies! If we allow Netflix to monopolize the business, it will obtain the power of ridiculous pricing, concluding with the end of movie night, as we know it.

Speaking of foreboding conclusions, we must not surrender to temptations that entice us to sell our souls to the red logoed devil we know as Netflix.

Bennett Word, Grade 9
Saint Mary's Hall, TX

Courage

I had courage when my friend Abbie and I tried out for Dance Company at UDA. We walked in the door and found our names on the list. We walked into the studio and saw the teacher Ms. Brooks. She was the meanest teacher out there. "Well are you just going to stand there?" she said. We worked as hard as we could trying to impress her. After two hours she walked out of the room, Abbie and I collapsed on the floor pouring sweat.

We would not know if we had made the team until at least five days later. We walked into hear the phone ringing. On the caller ID it said UDA. We looked at each other thinking the same thing, we didn't make it. Abbie answered the phone in a soft voice, "Hello?" I couldn't tell who was on the other end of the line. Twenty seconds later she said thank you and hung up. I stared at her not knowing what to think. That second her face lit up. At the top of her lungs she screamed "We made it!!!" Ms. Brooks had explained to her that we were good, and she knew right away that we would be great!

Monday was our first day. We walked in the doors ready to dance our guts out! After practicing step after step over and over again we had only learned the first 20 seconds of the dance. But already, I knew dance had changed my life. I felt exercised, relieved of stress, and dance always made everything better!

Madison Anderson, Grade 9
South Jordan Middle School, UT

The Dark Side of the Olympics

People scream with exhilaration; gossiping crowds cluster on the streets — the Olympics are coming to town. The citizens anticipate the entertainment; it will surely be wonderful. But what about the devastating disadvantages the games bring?

One huge and obvious problem presented by the Olympics is that not only are the costs outrageously high, but they are also notorious for going over budget. Athens, Greece budgeted $1.6 billion for the 2004 Olympics, yet that wasn't enough. The final cost was $16 billion, ten times the amount budgeted. Beijing invested the same amount of money in 2008 and ended up spending $40 billion.

Another problem comes from the eviction of thousands of citizens. To make way for the Olympic Village (a housing structure for participants), the hosts simply force people out of their own houses and destroy their homes. For the South Korea Olympics, 720,000 citizens, mostly poor, were evicted. The Athens Olympics resulted in the demolition of 2000 housing units, leaving 6000 people homeless. 2008's Beijing Olympics brought about the eviction of 1.5 million citizens. Finally, the Olympic Village isn't even permanent. Once the Olympics are over, this $1.1 million structure is destroyed.

Of course, the Olympics are not completely bad. They allow many countries to peaceably assemble together and create inspiring role models. The losses sustained by the host city, however, remain enormous. Those must be changed. It is time to take action.

Allison Yuan, Grade 7
Stratford Elementary/Middle School, CA

Instant Gratification

Ever since I can remember, either as a child wanting a toy or as a nouveau teen wanting to beat the high-score on that new game, I had always wanted it right now. Though I have tried to balance instant and delayed gratification, a recent quote showed me what is really happening in society: "We are a society that revels in our need for instant gratification where we want most things instantly when it would be better for us to wait." The article expounded the famous marshmallow study where four year olds were offered two marshmallows if they could wait twenty minutes; however, only one-third could resist. When tracked through high schools, those who resisted were more self-motivated, while those who couldn't were less confident and had poorer SAT scores. The key reason why society is not able to resist the marshmallows is that our pervading environment of the "right now" does not allow us to conquer our need for instant gratification. As a result, we simply fail to mature because we live in an environment that caters to our ever-wanting id, while not listening to our reality and morality principles, our ego and superego. Instant gratification is persistent because we normalize it, from the instant coffee to that instant fudge brownie. What society needs is the belief that happiness is not a matter of intensity but of balance and harmony. The aim should be to turn the right now into when the time is right.

Abhinav Suri, Grade 9
Saint Mary's Hall, TX

The Best Coach

I have a coach and he's been my coach since 6th grade. He always sets the example for me every time I see him. Coach Rivera has coached me not just in basketball and football but also in life.

He's the best coach I have ever had all my life. Whenever I'm not playing good and I'm mad at myself or I'm just having a bad day he's always the first to bolster me up. He's not perfect but he's a very good person. In any situation he always knows the right thing to do.

I feel very comfortable around him, talking to him and just being there with him. We always banter with each other and every day I spend with him we get even closer. I'm really going to miss him next year when I'm in high school.

I don't see him every day anymore since basketball season ended, but I will be seeing him still because he coaches track. Hopefully I will stay close with him because I really love him as a coach and really as an extended family member. I would do anything he needs me to do when he asks.

It was an honor playing for him this year, last year and sixth grade year. I will always remember him as the coach that really pointed me down the right path. I can honestly say that he is the coach I will never forget throughout my life. He stayed with me through thick and thin, he pushed me to the best that I could be, and he was there for me as a friend when I really needed one. I love him so much and I would trust him with anything.

Alec Huriega, Grade 8
St Matthew Catholic School, TX

Do You Really Need It?

While food can be healthy, it can also become addicting, making it unhealthy by over eating. You see, people in some countries stuff their faces with food, becoming overweight, while others struggle to provide food each day.

Did you know that some families such as those in the U.S. and Italy, can spend two to three hundred dollars a week in food?

In some places such as in Germany, people can eat nearly five hundred dollars in food for one family per week, while at the same time an African family struggles to live off of a little more than one dollar a week.

So, basically the money used to buy a week's worth of food in Germany for a family could feed an African family for roughly five hundred weeks. Personally, that is quite astonishing. Now I'm not writing this to say Germans or Americans eat too much. Some families are more fortunate than others. You see, the problem is when people who are fortunate, sit at home simply stuffing their faces with food! But instead of stuffing your faces you can help those in need by participating in can drives or at shelters for the homeless.

So before you shove another Twinkie down your throat, or get that next piece of pie, or open a second bag of chips, ask yourself if you really need the extra food. I can almost guarantee you that someone else needs it more than you.

Josh Baker, Grade 9
First Baptist Academy, TX

The Happiest Place in the Happiest Place on Earth

Joyful screams ring in the air as children stand jittery in the line feeling cool mist from the log crashing into the bottom of the massive drop. The excitement from Disneyland's Splash Mountain fills the air in the happiest place on Earth on my favorite ride. People chatter with anticipating in twisting paths of the stony cave that leads to the beginning of the ride: a moist log with squishy seats and glossy silver handle bars to hang on to. Cheery songs of wonderful days merge with the happy screams of people as their log drops down the first leg of the ride into a colorful world of fantasy. Colors and lights fill the room and everyone's eyes swivel back and forth trying to absorb every little detail as singing animals tell the story of one mischievous rabbit, and the mistake he makes playing a prank on a sinister fox. So much is going on that it is almost easy to forget that this ride plummets and whoosh, cool crisp water sprays at the log and into the giggling faces of people. The ride comes to an end as the cranking of the conveyer belt pushing the log blend with the sorrowful tune of a mother rabbit despairing over the fate of the mischievous bunny. As the log reaches the top of the mountain, adrenaline pumps and people gasp for their last breath of air before the log gradually tips and plunges, and a shower of cold water splashes the riders. The log then enters a dazzling room of singing and dancing animals, and people hum along to the familiar tune. The log comes to a halt and everyone steps out dripping wet while children plead with their parents, "Can we do it again?"

Josephine Horst, Grade 7
Placerita Jr High School, CA

My Role Model

J.K. Rowling influenced me to be a writer. To me, she is the best writer because of her attention to detail, and her ability to create a fantasy world out of scratch. She is my role model because of her ability to come out of a rut even when times were hard.

When I was in 4th grade, I read Harry Potter for the first time, and I instantly fell in love with the book. I still didn't know anything about J.K. Rowling after I finished the series on January 17, 2010, and I really wanted to know about her. Last month I was flipping through the channels on my TV and I saw a biography movie on J.K. Rowling. As I was watching it, I learned that she had a bad marriage, had a dependent child, and was unemployed. During that time, she was diagnosed with clinical depression, and contemplated suicide. Although she'd hit rock-bottom, she rebuilt her life. J.K. Rowling finally published, *Harry Potter and the Philosopher's Stone (Harry Potter and the Sorcerer's Stone* in America) on June 1997. She won eight awards for best series, and best author.

I admire her because of her decision to get back up and not give up. She won eight awards for best series, and best author. It is really inspiring how she got out of her rut and became successful doing what she loved. I can only hope to be like her when I grow up.

Madison Hoke, Grade 7
League City Intermediate School, TX

Love Changes You

It was November 13, three days before my birthday. I was in the bathroom getting ready for school, when my mom came in and said that my aunt was getting a foster kid. At that moment, we didn't know very much about him, except that his name was Micah.

After school that day, we went over to my aunt's house so we could meet him. When we got there, he hadn't woken up from his nap yet. My aunt was telling us that he wasn't going to be with us very long, probably only a month. After a few minutes, he walked into the living room. He was two years old, was thin, and had white blonde hair and blue eyes. He walked slowly, cautiously looking around at all the people he had never seen before, then sat down and started playing with his trucks. Slowly, my sister and I went over to him and started talking to him. It took him a minute, but then he began to play with us.

Almost a year later, my aunt told us that Micah's mom was finally doing better, and that he would be going home the next week. I couldn't believe that he was actually going home this time. They had told us it was only going to be a few weeks, then a few months, and now it had been almost a year. I loved Micah like he was really my cousin, and now he was leaving forever.

Having Micah as a cousin taught me that life is always changing, and I will have to accept whatever happens, and that I can't always control the outcome. I knew that no matter how much I wanted Micah to stay, I knew his mom loved him, and he needed to be with her.

Kelsey Crews, Grade 7
Lindale Jr High School, TX

What Inspired Gymnastics

Almost every little girl yearns for gymnastics classes. They entreat their moms for just one class which turns into a few months of classes. Well, I have been doing gymnastics for almost five years now, and I am still loving it. If you think gymnastics take just an iota of your life when you are my age, then you are fallible. It is a real commitment when you are at this high of a level. Here is an anecdote on how I got involved in the world of gymnastics.

When I was in third grade, there was a new gymnastics program at my school. I didn't really want to do it until one of my friends convinced me. The classes were on Thursday afternoons right after school, so we would change and eat a snack at school in about 15 minutes prior to the classes.

My coach said that I was very dynamic and prominent. She also said that I was so good that she wanted me to go to an actual gymnastics training center. On my first day, I made a lot of friends, but my old coach still nurtured me on Thursdays. She was my inspiration. I was still a fledgling, so she made sure that I got the extra practices.

After about a year in the same level at the gymnastics center, my coaches thought that I was proficient in that level. I got moved up to the next level with one of my friends. We were both so excited to get better. Through that whole process, my old coach had been helping me the whole time.

Aubrey Rosilier, Grade 7
St Matthew Catholic School, TX

Singing My Praise in Faith

I have an ample amount of people in my life that have helped me grow in faith. I have felt many things that have left me thinking "Is there even a God?" or "If there is a God, does He hate us?" I always try to think of ways to say "yes" to one of these questions, but my attempt is always futile. The more I think about the questions I always come up with more reasons why He does love us. Even though there is no strong, rock hard evidence, I still believe. People tell me I have a strong voice, so I will start there.

My teacher, Mrs. Cropper is one of the main people that have helped me. In my seventh grade year at St. Matthew, Mrs. Cropper was my English and religion teacher. To be honest I daydreamed during her lectures. When we were a month away from leading the school mass we would start practicing. During this month I would lead my class in the songs and practice the Responsorial Psalm. I would count down the minutes until I was in that class.

Mrs. Cropper called me her prodigy. My sister said with my voice I had the right to flaunt, but I would only banter with my friends. Every time I sang I would handle it with finesse. The more I sang my praise to God, the more I saw that He had given me a gift. Mrs. Cropper showed me that I can sing and proclaim the word of God at the same time. She taught me how to make my singing genial so people will listen to everything I was singing. With my voice everyone would listen to me praising God. I have grown so much since then.

Cassidy Crane, Grade 8
St Matthew Catholic School, TX

You Can Do It

My basketball coach, Monica, graduated from the University of Texas at San Antonio. Monica is probably the funniest person you will ever meet. She is genial and easy to get along with. She was so successful there that they were able to retire her basketball jersey. She had such finesse that she got to play in Europe, on an elite team.

Monica inspires me to do the best I can, and to never cut myself short. She makes us run at a college level, and says that she would not put us up to something that she doesn't know that we can do. When we get tired she always says, "When they want to walk we'll be able to run." Or, "To be a top player you got to be in top shape." That pushes us to the finish. She would always bolster us to keep on going. But it wasn't always about running. During a game she would make facetious jokes to remind us to box out. She would say, "Do the booty-doo because if your hands don't your booty do!"

We venerated Monica because we know that she gluts us with skill and mental tricks to be better not just in basketball but in school too. Every time we got fouled she said to visualize yourself making them and you can do it, and we did. We were apt to her doctrine of basketball. Monica has attributed all of her basketball skills to us. We know that she will always be there for us and remind us to push ourselves and to always have faith.

Kayla Alvarado, Grade 8
St Matthew Catholic School, TX

Traitor or Hero

"Traitors are the growth of every country." These very words were said by George Washington. Although there are an indefinite amount of meanings, one hidden meaning can be seen. That meaning is Benedict Arnold. The traitor we know was actually Benedict Arnold VI. Benedict's childhood experiences give some explanation on his personality. Benedict Arnold VI was born on January of 1741. Benedict Arnold VI was described altogether as a naughty and mischievous boy. He was also described as a boy of "middling height." At about that time, a diphtheria epidemic swept the whole town, and out of the eight members of the family, only four remained. Soon after that, the French and Indian War emerged which stopped and ended the trade with the West Indies. While slowly going into debt, his father soon died from acute liver failure. His mother then died soon afterward in 1759. He soon joined the militia, training to fight in the army. After hearing about the Battle of Lexington and Concord, he went to Massachusetts to join with the thousands of Patriots. After winning the Battle of Ticonderoga, Benedict forwarded his military career, victory after another; sometimes leading the charge himself. Although he was the one who led the battles, he was never given credit; partially because of his jealous superiors, who took the credit for themselves. He then betrayed America by giving the structure and plans of West Point to the British. The reason for this is that he did it for honor Even though he is known as a traitor, his merit still lives to protect our independence.

Nathan Yung, Grade 8
Carmel Valley Middle School, CA

The Healthy and Unhealthy Ways to Deal with Depression

Depression is a hard thing. It has its ups and downs and many people take medication for it. I know at least three people who take medication for depression and anxiety, my aunt Angie, my grandma, and my "sister" (best friend) Tristyn. Some other people deal with depression in an unhealthy way like cutting, using and/or abusing drugs, drinking, and worst of all…suicide. I know at least five people who have dealt with it in one of these unhealthy ways. One of them was me. I used to cut because I thought there were no other ways to deal with it. Now I cope with it by talking about my issues to my boyfriend or just simply writing. I think writing helps me more than talking does.

You feel like the pain of depression will never pass by, but eventually it will. The fastest way I try to convince myself it will pass is by thinking of all the things I am thankful for. I try my best to help people who are depressed and don't know any other way to deal with that *pain*. I don't like to see people hurting themselves in any way. I know from experience that it's unhealthy and I don't like people using an unhealthy way to deal with it. Depression is a hard thing to go through, trust me I know, but you must know you're never alone and know that you're beautiful!

April Snyder, Grade 8
Excelsior Academy, UT

Enjoy Nature

Nature is something that people need to appreciate more often, and not take it for granted. We need to take some time from our lives and take walks and hikes and enjoy nature at least 4 days a week. If you don't live near a place where you can enjoy nature, then go to the park or walk to work if you live close by.

We need to set goals such as hiking Mt. Timpanogos or Deseret Peak instead of wasting your time playing video games or playing with electronic devices. We need to plan family vacations such as going to Yellowstone National Park, Arches National Park, or Zion's National Park. By visiting these places, you will soon appreciate the wonders of nature. There are many wonderful things to see at these places. For example, at Arches National Park there are many beautiful arches that are mind-blowing to think about how long nature took to create. The dirt at Arches National Park is an orangish-red, which I think is really cool. There are many fun arches to see, such as Double Arch a.k.a. Indiana Jones Arch. Yellowstone National Park is amazing because it has geysers such as Old Faithful. You can see a lot of wildlife such as buffalo, bears, and deer. Zion's National Park is amazing because you can take hikes, like the Angel's Landing hike.

People need to appreciate nature more often and not take it for granted. We should spend more time outdoors and spend less time cooped up inside. We should all set goals to enjoy nature 4 days a week.

Derek Redmond, Grade 7
Excelsior Academy, UT

Chinese Foot Binding

It's interesting what people will do to make themselves look "beautiful." They'll pay very high prices to be accepted. One of these things is Chinese foot binding. Foot binding began in the 10th century and was outlawed in 1912, but even after being outlawed, people did it in secret.

There are a couple stories that explain the origin of foot binding. One is of a prince who had a favorite dancer. He ordered her to bind her feet so they'd be smaller. Then there's the story of an empress who was born with a club foot and had all the young girls bind their feet too.

Foot binding is when your feet are tightly bound to keep them from growing. Girls would have their feet bound at a very young age of about 4 to 7. First, their toes were pushed under their feet and broken, then pushed up into the sole. Their toes and heels grew closer together and made their feet deformed. Because of the deformation of their feet, it was very hard for the women to walk.

Foot binding was supposed to be beautiful. It also represented a high-class woman. It soon became a necessary thing to do for women to get good marriages.

This is a horrible thing that went on for a thousand years. Many women still have their feet stuck like that and hate it. I think it's just crazy how a trend can be ugly and painful, but people still do it.

Amanda Logan, Grade 8
Excelsior Academy, UT

The Power of Sight

I am 16 years old, and the horrors of reality hit me harder every day. Adults expect me to have a boyfriend, dreams of marriage, and interests in everything that I am not ready for. It's scary how the new generations are "growing up." I say "growing up" sarcastically only because The Teens of Today — as I like to call them — think that they are mature, when in fact, their brains are as small as seeds. You may wonder, who am I to say the things I say? I am a voice that's not afraid to tell the truth. A few days ago, I sat in Geometry class watching an episode from a show called *Numb3rs*. The teacher claimed the episode is educational because of the interesting number sequences. Halfway through, I hear the disgusting sounds of tormented people, and I start to question just how "educational" this show is. Later, my teacher's daughters come in from their Elementary School and sit down next to me, watching the episode. I stare in awe as their faces are indifferent to what they see. The gruesome images and horrific events make me cringe and crawl in a box, but they remain fearless. A few months ago in speech class, my teacher put on some "funny" commercials from the *Saturday Night Live* TV show. Teens my age laughed at the perverse images, while I covered my eyes and ears to keep from taking in the vulgar words. Sometimes I find myself questioning the reasons why I'm not like them. Why I hate the things I see and hear, and instead prefer to sit safe in my bedroom, away from everyone else. Now I know the answer.

Ana Done, Grade 9
Western Hills High School, TX

The Rocker Inside of Me

The thump of a textbook tossed on the floor is intermingled with the haphazard fluttering of the escaped flocks of paper. Sick of completing all of the assigned work, I sighed and attempted to calm the furious equations that swirled within my brain. Frustration welled up inside of me, seeking a chink in my composure to explode through, but before I did anything that I would later regret, I pulled out my iPod and played the first metal song I beheld.

The heartbeat of the drum played along with the screaming guitar, the two sounds completely different, but meshed perfectly. If I did not have a buzz cut, my hair would have certainly been flying in every direction, a flock of birds disturbed by a thrown rock. Why do I love this "devil music?" Why do the yells emanating from the ear buds intrigue rather that repulse me? Because when my foot starts to tap and my hands play an awful air guitar, all of my worldly concerns fade away. The melodies crowd out all other sounds, but more importantly, they crowd out my malignant thoughts.

The music is a siren, calling different me to emerge. I become a person who does not care what is expected of him, but does what he wants — regardless of the repercussions. In reality, I cannot be this reckless, impulsive person, but while the song plays, all of the shackles and chains that bind me to my studious alter ego are gloriously removed.

Joshua Winnert, Grade 9
Saint Mary's Hall, TX

The Gardener Who Sings

Steven Curtis Chapman is my inspiration. He is also renown for being religious. He is an amazing singer, not only that, but he sings about faith. He is planting the seeds of faith in me by teaching me about God while singing. While making a few catchy tunes, he also teaches us about God, faith and love. He had been a prodigy as a child, but got even better.

The first song I heard from him was "Cinderella." I was at a Girl Scout party where you brought your dads and danced with them. And if you don't know, the song "Cinderella" was made by Steven for his young daughter who died. The only way he could handle the pain was to pray, and sing. He is a strong man, who if ever feels anguished or belated, turns to God and praises Him by singing.

Hopefully I grow up and be a follower of God too. He teaches me how to be loving, kind to others, forgiving and understanding. He has had a lot of bad things happen to him, but he lives through it by turning to God, and praying every day. As he says in his song "When I see you, I see the fingerprints of God." He is telling us that God made us, and he loves us deeply.

I know that I can't sing like he can, but I can pray, and be strong in my faith like him. I had been incognito and he helped me find myself. If I ever need help from anyone and I feel like no one else can help, I listen to one of his songs and I remember God is good, all the time. Steven Curtis Chapman has two very, very strong things: his voice, and faith.

Ashley Gonzalez, Grade 8
St Matthew Catholic School, TX

The Amazing Teacher of Faith

My grandfather, Archie Titzman, always plants the seeds of our faith. He always goes to church every day to get even closer to God. He always thinks about everyone but himself.

My grandfather teaches others about our faith and makes everyone he talks to a strong believer. He always dissuades many people from doing the wrong thing and persuades them to do the right thing. He is never indignant; he is always very fruitful to anyone who seeks help from him. My grandfather is always very spirited no matter what the case.

Everything about God is never indispensable for him. He is always available to anyone who has a question to ask him. He can make even the most melancholy person luster and be animated with joy. He has had a very big potential of teaching others about our beautiful and awesome God. He is the most amazing person that I know. He loves to talk to anyone who would like to talk with him.

My grandfather prays more than anyone that I know. If anyone asks for him to pray for them or for others, he will not even hesitate and will pray for the person. He is the most loving to everyone. If somebody gets mad at him for something that they did and then come back to apologize he will never hesitate to accept their apology. This is why I wrote about my amazing grandfather who plants the seeds of faith in everyone every day.

Devon Titzman, Grade 7
St Matthew Catholic School, TX

The Day My Dad Met a Black Bear

Ever since my dad was nineteen years old, he has gone to Alaska once every year. When he goes, he usually goes to the town of Klawock on the Prince of Wales Island. He normally goes with his friend, Jason, who grew up in Alaska.

One day my dad and Jason decided to go river fishing. They got in the car and took a logging road that would take them to the river. In Alaska they do a lot of logging, so there are a lot of logging roads. Along the way they stopped and found a game trail made by deer or other animals. They followed the trail until they got to the river. When they got to the river they walked in in their jeans and shoes. Then, they began to fish. Soon after, Jason caught a silver, which is a type of salmon. Jason put the fish on the river bank and started to fish again. A few minutes later he told my dad to look back. My dad looked back and saw a black bear eating their fish. Eventually the bear left, but it had been really close to them and was watching them. That night they made it home safely and everything was okay. That was the time my dad met a black bear.

Emma Piziali, Grade 7
St Joseph Catholic School, CA

The Wonderful World

You are scared out of your mind, standing ten feet above the water, and the encouraging shouts from your friends are background noise to the pounding in your ears. Everything stops for just a moment as you tense. You take one moment and absorb your surroundings, the baby-blue sky, the bright yellow sun, some luminous white clouds and the turquoise water; then you jump. You forget how pretty the water is or how blue the sky is. All you think about is jumping into the water, not knowing what to expect.

No one really stops and thinks, "Nope, there will never be another day that the sky is this exact same shade of blue," or even, "Wow, the clouds will never make this exact shape again." Isn't the world a wonderful place? We need to slow down. Don't rush into things. "Stop and smell the roses," people!

Alexis Topham, Grade 7
Excelsior Academy, UT

Power Has Two Meanings

"When the power of love overcomes the love of power, the world will know peace." —Jimi Hendrix. Everybody has someone or something to love, and that something can be power. Whether it is the president of the U.S. or the top of the group, power can take control of your life and put you in a deep dark hole. Power is a strong force that you need to decide its path in your life. Power can be used to control others or it can be an emotion or feeling. Power takes a part in my life in the form of friendship. I never would be able to stand my life without best friends. They are always there for me when I am sad. They back me up and help me out when I am mad. Finally, when I am happy, they share it with me. My friends are the power that supports me through rain and shine; remember that power has two meanings.

Miette Walton, Grade 7
North Star Academy, CA

Taking a Stand Against SOPA

In a world where the Internet is a major highway to information, the Stop Online Piracy Act (SOPA) takes away freedom in the online world and must be stopped. SOPA, a bill introduced by the House of Judiciary Committee Chairman, Texas Representative Lamar Smith, and twelve co-sponsors on October 26, 2011, is designed to prevent copyright infringement online by blocking websites from search engines and payment facilities.

Although seeming reasonable, SOPA poses a serious threat. According to guardian.co.uk, it can interfere with the Domain Name System (DNS), the center data service of the Internet that holds website addresses. With this ability to look into the information of websites, U.S. law enforcement agencies may prevent the DNS from releasing the address of a website, causing that site to vanish from existence. The Digital Millennium Copyright Act (DMCA), passed in 1998, has already removed infringed material online, as referenced on the website gizmodo.com.

SOPA also justifies shutting down websites for a single infringement link, even if the link is not endorsed by the original website creator. Websites, such as Youtube, Facebook, and Twitter, that have users linking to copyrighted material, could be "taken down." Adults and teenagers from all over the country, who link to online copyrighted material, could face legal action with SOPA. Whether it's singing (covering) a song or videotaping the footage of a video game, the prosecuted could face up to five years in jail. According to 1stwebdesigner.com, the U.S. government hopes to start a worldwide change on the Internet by promoting bills like SOPA in other countries.

The Internet represents our freedom and should not be controlled by governments that can create blacklists for sites that they deem "wrong." Considering the dangerous impact SOPA may have, it's crucial that we take a stand and keep the Internet liberated.

Nathan Phan, Grade 9
Schurr High School, CA

Best Buds

Friends can help you become a better person, but this is only true if you pick good friends. Many people have friends that get themselves into trouble. When I see my siblings become friends with troublemakers, I always wonder why they would pick those people. For me, it is pretty easy to make friends with people. When I choose friends, I always look for people who will help me when I am in a jam, a person who will laugh with me and not at me, even though I occasionally make a fool out of myself. When I used to be in home school, I didn't have as many friends; the friends I had were my neighbors and people at church. When I came to this school I made lots of friends that are still my friends today.

Over the years, I have learned that friends can help you become a better you. Friends are people who smile at you when you are having a bad day, people you can tell secrets to. Friends are the bomb!

Matthew Wells, Grade 8
Excelsior Academy, UT

Internet as a Tool

Is the Internet giving out bogus information? Some people seem to believe that we shouldn't trust the information found online. However, what they may not realize is first, the Internet isn't just used as a source of information. Second, if you look something up and are uncertain if the information is reliable, check another site. Third, the Internet isn't the only source available for finding information.

There are a ton of websites that aren't used to find information. They're used for interaction and communication. For example, in today's society we use Facebook, Twitter, and Gmail to interact. These sites give us the chance to interact with loved ones. Taking away this privilege would be unnecessary because some people use these sites as opportunities to interact with people they can't see for whatever reason.

If you look something up and you're not satisfied with your answer, look it up on another site. If you end up getting two different answers use a third site. If you're lazy and don't want to do that, that's your fault! Not the Internet's. If you've looked at multiple sites and are still uncertain about the information, find another source. There are plenty of other sources that are available. There are different varieties of encyclopedias and books for you to use. There are also a ton of people who will probably know the answer that you are trying to find out.

Brianna Robbins, Grade 9
South Jordan Middle School, UT

Beyond the Flames

Many things can happen in a split second, as if your life flashed before your eyes. My father, Jason Schechterle, experienced that event March 26, 2001. The life he knew was erased by the roaring fire he faced and the three-month coma he endured. The taxi driver was oblivious of what was happening. He had suffered an epileptic seizure. His foot was frozen on the gas pedal going at lightning speed, crashing into the start of my father's new life.

My father missed a lot throughout his coma, including my birthday. Who could blame him, he was already in enough pain without knowing it yet. One day, I was fortunate enough to visit my father in the hospital. When we arrived I was ecstatic until I looked upon his face. My face drowned in darkness as I looked upon bruises, stitches, and scars. I flew out as a waterfall of tears dropped, leaving a heartbroken father behind.

The recover of my father was quite challenging. He had difficulties with all sorts of things. We recently celebrated my father's "Burn Day" on the 10th anniversary of his accident. His life now is a true gift to his family and himself. He currently has a foundation called "Beyond the Flames" which raises money to help support those who have gone through what my father experienced. My father did not give into the fire but embraced it, inspiring hundreds of people, including me, his son, Zane Schechterle.

Zane Schechterle, Grade 8
St Gregorys Catholic School, AZ

All People Can Serve God, No Matter What

All people can serve God, no matter what. "Serve: to be useful or of service to; help." Women can be religious sisters, and be single or married. Men have more options. They can be priests, deacons, religious brothers, and can be single or married. God can be served in more than one way.

One vocation is becoming a religious sister. One example of a sister serving God is Sister Eloisa, she teaches at Saint Rose Catholic School. She serves God by teaching the middle school religion, and teaches the confirmation class at the parish. Other sisters work in hospitals and volunteer at homeless shelters. The sisters serve God in the way He has chosen for them.

Another vocation is getting married. Married people serve God in many ways. An example is my parents. They send their children to a Catholic school so their kids can learn about and serve God. Married couples have a harder time serving God in big ways because they have to make commitments, but they do serve God. Many married couples volunteer at local soup kitchens and organizations. Others serve at their church on Sunday.

Another vocational option is living a single life. Single people have more options in serving God. Many don't have big commitments like married couples do, so they can move around whenever necessary. An example of a single person is my uncle; he is able to volunteer in faraway places without having to worry about a wife and children at home. Single people have more opportunities but aren't always willing to accept them.

In conclusion, all people can serve God, but it's up to them whether they take the chance or not. God has many paths for us to follow and ways to serve him. How will you choose to serve God?

Mishta Stanislaus, Grade 7
St Rose Grammar School, CA

Volleyball

Volleyball. It is my favorite sport. Unfortunately, I only do my school season, which isn't very long. In fact, it's too short. Every time it ends, I wish it could be longer. However, it's all I can do, so I manage. I really want to play on a club volleyball team and keep improving. Volleyball encourages me to work harder in school. I have always wanted to play on a collage team such as Stanford, but for that you have to have a lot of talent, and very good grades. If it weren't for volleyball, I would have given up on that dream a long time ago. But I have, and will always, love volleyball, so I won't give up. I kept my impossible dream and I intend to follow it. Volleyball is a part of my life, and I hope it will stay that way. I plan to play all through high school, collage, and beyond. If I succeed in my collage volleyball dream, my next dream would be to play in the Olympics. I would play beach volleyball with my best friend. I would love that because I obviously love volleyball and I love the beach and my friends as well. I hope to play volleyball until the end of my life.

Jesse Crowley, Grade 7
North Star Academy, CA

A Way to Live Everyday Life

Fairness is an element that we learn as we grow up. When we were younger, our parents taught us that we always have to be fair no matter what. For example, in the first grade, if we were playing kickball, we always made sure that everyone had a chance to kick to make it fair. There are many ways of showing fairness and it is a good way to live life. We must treat everyone fairly no matter how they look, where they come from, or what they wear. God put us on this Earth to do good deeds and treating others fairly is one of them. Being fair can show a lot of your personality. If you go for a job interview, they look at your strengths and your weaknesses. Sometimes they even check if you are fair and if you are able to work with others well. No matter how old you are or whatever you do, you always have to be fair. I remember a while back my grandma and I were at the market getting some groceries and when we were waiting to pay, another line opened and the girl working there said she would help us. Right then, when we were about to go in line, a man cut in front of us. I was a tad upset, but my grandma told me he wasn't worth it. My grandma told me people who aren't polite and fair don't have proper manners.

Melissa Rogero, Grade 7
St Ferdinand Catholic School, CA

My Family

My family is the most special part of my life. My mom is so sweet, kind, and caring, but she also has that sense of discipline that every mother should have. She helps me with schoolwork and always supports my choices. Driving me around to the multiple places I have to be is a pain, and yet she does it for me. She will always love me.

My dad is so comforting and loving. He understands me in whatever situation I'm in. There is no time or place that could take that away from him or from me. He knows how I'm feeling, and always knows how to make it better.

Kelly and Catherine, my two sisters, are girls I hold dear to my heart. They love me so much and always look up to me. They will never not want to play with me. As my sisters, they will always be there for me, no matter how rough things turn out to be.

Nicole Greenberg, Grade 7
North Star Academy, CA

Honesty

Honesty is one of the most important character traits a person could have. It plays a major role in trust. If a person constantly lies to you, you never know if they are being truthful. It becomes very frustrating, and you start to believe nothing that person says. Even though being completely honest is hard sometimes, it is essential. For example, if someone asks for your opinion on an outfit they are wearing and you don't like it, you can let them know what you think in a kind way. Also, if you do something wrong, it is better to say what you did rather than to hide it, because people will have more respect for you. Overall, honesty is the best policy.

Sarah Bennett, Grade 9
Foothills Academy, AZ

The Reason to Live

Something that I can remember from a long time ago is when my family and I were down in St. George. We were climbing up in the mountains. When we were leaving, I was heading to the car. I didn't see a big gap in between two rocks. I fell down into the gap, which was about 6 feet deep. I was only 4 years old so I couldn't just climb out. I was stuck, and there was nothing that I could do. To make things even worse, I was positioned in such a way that I couldn't even breathe. I could have died right there between those rocks. Finally, I saw my dad. He saw me fall into the gap. He pulled me out and saved my life.

When I think back 10 years to that day, I realize that I was saved for a reason. I needed to be saved. I don't know what I need to do in my life, but I do know that I could have died right there, and people need me to accomplish something in their lives before I can leave their lives behind. Everyone has a purpose in life, I don't think that a person leaves life until they serve a purpose. Nobody is useless; we all have something we need to accomplish in life. We don't die until we have completed that purpose.

Nate Skelton, Grade 8
Excelsior Academy, UT

Music

"All things shall perish under the sky. Music alone shall live never to die." Music is the most important thing in my life. It really ties together my chaotic existence because when I sing, or play the piano, all of my troubles seem to wash away. When I grow up and go to college, I hope to study music more than I ever have and enrich my future life, no matter what I become. I love music the most because it is beautiful to listen to, like candy to the ears. I go into a world of happiness and zone out from my distracting life when I make music. When I sing in a concert or perform in my annual piano recital, I always feel great afterwards because I have jumped a hurdle to become a better musician. Music connects me to some of my favorite subjects. Counting rhythms and singing scales are intertwined with math. This makes me feel even better about music because I learn while I have fun. To pursue music is my dream and I will always try to fulfill it as best I can.

Colston Rienhoff, Grade 7
North Star Academy, CA

The Golden Guitar

When I play my guitar my mind and my hands become an amazing harmony of mind and music working together. My guitar, put in the hands of a musician composes a dazzling orchestra of notes and riffs. When I play the whole world around me collapses and turns into a cave full of unexplored chambers and secrets, just waiting to be probed and learned. Roads and paths are all dormant. When my hands slide down the neck they make musical streaks of gold. But when I'm done, and my hands leave the neck, the adventurous cave slowly turns into reality, and the rhythm is lost.

Matthew Stephens, Grade 8
Monte Vista Christian School, CA

My Cousin

Ever since I could remember, there has always been that one person who was always there for me. It isn't my mom or dad, or even my older brothers. It's my oldest cousin, Nikki. I personally think she is the coolest person, and I look up to her for many things. She is my main influence.

Even today, I am thirteen years old and she is twenty-five years old. Sometimes I forget that she is that old because she doesn't act like it. It is not that she is immature, it is just that she is just a fun-loving spirit. She graduated from the same Catholic school that I am still attending, St. Gregory's. She was in the class of 2000, and I will be in the class of 2012.

We do everything together, but mainly we go shopping. She is like my older sister since I don't have one. I only have two brothers. She tells me a lot about her past mistakes and informs me not to do the same. I really appreciate her looking out for me. I really appreciate everything she does and I know she will always be there for me. I thank God for having her in my life. I believe everyone should have such a caring influence like her.

Monique Hasbun, Grade 8
St Gregorys Catholic School, AZ

Disneyland

My Mom, Tata, Nana, my cousins Maya, Ray, Frank, Abie, my Aunt Liz, my Uncle Frank, my brother, and myself were getting ready for our big family trip to Disneyland. It was really hard getting everyone's luggage together. We couldn't wait till we arrived at our hotel. I couldn't wait to get on California Screamin'.

I was so excited because we were going to stay in California for five days. Disneyland was so much fun! I couldn't go on many rides because I was too short. That really disappointed me. The atmosphere was amazing though, so that made up for me being too short. I had so much fun.

When we went back the next day, I still had fun. Knott's Berry Farm was also fun. I had more fun at Disneyland though. I loved the rides there. I had fun hanging out with my family. The drive home made me tired. It was the best vacation ever.

Sammy Rivera, Grade 7
St Gregorys Catholic School, AZ

God

God in general is the savior of many people, people who are Christian and have accepted Him into their lives. God is a good person and guides us through our life and gets us through our bad times. God is always there for you, when you're in trouble or even if you just need to talk to Him. He never forgets you and will cleanse you of your sins when you repent to Him and He will forgive you of them as well. He sent His son to earth to die on a cross for us so we would not have to suffer for all of our sins. God also has made a plan for you and it is a good idea to follow that plan even if it is difficult. God has done so much for us and we should be thankful to Him for giving us life and so many good things in this world.

Austin Gudgel, Grade 8
Monte Vista Christian School, CA

A Simple Welcome Can Change Lives

When we look past diversity, we discover that everyone is special and has a unique purpose in life. We must incorporate equality into our lives so that others may feel accepted and special. My family had the opportunity to go to Morocco, Africa. When discovering the news, I was elated, but then suddenly a fear overcame me that our racial differences would make it difficult to feel accepted. Upon our arrival, we realized that United States differed greatly from Morocco. The airport had no air conditioning and the security system was very poor. We noticed many miniscule mud huts and realized what challenges we would face throughout our stay, such as the overwhelming heat and living without some modern conveniences. Soon after our arrival, we began to feel peace and were not judged for our differences. We spent countless hours with a group of Moroccans because of the loving treatment they gave. The acceptance of our differences made it easier to communicate and still have a learning experience.

After receiving their kind regards, we realized that the Moroccans had an understanding of our equality. If we had not received such a great welcome, we would have never fancied to stay there. We must always emphasize to others the importance and equality that they have within themselves. By accepting those with differences, you will radiate an example of someone who truly knows the equality that we all have within ourselves. Those who have the "guidance of understanding" will abide by the example omitted.

Megan Bateman, Grade 7
White Pine Charter School, ID

Best Summer Ever

My favorite trip took place in the summer of 2010. My family and I were heading to Michigan to visit my step-mom's parents, brother, sisters, aunts and uncles. We passed through the states of New Mexico, Colorado, Nebraska, Iowa, Wisconsin, and finally, there it was, the big sign with big letters saying Michigan.

My family decided to get there as soon as possible so we could go places on our return trip home. It took about three days to get to Michigan. Every time my family and I travel to Michigan we try to fish in Lake Michigan, but this year the wind was too strong to fish. I spent time with each family member while I was visiting with my family. Then it came so fast, the last day in Michigan. We said our goodbyes. The next morning my family and I left.

On our way back from Michigan, we stopped in Minneapolis, Minnesota. While we stayed there, we wanted to visit the Mall of America. This is probably the best mall that can ever be made. The next day we stopped in Sioux City, SD. The hotel was awesome because of its pool accessories. The next stop was in Denver, Colorado. We were a little scared because there was a tornado warning the area. Thanks to God there wasn't a tornado. Our next stop was Phoenix, Arizona. It was exciting because I hadn't seen my family in over two weeks. This was my best trip ever.

Angel De Los Reyes, Grade 7
St Gregorys Catholic School, AZ

A Man's Best Friend

A dog is a man's best friend, nothing more, nothing less, just your very best friend. For me, I was able to experience this first hand. It all started when my mom rushed me home from school, I was curious but unsure. Oddly, when I found the house vacant, still, and quiet, I was disappointed. When I turned around I saw a goofy blond golden retriever puppy. My life was never the same after that day.

Max was a year old before we knew it! My younger sister even sat him on a dining room chair and let him eat a hamburger, with a birthday hat on. We took him and our other golden retriever, Rusty, with us everywhere.

He loved to travel with us. That dog had probably been to more places than the average human. He traveled through seventeen U.S. states in all! Every summer we went on a long road trip, just the four of us—six if you count the dogs. Swimming in the North Fork of the American River was one of Max's highlights.

Until the summer of 2010, Max was at the height of his life, but sooner or later good things come to an end. The vet said that it was just an ear infection, but when he didn't get better the doctor took x-rays. With two massive cancerous tumors, it wasn't hopeful. For two months, Max lived on a daily dosage of painkillers, leading us to make the decision to put him down. He was only six. After having Max, I understand the meaning behind the saying, "a dog is a man's best friend." Like I said, my life was never the same after I got Max and will never be the same after losing him.

Stephen Oakley, Grade 8
Aviara Oaks Middle School, CA

The Accident

My dad used to travel with my brother and me on an old bicycle. One day, a motorcycle rammed us as it drove by. It was a humid and sticky day. The road looked like a murky black river. Suddenly, a rip-roaring sound rang out, and I collapsed onto a dusty sidewalk. Voices rang through my ears as someone picked me up and carried me away from the scene. I saw a sleek and incandescent motorcycle race away.

I started to wail because there were so many unfamiliar faces surrounding me. A numb sensation covered my leg, and there were scrapes and bruises encasing me. Someone rushed me to the local clinic. That's when I found out my brother almost fell into a 10-foot ditch along the roadside. My dad seemed fine, but he was really shaken from within.

My mother came fifteen minutes later and held my family tenaciously. I had never been happier to see my mother in my life. Even though we were covered in painful bruises and tiny scrapes, we were never happier to be alive and together. Somehow, we had survived and we were lucky to be alive.

This experience has taught me to love the things I have taken for granted. Family is something I have kept enveloped around my heart. Wistful moments like these can wrench your heart and really teach you a lesson that you will cherish forever.

Shaloni Pinto, Grade 8
St Gregorys Catholic School, AZ

Inspiration to Become a Better Catholic

In my life I have never been that big of a religious person. I'm not perfect. Some weeks I wouldn't go to church and half the time I would forget to pray. Over the summer though, my family decided that we would visit Rome for a few weeks with my grandpa.

One morning we woke up bright and early to walk the mile and a half distance to arrive at St. Peter's Basilica for a mass said by the Pope. As we got closer to the Vatican we began to see the citadel, castle Sant' Angelo, which looked over the city. When we arrived we saw the prodigious amount of people who were there to attend the vigil. We took our seats and waited for the ceremony to start.

When the pope came out, the crowd roared with loud plaudits. When he made it up to the stage he began to say the mass in Italian. Throughout various parts of the mass, translators would begin to speak in the languages of the people who attended the service. From my perspective being in the presence of the Pope I felt holy. I felt such respect and loyalty to God. I had never felt that way before in my life and I didn't know what to think. After we prayed in unison in Italian we all left to get back to our hotel.

When I came back from Rome I became obsessed with prayer and church. I now pray before I eat and before I go to bed and I am more watchful of the things I say and do. I venerate the Pope for inspiring me to become a better Catholic and planting faith into my life.

Makena Shaughnessy, Grade 8
St Matthew Catholic School, TX

Tim

Tim Haviland was my cousin, my role model, and best of all, one of my best friends. Even though Tim was five years older than I, he treated me like his closest friend. We did not see each other often, but when we did, we made the best of it. Whenever he came to Phoenix, I wouldn't leave his side. I remember countless hours of h-o-r-s-e- and talking about girls as well as card games like poker and twenty-one. It was always a treat to have Tim over.

Tim was a die-hard Lakers fan, and I am a die-hard Suns fan. We would spend hours talking smack about who would win the upcoming game. Tim would never let me forget about Kobe's last-second fadeaway in overtime when they beat the Suns. Tim nicknamed his favorite player (Kobe Jelly Bean Black Mamba Bryant). Every Easter we were corn hole partners, ever since I learned to toss a beanbag. We challenged many uncles and family friends. In 2011, Tim and I went undefeated in the family corn hole tournament.

Tim and I would text each other about sports and chat on Facebook about everything. It was a shock to everyone that knew Tim that he had passed away. God is the only one who knows why. My opinion is that God called Tim's name because someone was lonely in Heaven and that person must've needed a friend like Tim. Tim had a one-in-a-kind personality that I will miss forever.

Ben Fairbanks, Grade 8
St Gregorys Catholic School, AZ

Broken Day

When I was younger, my days never failed to satisfy the feelings of happiness and reassurance I needed. I had free time every day; life was so much easier being able to fish, swing, and play games in one day. Then, the most extraordinary weekend would take place without my knowledge. It had the perfect weather; warm enough to be scorching, yet containing a small breeze that would push the heat waves off the sizzling skin. I sat on my swing in my backyard to embrace the weather. My dad peeked out the door, informing me that we would be shooting rockets. I got excited, anticipating the fun I would have. I didn't know it would end in quite the opposite way.

I jumped out of my swing as I was at my highest point. I slowly began falling forward and realized I had no control. I instinctively pulled out my arms, then I felt excruciating pain. I crawled into my house and shrieked as loud as possible. I saw my mom run to me, and I can't remember anything after that. I then found myself on a hospital bed with a broken arm. It altered my great summer; I could no longer do half of my activities. Swimming, fishing, and so much more were impossible. Yet, I found other activities, and best of all, people were nice to me. People were suddenly interested in my injuries and wanted to sign my cast.

I learned that day that I could become strong when needed and that others would help me through. For the last few weeks of school, others carried my books and did other good deeds for me. I noticed how, at the worst of times, people give support.

Eric Lyne, Grade 9
Brush High School, CO

Weird Weather

It began as just regular rain, and then it became very cold. My mom runs a daycare at our house, and the little kids think the rain is cool. Then, thunder came. It was very loud, and I understood why toddlers think it's frightening. We lost power, and the house got very dark.

When we heard the first window shatter, Mom yelled, "Get in the hallway!" The hail was terrifying. Everything became cold, dark and loud. Each hailstone was as big as a golf ball and moved extremely fast. The storm was like being struck with golf balls, relentlessly and painfully.

After the hail stopped, I found cardboard to temporarily fix a broken window. I propped it up in front of the living room window; otherwise the rain would soak the floor and everything on it. The ice that had gotten in was melting on the furniture and carpet. There wasn't much we could do about the electricity, but it was only out for a little while. Once everything calmed down, we walked outside to see the damage.

It was catastrophic! Trees, flowers and bushes were stripped of their leaves, a neighbor's tree was toppled over, the sturdy plastic garbage can had a huge hole right through it, the newly pained fence had holes in it and the paint was completely eaten away. We had just redone our roof and AC, so those remained in good condition. I'm sure some people were hit worse, but it was terrible for me.

Alex Wille, Grade 8
St Gregorys Catholic School, AZ

Taxing the Cause

Tobacco use is a major preventable cause of premature death and disease worldwide. Smoking harms nearly all of the organs of the body, is an expensive addiction, and causes memory loss and other adverse health effects such as an increased risk in hip fractures, and lower bone density throughout the body. These effects can cost millions in insurance for the people of America. Nicotine, the tobacco plant's defense towards insects, is a toxin more lethal than strychnine or diamondback rattlesnake venom and three times deadlier than arsenic.

Long-term smoking can lead to diseases such as the Mosaic virus, cardiovascular diseases, respiratory diseases, and cancers. Nonsmokers have to pay higher medical costs for people who have smoked and gotten diseases, and cannot afford to pay the cost of the treatment. Smokers are considered a high health risk due to preexisting conditions that make it hard for them to get medical coverage, causing an increase in health insurance premiums. A yearly checkup for a nonsmoker costs about $150 for a physical and routine blood work, while a smoker's physical can range from $150 for a consultation, plus additional blood work and treatment including x-rays ranging in the thousands of dollars.

The tobacco companies should dramatically raise the prices of tobacco whether it damages the company financially or not. Higher tobacco taxes save money by reducing tobacco-related health care costs, including Medicaid expenses. States can realize even greater health benefits and cost savings by allocating some of the revenue to programs that prevent children from smoking and help smokers quit. With the increase of taxes on cigarettes the state can save money for better revenues and slowly stop the use of tobacco and smoke pollution.

Josiah Guzman, Grade 8
Vacaville Christian Schools, CA

Life

Life is one of the hardest things to learn about. No one will ever know everything about it. No person's life will ever be perfect. It will have highs and lows, and many interesting moments with friends and family, you just need to make the best of it. Learn from your mistakes, don't let the bummers (lows in life) bring you down, and don't ever let anyone bring down your dreams. Live like you will die tomorrow. I personally have had an eventful life. I've lost some of the people closest to me, had some great times with friends, laughed, cried, had to deal with some major family matters, found out who my true friends are, and much more. I'm still trying to figure it out, who I am, and what I want to do with it. I definitely learned from not just my mistakes, but my friends' and family too. After having my cousin die from drugs I realized how important life truly is, and what it is to me and my peers. With any kind of experience you find out a little more about everyone, including you. Just live like you will die tomorrow, and dream like you will live forever and see where your life will take you.

Kasey Barker, Grade 8
Monte Vista Christian School, CA

The Essay

December 21, 2011
7:56 A.M.
What!?! I only have until the end of the semester to enter a writing contest?!? That's ridiculous! She said we had to enter one writing contest during the year but she never said it had to be before the semester ended! Of course I didn't actually say this out loud. I merely screamed it in my head. That's only three weeks from today not including winter break. I haven't even found a contest to enter.

January 9, 2012
7:42 A.M.
Ugh. English, first period. I have that essay due in three weeks and I haven't even found a contest to enter. After class, I'll grab a few of the contest flyers and look them over. For now, I'll try not to worry about it.

8:36 A.M.
Awe, I forgot to grab the flyers! I'm right outside the classroom but I guess it'll be fine if I get them tomorrow.

January 13, 2012
8:36 A.M.
Yes! I got the flyers and shoved them into my backpack.

6:31 P.M.
Okay, time to start homework. The first things I pull out are my 3 flyers on essay contests. The first of which is about some Greek people it seems. No, too much research. The second is about women who do math. No, just no. The third is titled "Creative Commons" and has to do with writing a nonfiction essay. It's better than the other two but unfortunately it's due in only one dwarf sized week!

January 19, 2012
8:07 P.M.
Now I have to think of an idea — the hardest part. It has to be nonfiction, so I can't do that idea about flying llamas. Hmmm…how about an essay about me writing an essay?

Scott Huppert, Grade 8
Aviara Oaks Middle School, CA

The Time I Went Snorkeling

I remember the first time I went snorkeling. I went with my dad and brother, Alex. We were in Hawaii, and the water was so crystal clear, you could see straight down to the sand. Alex was too scared to go far into the water, so I decided to go out by myself. I was a little scared, because to see the fish you had to go where the waves got big, and near the rocks. After I saw the first fish it was amazing. It was like I was floating in air seeing the most wonderful assortment of colors: the purple sea urchin, the orange and pink fish, and the blue water. As I went further out, I remember seeing eels and bigger fish. Then I saw the most beautiful fish of my life. It is called the parrotfish, it has all of the colors of the rainbow, and swam in a perfect way. I followed it for a long time, to see where it would go. It swam farther out and turned back around, then it led me to more parrotfish. I think there were four or five. Soon it was time to go, I was sad to leave. I hope I can go snorkeling again.

Maiah Yanni, Grade 8
St Joseph Catholic School, CA

The Insane Skiing Vacation

The mountain crouched silently like a lion hunting its prey. The strong smell of pine trees filled the chilly air.

I was going snowboarding for the first time with my two friends Kyle and Mathew. They were excited, while I was scared. I knew my friends could get very pushy. My palms started to sweat and my mouth was getting dry. We got on a chair lift and up we went. My snowboard dangled off the end. Snowboarders and skiers zoomed under me with ease. As I got off the chair lift I face planted into the snow.

My friends laughed, "Are you kidding me?"

I was thankful that my helmet and goggles masked my identity.

I slid on over to Matthew and asked, "What run are we going down?"

"Gold Rush," he replied.

"That's a Double-black diamond right?" I asked.

"Yah, so what," stated Mathew.

"I am scared to go down the run," I stuttered

"Don't be such a wimp," replied Mathew.

I reluctantly strapped my boots to my board. One push and I was flying down the mountain. I felt the whistling air sting my face. In just a split second I was soaring through the air. Once again, I fell face first into the snow. Everything went black.

I woke up on a snowmobile escorting me down the mountain.

The driver asked me, "Do you feel like you're going to throw up?"

"No," I responded.

"Then you'll be all right!" he said.

I was dropped off at the bottom of the mountain. My friends were ashamedly waiting, feeling guilty for intentionally taking me up to a double black on my first run. There was one big lesson that I learned that day— never get overpowered by peer pressure. Peer pressure will never affect me again!

Nils Methot, Grade 8
Aviara Oaks Middle School, CA

Beaten Face

Most people think a flawless face is a beautiful face. I believe a face that tells a story is the best kind. Every mark has a tale to tell, every flaw is a moment of glory. The thought that a single scar could be the adventure of a life time can make one begin to wonder how far they can go in life. The lines of hurt through the ages, the wrinkles of shame and humiliation allow me to take caution and expect the unexpected. Every smile is a memory of complete satisfaction; every grin is a hope to continue on through the few short days of the rest of your life, confident to pass it down generations to come. You may have just another old face to people passing by, but to me it's a story I can read over and over, never getting tired of the adventures. To me you're a children's book that never dies, that never fades, that keeps its shine no matter how many times I turn the page. On the outside you may be scarred and torn, but to me you're something much more. To me you're truly beautiful.

Brittney Welter, Grade 7
Salida Middle School, CO

My First Volleyball Tournament

It was up to me. The last point. Game point. The crowd was wild. My coach had her fingers crossed.

It was my very first volleyball tournament, and I was nervous like crazy. Everyone around was talking, and the noise was almost unbearable. There were babies crying and screaming. The captain for our team won the coin toss. That meant we served first. The whistle blew and the game began. The smell of stinky feet and new nets filled the cool tournament complex. My hands were shaking and palms sweating. We volleyed the ball back and forth many times. Sometimes we would make errors and sometimes we didn't. The game continued on for about 15 more minutes. I could taste the fear, anger, and worry that we would lose. I could see the brand new, white Tachikira whizz by. My heart was pounding as I went up to serve the ball. It was up to me whether or not we would win the game. Everyone had their fingers crossed. My hand hit the ball and it went to back row. My coach was happy that it went in. The game finally ended. It was a good game, but sadly we fell short of a win. We went back to our hotels thinking of how we played that day. The same thought kept crossing our minds. Here we go again…time for Day Two of the tournament to begin.

This event gave me the confidence to not be afraid on the volleyball court. I was really happy with the way my team and I played for our very first volleyball tournament.

Hailey Holland, Grade 7
Lindale Jr High School, TX

Pilgrims

Worn soles travel the naked terrain. Gusts as daggers pierce thin cloth, sending needle-pricked pain up numbed, stiff spines. Leathery skin, tanned by dirt and mud, wrinkles with age as the ground slowly erodes with passing rains. Condemned by the elements they trek, pilgrims in search of relics. Warm souls, roam the Earth. People, whose souls are blazing fires, from which flames leap and lick at throats and emerge as speech. Hearts contracting, pounding, and flowing; blood, the essence of life runs deep red. They live to travel freely yet are controlled by the natural world. They are on a journey for the foreseeable future; people in search of answers. People, who like the pilgrims, wander, though ceaselessly. All with tales crackling in their depths, crouching, ready to leap forth, spraying a spew of glowing embers over the groundlings, and warming the chill-bitten faces of the audience. Though not through rain, and sun and ice, they travel, they travel a rough path: rough life: divot, embankment, rut, until they run out of road. Clutching that grasp of thread; grasp of life, which leads them down their trail. They are all pilgrims "passing to and fro;" no matter their social relationship they are one. In a world shrouded in a cloak of darkness, the beautiful, soft flames, stories, flowing from their lips illuminate the lurid, tenebrous land and new tales form as the people wander farther and their blazes stoked. We are all pilgrims with our own histories, journeying through life.

Naomi Suminski, Grade 9
San Diego Jewish Academy, CA

California SB48 Should Be Stopped

California Senate Bill 48 proposes teaching gay history in school. This Bill should not be allowed because it infringes on parents' rights to protect their children's beliefs, may cause students to get in fights over their beliefs, and will expose children to sexual preferences at too young an age.

Parents have the right to protect their children from things they consider harmful. Courts cannot interfere with parental decisions except when the child's life or physical health is threatened. The California bill does not give parents the option of whether their child may receive the school-mandated sexual orientation instruction. The gay history instruction unwanted by many parents may lead to confusion by children who may get involved in fights over their beliefs, ultimately leading to harassment, emotional distress or physical fights. Children should not be exposed to sexual preferences when they are too young even to discern from right and wrong, but the government wants to teach kindergartners about sexual preferences. The California bill will violate the innocence of seven million California children.

Teaching gay history in school should not be allowed because it violates parents' rights to protect their children from unwanted information, may cause arguments over their sexual beliefs, and young children are unable to discern from right and wrong about sexual behaviors. The California bill does not give parents the option of whether their child may receive the school-mandated sexual orientation instruction. Teaching about sexual orientation in schools will expose young children to sexual preferences, causing confusion and gender experimentation by some. All concerned citizens should unite to educate parents, neighbors, friends and relatives about the harmful effects of this legislation and tell our local, state, and federal government to repeal this California law.

Summer Wary, Grade 8
Vacaville Christian Schools, CA

Still Proud!

Have you ever tried to do a Canadian accent littered with "aboot" and "eh?" The answer is most likely yes. The definition of Canada is filled to the brim with discriminatory stereotypes, yet I'm still willing to say I'm proud to be a Canadian. Only those who've visited the wonderful land of Canada can begin to understand its amazing qualities. My brother is Canadian, as are my parents and grandparents and all my relatives I'm aquatinted with. People have such odd misconceptions that our blood is partly maple syrup. None of those are true (except maybe "eh"), and like most other countries, Canada has sad stereotypes to deal with. Canada is still my home, and always will be. There is a love for that country that only people born there can understand. It's deeper than just a citizenship and place of birth. With snow as fluffy as goose feathers, food so delicious that the 10 lbs. you gained eating it doesn't bother you, and people so friendly, it's like the whole country knows your name. It's hard not to love Canada, and I'm proud to say I'm a Canadian citizen.

Jayden LaBas, Grade 8
Monte Vista Christian School, CA

Teens and Responsibility

A girl should not have to have her parents' permission to get birth control because use of birth control reduces teen pregnancies, parent notification is not going to stop teens from having sex, and birth control could be against her parents' religion, but not hers. The abortion and teen pregnancy rates have dropped more than 50% since birth control has been allowed for minors without parental consent. Texas and Arizona are the highest in teen pregnancy rates because birth control is not allowed without parent permission. In places like California and New York, the pregnancy rate is much lower because birth control is allowed without parental consent.

Some parents are against birth control, which does not stop teens from having sex which can result in pregnancy. More than 1,500 girls said they would not use birth control if they needed parental consent. Parents who are religious are not as likely to talk about birth control because they believe in abstinence, even if the teen does not. The parents are more likely to talk about the morality of sex, rather than the ways to prevent pregnancies. 1,500 more girls a year could get pregnant if it is necessary for parental consent. Teen pregnancy rates are almost doubled in the states that require parent permission. Girls are most likely not to ask their parents to use birth control because it is against their religion and they know the answer will most likely be no to using birth control. Even though many parents would oppose the idea, statistics and researchers show that the teens with access to birth control are more responsible, resulting in fewer pregnancies and welfare costs than teenage girls who do not use birth control because they need parental consent.

Julia Hinojosa, Grade 8
Vacaville Christian Schools, CA

My Escape

There are bad days that haunt everybody, days swamped with emotional pain. Each person has a particular way to scare this pain away. For me, music is my escape. One night, I was overwhelmed with family situations. I was a boat sinking in a sea of sorrow, fighting to reach the sunlit shore while something was hauling me back, deep down into the dark water. Aggravation and frustration overpowering me, I urged to abandon this agonizing pain. With my keyboard in front of me, I began to write a poem, which then was blended with a unique chord progression. In no time, I was improvising the melody by singing the words off the paper while accompanying myself on the piano. The strain, the fury — they all came alive with the music. Sensing as if the doubt and concern evaporated, I encountered a new way to express myself: music composition. Allowing me to convey my own stories through melodies I create, music composition drives me to release my emotions and learn more about myself. As an artist needs his brush to paint a captivating image that expresses his emotions as if no other thing can, I am a musician who needs music in order to connect with myself and craft pieces that enable me to embrace who I am.

Jasmine Liu-Zarzuela, Grade 9
Saint Mary's Hall, TX

Reducing Teen Crime

Teens who commit violent crimes should be tried as adults because the severity of crimes is not determined by age, teens have the mental awareness of right and wrong, and society needs to remove violent teens from society for the protection of the public. Even though some adult crimes are committed by minors, those who commit those crimes should be tried under equal laws.

An ABC news poll showed a majority of people believe the crime, not the perpetrator's age, should be the determining factor in sentencing. The justice system depends upon holding perpetrators responsible for their actions, and should not give someone a lighter sentence based solely on age. While juveniles may not have the same cognitive development as adults, it is widely accepted that they do understand and can evaluate the difference between moral right and wrong. Teenink.com states that even if a teen did not know what they were doing is wrong, it does not make it right. They should be punished because if they are not, they will think crimes are acceptable and continue to commit them, while American society deserves protection from all criminals, even teens. Light sentencing does not teach juveniles their lessons, so when they go back into the public they have a higher chance of committing another crime.

Violent teens should be tried as adults because crime has no exceptions, especially when teens know exactly what they are doing, which is why society needs guardianship from all perpetrators. The sentencing for a flagitious crime should have the same outcome if it is committed by a teen. Although some people believe teens should not be tried as adults, it would keep society safe and give teens more discipline.

Olivia Petnicki, Grade 8
Vacaville Christian Schools, CA

Music to My Ears

Imagine your favorite song or music. How does it make you feel? Happy? Inspired? As if you're part of something? That's how music makes me feel, which is why I am so passionate about it. I can focus my energy and emotion into music. Sometimes it's for my benefit, but other times, I can make something beautiful that others can enjoy. Music can make you laugh and it can make you cry. If I am angry or upset, I can listen to music that has that feeling and it clears my emotions. I love soundtracks from movies because I feel as if I am there. They have no words but can make you feel more than songs with words do! I don't have a favorite type of music. Honestly I like them all. I am addicted to music. Whenever you see me, I usually have my iPod. I sing, play instruments and dance. Music is my life and it is what I want to do. Music is a universal language and loved all around the world. It is strange and rare to find someone who doesn't like music. You don't need to see the beauty in music, you must hear it. Music unites people. I love the diversity in music. There is something for everyone. There is no judgment in music. No matter who you are or what you look like, there is a place for you in music.

Jaden Kendall, Grade 8
Excelsior Academy, UT

Dolphins

Have you ever wished you could ride a dolphin? Do you want to feel the waves press upon you and feel the freedom as you jump out of the water?

Ever since I was little, I remember being called "Muchalee" which means fish in Urdu. I love to swim. It is my favorite thing to do. I had dreams and saw me swimming with them. Finally, I could swim with dolphins because we were going to Hawaii for vacation. We went to Oahu, the main Island. At midday when the weather felt stiflingly hot, we went to Sea Life Park. It is a place with animals under the sea.

At Sea Life Park we saw sting rays, turtles, sharks, fish, seals, and the thing that caught my eye was DOLPHINS! My parents knew how much I liked dolphins so they blessed me, by buying tickets so that I could swim with the dolphins.

As I put on my suit and jumped in the water, it felt cold, and had a peculiar fragrance. The dolphin trainers explained to us what to do. Two dolphins swam by they felt hard which I did not expect. They made a weird noise like a bird.

Then we got the real deal. The dolphins swam by and lifted me in the air on their noses. It felt like I was flying, at least that's what I thought I was doing for a minute. After that, the dolphins pulled me between them. I was smiling so some water got in my mouth. It tasted salty and nasty. That was all we did but, it was a huge blessing.

I felt blessed. As I look back, I want to remember the good times. It made me believe dreams can happen.

Sarah Crosby, Grade 7
Lindale Jr High School, TX

Changing the World

Who hasn't dreamed of changing the world for the better? Nobody. Everyone, at least once in their lives, has wanted to make a positive difference in the world. Why, then, do so few dare to make changes that better the lives of everyone on this Earth? The answer is distressingly simple. Other things, other goals, cloud our perception of what is important in our short lives, and we begin to lust and struggle for power or money, neither of which can bring satisfaction. Power is a mere illusion, for our leaders, try as they might, can never truly have dominance over our thoughts or our actions. Money is an even more powerful deception. We humans are slaves to it, yet it does not exist outside of our minds. Even those who have no desire for these fleeting daydreams have not the ambition to change the world, and again the reason is simple. Fear. Fear of being wrong, fear of having others disagree with the helpfulness of their change, fear of being hurt, just plain fear. This fear can consume one's sense of righteousness and choke the desire to change the way we live until we are blind to the knowledge that we can change the world.

What is the answer, then? How can we solve problems that have been around since the beginning of humanity? Once again, the answer is childishly simple. Love. Love everyone and everything absolutely and utterly unconditionally. The rest will follow.

Sarah Rodriguez-Soto, Grade 7
North Star Academy, CA

Friendship Has No Cost

A trait that I value is friendship. Without friendship a person would be lonely, depressed, and upset. Without friendship you would not find a husband or wife. A true friend is there for you through the ups and the downs, from preschool until you are in an old people's home. When I think of a friend, I think of trust, love, and strength, and these three things define my best friend, Julie. I can trust her with all my secrets. I love her to death, and she has to be strong in order to defend me. Friendship makes me want to get up every day and go to school, it makes me want to go to sports, and most of all it makes me want to live. The thought of having no one to be able to share all of the special moments in your life with makes me want to cry. In order to have friendship, I believe that you and that person need to have those important three traits. You can't buy a true friend no matter how much money you have. You can only earn friendship. Friendship can be sad, but it can also be the happiest thing on Earth. Friendship makes the world go round.

Leah King, Grade 7
North Star Academy, CA

The Game

"There's no better feeling than lying on the field of battle exhausted, but victorious. Knowing that you could not have done any better to help your team, and even if the points on the board say you lost, in my mind you're a winner."

"Koonce, get out there, it's their ball," my coach hollered. It was the all-star football game and I wanted this win bad. The main reason for this was because half of the other team was from the "BUCS." They were the only team in the regular season that could beat us, and now with some new players, it was our turn to win.

"YES!" I yelled. I was having a blast. Our team was dominating and our defense was like a brick wall letting nothing by. I was playing hard and it was great.

By now our team was winning with a minute left. As the clock wound down a surge of energy arose inside of me. I trotted onto the field smiling—victorious.

Drew Koonce, Grade 7
League City Intermediate School, TX

Firebird Football

Crack! The sound of football helmets colliding together, then the whistle blows. When I'm on the field I get a rush; I played on the Chaparral Firebirds Competitive Track Football team. Our season record was 5 and 8; we didn't have a winning record, but I had a blast. I had one friend on the team when the season started and 25 friends by the time the season was over! Our practices were three hours long, six days a week, and our games were about two hours every Saturday. Our practices were tough with a lot of sprinting, hitting, and tackling, but I still loved them. Our games were amazing and I was the running-back and safety. Firebird football: blood, sweat; glory.

Steven Senatro, Grade 8
Foothills Academy, AZ

A Pencil's Artwork

Lines in art are some of my favorite things. Art can be anything and one piece can mean many things to many people. Two people can look at a piece of paper with some smudges and lines, and it can be a sun setting over the mountains with an explosion of pink and yellow. Or it could be a flower opening its bloom. Lines in art can be a square, a triangle, or a circle. If you combine them, you can make whatever you want. Those lines could be a soft cloud or a solid brick. It could be the joy of sliding down a slide. Lines make you feel that you can make whatever you want. They can bring anything to a blank wall. With them you can make anything more lively. Lines will confuse you. Seeing some lines will confuse you, while others can make you happy, sad, joyful, lonely, energetic and slap-happy. Free your mind if a line is only a line to you. For a line can be so many things. But it is only these things to people who have their eyes and minds open. Then, if you study a piece of paper, a line or two can tell of a person's life, a life that can be told by a pencil's gentle stroke across a piece of paper hung on a wall.

Caleb Barnes, Grade 7
Salida Middle School, CO

What I Felt Like in Costa Rica

I take a deep breath and open my eyes. The wind tears at my hair and quickly touches my cheeks before it reaches my brother. The cold, clean air breathes upon my ears and makes them as cold as the ice in winter, but as the little gray car turns away from the wind, the sun shines across my face. It slowly creeps under my skin and I feel comforted by the warmth of the glowing sun ruling the skies. As I gaze upwards, I see the huge, green mountain, standing tall and proud like an old warrior. Greens of all kind surround me, swaying; welcoming me into their kingdom. There are trees hovering above me and birds of many bright colors soaring and chirping in the brush. The car continues on and everything becomes a blur, like one of those colorful impressionistic paintings in a museum. The smell of ripened fruit travels to my nose and I take a deep breath again, enjoying every moment of being in this worry-free paradise.

Varesh Gorabi, Grade 7
Salt Lake Center for Science Education, UT

The Movie

Your life is a movie, every scene counts so make it better than the last. Just because the scene looks like it is headed for the worst just remember the plot will always thicken and change for the best. Make the movie count so the director will be happy with you, because the cast party is better than anything you could think of. The director will always have all the power and all the applause; you could say he "made" the movie. Just because the movie is coming to an end don't be sad, you are the star and the reason the movie was great. Make the end count so others will remember it and most importantly when you and the director watch it together you are proud of it and so is the director.

Justin Tadros, Grade 8
Monte Vista Christian School, CA

Female Police Officers ~ The Advantage

There are many advantages to women serving as police officers because women are better communicators, they are less aggressive than men, and are more effective at dealing with domestic violence. One study showed evidence that women officers rely more on communication in police work than do men. Women officers receive better evaluations than male officers based on communication, problem solving, and working with community members. Female officers tend to rely on an inner strength to deal with the challenges in their daily work, and tend to use strong communication skills rather than the use of excessive force.

A number of studies show that female officers rely less on using physical force to be effective, and are less likely than male officers to be involved in fights on the job. One recent study of seven major US police departments showed that female officers are named in only five percent of citizen complaints for excessive force. Listening before reacting has helped many women officers to avoid using physical force. Female officers have the advantage of interacting with more empathy which is beneficial in domestic violence situations.

Research shows that approximately two to three million women are assaulted each year in the US by their male partners. A 1985 study found that battered women who had a women officer in contact rated the act of female officers more receptively. Female officers show more concern, patience and understanding when responding to domestic violence calls. Inadequate police response deters victims of domestic violence from reporting future assaults, therefore it is crucial to have women officers at the scene. Given that domestic violence accounts for approximately half of all violent calls to police, it is critically important to have female officers in the community.

Kailey Barandas, Grade 8
Vacaville Christian Schools, CA

My Best Friend

I have a lot of friends, but my best one is Lori Massey. She is a punk, but I love her to death. She can be mean at times, but she's my friend.

Lori is a fun-loving, caring, mean, sweet, and a crazy girl. We know everything about each other. For example, her favorite colors are blue and lime green. Her favorite animal is a horse. Okay, back on subject, Lori is fun to be around. Sometimes she beats up on me, but I always get her back. She comes to me for advice, and I admit I go to her for advice, too.

Lori is very supportive. She helps me when I fall…literally. I'm freakishly clumsy. Anyway, when we are playing sports, she points out what I need to work on and helps me with it. When I'm sad, she comforts me. When I text her she always texts back.

Lori is my best friend. I love her with all my heart. You could say that she is like a diamond; I won't let her slip out of my hands. I won't let anyone steal her, and I won't let anyone hurt her.

Keely Clark, Grade 7
Dew School, TX

Nature

In my busy and chaotic life, it's hard to find something that I can use for relaxation and peace; everything that is commonly used for other people is either too expensive or doesn't work. So, I have resorted to something priceless and that works: nature.

Ever since I was a little girl, I've always loved nature. Every time I used to go to the local playground, I would always spend more time climbing trees then climbing the jungle gym. "The smell of the trees should be bottled into a fragrance," I have always said.

My father just thought I was crazy, but nature has so many mysteries that make me wonder. How did the trees, which have been around forever, get so tall? Why are flowers rainbows of colors?

Of course, now that I am learning biology, the study of life, all my questions have been answered. But I'm not going to let that ruin my fun.

When I took an overnight trip to Yosemite, I was in nature heaven. Around every corner, breathtaking views would fill me with joy.

My favorite picture of Yosemite is one of Half-Dome. I really can never get enough of this rock. The picture is in a grassy field with a pretty view of Half-Dome at the back. North Dome pokes its rounded top through a top-left corner of my picture. The picture sits on my desk in a pretty frame.

Nature. My natural soother who helps me relax.

Kiran Rao, Grade 7
North Star Academy, CA

Cheerleading Is a Sport!

Cheerleading should be considered a sport because it involves physical exertion, evaluated competition, and requires a certain amount of skill. Cheerleading includes a great deal of physical activity and effort, and part of the definition of a sport, defined by the Women's Sports Foundation (WSF), is that a sport shall be defined as an institutional activity involving physical exertion. Cheerleaders tumble and perform stunts that require large amounts of strength, endurance, flexibility, and technique, filling one of the requirements from the WSF: a physical activity which involves propelling a mass through space or overcoming the resistance of a mass. Other sports fill this requirement, using a ball as their mass object. Rather than using a ball, cheerleaders use a person, which takes more physical effort, strength, and training. Cheerleaders compete against other squads at competitions, as do other athletes at games or tournaments, and compete against many other teams in one day, rather than one like most sports.

Cheerleading is a team sport requiring cooperation, concentration, and a high level of athleticism, body control, precision, and synchronization, requiring every member to be in tune with the rest of the team. Cheerleading, as a whole, is equal to or even more demanding than other sports. Although some may argue that cheerleading is not a sport, they state this without analyzing cheerleading as a whole.

Briana Morris, Grade 8
Vacaville Christian Schools, CA

My Family Tragedy

It was a normal day. Then the phone rang. All of a sudden, I heard my mom screaming. I couldn't really hear what she was saying. Then she called me saying, "Mommy's house is on fire!"

Mommy is my grandma. My grandma and grandpa had just left for a vacation. They take lots of vacations because my grandpa, Deddy, owns a warehousing business.

We all ran to our tiny red Yaris and drove to Mommy's house. When we got there, there were 4 fire trucks and 16 firemen. Some of my other aunts were already there. My grandparent's house had black windows and black smoke from the air vents.

My mom got emotional and my dad tried to comfort her. I was a little scared so I prayed. I didn't know what else to do. My family was not prepared for a tragedy like this one.

Before my grandparents had left my grandma had paid the next-door neighbor $50 dollars to water the lawn every day while they were gone. That same neighbor was walking with some kids asking if we needed anything. He seemed a little suspicious to me.

After a while the firemen left. One truck stayed just in case. When I walked in everything was black. My grandma's prized possessions had been burned.

We found out the next day that the neighbor had broken into the house, stole stuff and burned it down. The worst thing was my grandma didn't know yet.

Mireya Bustos, Grade 7
Arbor Christian Academy, TX

Roller Coaster

My family and I normally don't go to fun places like Six Flags. We did a few months ago, though. My older sister and I went on a lot of rides when we went to Six Flags. We went on a few roller coasters some scarier than others. Of course, I was scared to go on most of the roller coaster rides. My sister, on the other hand, was courageous, she was fearless. Out of all the terrifying roller coasters to pick from, she wanted to ride the worst. She wanted to ride the Titan. I didn't think it was such a great idea to get on it. It was long and really fast. Seeing the people get on it and hearing the people screaming made me want to back out, but, I was already in line. Me and my sister were next to get on the ride. As the passengers stepped out of their seats, my sister, me, and the rest of the people waiting to get on the ride stepped inside the seats. Scared, and terrified, I could hear my heart pounding over the people in line talking as we sit in our seat. The roller coaster started moving slowly, then faster, and faster. We screamed most of the ride, as we grabbed on to the seats that were in front of us. Later on I realized that, it wasn't as bad compared to other stuff that has happened. It calmed me that it was over, though. After this event happened, I felt good about myself. Going back and thinking about it makes me feel proud. As scary as that roller coaster was it changed me somehow, the saying, "You could do anything you set your mind to," makes more sense to me now.

Viviana Ramirez, Grade 7
Lindale Jr High School, TX

Friends for Life

The County Fair is always the best time of year. Between water fights and gorging yourself on water melon, you make the best friends possible...friends for life...

The kind of friends that can make you break out in a rib-splitting fit of laughter, just by looking at you. A friend like Madelyne. Someone positive, hilarious, intelligent, and totally awesome. She is a friend who you trust with your deepest secrets, and you never have to worry about being made fun of. She is the type of friend who you can be yourself around, and she won't criticize you.

She is the kind of friend that will take your side on anything and stick up for you no matter what. She is brave...

She is my best friend...

Even though I thought I knew everything there is to know about anything, Madelyne proved me wrong. Every day I am around her, she teaches me something new, and important. She has shown me that no matter what, there is always someone who can teach you something and make your life so much better and more enjoyable.

Even though I am pretty thickheaded, Madelyne still puts up with me, and I hope nothing ever comes between us. After all, you don't get a second chance at a friend like Madelyne...

And even though we are so different, we are so alike, and for as long as possible, I will cling to that. I will always be there for her, no matter what...

We are best friends for life.

Kylie Poole, Grade 7
Salida Middle School, CO

A Colorful, Wonderful Adventure

My favorite time of the year is when the leaves are turning from colors of light and dark green, to fiery, bright colors of orange, red, and brown. When I look down the road, it looks like a fire is emerging. I look to my left, and to my right. All I see is beauty. Running down the road, wishing they would stay forever. When I go home the beauty is still with me. I decide to rake the leaves with my dad. After we are done, we talk about the beauty that I saw. "The colors remind me of all the camping trips." We both erupt with a round of laughter. My dad decides we should go camping that night with the family. When we get onto the mountain, the sun was setting, the dark mysterious colors of pink, purple, and blue. The colors shoot out of the sky like we are in a rainbow. As we look at the trees, the sun is setting off of them. As we "Ooh" and "Aw," I capture the moment. As we start a fire, I watch the sparks fly into the trees. Then I think, is there anything more heartwarming than this? The stars and the trees reflect against the pond. I get my camera. "Click," I capture the ivory brown, the roaring orange, the mellow yellow, and the daring red. As I lie in bed and stare at the stars, I fall asleep. "Crack!" I wake up. My family is packing up. I look all around and wish I could take all the trees home with me. I gather the three leaves of orange, red, and yellow. We say goodbye to our home away from home, and hello to the loud city of Austin, Texas.

Veronica White, Grade 7
Salida Middle School, CO

The Internet: A Tool or a Terror?

Where do students go to probe information for a research report? How do businesses send documents to all of their workers in a hurry? What is the easiest way to communicate with loved ones? The Internet is a useful and helpful tool because it is a facile way to find information, very accessible, and a speedy way to communicate with friends and family all over the world.

First, the Internet is an effortless way to find information. Search engines help narrow down our search. Searching for any topic is simple, because the Internet is worldwide and information about anything and everything is available.

Second, the Internet is also very accessible and convenient. When in a hurry, someone can search something quickly on a portable device. In this generation, mostly everyone has access to the Internet.

Finally, most people use the Internet to talk with family and friends. Businesses communicate via e-mail and people can keep in touch with families.

In conclusion, the Internet is a tool with myriad uses. This has been a tool that has really changed the world in a positive way and we will continue to grow with all of these opulent developments. There are countless useful things that the Internet has in store. It is severely easy to find information, vastly accessible and convenient, and the Internet is a fast way to communicate with family and friends. Go and explore all the Internet has to offer today!

Shalee Bullock, Grade 9
South Jordan Middle School, UT

Schools Are Not Meeting Their Goals

Schools in America today do not function as they were originally intended, because students do not get a chance to assimilate and generalize what they have learned, while many of the topics taught are not relevant to the demands of living in today's society. Schools should be teaching kids how to do more than read and write correctly, and add two numbers together; they should be teaching children the skills they will need to survive in the adult world. Students need skills such as managing finances, negotiating, using contracts, reading financial statements, managing time, and marketing. Sadly, in a poll of 1,000 students, nearly half in their final year of high school said they felt unprepared for the work world, showing that schools are not meeting their goals.

On top of this, schools are not teaching their students good character. Respect and self-discipline are vital; however schools are doing little to promote these character traits. A paper on freedomforum.org says that, "The very qualities that today's work force needs are character traits and skills that form the building blocks of character education."

Schools in America today do not accomplish what they were intended to do, preparing students for work and life in modern society. Although American schools have many benefits, the schools are not functioning very effectively and significant restructuring of goals is needed.

Stephanie Shatell, Grade 8
Vacaville Christian Schools, CA

Perils of Animal Testing

Animal testing must cease because testing on animals often produces inaccurate or misleading results, animals are killed due to the ingestion of harsh toxins or chemicals in a product, and the federal government should spend their money on studies of more relevance to the health of humans. No matter how many animal tests are undertaken, someone will always be the first human to be tested on, and with the results of animal tests so unreliable, they make those human trials even riskier.

The FDA states that 92% of all drugs shown to be effective in animal tests fail in human trials. Animals might have similar attributes to humans internally, but since they are not identical, most people will vary in response to certain products, making applying test results to humans problematic. Furthermore, the animals held in laboratories frequently express psychological distress, and it is acknowledged that the use of these troubled animals makes the validity of the data produced precarious.

The Animal Welfare Act allows animals to be subjected to torturous procedures such as for the use of experimentation. Better options are available and should be used. Non-animal methods usually take less time to complete and have proven more effective, affordable, and humane than the crude, archaic animal tests they replace. Laboratories that have animal testing claim to be making sure humans do not experience any side affects with their products, but non-animal methods are more germane to human health, so there is no reason for companies to even consider animal testing when facts prove otherwise. Although, some people argue that people have greater value than animals, and testing on them aids humans, there are other far superior alternatives that will save animals' lives and give more promising results.

Kaila, Grade 8
Vacaville Christian Schools, CA

The Clutch

It was a hot summer day when I was eight I learned how to ride a dirt bike with a clutch. I was at my uncle's pasture.

My dad, my brother, and I were riding dirt bikes. If I learned how to use a clutch, my dad said I could ride my brother's dirt bike. I was daring to try it so I did. I fell, but I wasn't injured. Brave, I tried it again and again, and I kept falling. Irritated, I got up over and over, and luckily I didn't get hurt. Hesitant, I kept trying and I would get it sometimes then I would fall. I kept telling myself if you can do it you can ride your brother's dirt bike. Another reason that made it harder was I couldn't touch the ground. Even though I couldn't touch the ground I didn't let it get in my way and stop me. I was determined to get it, and I got it in the next couple of tries. It's so much fun riding one with a clutch. It was fun riding my brother's dirt bike.

When it happened I was relieved, to this day I still have fun using a clutch. That day taught me that you need to keep trying and to never give up.

Seth Shacklett, Grade 7
Lindale Jr High School, TX

Animal Rights

Animal cruelty is a problem that can be characterized as either deliberate abuse or failure to take care of an animal, and perpetrators should be prosecuted. Many domestic animals are beaten, neglected or forced to struggle for survival by abusive owners. For many, the word "circus" evokes imagery of popcorn, candy, wild animals, and fun; however, one of the most common cases animal abuse in the country is the treatment of wild animals in circuses, starting with lack of exercise, lack of social contact, and poor quality of life compared with life in the wild.

One of the negative effects of animal testing for human cosmetics or cleaning products can be the death or suffering of animals. Many say that human life is more important than animals, but God created animals for love and care rather than suffering for beauty. Animal rights are lost in oblivion when it comes to animal testing ethics. To discover new medicines and vaccinations, millions of animals are killed every year. A small amount of animal testing may be vital to understanding of complex human diseases, but the welfare of the animal must always be considered.

While animal abuse and cruelty is a problem, and the animal abusers are often known, little is done by the law to stop it from continuing. In the year 2011, there were about 2 million animals that died from their abusive owners, or neglect. The laws for animal abuse need to be and should be properly enforced. In California, the law states that cruelty to an animal is a $20,000 fine or one year in jail. All kinds of animal abuse should be taken seriously and abusers dealt with in a proper and serious fashion.

Brittney Hockersmith, Grade 8
Vacaville Christian Schools, CA

The Ultimate Joy

Friendships are very important to everybody, especially me. My friendships bring joy into my life. I want loyal and kind friends, those who I can trust. I'm never going to be the type of person that says cruel and demeaning things about my friends. I try to be a friend myself. School is a lot more fun when there are friends around, because they make the mediocre boring parts interesting and fun!

Once time I was having a fight with a friend, and another friend comforted me and gave me some good advice about how to solve the problem. That helped a lot!

I think friendships are meant to be long-lasting, instead of just a five minute thing. I know that I will remember my friends for the rest of my life, because they have changed my life in ways I *can't* forget. Friendships should be something to make one's life better, and I know my friendships have improved my life immensely.

I think friends should be examples to each other. Friends give vivacity not normally had! Friends should stand up for each other, and should be comforters when needed. You should be able to laugh and cry with your friends. Friends are the ultimate joy!

Allie Palmer, Grade 8
Excelsior Academy, UT

Let It Go

A year ago as my New Year's resolution, I promised not to drink soda for a whole year. You may think, "Why would I ever do that?" Well I have realized it is because soda is bad for my overall health. Soda has so much sugar that if I drink them every day, my tooth enamel would get soft and become prone to getting cavities. I would always get at least two cavities when I was getting my dental checkup before I stopped drinking soda. I am not saying soda was the cause of my cavities, but it probably played a big part in it. now I barely get cavities.

My physical strength was also poor and I got tired very quickly. Playing sports was not extremely hard but it was not easy either. I'm much faster, more agile, and stronger while playing sports. I am not saying soda is always bad for you, but if it becomes part of your diet, your health may deteriorate very slowly or fast depending on how much you drink and weigh. Soda is advertised as a product that is consumed by millions, but I believe that less is better.

Soda has many other health concerns when taken in large quantities. Soda is associated with obesity and low nutrient levels. it can cause weight gain depending upon how much soda you consume. Researchers say that in some cases, soda consumption can be associated with obesity and low nutrient levels. It can cause weight gain depending upon how much soda you consume. Researchers say that ins some cases, soda consumption can be associated with many weight-related diseases, including diabetes, cardiovascular risk factors, and elevated blood pressure.

Emili Futagawa, Grade 9
First Baptist Academy, TX

All Hail, Hail

Witnessing storms is terrifying. You go through crazy emotions and feelings. My worst weather would have to be when the "Mother lode" of hail scurried through Phoenix. It was like going through a real hurricane in Florida. I could not see anything through my windows, and it was all pure white everywhere.

It all started on a normal school day. Beautiful weather, sunny grounds, and lots of school work. By the time the school day was over, the clouds had come in and created a foggy look in the sky. When my brothers and I arrived at home, we enjoyed the TV and snacks, such as pudding and chips. But, that didn't last very long. I peered out the window for a quick glance of beauty, and that's when I saw the big wall of rain and hail.

It came within minutes. The windows were white, the door swung open, there was loud banging everywhere on the roof and we thought for sure that the place was going to fall down, until the hail disappeared into thin air.

The ground was white, green and filled with twigs, hail, and sticks. We smelled the air, which was quite wonderful because it smelled like a wet forest. Our mom was in complete shock and my brothers had open mouths. I just was amazed that a storm like that could create such a smell and mess. Everything was a complete disaster.

Eliana Benites, Grade 7
St Gregorys Catholic School, AZ

Camera Obscura

It's what we strive for, what we all need; without it we are nothing. After all, what is the point of life if we are not truly living? Passion is what everyone is looking for, but most don't know they are looking for it. Of course, passion does not have to be one thing, some people have more than one, and I am no exception. I have many passions, yet I have one particular favorite: photography. Photography allows me to capture the beauty of nature that I see and share it with others. Photography is an addiction. You can't just take one picture of something; it's a necessity to continue taking pictures until the opportunity is lost.

This is what you may call a summary of my every morning. The birds in the trees outside my house chirp and sing as I walk past them, just like every other day of the week. I gasp as I glance up at the rising sun, while I raise my camera. All other thoughts drone out, as if they have no meaning to me, when I take my pictures. I hold the cycloptic device close to me, an extension of my body that focuses only on the task at hand. I feel the tip of my finger gently slide to the smooth button, nearly unconsciously. I steady the camera and press easily on the button that will capture this magnificent sight. In response to this action, the camera replies with four low clicks as I take multiple photographs of this vibrant sunrise. I can't stop my smile from showing, as I look at my newly captured masterpiece. I then shiver as I remember that it's 6:20 in the morning. I then walk off, looking for yet another breathtaking sight.

Ben Senter, Grade 7
Salida Middle School, CO

The Path to Peace

Fairness is needed in everyone's life to keep a peaceful environment. Without it, people can be hurt and feel sad that people do not include them or, in other cases, do include. There are many different ways that may lead you or others to be fair or unfair. Once in everyone's life, people feel like some decisions are unfair for themselves or another. For example, one reason why this happens is because one person, who can be under favoritism, can make a person feel like they have been treated in an unfair manner. This can lead the person who is treated unfair to feel different emotions toward the person under the favoritism or the person who is treating the man or woman with favoritism. They can either feel angry, irritated, or even some level of envy toward that person. In some cases, the person being treated unfairly can feel sad and be let down, or they might even feel a sense of hatred for one of those people. In life, people should not be treated unfairly. Sadly, this is not true in all cases. No one should ever have to feel being let down or to be hurt by someone else. You too should try to be fair. If you have been treated unfairly, which you probably have, you would know the feeling of being put down as if no one cares for you, so why should you, or others, hurt another human being by treating them unfairly? No one is perfect, but people should try not to hurt others by being unfair.

Nicolas Ramos, Grade 7
St Ferdinand Catholic School, CA

Our Family Dog Roxy

The love and care we have given our dog Roxy has helped her recover from past abuse and cancer. She'd been tortured and beaten. So for that reason and so many more, we love that cute and amazing black and gray face; so enduring, so happy.

Abusers abused, beaters beat, and the torturers tortured most of the bad and some good out of her, leaving her and her ego for us to love and care for. Recovery has taken much time; winning her a place in my heart, of warmth and happiness, forever. She, a princess, has been through many of life's troubles, and gets every drop of my love and compassion.

The reason I tell you this, my reader, is because our pets have feelings just like us. We should not abuse these lovely creatures and their feelings. We must love and care for them. So save the supernatural feelings of our pets. I've loved this sweet amazing face, since I met her six years ago. More recently we found out she had four pounds of tumor in her belly; she had surgery and we cared for her even more during the busy schedules of our lives.

This amazing dog has won over my heart, and continues to warm it every time I see her. It's as if I had been brainwashed twenty times or so that evening, the evening that I met this amazing dog. Roxy has brought so much love and compassion to my heart. Though life has many challenging times, I try to remember the better parts of each and every one of my memories, especially those of my pets. Roxy, our family dog, has been through many hard times, and yet we still love and care for her.

Danielle Riggio, Grade 7
Salida Middle School, CO

Fairness as a Guide

The act of fairness is showing justice, not only for yourself, but for your neighbors. When you are fair, you are being equal to others. Showing fairness is to treat others the same, it means treating everyone the same. Being fair to your classmates and friends shows you are doing what is right. The characteristic of fairness is right for both boys and girls. Fairness is also shown as equality, in which fairness can also be shown through liberty. Fair is not everyone getting the same thing, it is everyone getting what they need to be equal. Fairness is a role in our lives. Fairness is not being on top or beneath anybody. It is being the same as everybody else, for everybody ranks the same. To show righteousness is to show fairness and that is a strong characteristic. Fair is the state of being just, to keep away from injustice, and do what is good. It is not to always judge a person. To be fair, you treat everyone with justice, not only yourself or your friends, but everyone. To be fair you share with everyone; the action of fairness is for all the people in your class or your family. These are the qualities of fairness, equality, and justice. These qualities are full of benevolence; they are good characteristics for you, your family, and your friends. In the end, through your good actions, and all your bad actions, fairness will always rank supreme and high above all.

Pamela Hernandez, Grade 7
St Ferdinand Catholic School, CA

He's My Brother

Jonathan has always thought of himself as different, but I just see him as my brother. Jonathan has ADHD, a disorder where the person has a difficult time focusing and acts overly excited all the time. Jonathan was adopted when he was a newborn. His biological mother drank and smoked during the pregnancy, which is a main cause of this disorder.

When my parents told me in 5th grade about the disorder and that Jonathan's disorder makes it difficult for him to grow and gain weight, so he will be smaller than other people his age, I did not understand at first. But then I realized that it helped me look at other people with disabilities differently and see them as normal people who have a harder way to live than me. It also helped me grow up by coming to the realization that not everyone is perfect and that many face problems in this world.

Most people see a disorder as weird, but for me it helped me in my life to have a better understanding of what it will be like for the rest of my life growing up and living near ADHD.

Many people take ADHD as a joke, but living with it is not funny, knowing that my brother struggles with it every day. I have changed immensely by having a front row seat to how it works, because with a friend the person puts on a mask, but when you live with it, nothing holds the person back from being himself. It's not one event in particular; it is more like while the whole of my families lives with ADHD, we will never love Jonathan any less. The lesson is never let a disorder stop you from forming a friendship or loving someone unconditionally.

Piercen Gaborko, Grade 8
Vacaville Christian Schools, CA

Favorite Memory

It was an average day at school, math, and English then lunch. When I was eating, Jeffery introduced me to a Japanese anime called Bleach. At first I thought he was talking about the detergent, and then he told me what it is. He said it's about a 15-year old boy named Ichigo, who is a Soul Reaper, or someone who helps lost souls find their way. I said I might have seen an episode or two.

After lunch I went to science. Jeff let me borrow a book. I got in trouble for reading. That was when Justin's phone went off; the noise distracted me, so I put the book down and looked. Coach Cowart let him get by with it. On the bus I never stopped reading Bleach, I read from the second I got on to the second I walked in my house.

The next day I asked if I could borrow it a little longer, he said yes. When I got home I did my chores, and then got ready for church and left. Paying no attention to Shane, my youth pastor, I just read Bleach the whole 2 hours. When I got home I ate, watched a movie, took a shower, and got dressed for bed. Then I got the book out and started reading, I read from 10 o'clock to midnight. I learned I love manga and anime. That moment helped me find something new to read, and extend my love for manga.

Michael Cooley, Grade 7
Lindale Jr High School, TX

A Special Gift

It is not an accident that I attend a Catholic school. My mother purposely changed her employment to come and teach at St. Matthew School. When the time came for my older brothers to attend school my mother made herself available to teach at St. Matthew. This gave her a unique opportunity to place my older brother Andrew in PK4. You can easily see that my mother was planting the seeds of faith into each and every one of her children to flourish.

My brothers and I have only known one school, one place, one educational environment that our parents have so graciously sacrificed to give us. My parents have a mutual appreciation of a faith-based education. My father unfortunately had a very disruptive primary and secondary education. He attended numerous schools and it left a large void in having a connection to a school. He and my mother wanted to give their children something special and dynamic. He wanted a more nurturing educational experience for his children. My father and mother wanted us to have a special connection to a school that we could hold special in our hearts. He always has said that it is important to have stability in your young life and attending a Catholic school will give each one of us that stability. I guess my father was also planting the seeds of faith in his children. My parents wanted their children to reach their full potential not only in school, but in their faith.

My school is a special place for me and I will cherish the time I have spent at St. Matthew. I sometimes wonder what kind of person I would have turned out to be if I did not get this special gift.

Elyssa Barrientos, Grade 7
St Matthew Catholic School, TX

Being Fair in the Decisions You Make

Being fair in all situations makes you a good person. It also shows that you are a responsible person. Making unfair decisions sometimes doesn't make you a bad person, it just shows that you need to work on making fair decisions. Fairness to me means to make the right decisions made by you to a group of people, or any living things, such as animals. Fair and unfair decisions are made a lot in this world. The law is considered fair because it keeps our country under control, and they are also fair rules. Fairness is also in campaigns because people vote on who they want to choose, which makes it fair on who wins. Being fair helps solve problems the best way. Being fair leads you to the right choice in making a right decision. Fairness also applies to laws and rules. I agree that fairness can mean justice to someone. If you are unfair to someone they might lose respect for you, and be unfair with you too. Fairness also means equality toward people when making decisions. If you are fair, people are able to trust you with making the right choice. Every day people are either making fair decisions or unfair decisions. Examples of unfair decisions are everywhere. One example is if you are in line to purchase something, then someone cuts in front of you, that is an example of an unfair situation.

Gia Velasquez, Grade 7
St Ferdinand Catholic School, CA

Coaches and Teachers of Faith

Some of my favorite coaches and teachers of faith this year are my football coach (Rene), basketball coach (Alex), and Fr. White. Coach Rene always told me this adage since I am small: I needed to "Do my best let God do the rest." This inspires me to grow and help others who are small like me. This invigorates me to do my best at whatever I do, not just football. In school, this helps me tutor younger kids. Coach Rene has been a prodigious person in my life.

Coach Rene always pushed me to work as a team and to collaborate as a team because Jesus is in everyone; all you have to do is to look and find Him. He also teaches me that God is the answer, not drugs.

The other person in my life is Coach Alex; he motivates me to inspire others to grow in basketball and religion. Since David and I are the oldest ones on our team, we have the job to lead the team in basketball, religion, and faith. He also says God comes first, then family, third is school, and last is hobbies or pastimes.

The teacher of faith that I want to talk about is Fr. White. He would always come into our class every other month at his old age. He gives us a lesson every time he comes. He would either talk about love, family, or just came in to talk about God and take any questions we had about God. Even though he has died recently, I would always remember him and encourage others like he has inspired me.

Overall Coach Rene, Coach Alec, and Fr. White has helped me in football, basketball, school, religion, leadership, and inspired others to grow in religion, school, and sports.

Joseph Pina, Grade 8
St Matthew Catholic School, TX

Had It Happened?

Pain was streaking through my side causing me agonizing pain with every step. Then it all went black. Had I done it?

Adrenaline started to pump through my body as I reached the starting line for the sixteen hundred meter relay. It was the last track meet of seventh grade and I had just finished my race when my coach told me I would be racing for an injured teammate. I had never raced in anything more than the hurdles and I wasn't a competitive distance runner. As I finished preparing for the race a man yelled for the racers to get set. I rose up, set my feet and waited for the sound of the gun. BANG! I leapt forward trying to find my stride. I could taste the cold wind as I started sucking air like a vacuum. I hadn't gone very far when the pain hit me. I instantly slowed but refused to give up. As we reached the last straightaway I kicked it into overdrive. I sprinted through the agonizing pain finally reaching Dalton to hand the baton off. Immediately after the baton left my hand a rush of relief came over me but was quickly replaced by the pain in my chest as I started to hyperventilate.

After the race I had a bittersweet moment. I had stayed in the pack but was suffering dearly for it. From that day on I decided to never race the 1600 meter relay again.

Kale Ridge, Grade 7
Lindale Jr High School, TX

Basketball

Have you ever gotten that adrenaline rush where there is five seconds left in the game and your team is down by one point? Well, I have and the definition of this is called basketball.

Basketball is a very common sport. I play basketball because I love it. I love it because it's competitive and something fun to do. Basketball is a team sport. From this sport, I learned it cannot be one person doing all the work. I love playing on a team because it's much more fun and enjoyable. Basketball to me is more than a sport. Every time I walk onto the court with my team, everything goes away. The only thing I am focused on is basketball. In order to play with a team, you have to get along with them. On the basketball court, you have to like the people you are playing with. You do not have a choice. Although off the court, it's a different story. Basketball is not a one man show. It is a team sport.

Basketball is my life. I can never go a day without playing. I hate when I get injured because I have to stop playing. I love playing club basketball and I can never get enough of it. Basketball is my everything. I will always love it. I will never get tired of it. I know that basketball will always be there for me. Basketball is my sport and no one can take that away from me.

Every day I dream about making it into the Women's National Basketball Association. That dream will come true someday. I need to work harder and stay on my "A" game. Basketball is a sweaty, competitive time consuming habit. You just have to love it!

Faith Williams, Grade 8
Santa Clara Elementary School, CA

Kindness and Love Lead to Fairness

What is fairness. Is it balancing things so that everyone receives equal rights, material things, and treatment? Or is it taking away advantages for these who are more intelligent, physically more gifted, and even plain lucky? It could also be a balance scale for mediocrity. Or maybe it is the kind act of making things right, not favoring, and doing things that only the heart can explain. I guess it all depends through what point of view people choose to see the word; it all depends on your life experience and what the word means to you. Just because everyone is treated equally, that does not mean that it is fair. Everyone's situation is different. No one is exactly the same, not even identical twins. We could not assume that treating everyone equally is the same as treating them fairly. An example of this would be: let us say one day a teacher decided to bring twenty candies to her class, and she was going to give her twenty students a candy each. Unfortunately, that day ten of her students behaved really badly and were not listening to her request. That made the kind teacher become a frustrated teacher which cause her to change her mind and only give the good students candy, not just one candy but tow candies, was she being fair? That all depends. It all comes down to what side of the fence you are on when fairness is being handed out.

Cassandra Marquez, Grade 7
St Ferdinand Catholic School, CA

Perfection

Students make up the majority of schools. Procrastinators, social butterflies, athletes, and class clowns are typical types of individuals I've encountered at school. Among these adolescents, perfectionists are always present. How does one go about naming one of these human beings? Has anyone ever set a full definition for someone of this adjective?

The "perfectionist" tends to be associated as a "fusspot" or "stickler." However, these adjectives don't necessarily capture the attitude of a "perfectionist." A "fusspot" and a "stickler" seem unreasonable and selfish; a perfectionist is guided with a good sense of reason, and doesn't inevitably care only for oneself.

A perfectionist is a person who strongly dislikes failing at something, especially something that will affect them long-term. They take pride in all of their work, completing it fully and thoroughly. Most of the time, they feel like something isn't quite right, or doesn't fill its potential. It will take the individual more than one try to get it just right, finally fitting the criteria of the perfectionist's own perception of achievement. Perfectionists will continue to climb the endless ladder to his or her goal, even though, to the average person, it seems unreachable.

The perfectionist is a man or woman who believes in correcting things until they are absolutely flawless. They are individuals who sometimes "sweat the small stuff," yet are humble. Everyone tries to succeed at school. The difference between a regular student and a perfectionist is the perfectionist almost always does.

Carson Kessler, Grade 9
Saint Mary's Hall, TX

My First Game

I tried out for the Monte Vista 8th grade basketball team. I was named a starter on the team. I was really excited because at the school I went to before I was a bench player. Our first game was a home game. It was against a school nearby. I was nervous before my first game.

In the first half, I only had one basket and I was terrible. My coach told me to take my time with my jump shot. As we started the second half, I followed his advice, and I was confident. We were losing by four.

In the first part of the third quarter, I did almost nothing. Then, all of a sudden, our coach called time-out and set up a play. It was where the other wing player and I started on the baseline and came up to about fifteen feet for a jump shot. That is when I caught on fire. Every time I shot the ball I would make it. I had ten points in that quarter.

At the start of the 4th quarter, we were ahead. I was confident our team was going to win. Then, the other team went on a run. They got the lead with ten seconds left to go. We had the ball in the backcourt. Our point guard dribbled the ball up court and went to the basket. Everyone cleared out so that he would have an open lane. He scored, and we won by one.

Robert Hill, Grade 8
Monte Vista Christian School, CA

Forever and Always

You may wait ages on them, or so it feels like. You probably think that they're no use to you. You may think that they don't understand you. I'm sure you think that you don't need them and you can live without them and you couldn't care less about where they're at or what they're doing. Truth is, you know inside, in the back of your mind, you're thinking about your family. It could be anything, but no matter what it's about, you're still thinking about them. When you're separated, you can feel the difference in your personality and mood. You know that spark in you is there, but you hide it. Why? Why do you hide this? You're scared; you think that you're the only one. You're not. Everyone has it, even the desperate and hopeless. People wish it away. They think that they can be stronger without it, but honestly, your family are the ones that build you up, they're the ones that make you stronger, they're the ones that wish you luck when you need it. They may choose wrong and go different ways from you, but you know, they will be waiting for you forever and always.

Bailey Howe, Grade 8
Excelsior Academy, UT

Midnight's Drive

The moon is serene, glowing and shimmering in the midst of the dark, quiet night. It soars in the deep nothingness above, watching the tranquility of the world below it. I watch it too, its shape barely visible from my fogged up car window. With every stop, turn, or movement, it treads alongside us, like a whimpering, lonesome puppy. It used to fascinate me when I was younger, with its waxing and waning and changing forms. The moon is mysterious, gone throughout the day, coming out late at night. It stays calm and peaceful, finding joy in the stillness in the air. I wonder if it ever dreamt like me, forgetting all its pains, fears, worries, and sorrows. I gaze up, just watching, waiting, listening. But the silence causes me to drift away. When I wake, brightness strikes me. And the moon is gone.

Krisianne Aromin, Grade 8
Our Lady of Guadalupe School, CA

The Hail Extravaganza

On October 5, 2010, the worst storm since 1980 hit Phoenix, Arizona. it was very unexpected. This is my story.

We were driving home form school, and there was not a cloud in sight. Then the ominous clouds started rolling in. Out of nowhere, one piece of hail falls. Then several pieces fall! They all were the size of baseballs! My sister started to freak out. Good thing my family and I were down the street from our house. My mom pulled in to the driveway and ran into the house! My sister and I opened the blinds and watched the hail storm until the very end.

When the hair storm was over, my sister and I ran outside and started playing with it. My sister shouted, "This is so cool!" I said, "Maddie, don't act like you weren't crying." We both just laughed. This hail storm was an experience of a lifetime!!

Alex Farren, Grade 7
St Gregorys Catholic School, AZ

The Wonders of Books

"There is no friend as loyal as a book"— Ernest Hemingway.

Books are good friends to keep for entertainment and enjoyment. Because of the information it contains, books are great imagination and creativity-builders. Moreover, books can also reduce environmental harm. Old and modern books are doorways to inspiration that increasingly shape our world.

In ancient times, the Romans used the layer between bark and wood as parchment. These types of ancient materials are undeniably expensive now and unlike other books, can be priceless. Modern books cannot match the importance of a rare, old book. In fact, a rare original 1865 edition of Alice's Adventures in Wonderland by Lewis Carroll, was sold in New York for $1.54 million dollars. Unlike modern books, old books hold importance to readers and collectors because of its rarity, facts, and physical changes.

Today, some modern books have 100% recycled content that can reduce total energy and gas emissions by 38%, wastewater by 41%, and virgin wood use by 100% (Earth 911). By reading books, people can be distracted from mind-wasting computer games and television programs. Reading books saves the brain from cell wasting and help increase one's reading skills.

In any case, books are more than just bound papers. Books are beneficial resources that provide skills, encourage creativity and help save the environment. Old books are kept and owned for its rarity and informational worth. In other words, books are extensions to the world, heart, and mind. Despite the difference, books are essential and loved either way, old or modern.

Mikaela Magwili, Grade 8
Queen of All Saints School, CA

October Storm

It was a cold day at St. Gregory Catholic School. The classrooms were so warm, but when you stepped outside, it was a different story. The wind was so cold that it stung my skin. I was only wearing shorts and a polo shirt. I had lost my sweater the week before. I couldn't wait to get home and just relax and not worry about the cold. My class and I were finally dismissed.

I was so happy when my mom drove my siblings and me back home. We rushed into our house and found refuge from the cold. My mother made us hot chocolate. Suddenly, we heard someone throwing rocks at our windows and doors. I looked out the window and discovered that it was hail. It was kind of ironic because Arizona normally doesn't have hail storms. I had a sleepless night because the hail storm was too loud and violent. One of my sisters actually managed to sleep through the storm.

The next day, I woke up with a backache. Apart from being scared, I received two hours of sleep. On my drive back to school, I was looking out my window at all the damage caused by the storm. There was a broken trampoline on the street, broken trees, and cars with holes in them. When I arrived at school, I saw a huge broken tree on the blacktop. All my friends had different stories about how the storm affected them.

Danny Murego, Grade 8
St Gregorys Catholic School, AZ

Christofer Drew: Mentor, Life Changer, Inspiration

It was a warm spring break and a friend talked about this new band. I decided to Google the band "Never Shout Never." I did not know that the lead singer, Christofer Drew, would become a big part of my life. I listened to one song called "Happy." I then searched for other songs. Soon I knew all the lyrics to every song. I discovered that he was an amazing person. Through his music lyrics, interviews, poems and quotes, I learned how to live in the moment and learned more about myself.

He is someone who inspires me and will always have a place in my heart. I feel he will always be there for me through the cries, laughs, heartbreak, and stress. Friends may come and go, but he will always be there. He is like a big brother, always there.

How Christofer Drew inspired me to grow was through his music and quotes. He taught me that the past and the future don't matter, just focus on now. He taught me to be kind and faithful, and to love yourself and others, especially Jesus. He inspired me to try to follow Jesus' ways. He taught me that it is okay to be different and outlandish and be audacious and whimsical. Just a few months ago, he inspired me to play piano again. I started playing piano in first grade and stopped playing in sixth grade because I thought I was not good enough. Actually, I love playing! It is one of the best things that has ever happened to me. Now I practice every day. He also inspired me to write songs. Thanks to him, I have evolved into a wonderful pianist and construct my own songs. I have become a better person and have now accepted myself.

Morgan Gimblet, Grade 8
St Matthew Catholic School, TX

Arizona, the Good Life

My family is large and obnoxious, but we love each other. That's why my family had a hard time when a piece moved away. The piece that moved away was the Benson's. They moved all the way to Tennessee. When they moved away, they let their daughter Hannah stay for the remainder of the year.

"Guy's, I'm back!" was the first thing Hannah said as she walked off the plane. Hannah was really lucky her parents were going to let her stay in Arizona. We had so much we wanted to do. We didn't expect time to pass so fast. Before we knew it, it was almost time for Hannah to go home. He knew we had to do one last thing before Hannah left. We would have another grandchild's sleepover. Grandchild's sleepover is an annual sleepover at our Nana's house. It is fun because all the cousins are there without any adults. It was so much fun! There were games, food and movies. When it was all over, we said a memory we had with Hannah and a prayer that she has a good life in Tennessee.

Have you ever heard the saying, "You never know a good thing till it's gone." I never thought about a life without Hannah, but now I have to live it. I know with all the other people in my family, I am overwhelmed with people to love. But Hannah will always have a special place in my heart.

Emily Richards, Grade 8
St Gregorys Catholic School, AZ

Abraham Lincoln

Abraham Lincoln was the 16th president of the U.S.A., and in my opinion, he was the best one yet. Abraham Lincoln lived in the time of the Civil War, back when there were slaves. He was a hero to the country.

When Abraham, or Abe, as he was known by, was a little boy, he lived in Kentucky. He was born on February 12, 1809. Abraham's mother died from milk sickness when he was nine. His sister, Sarah, looked after him until his father remarried to Sarah Bush Johnston. Abe was very close to his stepmother. He called her "Mother" instead of something else.

When Abraham was 22, he set out on his own, sailing down the river and eventually ending up in New Salem. When he got there, he was hired to take goods to New Orleans. When he saw slavery in New Orleans, he walked home.

Abraham was going to be married to Mary Todd, but then canceled the wedding, ending their relationship. A while later they were officially married after meeting at a party. Abe had four children: Robert, Edward, Willie, and Thomas (Tad). Only Robert lived to adulthood.

Abraham ran for president and failed due to lack of money and other essential items. A little while later, he ran for president again and succeeded. Abraham Lincoln helped this country quite a lot in the Civil War. He was the sixteenth president and one of the greatest presidents so far.

Abraham Lincoln was a great president, father, lawyer, and many other things. He died on April 15, 1865, after being shot in the head by John Wilkes Booth. His death was a sad time for a lot of people. Abraham Lincoln was a good president.

Cort Lawrence, Grade 7
Sunrise Ridge Intermediate School, UT

Art

Art is a passion of mine. It makes me feel free and feel like I can do anything, if I put my mind to it. People who have seen my art always tell me what a great talent I have. I know that art is a big part of my future.

My artistic journey began when I started taking art classes in 2007. I took drawing for over a year, before I started painting. Then I took drawing and painting together for two years, until I switched to only painting. The medium I enjoy most is acrylics.

My artistic ability runs in my blood. My great grandfather was actually a professional artist. My mom has one of his paintings hanging in our house, and every time that I look at it, I know that I was meant to be an artist, like him.

I have won many awards for my art. I have entered my work in the Washington County Fair. I won many ribbons, representing a variety of awards in the two years that I had entered. One of them was a grand sweepstakes. I was also on the front cover of the local newspaper called the Spectrum, twice, showing my work. In fourth grade, I entered the yearbook cover contest at my school, Little Valley Elementary. I painted a picture of a lion. I won, and my painting was on the front cover of our yearbook. I have also won many more awards.

Art is about finding out who you are, and expressing yourself on canvas. It has been a great journey, and I have achieved a lot through art. I hope to become a famous artist, who is very successful. I look forward to many years of success and glory through the amazing world of art.

Bailee Danklef, Grade 7
Sunrise Ridge Intermediate School, UT

Rekindle the Flame

Have you ever had a boyfriend or girlfriend who went to a different school, or who moved to a different state? Perhaps they once lived close to you, but you did not see each other all of the time. As the time spent apart increased, that little spark or feeling you had for them started to quickly die down. However, when you finally were able to spend time with them again, you remembered why you valued your relationship in the first place. Without that little reminder, your relationship might have continued to dissolve until you are almost strangers.

If you think about it, your relationship with God can be like that. If you do not have a daily relationship with Him, other people or things step in to become more important. You might drift away from Him, or maybe even push Him away, but He is always there with open and loving arms when you come back to Him. Like going on a date, going to church can be the spark that rekindles the fire or the flame for the love of God. Consider church to be like a date with God. Sure, you can always talk to Him by praying, but in any good relationship, you need that quality time with the one you love. Without that, you will drift away from the blessings and favor that God who gives to those who walk in step in their relationship with Him.

Emma Womack, Grade 9
First Baptist Academy, TX

The Magic of Music

Music: joyful, melancholy, funny, strange, or magnificently beautiful. What could be more mysterious than a series of notes creating feelings of infinite depth? When I play a song, whether it be bluegrass or folk, a sensation often bubbles up inside me. It causes me to reflect on a memory or sense a strong relationship with something, somewhere deep inside. Bluegrass and folk music open up my voice, and a sense of calm and purity enters my body. My fingers chase the notes of my guitar and settle on them at the exact moment that my voice soars up into the land of music. For a moment I am in a different world, full of clarity and near perfection, as my feelings harmonize with my voice. A surge of gratitude, joy, or sadness passes through my body as the words find their way into my heart. Whatever I'm thinking or feeling comes out through my hands and voice in a wave of love, melancholy, or hope. Soothing my anger or amplifying my happiness, music takes the sadness or optimism in the words and generates energy that enters into me and anyone listening. Music is the art that I hear, the spice of life that can turn me into anything I want to be. It is the passion that consoles me and fills me with satisfaction. Without music, the joy and adventure in life would forever be buried deep inside me.

Harper Powell, Grade 7
Salida Middle School, CO

My Cat, Rocky

Do you have a companion you can turn to any time? I do, he is a cat named Rocky. Rocky is either wanting to play or snuggle. He can cheer anyone up at any moment! I think Rocky is a very intelligent cat because he always knows exactly what to do.

My cat, Rocky has black and white fur. He is a tuxedo cat. Rocky has black arms with white paws. His white paws make it look like he is wearing boxing gloves. Rocky has black spots on his fur, I call them freckles. Rocky has bright green eyes. Rocky is so cute that even if you do not like cats you will love him!

Rocky is special to me because he is a million dollar cat. Christmas 2010 was very sad because Rocky was getting very sick easily. My mom took him to the vet. I remember that moment feeling so scared and alone I could not breathe. The vet said he had a rare red blood cell disease. Later about two days before Christmas a miracle in my eyes happened and he regained strength.

I have a lot of memories with Rocky. One of my favorite memories is when he chased a laser light in circles! Another is a time he had to take a bath. When Rocky saw the shampoo and water he jumped out of the bath tub. There was a time when my mom was playing with him and he looked as if he was boxing an opponent.

As you know I have had great times with my cat, Rocky. To me, Rocky is more than a cat, he is a friend. Rocky will always be there, whenever I need him. He will always be in my heart.

Bailey Estrada, Grade 8
Santa Clara Elementary School, CA

Good Stories

What could be more sublime than a good story? The orator spins a web of words that whisks you off your feet, making every new word another moment of pure glee. Imagine a crackling campfire, then add the chirping of crickets filling the hollow night-sky. Soon a low voice softly flows over your ears. It speaks jokingly and lightly about near-death experiences, or funny stories, carefully enunciated to ensure maximum clarity. These words, that I consider an atheist's godsend, create the stairway I ascend into a land of excitement and uncertainty.

I love all kinds of stories. I love the kind told sitting around a kitchen table, fraught with dim light. Or the kind told in a bar, after you don't really consider the storyteller "sober." I even love the memories of being tucked in at night and pleading for yet another bedtime story.

Stories are the bread and cheese, even meat and bones, of my very own dreams and many others'. I remember, at the age of 4 or 5, being told all of my mom's old rock-climbing stories. I would sit and listen, in awe, as my mother would romanticize about every aspect of climbing, whether it was different holds or embarrassing adventures. Whatever the topic, I was captivated, stuck in a web of entertaining words.

Stories unplant me from my earthly form. They let my thoughts fly about through the various nooks and crannies of my mind, free as a bird. From them, I discover and learn new things about my life. Without a good story sprinkled here and there in my history, like a fine coating of powdered sugar, I would not be the person I am today.

Seth Minor, Grade 7
Salida Middle School, CO

Inspiring Others to Grow

We inspire others to grow like we did when we were younger and fallible. We are the role models of our siblings and the teachers of their growth. We inspire them to achieve what we achieved and to do what we learned from our elders. Our feeling of radiance entices them to be happy, sad, angry, or even act like a buffoon.

Our notable teachers help us to grow by helping us with what to do. They inspire us to be responsible and vigilant and to help others when they are in need, to get help or to tell someone to get help, and to do what you need to do in a situation when in trouble.

We can influence others on the job or which affects our future endeavors. If we provide the wrong influence, our students could go to jail and be fugitives. How we hold ourselves can determine how they succeed in life. We learn every day from our teachers and elders, and these teachings will pervade the community.

We are always being watched and studied, no matter what situation we are in, by all the bystanders around us. No matter how troubled we might be, we are planting the faith in our community and nurturing the next generation. These seeds are instilled in us from birth by our parents, teachers, friends, and God who help us to be poised for the future.

Duncan McLauchlan, Grade 7
St Matthew Catholic School, TX

Disabilities

Disability is serious. There are three reasons why you shouldn't make fun of people with disabilities. One, it can and will hurt disabled people's feelings. Two, you can offend people who may be close to people with infirmities. Finally, you may end up with disabilities.

First, making fun of disabilities can hurt disabled people's feelings. Say that you are walking through school and are joking with your friends about autism. An autistic kid hears you and tells the principal. You're now suspended and also feel bad about making that joke.

Second, you can offend people who are close to disabled people. Now you are walking in the park and talking to your friend again. You were making fun of amputations. The frail lady next to you glares at you and whacks you with her cane. Hard. Apparently, her husband lost a leg due to war injuries.

Third, you may end up with injuries. You are seventy-five and fall down the stairs. You already have Alzheimer's and you never walk again. You should not have made fun of those disabled people when you were younger.

In conclusion, you should not make fun of people with disabilities. It can hurt people's feelings, offend people, and even you may end up with disabilities. It's not very nice to make fun of people with infirmities.

Kayla Redmond, Grade 8
Excelsior Academy, UT

Should the NFL Have an On-field Doctor or Not?

In a recent game, Colt McCoy was hit and got hurt, but was told he was fine to go back in the game by the coach and the team medical staff. After the game he complained about still having headaches, and he went to a doctor and was told he had a concussion.

The NFL needs to have doctors on the field that do not work for the team. They should have a doctor on-field to make sure a player doesn't go out too soon and make sure he doesn't need immediate attention from a more specific doctor, regardless of what the coach or owner thinks. These doctors would be able to make a quick analysis on the player before he went back to the field and only worry about the player's safety, not winning the game.

Coaches, players and owners are very competitive and want to win. Even players that are injured want to keep playing as they love to win. Having a doctor that works for the NFL and no one else would allow only a medical opinion to matter.

On the other hand, team owners pay a lot for their starter players and would not want them to be hurt. Concussions are not easy to detect and a doctor can't always tell. A NFL doctor might be overprotective and not let a player keep playing because they don't want to be sued.

In conclusion, player safety must be first and the only way to be sure is to have a doctor on the field that does not work for the team or the player. A NFL doctor could prevent players from continuing to play while injured, helping them recover faster and prevent long-term injuries.

Travis Spangle, Grade 7
Beacon Country Day School, CO

The Story of My Heart

When I was six months old, my mother took me into the doctor's for a checkup. The doctor told her that my heartbeat did not sound right. I was instantly taken to a pediatric cardiologist at Stanford. The doctor ran tests on me and looked at my heart with a machine called an echocardiogram, it is a type of ultrasound test that uses high-pitched sound waves that are sent through a device called a transducer. These echoes are turned into moving pictures of the heart. The doctor told my parents that I would need immediate surgery and he explained to them that I had a congenital heart defect. There were two major issues going on with my heart. I had what was known as ASD and a problem with my valve. ASD, which is short for atrial septal defect, are holes in the heart. I had seven large holes in my heart. The mitral valve is a dual-flap in the heart's chamber; it controls the blood flow through the heart that provides us with oxygen. Your valve normally has two cusps. I was born with only one and I was not getting enough oxygen. My parents were told that I would need to have open-heart surgery. I was taken to UCSF in San Francisco and I underwent open-heart surgery. The heart surgeons patched up all of the holes in my heart and fixed the problem with my valve.

Thanks to modern technology and great doctors, I am alive and healthy today.

Katie Teresi, Grade 8
St Joseph Catholic School, CA

Football

Football is a common sport in America. It is played at nearly all ages from kids to adults. Some kids play for a city in a league or for their school. I used to play football for the Oxnard Warriors and now I hope to play for a high school football team.

Football is a very fun sport. You get to meet a lot of different people and have lots of fun memories. I find football amusing because you can make big hits and you won't get in trouble for it. Once you get hit it doesn't hurt because you are covered in gear. The only bad part is going to practice every day and conditioning a lot. On game day all the practice is worth it because in the game you can show people what you are capable of.

I play football every year and I have been playing for five years. Every year I got better and better and every year I stayed with the same coach and the same teammates. My team was really good because we would always make it far in the playoffs. This was my last year for playing for the warriors, and we lost our championship game. Luckily, I still was able to play another game because I was chosen to play linebacker for the North all star team. We played the South. We beat the South and I had a great game. Once I thought that youth football was over for me, I got a call from an All-American coach and he asked me to be on his team to play one final game.

This was the best season I have ever had. I'm going to play football in high school and I hope I have a lot more good times.

Daniel Luna, Grade 8
Santa Clara Elementary School, CA

Hope

Hope can mean many things to many people. It can be hope of getting the newest toy, hope of a snow day, or hoping the health of another will escalate. Life is filled with many obstacles, some can even seem impossible, but with hope, anything that felt unachievable can be accomplished. Without motivation (hope) in who you are and what you are capable of, you can never reach your aspirations. Whenever you feel every chance is lost, or your limits have been reached, just remember there will always be hope for the last second buzzer beater, the open lane in traffic, or the last slice of pie. There is no boundary for hope. It is a tidal wave of ambition and dreams without a conclusion, it is eternal; a vast frontier without limitations. Hope can only come from within the heart of those who never impart on their desires, hope is always going to be by your side, it is always going to be there when you're down, and when you are not, it will always be the catalyst between second half domination being on your side or second half domination rooting against you. Life is too short to waste wondering what could have been, those who take action and rely on hope are always going to go down in history; instead of reading, or hearing about that person, be that person. Hope is shooting for the moon, even if you miss, you will be with the stars.

Mario Santacruz, Grade 9
Brush High School, CO

Growing Up

All children love Disney World. It is a mysterious, magical place that anyone can escape to from the problems of the world. As a kid, I loved Disney World. Everyone would always be smiling and families would enjoy time with each other. The roller coasters were huge and fast and I could meet the famous Disney characters that were on TV. I would go to the magic shop and try to impress my family with the magic tricks that I learned. Every time we would have to leave Disney World, I would cry myself to sleep on the plane. As I started to mature though, I began to have a different view on the park. Everything would seem childish and the songs they played on the loud speakers annoyed me. But when I saw the face of excitement on my little brother's face, it reminded me of what I thought of Disney World as when I was a kid. Everything that excited him is what I was excited about when I was a child. I try to view the park as a younger child so I can make the experience better. I am now familiar about everything in the park, and when I am an adult and start to have a family, I will make sure that my children have the same experience that I did.

Cristian Bonilla, Grade 9
Saint Mary's Hall, TX

Like Two Peas in a Pod

Friendship is a weird thing. Sometimes you think you have a friend but you really don't. Sometimes you think you don't have a friend but you do. Sometimes you want to be someone's friend but then you find out you have too many dislikes and that it's impossible. Sometimes you think you dislike someone but in the end you become really good friends.

And then there's the times when you are really good friends and then they do something that makes you so mad that you never talk to them again. If they move, try to stay their friend. Friendships can last forever, and it's really nice to have some.

I have a friend, and she's my best friend, and she moved. She now lives an hour and a half away, but we are still friends, we write letters, and see each other a few times each year. Without friends I wouldn't be able to make it through the school year. They are what keeps me going.

Spencer Goodworth, Grade 8
Excelsior Academy, UT

My Life and Dreams

My life and dreams are very important to me. I have many dreams in life. Your dreams should be important to you too. I hope you have many. One of my biggest dreams in life is to be an FBI agent. I want to be an FBI agent because I want to get as many bad and troubled people off the streets as possible. If I am not able to be an FBI agent then I want to be a nurse or a paramedic. These dreams are important because they will help me with my financial future. These are very important. When I am out of high school I will go straight to college and study criminal justice. It is very important to have life goals and dreams.

Brynn Colton, Grade 8
Excelsior Academy, UT

Class of 2012

She's leaving me. The class of 2012 is going to graduate and leave to go to college and start their lives, taking my big sister with them. I don't really know what I'll do with my life once she's gone. She's my everything and I love her dearly; more than words could ever describe. Just knowing that I won't be able to see her smiling face every day breaks my heart. I guess I'll be able to see her when she comes home for the holidays, but it will be hard for me to wait.

On one hand, I want her to go and be successful with her life, but on the other hand, I do not want her to leave me and my family. She is one of the most intelligent, strong-headed, beautiful, and talented women I have ever met. I know that whatever it is that she chooses to do with her life, she will be successful because she is the type of person who strives for excellence.

When she is gone a great big chunk of my life will be gone with her. She has already told me that she doesn't want me to dwell on her absence, but it's kind of hard not to. She wants me to move on with my life. It's going to be really hard, but I know that I will make it through.

Allison Payne, Grade 8
Young Scholar's Academy, AZ

Cream-Colored Skies

The sun burned my face as I got off of the Le Bus. The sun was hot and everything was dry. I searched for trees or anything to remind me of home, but nothing was found. We all formed in a group, planned what trails to take, and began on the hike. Although it was hot and hard to go on, we went on. There were no trees, just dry desert bushes. It was different from home, but the sights in front of my eyes were amazing. The sun always glistened perfectly over the sand with every sunset.

Nature is your surroundings. You may not notice how beautiful nature is until your backyard, which was once a garden, is sold and turned into a grocery store. Then you regret selling it. You need to stop, look around, and enjoy the beauty that comes naturally without all the backbreaking work. Enjoy what you don't have to work for. Enjoy the wild!

Karlee Brandt, Grade 7
Excelsior Academy, UT

Friendship

Friendships are essential for life. One reason for this is that people need someone to cheer them up when they are down. For example, if a family member dies, you need someone to be there for you. A friend should make you think about other things to distract you from you sorrow. People need someone to talk to other than their parents. For instance, if you have feelings for another person, it may be embarrassing for you to talk about it with your parents. A friend can give you helpful advice because they go through many of the same experiences with you. Overall, true friends are necessary for a happy life, and they cannot be replaced by anyone else.

Shannon Munn, Grade 9
Foothills Academy, AZ

It's Not a Necessity

Unnecessary cosmetic surgery should be restricted because of the risk of the client's addiction to the concept of the surgery, the high risk of danger during and after the procedure and a high possibility of unsatisfactory results. With these things as likely occurrences, unnecessary cosmetic surgery should be restricted and cosmetic surgery should only be used for constructive surgery.

Often the results are not satisfactory or equal to a client's expectations, and dissatisfaction with the results may lead to more surgeries. Although the results are not always repairable, people will either persist in having more done, or they will have to live with the bad results. On the other side, pleasing results may also lead to addiction to the concept of the surgery. When the clients are content with the results, they are likely to want additional surgeries. Clients often have get implants redone every so often, and the same happens with Botox. Often many people will want to get more done as they age, to deny the aging process, even though it may be dangerous. The procedures can be deadly and may endanger the client's health during and after the surgery. The risk of infection is high and experts say 70% of people have complications because of the procedure.

Unnecessary cosmetic surgery should be restricted. There are many complications that can endanger the client during and after the surgery; therefore, there is no 'must' for this type of surgery other than reconstructive surgery for people who truly need it. Nobody 'needs' cosmetic surgery.

Mandy Santiago, Grade 8
Vacaville Christian Schools, CA

Germany

My mother was born in Germany and she lived there with her family until high school. After high school, my mother came to America to attend college. Every year, she goes back to Germany to see her parents and brothers. Since I was born, every year my mom has taken my brother and I with her. Going to Germany has opened my life up to accepting different cultures. The style of life is different, but in a good way, and I am very fortunate to be able to experience it.

One of my favorite parts of Germany is the food. In the morning, they eat rolls with jam on it, which is sort of like eating bagels and jam here. Lunch in Germany is like dinner for us. That is when they eat warm foods and it is the most important meal for them. In fact, when my mom was in elementary school, the kids would go to their house for lunch. For dinner, they usually eat simple foods. A typical dinner at my grandparent's house includes meat on bread, and vegetables from her own garden.

Even with the great food and everything else we get to experience, seeing my grandparents is by far my favorite part. They are the ones that make sure everything goes the way it is supposed to go. Seeing what Germany is like makes me accept more foods, people, and so many more things. It makes me a better person.

Max Fitzmorris-Johannes, Grade 7
St Joseph Catholic School, CA

Family Is a Unique Thing

Family is important and personal to me. When your friends or other people leave you or don't trust you, then your family is probably going to be there for you. I have learned in personal experience that friends go, but family stays forever. Your mom is there when you are having friend trouble, your goofy little brother is there when you need a good laugh, you strange sister is there to make you feel normal, and your dad is there to make sure you stay strong. Think about it. How many times have you been sad and your family has been there for you? I know mine has been there for me when I'm sad. The success of my family's relationship is in knowing that, if you're sad, or need someone to talk to, your family will be there for you. In life, you're going to lose friends, lose jobs, and sometimes need someone to get you on your feet again. Well, again, your friends won't be there for you all the time, and friends don't stay. If you are in high school, some of your best friends might not talk to you anymore and then you wouldn't have any best friends and you would have to make new ones. Family won't leave, your family will be there for you financially, and for friendship.

Erika Ringwood, Grade 8
Excelsior Academy, UT

How to Brush Your Teeth with Braces!!

Have you ever wondered how people with braces brush their teeth? You came to the right place; I will tell you how to brush them in 4-5 easy steps. The first thing you need to do is pull out your toothbrush, toothpaste, mouthwash, and a glass of water. Then you squeeze the minty green substance onto your tooth brush. Once you think you have enough toothpaste on the toothbrush, put it in your mouth and swirl it on your braces. You then start on the top of your bracket or wire, and scrub all around your mouth. When you are done, go down to under the bracket and scrub again. Scrub very gently, yet hard at the same time, so you can get the plaque off from eating. When you are done making sure they are plaque free, you are done. Finally, put up your utensils and now wash out your mouth with water, or you can get a more minty taste. If you follow the rules above, you should have straight white teeth, and a beautiful smile.

Chase Walker, Grade 7
Lindale Jr High School, TX

A Dreamer or a Seeker

Don Quixote was a dreamer. He imagined his own life. He would imagine that he was a knight and would go to buildings with his sword and dream that he was at a castle.

I think of myself as a seeker, always seeking answers. I elaborate on everything I see, seeking to always find out more about everything I encounter in my life. I always seek improvement and push myself to do better. My personality is usually laid back and easy going, but inside I am constantly going over things in my head, analyzing everything I come in contact with on a daily basis.

Dante Matero, Grade 9
Athens Christian Preparatory Academy, TX

Nature And All Its Glory

I believe that nature is the most outstanding creation in the world. Every chance I get, I want to go to the forest to enjoy everything and clear my mind. Walking through the crisp, clean forest makes me love it even more; from the tip of any mountain to the smallest grain of dirt on the Earth's crust. The serene environment makes you clear your head. The most beautiful sight is watching majestic butterfly wings gliding past me, as if he is saying "Follow me to a magical place."

Watching a little breeze flow freely throughout the trees is calming. I remember many picnics in the forest with my grandparents. I sat under a tree and stayed there for hours on end observing my surroundings. I remember watching the river throw the sun's golden gleam off the surface, blinding me at times. A vibrant blue bird whistled a marvelous melody. Nature is always different every time I go.

Nature is how we live; that is why we should have respect for nature. In nature, you could ponder solutions or clear your mind completely of any stress. The next time you need either of these, go into the mountains. Enjoy nature every chance you get.

Alexus Kelso, Grade 8
Excelsior Academy, UT

Lightning Storm

The "Boom! Crash!" of the lightning and thunder make my heart race with excitement. The hard thump of the rain droplets helps me relax and eases my mind. Waiting for the next lightning crash is the most exciting part yet, and when you see the light streak across the sky in jagged and long lines, you're left amazed. The thump of the thunder is so strong, it makes your house shake; as soon as that happens, you jump off the couch and run to the porch. Standing on the porch, smelling the sweet, sweet smell of rain makes your senses tingle. The water falling from the sky soon turns to hail, and pea-sized ice starts to pelt your body. You run inside with water dripping off your clothes and down your fingertips. As I run to get a towel to dry off, I look out the window and see a car drive by. It makes a wave of water, splashing a puddle into my drive way. The rain stops and I am left satisfied with what I have smelled, heard, and watched.

Phillip Vigil, Grade 7
Salida Middle School, CO

Volleyball

My blood rushes through my veins every time I hear the words "bump, set, spike." The thrill of hitting is addicting like candy. I watch the opposing team scramble to dig the ball. They are a second late and the ball hits the ground with a loud smack; the crowd roars with excitement. I hear my hitters screaming for the set as the ball is passed high to the middle of the court. In a split second, I choose my hitter, let her know with a loud yell, and set the ball. The ball rises high above the ten-foot line as the hitter takes her approach, a perfect kill. I live for volleyball.

Nicole Blair, Grade 8
Foothills Academy, AZ

Feral Pigs: They Make People "Wallow" in Frustration

What do you think when someone says the word "pig?" A cute, pink ball of fuzz or a vicious, charging beast?

Also called Sus scrofa Linnaeus, a feral pig is a pig which is not kept or bred in a holding. An average adult feral pig can range from 200 to 400 pounds, with nasty-looking tusks and a frightening snort.

Biologists say that these pigs are a menace to the bird population, and they nibble on new-growth trees, hurting areas struggling to recover from wildfires. The pigs also like to dine on acorns. The coastal live acorn and the black oak acorn are favorites of the pigs, officials note. "Further stress caused by pigs could present a significant problem in oak habitats in the Cleveland National Forest," said William Metz, a forest supervisor in the Cleveland National Forest.

These deadly creatures also spread harmful diseases. Swine brucellosis, an infectious disease carried by feral pigs in at least fourteen different states in the United States, causes abortion in sows and infertility in boars. The feral pigs also contain a disease called pseudorabies, which can be fatal to cattle, sheep, goats, dogs, cats, raccoons, skunks, foxes, opossums, small rodents, and many other animals. The virus attacks the nervous system in these animals and can produce intense itching, followed by paralysis and then death.

How will the government deal with these beasts? They reproduce extremely quickly, destroy property, and spread diseases. Can we find a solution to this puzzle, or will eradication be necessary?

Johnny Liu, Grade 7
Stratford Elementary/Middle School, CA

Giving Back

"You know what we should do!?" my sister Annie asked. "What?" my mom and I asked. "We should donate our clothes to the homeless!" she exclaimed. "That's a great idea!" my mom shouted. Disagreeing, I managed a nod. I didn't really want to donate any of my clothes.

We got home from school. Annie ran straight to our closet. I sat on the couch doing nothing for a while and finally decided to go check on my sister. She had at least three piles of clothes scattered around the room. I couldn't believe how serious she was about this. Who would want to donate clothes? Especially to the homeless.

As I thought about it more, why she was doing it and who it was for, it gave me a change of heart. It's the coldest part of winter and there are people on the streets freezing like popsicles, catching diseases while I sit in a loving home with clothes to keep me warm. How could I be so selfish?

I dashed to my closet, going through it at least five times. I gathered up two bags' worth of clothes. I was so excited to be giving my clothes to those in need; not to mention they'd be warm as well as stylish. I felt so proud and a weight lifted from my conscience. It was all because of my little sister influencing me to do something selfless, donating clothes to those in need. Thank you, Annie!

Donna Sciascia, Grade 8
League City Intermediate School, TX

Miracles

Many people have inspired me to learn about my faith, but the one person who has inspired me the most is my mom. My mom tells me about all the miracles that have been performed. Some have actually happened in my family and have saved lives.

One of the miracles that I think is so stunning is what happened to my cousin. My cousin had kidney and liver problems and she was worried she would die; she was in dire need of a miracle. She was perturbed at thinking of what would happen to her son if she died. She wanted to present a sacrifice to Mary and pray to her, so she wanted to get some roses. She found some growing in a field and picked them. She put them in a vase and prayed.

When she woke up she was aghast at what she saw. All the rose petals were scattered on the floor and dried out. Every single petal had a picture of Mary on it, even the candles she put out for her had the image. She went to go tell her family about the miracle. When she was telling her family what happened her son told her an apparition of Mary came to him saying his mother would live. She went to the doctor and the tests proved that Mary was telling the truth. She wanted to give more prayers to Mary to thank her for saving her life. When she went back to the place where she found the roses, there was no trace that there were any roses there. Mary was a recourse sent from heaven and showed her the roses.

That's just one story over many. I am glad my mom told me about this miracle. These miracles inspire me to grow in my faith and show that God is always watching over us. Mary still watches over my cousin today sending signs, starting with the scent of roses.

Desirae Imad, Grade 8
St Matthew Catholic School, TX

Love for Basketball

Is playing sports your thing? Do you love to have fun playing your favorite sport, especially with friends? I love sports and play a lot.

Basketball is my favorite sport. I always play whether I am by myself, on a team, at a park, or with someone else. I am also very tall, which gives me an advantage in basketball. I am good at playing it. I would never get tired or bored of playing.

I like to practice basketball a lot. I practice my basketball skills to improve how I play. Sometimes I will go to a park with my friends to practice my skills. We will just shoot around or play a game like Horse or Around the World.

I play for the basketball team at my school. We have practices every Wednesday and Friday. In order to play, you need to have certain grades. You cannot have anything lower than a C-. If you start going down, you get put on probation and cannot play that weekend until you bring up your grades. Bringing up your grades gets you off probation.

As you can see, I am all for basketball. I am very committed to the sport. Someday I hope to be a professional basketball player.

Trevor Cobb, Grade 8
Santa Clara Elementary School, CA

The Strength of My Faith

My faith is the most important thing in my life, because without it I would be lost. Let me tell you how I influence people and how they remind me how strong my faith is and where it began.

The story of my faith began when my religion was born. It is called Catholicism and it was created by a man named Jesus. He was born in Jerusalem. Many people believed that he was the prodigy or Messiah. It was not long before the people that did not like him wanted him executed. The Romans had him carry a cross up a mountain, while whipping him. Three days after he was crucified his disciple Mary went to his tomb and found he was not there. Only the burial cloth he was buried in remained. On the same day, Easter Sunday, the apparition of Jesus appeared to his disciples. He told them not to be afraid and to go and be fishers of men. He armed them with the Holy Spirit.

There are times when I have tried to learn more about my faith or share it with someone. For example one day I met someone who looked lost and confused. I told them to come with me and to see what mass was like. When the mass started I explained all the parts of the mass, why we read from the Bible, and most importantly, why we have the body and blood of Christ at the altar.

The world can bring you down at times, but don't capitulate when it happens. God will help you if you only have faith and trust in God. Through the experiences I have learned, my faith has gotten stronger and I will carry that through my high school years at Antonian.

Eleasar Valadez, Grade 8
St Matthew Catholic School, TX

The Day

Have you ever had a day where all your talent counts? Did it make you feel like the start of a new season? From all the pressure did you think you couldn't do it?

As I walked onto the basketball court, you could smell everyone's nerves in the air. All of my friends were here, and we were all trembling with fear of not making the team.

When practice was over, everyone went to go sit where the coaches were. Everyone was sweating bullets. If I would've licked my lips, I would've tasted the sweat pouring down my drenched face. All of a sudden Coach Ogden started calling back people who she wanted to stay. My name wasn't being called, so I was getting more and more nervous. Frightened and panicked, my hands started getting clammy. When all of my hopes were lost, my name was called. The feel of the cold floors was comforting now, because I was so warm with joyous praises. I couldn't wait to tell my mom that I had made call backs. Once we broke out, I just started jumping up and down with exhilaration and delightfulness.

Ever since I made the team, I've loved basketball. I didn't think I would make the team, but I overcame it. Basketball is soothing to me now. If I ever get mad, I will just go outside and shoot.

Bonnie Smith, Grade 7
Lindale Jr High School, TX

A Single Clearing

There is a lot of life in a single clearing alone, but it would be nice if all of us could be able to see it, so we could treasure it while we can. You may see a rabbit streak across the clearing full of exotic flowers. Or see a few bumblebees buzzing from vibrant scarlet roses to indigo pansies. Maybe you hear a blue jay harmonizing in the tall conifers with a chickadee in a grove of quaking aspens. You may see a stream that gurgles down a hill toward a pond as blue as the sky, where small fish dart among emerald green seaweed, beside glinting pebbles and color rich seashells. A doe and its young fawn drink from the pond while the buck stands tall, watching for danger. Maybe a copper rattler with a flashy diamond pattern sliding down its back slithers through the tall grass, using its senses to find a trace of the rodent for its meal. Now this may be only a fraction of the life in this single clearing, but what you don't go looking for, you won't find, and if you don't find life and beauty, you'll never be able to treasure it.

Caleb Smith, Grade 7
Salida Middle School, CO

The Melody of Music

To me, music has got to be one of the biggest things in my life. I absolutely can't imagine my world without music. Ever since I was able to walk and speak, or maybe even before that, I loved to dance whenever I heard music playing and sing along to it in my cute little baby voice, which my family thought was adorable! Even now, I hum along to favorites that come on the radio, I sing in the shower all the time, and sometimes, whenever a really catchy song gets stuck in my head, I burst out singing it in my room. Whenever I come back home from school, the first thing I do is grab my guitar from its stand and play it for at least half an hour every day before I get on to my homework. On weekends, I spend forever on my guitar playing random tunes. By now, you can probably assume that I'm totally obsessed with music, right? Because I really am. It's my passion, and almost nothing in the whole world can beat the power of music.

Pooja Tipirneni, Grade 7
North Star Academy, CA

Sarah

Having my sister as my best friend is one of the greatest things I could ever ask for. She is so willing, kind and helps me when I need it. She is always filled with love and joy. Sarah always had, and will have a big influence on me. She has that special touch to make everything we do more interesting, like when I'm not tired at night, she will ask me if I want to play "temple run" on our iPods, and listen to music. Sure, we fight like other sisters, but not very often, because she always tries stop the argument and make me laugh. We spend a lot of time together, which I believe makes our relationship stronger. She is truly like the sun to me, lighting my way. I think it is hard to know how good life is with a sister, until I imagine it without her.

Rebekah LaCroix, Grade 7
Salida Middle School, CO

How FIRST Robotics Changed My Family's Life

FIRST, was started in 1992 by Dean Kamen. His mission is "To transform our culture by creating a world where science and technology were celebrated and where young people dream of becoming science and technology leaders." FIRST has transformed many lives since 1992. An example of this is one of the FIRST alumni's dreams. When he started high school, his goal was to be an actor or a model. He found FIRST. After doing four years of FIRST, he wanted to work professionally with robotics. He ended up at NASA. He helped build the 2011 Mars Rover. This is amazing! Neither of my parents completed an accredited college degree. Finishing college is important to me. I thought I was just joining a team to build a robot, but I have seen my own life change. My confidence has increased. I am more outgoing. I am more comfortable with public speaking and much more. My whole family is doing this with me and we love it. My mom is single but she makes time to be our coach. We spend 21-30 hours a week building and working for our team, Bots of Prey 4106 FIRST 4H Team. My two year old sister, Madeline, comes with us to build. Saturday, she was sick. Madeline still insisted on going. Even at two, she enjoys robotics. I think my family has come together because of FIRST. I love this program and I would like to thank Mr. Kamen for starting this wonderful program. I am now excited about attending college and know I can accomplish anything. What I have shared is just the tip, there is so much more. I am MacKenzy and these are the ways FIRST has changed my life and my family's.

MacKenzy MacCleary, Grade 9
Heritage Community Charter School, ID

My Papa

I was on my papa's lap.

The smell of old cologne swirled through the air with every breath. The warm hug of my Papa and the voice of my Grammy flew throughout the house. It's all part of a recurring memory. This image of warmth spreads throughout my mind every time I think of the soft spoken, loving man I once knew. This was my Papa. He was only 84 when he passed 3 years ago.

My life, until I was seven, was spent learning under the halcyon wing of my Papa. He taught me what he knew about the good and the bad of the world. He knew, having been an army meteorologist during WWII. He understood. He understood the bond between a Papa and his granddaughter. I couldn't be there for the last couple years of his life, but we kept in close contact through letters. I always sent him art work, and he sent me compliments. This went on for 4 years. Until he passed.

The haunting, lingering memory of how I felt the day he died will never cease. I felt like I was in an oblivious world that only focused on the fact that he was gone. The day of his funeral was the day I found the peace that I'd been seeking. It seemed like he whispered to me that he was happy in heaven, and that I would see him once again. I had never felt such happiness in my heart until that day.

Katie Roche, Grade 8
St Joseph Catholic School, CA

How I Live My Life

"Treat each day as if were you to die tomorrow, learn as if you were to learn forever." — Gandhi. I also have three ethics I use to live my life. They are: treating others with respect, try my best at learning, and live life to the fullest.

I have always treated my friends with kindness and they will always treat me back with kindness. For example, I always say good morning to my friends when I get to school. That hopefully puts them in a good mood for some time of the day. That's basically how I express my respect.

I also always try my best at learning. As I am writing this, I am learning how to write better! This ethic is important to me because it is basically my future. If I do bad in school, I won't get in any good colleges, but if I do good, I'll get in a good college with a good job. For example, I study one hour before a test day. That's how I get good grades on my test.

My third and final ethic is living my life to the fullest. I always treat a normal day at school as if it were my last. This keeps me motivated for the school day. I also finish my homework almost every day so I feel proud. Then I spend my time with my neighborhood friends playing football or soccer and it's always fun! So this also keeps me motivated to do my homework so when I'm done I get to hang with my friends.

The reason I am sharing this with the reader is to encourage all to try my ethics and see how it makes life much easier! It certainly made mine easier.

Pedro Ramos, Grade 8
Palm Desert Charter Middle School, CA

My Bird Dog

Bam! Dead! Woof! Point! The sounds just blow me away, and it's never just the dogs, it's everything. The birds, the dogs, the guns, and the long exhausting trips make me love this organization to the moon and back. The North American Gun Dog Association has been pleasing people for a long time.

It's has always been a dream of mine to stand next to my dad with Jake in-between us. We both look at Jake together. I can see the excitement in his melting dark chocolate eyes swirled with a light caramel color. Dad hands me my bullets. I wait. I wait for something. I wait for absolute silence to come into action. I'm ready I say to myself to keep me calm, so I don't send my stress to the dog. As I tell Jake to search for a bird, I get so many goose bumps that I feel as if I am a chicken on a farm. Jake slowly stops in this very weedy but grassy area; I know he is on a bird. He stands as still as a rock. Then he looks back at me. I see his eyes popping out of his head because his excitement has nowhere else to go. "Release," I slowly say. Jake bolts toward the area of the bird. I shoot. I slowly yell, "Dead!" My dad cheers in excitement.

I know that dreams are dreams, but someday they will come true. If you work to the highest point of where you want to be, you will eventually get there. Sometime, someway, somehow just think about it. The North American Gun Dog Association has made me excited for my future. But I know right now it's just a dream.

Morgan Walker, Grade 7
Salida Middle School, CO

To Save a Life

Growing up with sisters that have a heart condition is kind of a challenge; Knowing that one moment they're fine and the next moment they're not. Using a defibrillator is not as tricky as it looks if you just follow these few steps. You can learn to save someone's life. Before you use a defibrillator, the person may need help first. The first step you do to use an AED (automated external defibrillator) is to de-cloth the top layer of the person, then you check for a pulse. If there is not one you turn on the AED. Next it will tell you the steps. Step one: take off the sticky tablets off of the handles. Then you place one right above the chest bone and the other right below the chest bone. It will check for a pulse and if there is not a pulse, then it will send an electric current through the blood straight to the heart and shock it where it will start working again. It will tell you when the person has a pulse again. Also, it might scare the person so make sure to tell them what happened and take them to a hospital. After you follow these few simple steps you could be considered a "hero."

Sarah Hall, Grade 7
Lindale Jr High School, TX

Trust

Something that I value as a human is trust. "Trust is like a piece of paper that once it's crumbled it can never be perfect again," — Joe Rappel. Trust can bring you down; it can also lift you up. Many times you feel that the person you talk to is the right person to trust but no, they betray you or turn their backs on you. On the other hand, trust can lead you to happiness. It can help you understand life in different forms. Before trusting you should know the person better and give yourself time. In this world you will need someone to trust; at least to listen. Trusting takes time and is just like learning to ride a bike; you need someone in your back to help you peddle in case you trip or fall. When you fall, someone helps you, and if you get hurt, they help cure you. Trust is a great way to gain support from others and to talk about your overwhelming emotions.

Maria Ceron, Grade 7
North Star Academy, CA

A Father's Voice

My father slips down in a chair. He swiftly turns the pages of a tired old book, and begins to read aloud. As he reads the words, the characters leap out of the book. The characters fill the room with mystery and adventure.

His voice makes the words wrap around my head like a crown. My eyelids begin to get heavy, and I start to slowly drift away into a dreamlike state. My father's reading voice makes me feel safe and warm inside. His voice continues to wrap a blanket of peace around me. His voice is my blanket of love, my compass home. It is encouraging, loving, and gives me confidence.

When he reads, his voice makes the words leap off the page in a book. It is my father's reading voice.

Savannah Krivanek, Grade 7
Salida Middle School, CO

Are You Ready?

I've always been intimidated by softball. Every game when my turn came up, I would pray to get hit so just maybe I could get on base, but for some reason today was different. The dugout was alive, the whole team was cheering me on while I waited to bat. As I walked up I looked at the catcher, who was down and ready, then there was the pitcher, who was waiting very impatiently. Her expression gave me the impression that she thought she was better, and if everyone else on my team hadn't hit off her, then I surely wouldn't. Man, was she wrong. I was tired of being pushed around, and I wasn't going to take it any longer!

I got up there and swung my bat like a dog running from a cat! Once I hit the ball, I ran until I felt myself get lower to the ground in order to slide. I'd never had this feeling before. Could it be the feeling of hitting your first home run??? Enthused and proud, I ran full of excitement into the dugout, knowing that I had done my team some good for once. My mom handed me water and gave me a pat on the back and said: "That was good but there's more to come."

Savannah Applewhite, Grade 7
Lindale Jr High School, TX

When Words Fail, Music Speaks

I love music. Music for me can block the world out. It can take me to a place where I can really think, a place where I can shut out the millions of imperfect things in my life. As soon as I plug my headphones in I can concentrate and think. I can think more creatively when I listen to music, and I am able to let go of what's bothering me.

Just one song can cheer me up or calm me down. A song can sometimes change my idea or thought believe it or not. Music is my own drug. When words fail music speaks. It's kind of crazy how music can have such power.

It can mess with your emotions too, sometimes in a good way and sometimes in a bad way. Some songs can make you laugh and cry at the same time all in the same rhyme. Music is great right? This is all how music can block the world out... music is like my own personal problem solver.

McKinley Mommer, Grade 7
Salida Middle School, CO

The Melody of My World

The softly ringing tone of a melody makes me stop and listen. There are different moods for different songs. One in a minor key might make me remember some of the several movies that I've seen placed in the desert. It might make me think of heat and tiredness. Another, such as the Star-Spangled Banner, would make me feel proud and strong, willing to do anything for America. Music brightens the world and makes it exciting and moving, not just staying the same for years and years. Music is a way to express yourself in ways that you could never have done before. Music is a part of nature itself, changing and going in the weirdest ways imaginable. Music can talk when your words fail you. Music is beautiful.

Ester Cox, Grade 7
Excelsior Academy, UT

How-To Shoot a Bow and Arrow

Have you ever wanted to shoot a bow and arrow? Have you wanted to hunt as quiet as a mouse? If so follow these few simple steps, and you can learn to shoot a bow and arrow.

For starters you need a bow, arrows, an open space, a target, and water. Now that you have supplies you are ready to shoot. First you need to go to your open space, and set up the target. Next, make sure nothing is in danger of getting hit. Then, once your area is clear position your arrow on your bow. Make sure your thumb is holding the arrow in place gently, so it doesn't move when you release.

Once your arrow is in place; pull the string back to your chin. It should feel tough at first, but as you shoot it will get easier. Next release; as you release you should here a slight pop. Finally you should see the arrow in your target. Depending on how many arrows and time you have you may repeat these steps.

Ah, the sweet smell of victory. I hope you feel proud of yourself. Have fun with this skill. It may come in handy.

Emma Harden, Grade 7
Lindale Jr High School, TX

Forgiveness

Forgiveness is a skill everyone must learn. There are many reasons why we need to forgive, such as saving relationships and keeping the peace. I forgava a friend to save our relationship when she did something very untrustworthy. It made me feel better to forgive her rather than to finish our friendship; thankfully, with forgiveness we are still friends today. In other words, forgiving is the best bet.

There are times I don't want to forgive my brother for annoying or teasing me. However, we love to have fun watching movies, playing video games, and eating junk food. If I did not forgive him for the little things, we wouldn't have as much fun together. Forgiveness is one thing in life that keeps all your relationships together, because all people have arguments. We need to be kind and be able to forgive people for their mistakes.

Jessica Hoffman, Grade 9
Foothills Academy, AZ

Hawaii

Swish! Swosh! The waves roll off the rocks. Hawaii's beaches are what make it such a beautiful place! There are so many things to do on the beaches, whether you like going to luaus, kicking back, surfing, building sand castles, playing beach volleyball, or going scuba diving. The beach is such a wonderful place to be on a gorgeous day! I love sitting back, relaxing, and just enjoying the waves hitting the sand! There are so many things to choose from at the beach, I have a hard time deciding what to do next! I think the most fabulous part of the beach is the luaus. At the luaus there is so much dancing, music, and great performers! The food there is magnificent! Hawaii is just one of the most exhilarating places to be!

Meghan Mansour, Grade 8
Foothills Academy, AZ

My Favorite Memory

The night of June 26, 2003 was magical. I think that's the best way to describe it because it's the day Phoenix Pittman, my baby brother, was born.

I rushed into the hospital room to meet my brother after my grandparents told me we could go in. We walked in and heard a loud, crying baby. I saw my mom holding the cutest baby I have ever seen! I was four years old when my dad told me "Layney meet your new baby brother." It felt amazing to see him with us.

My cousin Emma and I walked toward him and he grabbed our pinky finger and wouldn't let go. He held on for what felt like forever. Eventually he let go of Emma's finger, but he wouldn't let go of mine. It's like he knew I was his sister and that he loved me.

I will never forget the day when my brother was welcomed to the family, and that weird feeling I got in my mouth. Sometimes I wish I could go back to that day, because now he's really annoying, and he stole all my attention! Everyone can't help but love him though!

Layney Pittman, Grade 7
Lindale Jr High School, TX

My Sister

My sister, Bryce, influences me a lot. She is in 9th grade and runs cross-country. She is running varsity and she is the only 9th grader that runs with seniors. She has a letterman's jacket and lettered in cross-country and in FFA. She raises a pig. She is dedicated to school, cross-country, and FFA.

Sometimes Bryce can be annoying or irritating, but she is my sister. When she sets goals, she does them. She always helps me with my chores or sports. She is always helpful. The day I realized she influenced me was when she joined cross-country; she was always a good runner. She has improved a lot in cross-country and it made me want to do sports.

All because of her, I have done sports like volleyball and cross-country and I am going to do more. She is an amazing sister and the best one ever. One day I hope I can be just like her.

Sidney Velasquez, Grade 7
League City Intermediate School, TX

The Dog

The dog is an incredible and marvelous animal that is always ready to play and spray joyful slobber over your face. When your tasty, juicy food drops from the counter or the table, your dog is there, ready to help you clean up. They wag their tails and toss their toys; carefree animals, always happy, their slobbery smile is always present when you need to be cheered up. Dogs are faithful companions that will always be supporting you, telling you it really isn't so bad. Everybody should have a dog (unless they are so unfortunate as to have an allergic reaction to canine fur or drool) because dogs are wonderful pets. So, get yourself one of these wonderful, candid, slobbery, furry pets today. (It will never be too late.)

Denali Wilson, Grade 7
North Star Academy, CA

The Graceful Discipline

One of the oldest, and perhaps most widely known disciplines of dance is ballet. The dress code is much more traditional; a black leotard with pink tights is the standard. Much stricter than hip-hop, ballet emphasizes rigid rules and strict technique. The teachings are steady and ordered. Most ballet instructors teach close to the same curriculum, so no matter where a student attends class, she can rest assured that she is receiving the same education in ballet as others. Names of movements are consistent and accepted in most studios, and the origin of the majority of them are French, which adds to the regality and perfection by the way the words roll elegantly off the tongue.

Ballet accentuates that beauty in dance is simple, not vehement and startling like hip-hop. The easier the student can make her moves appear, the more enhanced of a dancer she becomes. Simple lines are stressed; a straight line is aspired from the top of the head to the tip of the toe. Gracefulness and ease of movement is a must in ballet. The goal of many ballerinas is to mimic the appearance and movements of a swan. Long necks and limbs are coveted, and the gracefulness esteemed. In fact, when ballet was first born, ballerinas were chosen based on their looks, and not on their authentic aptitude. It was only when society discovered how much expertise and practice it required to perform the meekest of choreography that it began to judge based on adroitness.

Alexandra Rae Theis, Grade 9
Saint Mary's Hall, TX

Happiness

It was written in our Declaration of Independence that all men are created equal, that they are endowed by their Creator with certain unalienable rights, and among these are life, liberty, and the pursuit of happiness. All people on Earth are created equal, and deserve the right of the pursuit of happiness. No matter what anyone may think, that is the truth. We may not realize this, but happiness is the basis of our lives. We depend on happiness, it is a critical emotion. Many of our actions take place based on whether or not we possess happiness. Without it, where would we be? There would be no importance to wealth, status, or charity, etc.

Different things make different individuals happy, it's just a well-known rule in society. Some people enjoy music, some enjoy writing. It's believed by many that the smallest things in life are the things that count. Buying a new puppy, rescuing a stray cat, knitting your grandmother a scarf — these are the things that make us happy. We all have a calling in life, and whether we answer that call depends on happiness. Many people do not live their lives to their full potential because they do not possess happiness.

What should be recognized in our lives is how happy one can be by helping others. This can bring so much joy and happiness it is almost unimaginable. Helping others is the key to happiness, however, it is your decision whether you wish to unlock it.

Gabby Peterson, Grade 9
South Jordan Middle School, UT

One Man Can Make a Difference

This is the story of my determination and my sacrifices to be the best and only the best. I strive to believe to succeed in all that I do. I made a promise to my coach and my fellow teammates to sustain and bolster my team. My baseball coach, Mr. Oscar Rodriguez, encouraged me to keep my head held high and to play with confidence. He has taught me not to cower in the shadows of fear and doubt, but to be audacious. He showed me the characteristics and necessity of being a good person, teammate, friend, and son. He planted the seed of faith in my life by his words and actions he displayed in my presence. He has been my baseball coach for the last two years in select baseball and with the St. Matthew School team.

Mr. Rodriguez is a great man on and off the field. He will have us pray on the way to a practice or a game. He tells me not to be abashed if I make a mistake but to go out and rehabilitate my game. Some of his players think he is too strict and tough and he can be sometimes, but he has taught me how to be a young man, how to always treat others with respect, and to always be aware of whom I represent. He is a legendary coach and role model to me in baseball and in my faith. I hope that I will be able to plant similar seeds in other people's lives like he did for me. I want to be able to encourage other boys and girls to go out and achieve their passions and desires regardless of what anybody else tells them they can or cannot do.

Cody Emmons, Grade 8
St Matthew Catholic School, TX

Music's in My Soul

Music has occupied a significant part of my life for as long as I can remember. Listening to music has provided an emotional cocoon, where I can feel safe and secure despite the tumult of my life. Occasionally, the commotion of my family's chaotic lives causes me to feel stressed. Between my older sister anxiously trying to decide where she will attend college, to my attention-demanding little brother singing and acting like a Broadway performer, it is easy for me to feel lost in my own home. When I need an escape, I dash up to my room, and turn on the radio or iPod. Music, to my ears, is like getting a massage — comforting and tranquilizing. Each song acts as a protecting blanket, providing an intimate relationship between the artist and me.

I was born with a love of music beginning with Music Masters class when I was three years old. In Middle School, I participated in Music Memory, a competition in which participants are asked questions about classical compositions and composers. I placed first in the regional contest and was selected to compete in the state competition that was unfortunately canceled due to the infamous Swine Flu scare.

Despite this bittersweet end to Music Memory, I have remained infatuated with music and hope one day to work as a music producer or talent scout discovering new artists and working with them to be part of their music and their professional journey.

Madeline Miller, Grade 9
Saint Mary's Hall, TX

The Odyssey

"The Odyssey" is an epic poem, it is greatly and intelligently written to fit the circumstances of some people's beliefs. Homer wrote this poem awhile back to give people an understanding of what it is like for Odysseus. Odysseus is out at sea to forage for food and to escape from Calypso's chambers. He is a son of the gods and is part of Olympus. He is out sailing the sea with his men unraveling mysteries of supernatural monsters causing mischief, and finding islands. The way that "The Odyssey" is written to pull you in with the first page of the poem, it makes you want to keep on reading. Everything about how it is written is perfectly spot on about what the people from a long time ago believed and what people still believe happened. Many people from Greece and areas around there, this is what they believe in and worship. Homer, being a believer, wrote this multipage poem about the gods and Odysseus. He wrote about Odysseus' journey, hence the name "Odyssey."

Odysseus is locked away in the depths of Calypso's Island as a love slave. He was broken out and given a crew and a ship to sail about and find islands and unobtained artifacts and creatures who roam the planet's islands and landmasses.

Some people may believe that the Odyssey is not an epic poem because they might not think that it is a true religion. However, they are incorrect because on the other side of the world this is what many of the people believe happened.

Eric Steffes, Grade 9
South Jordan Middle School, UT

The Internet

The internet, now since the invention of the internet, it has blown up since then and has taken all over the world. The internet can be used for a large variety of things. From emailing, to streaming movies, music, entertainment, etc. But most common for all people of all ages, using the internet to gather information. Now is it a reliable source? Could the internet be trustworthy to you? Does it provide good information? Yes, for an important reason. The internet is a great accessible source that can be accessed pretty much anywhere at anytime.

Thousands, even millions of websites are on the internet. Now what do people use the internet for? There is no specific reason, there are billions of different things you can find on the internet: pictures, movies, recipes, history, facts, and so much more. So what does this tell people? That the internet is a VERY advanced tool. For example, say someone needs to write an essay on "Benjamin Franklin." If you read a book on Benjamin Franklin you're only getting a certain amount of information that the so-called author provided. So in other words, you aren't getting the full details. But with the internet, you have access to EVERYTHING. Using multiple search engines that the internet provides, you can discover and find thousands of different links or websites about Benjamin Franklin. The internet gives you the whole package rather than just half of it.

Daniel Figueroa, Grade 9
South Jordan Middle School, UT

Cappy's Chips

The handmade potato chips served at Cappy's, in the center of Terrell Hills, are the most exquisite handmade potato chips ever created. When I eat a meal at Cappy's, I look around at the baskets of warm, handmade potato chips. I can conclude that I, myself, among others, love the potato chips more than any other side option. The generic French fries appear at every restaurant in town, no matter what type of food is served, but the potato chips are so uncommon that the sensation of a change is so exquisite. Potato chips, otherwise associated with yellow, overly salted, and fried until greasy, are made from locally grown potatoes and fried in organic oil, leaving behind the unappetizing associations. Once the potatoes arrive at Cappy's, they are sliced by hand, not too thin not too thick. Then the slices are tossed into the frying pan. The seasonings, salt, pepper, and herbs of perfect proportion are sprinkled atop of the chips. There are two unique things about these handmade potato chips, one is the optional but common, cheese melted to an ideal state on each chip. The other extraordinary thing about these chips is if they are not coated in cheese than ketchup dipping is highly recommended. Treated as a French fry, the chip with ketchup gives you the savory flavor of fries, but the crispy crunch of a chip. While examining the chips, no two are identical to each other; both have their own unique imperfections, making them delightful and delicious.

Olivia Nastala, Grade 9
Saint Mary's Hall, TX

Is Not Caring Easiest?

Under the dim lights, hot tears streaming down my pink cheeks, I witnessed the repulsive grinding of bodies between people who had never met. A horde of 1,500 people displayed vulgarities that disgusted me to my very core. My roommate in possession of the room-key, I had no retreat from the sight of my generation's societal plummet.

Society decays like a wilting flower before me, once a fresh and lovely bouquet, the rotting leaves of humanity made me wretch. Why have the unyielding stems of purity been pushed aside? Why does the youth of my generation tread with blind eyes? I do not understand their shameless display of the cherished flesh that they so irreverently expose, and their carnal motive condoned by a lack of parental prudence. When did it become acceptable to make such exhibitions of oneself? Perhaps my wholesome morals are what force me to so acutely see the impropriety in actions that have become today's norm, but then why is every other teenager not equipped with the same defense? My mother, who spent so many years explaining the straight and narrow path that one should presume, is the essence of my morality. I find the fault of such atrocities to weigh on the shoulders of the children's parents, for they are the societal threat. Lack of parental involvement and interest in their spawn is the true essence of our societal decline. The solution to our downfall remains as no more than a question: why do you not value your child?

Paige Livingston Lopez, Grade 9
Saint Mary's Hall, TX

The Seed That Built Me

Someone who has planted the seeds of faith in me is my grandma. Since I was born she was always there for me. She was there for my mom and me mostly after my dad left us. She has always yearned for me to do and be my best. She has always been very upright and will never tell me a lie.

She is always available whenever I just need to talk. Whenever she feels I'm doing something wrong she always tries to dissuade me into not doing it. She has a virtual effect on me that always keeps me spirited. I have never seen her being hostile towards someone or something.

She has always been very tactful even with the in-laws. My grandma is not inimitable, I have never detested my grandma nor will I ever. She has nurtured me since I was a fledgling.

My grandma is the only person I have ever been able to really talk to, like about how I'm feeling or if I like something or not. She understands. My grandma has planted the seeds of faith in me.

Kendall Schuchardt, Grade 7
St Matthew Catholic School, TX

Family

The thing that I value the most is my family. Everybody helps me so much and I do not know what I would do or where I would be without them. My parents support me in the sports I do and they have helped me so much with my schoolwork. They have paid so much money to feed me, put clothes on my back, put me in the camps that I have been in, and let me do the many sports I have done. My whole family is always there for me if I am upset or if I've just had a bad day and that is why I love them all so much! There are many people in my family and there are some people in my family that I haven't even met! I have received many letters and gifts from family members that live in Hawaii and in different parts of California, but even though I have not yet met them, we still get to keep in touch.

Ava Ocon, Grade 7
North Star Academy, CA

How to Straighten Your Hair

If you're going on a date and you notice you're having a bad hair day, then maybe you need to follow some simple steps.

If you have thick, long, and dry hair like me, you will need a straightener, mirror, hair clips, brush, and heat protector spray. First, you will need to brush your hair and get all the tangles out. Then you will need to pull up half of your hair with the clips. Next, you spray the hair that is down with the protecting spray. After that you can now start to straighten your hair, but be careful because it will be hot. You keep straightening your hair until you get it as straight as you want. Once you're done with that part of your hair, you do the same steps to the hair you had pulled up.

When you're done, your hair should be flat and look really pretty, so you are ready for your date.

Maddi Johnson, Grade 7
Lindale Jr High School, TX

How to Make a Bow

Do you like to wear bows? Would you like to learn how to make them? If you follow these simple steps, you will be able to make a beautiful bow.

To make a bow, you will need ribbons, scissors, twine, a hot glue gun, a lighter, some double-sided tape, and a hair clip. First, you have to plug your hot glue gun in and wait for it to get hot. While you are waiting, you have to pick your bow size and ribbons, depending on the color. After you design your bow, cut your ribbon at your desired length. Next, tape your double-sided tape on the end of the inside of the ribbon. When you have done that, take the white layer off and press down on to the other side of the ribbon so that it becomes a flat bow. Then, use a twine to bind the middle together. I would suggest fold it in to three sections. One you have done that, use the other piece of the ribbon and cut it at a length that will go around the bow and cover up the twine. Use a lighter to lightly light the ends of your ribbon to make sure it does not undo itself. Then, hot glue it around the bow, covering up the twine. Lastly, hot glue your bow on to your hair clip. Voila! Your beautiful bow is finished. When you have finished your bow, you will feel a wave of satisfaction in you. Wear it with pride. You should be proud that you have done such a hard and amazing task.

Once you have followed these instructions, you will be able to make a wonderful bow.

Christina Lee, Grade 7
Lindale Jr High School, TX

Hailstorm

I've been through some pretty crazy weather, but nothing worse than the hailstorm last year! Of all places for there to be a hailstorm, it was in Phoenix, Arizona! It was especially scary because both my parents were at work, so I was home alone with my brothers. We also had nowhere to go because in Arizona there are no basements and nearly every room in our home has a window. We were scared one of the windows might break.

It all began as a rainy day, then small pieces of hail began to fall. Before I knew it, the hail was coming down the size of golf balls. When I looked out the window, I couldn't see too far. It looked like a tornado was coming through. After about fifteen minutes it ended.

About ten minutes after the hail ended, my mom arrived home. She apologized for not being there to help us, but he was in a meeting that was about to finish when the storm started. It was so bad that the teachers there couldn't leave and had to wait it out. When the teachers came out of the room they were in, it was a mess of broken trees and ice.

Luckily there was one good result from the storm! The insurance company gave money for damages to our car and roof. With that money, we replaced our fifty year old roof and repainted our house. It goes to show that good comes out of bad.

Ella Sullivan, Grade 8
St Gregorys Catholic School, AZ

When I Met My Best Friend

You can never go wrong with a friend. Have you ever heard that before? When I was little I thought it was a bunch of ham. I have a totally different perspective now.

When I saw her wearing the exact same type of outfit as me, I knew we were destined to be great friends. When I walked over, I knew she was thinking the exact same thing. Every Sunday at church, I would complain because I was stuck with a bunch of boys and one girl who picks her nose. It was pure agony from the time I walked in to the time I walked out. The thing I realize, though, is that God didn't give me Peyton to save me from Miss Booger and her relatives. He gave her to me for a friend to tell my secrets to, a friend to cherish, and a friend to be there for me. I knew right then that when we would be old and wrinkly, she'd still be there for me. Now, being five, it's pretty self-explanatory that those weren't my exact thoughts. I was probably thinking "Hmm, who is she? Oh well! Oooh, I love her outfit." Now, I'm telling you this story because, though it has almost been ten years, she is still my best friend. That is something that will never be broken.

Some people think friends are like sand. When you finally have a grasp of them, they start to fade and slip through your fingers, just like your average teenage friendships. That doesn't describe the friendship that we have. She will always be there for me. Peyton will always be my sister.

Avery McMurray, Grade 7
Lindale Jr High School, TX

Cell Phones Are a Necessity for Children

Did you know that 60% of children over the age of 10 own a cell phone? It's true, but are children mature enough? Not all are, but I think it's a great tool to help kids understand responsibility. Cell phones are ideal for children who have working parents, or for those who participate in extracurricular activities. Sometimes a practice can run late. In these situations, children need to be able to contact their parents, and having a cell phone could make it easier to do so. I have had experiences where I needed a cell phone, and I couldn't reach my mom. One time, I got separated from my mom in the store. If I would've had a cell phone, I could have told her where I was, and we could have found each other quickly.

Cell phones can teach kids responsibility by keeping track of the phone, and taking care of it. It is a great tool for kids to keep track of their minutes and texts, and only use the limits they've been given. Children also need to recognize the real use for the phone. The real use should be for an emergency, although children can have fun with it.

Not all children should own a cell phone, but it's an ideal responsibility tool. Kids, if you want a cell phone, think about these reasons. Cell phones can be a significant help for parents and children alike.

Anya Brown, Grade 8
White Pine Charter School, ID

The Most Important Thing

The thing I consider most important in my life is my school. Without education, it would be really difficult to get a decent job. I want to work in the fashion industry as a photographer, stylist or editor when I grow up, but who would hire a girl without a degree? If I pay attention and do my work, however, I can, and will, get far in my life and my career when I'm an adult.

My school, North Star Academy, teaches me things outside of the textbook, as well. Some of those things are how to work in groups and get along with other people. I think these are really good skills to have, because then I can go anywhere and do my best to get along with anybody perfectly. I've also learned many great study habits at North Star, like time management and how to block out distractions.

This amazing school has taught me many things, from how whales evolved to why you shouldn't cheat. It's been a fantastic four years.

Nina Leopold, Grade 7
North Star Academy, CA

Why Are Dogs a Good Choice for Pets?

The dog is the most popular of all pets. They comfort, give friendship, and make the owner happy. They are good for any age, especially the elderly, because their children have moved out and they need someone to keep them company. Dogs also keep many safe. No matter what size the dog, it will protect you. For example, if there was ever a break in, the barking of a dog can scare the burglar away. Another occasion would be when walking the dog, and a suspicious person walks up, the dog can sense that they are up to no good and start barking, then tug on the leash to warn the person to walk away. Dogs can also bring the company of new people into your life. When petting dogs, they show their acknowledgment and appreciation of the person for petting and making them feel happy. Dogs are also very intelligent. They can tell when you're sad and need comfort from someone. They are capable of learning as many tricks as their owner will teach them. If trained properly, they will be the best pet you ever get.

Tehya Gibbons, Grade 9
First Baptist Academy, TX

Influence

On our way back from McDonalds we saw a homeless person on the side of the road asking for food.

When we were about twenty feet away from the homeless person, my mom rolled down the window and held her food out the window. She said, "I'm not hungry," and the homeless man had the biggest smile on his face and said, "Thanks!" The huge smile on his face made me want to smile and my mom and I both said, "You're welcome." When my mom did that nice thing for the homeless person, that influenced me in a positive way. I want to help others the way my mom helped the homeless person.

In the future, I hope to influence others in a positive way, too.

Nicholas Greer, Grade 7
League City Intermediate School, TX

Honesty

Honesty: the quality or fact of being honest; truthfulness, sincerity, or frankness. Honesty is an important attribute in our society for many reasons, one being that honesty is a form of judgment. Those who are honest tend to be thought of in a positive way. In everyday life, whether a person is attempting to get a new job or make a new friend, honesty leads to trust and forms a strong base for a good future. If one is known to be dishonest, they can't expect to be taken seriously. Honesty can be thought of as a reputation to uphold. Having an honest reputation could very well lead to a successful future filled with many opportunities. Much like the golden rule, "Do unto others as you would have them do unto you," be honest with others as you would want them to be honest with you.

Tatum MacCarter, Grade 9
Foothills Academy, AZ

Oliver

My cat is one of the most important things in the world to me. Some people see a cat as just a pet, but I see him as much more. I see him as a beautiful, sleek tabby. I see him as a light brown and cream cat. I see him as my cat. He and I are like two peas in a pod. Without him my life would be totally different. The scars he has left me remind me of the "good" times we have had together. The bond we share is indestructible. Nothing could shatter it. He is like the main prize in my treasure box. I am like a puzzle and he is the last piece. Sometimes he gets mad at me and avoids me, but he quickly comes back to my side, forgetting all the anger he had. When my cat comes and cuddles up to me, his pelt is so soft and comforting. I love my cat and always will, no matter what.

Tanner McCarty, Grade 7
Salida Middle School, CO

Where I Want to Go

The sound of wind blowing through the trees as if the wind whispers secrets because it knows something I don't. The clean, crisp air filling my lungs, taking away the stress. I want to go to Montana. I want to go to Montana because of the scenery. I want to see the tall pine trees and the running rivers. I want to see the lush green pastures and the beautiful open sunsets there. Another reason why I want to go there is to see the animals that live there. I'd like to see the horses that run burning the energy that's been bound up inside them. I'd also like to see the cattle that look so peaceful there, they take in the beauty of the world just by standing there and eating. So now you know why I want to see the lush beautiful things of Montana.

Jaqui Beres, Grade 8
Foothills Academy, AZ

Not Afraid

The person who influences you should change you in a positive way inside and out, and that person is my mom. One day we were on our way home, the sky was dark, and the mood was lifeless. The weather station was talking nonstop about a tornado watch in our area. I was very afraid, so I hoped changing the channel would take my mind off the weather, but every channel I went to, blaring horns would remind me of the horror.

I asked my mom some serious questions ending with, "Do you think we are going to die?" I was little then, so it sounded like a childish question, but to me it was very serious. My mom looked at me with a sweet smile and said, "If it is our time to go then it is our time to go, but the best part is that our family will be together in the great kingdom of heaven." I thought about what my mom had said and realized not to be afraid of death but to enjoy life.

The tornado never touched ground that day, but I learned something that still affects my life today. My mom influences me every day by being cool, calm, and collected in situations where I would most likely be afraid. My mom's attitude towards things inspires me to be who I am today. The person that influences you should change you in a positive way inside and out, and, for me, that person is my mom.

Kimberly Salazar, Grade 8
League City Intermediate School, TX

Adventures with Grandpa

When we find a book that we love, our imagination springs to life. Reading becomes physical and our mind tells us we are experiencing everything with the characters. This happened with my grandpa and I. Grandpa had a way with words that made the towering trees and undergrowth of Theodore Roosevelt's Island in the District of Columbia, feel like the banks of the Mississippi River.

Gingerly we snuck around the mysterious bend in that deep, dark wilderness. We knew they were going to jump out at us; we could feel it in the air. As we stepped around the last bend, they attacked, but we were ready, my grandpa as Mark Twain and I as Becky. We stepped into combat and fought for our lives with stick swords and spears. We fought like ancient knights, quick to defend and sly to attack. As we fought off the last pirates, my grandpa and I fell down in exhaustion. During this favorite adventure of mine, we acted out the novels written by Mark Twain, and we were in the middle of them.

A love of literature can create numerous experiences. As one's imagination ushers the reader into unmarked pathways, unreal adventures and wonderful worlds, they can feel as if they are within its pages. The journey provided through reading a good book, allows the reader to appreciate literature as a more full experience and to love it as well.

Mikelle Rogers, Grade 7
Excelsior Academy, UT

My First Important Concert

I remember when I performed with an orchestra in front of a huge crowd. The entire gym was filled. My parents and some of my friends' families were there. Before the orchestra played, we were part of the audience and listened to bands and choirs. When my turn came, I was nervous about messing up. The orchestra played three songs. I had to play a mini solo accompanied by some other people. I made a few mistakes but the audience didn't hear them. I did better than I thought I would. After we bowed and put away our instruments, we listened to more bands and choirs. I heard some exceptional music that day.

This experience has helped me become a better musician and audience member. It has also helped me understand music better. Now I am not as nervous before I perform. I have learned more songs that are harder and longer. I like playing and listening to music almost anywhere. Music is amazing because it does so much. I have learned it can influence everybody in their lives. I want to learn more music and be able to play many instruments, especially the string instruments. In my opinion, everyone should have the opportunity to perform so that they can try it out. It helps build your social skills. It can also help you find and show your talents.

Joshua Hales, Grade 7
Excelsior Academy, UT

T-Pud

My friend, Marquise would always joke around and say funny things when my friends and I talked about skating. If someone said something about Torey Pudwill, T-Pud for short, they would say his tricks were buttery, another word for really good. Marquise would say, "His tricks are so buttery. Every time I see him skate I want to run behind him and drag a piece of bread behind his skateboard."

We all loved Torey, but I knew that he was my favorite professional skateboarder. He created the reason for me to go outside and skate. I wanted to be like him. He was an influence to me. Torey is mostly known for being sponsored by Plan B skateboards and for his recent video, Big Bang. Some motivational things he would say would be, "Just go out and do what's fun to you." It made me think that skating isn't about trying to impress people by doing something you don't really enjoy. It's about going out there and entertaining people with something that entertains you.

Even though since I've moved here I haven't been able to skate as much as I used to, I realize I shouldn't give up. When Torey was ten years old, he attempted a trick off a ledge about eight feet high and fell and hurt himself really bad. Ever since then he's been doing better and better. This made me want to be able to do what Torey Pudwill does.

Jake Cleary, Grade 8
League City Intermediate School, TX

Family Struggles

I was diagnosed with leukemia when I was six. It all started when I kept getting sick. My mom finally told the doctor to do some blood work so that they could see what was going on. Well, the doctor and nurse cam running and said that I had to go to the hospital. When I got to the hospital, all of the nurses were doing things like putting an IV in my arm and hand and then they sent me to my new hospital room. The type of treatment that I had was called chemotherapy.

It caused all of my hair to fall out. Sometimes it would come out in chunks at a time. When this happened, I was struck with horror and so, so sad. Don't feel bad about these struggles that our family has had. They made our family stronger. The reason why I'm writing about this specific struggle is because once one person in a family gets leukemia, the whole family gets leukemia. The whole family has to go through all of the treatments, the whole family gets the whole package, not just one person. A lot of people are sorry for that one person, but really they should be sorry for the whole family. Have you ever heard the saying, "Struggles make your family stronger?" Well, you can look back on your own family struggles and see whether the saying is true or false. Because of the experiences that we have had, I know that the saying is true.

Saydies Griffith, Grade 8
Excelsior Academy, UT

Spiking

Volleyball allows me to release my emotions and stress, while causing me to have more confidence in myself. Since I first started playing around the age of ten, I have always been a middle front, also known as middle blocker. Whenever my coach directs me to perform in a different position, such as right back, I feel overwhelmingly confused and lost. However, when I am comfortably in my regular position, my individual job involves hitting — or spiking —and blocking practically every position.

I adore my role on the court because I get to spike. The exhilarating rush as I surge into the air and penetrate the doughy, pale ball, is inconceivable, the sense of power I experience, which I have never felt at any other time. With what seems a simple pop of the wrist, I send it tearing down. My hand stings from the forceful impact while my long legs come crushing down. I am very proud to have this ability and work tirelessly to improve it during volleyball season, and even occasionally after the fall has passed. All my diligence is worth it when we have a game. The entire crowd seems to hold their breath as I go up to take it and within that suspenseful moment, all the pressure is on me. I successfully spike the ball, and there is an eruption of cheer from the stands, the court, and the sidelines. Victory is ours.

Jenna Thomas, Grade 9
Saint Mary's Hall, TX

The Internet:
The New Way of Keeping People Connected and Informed

The internet is an emerging piece of technology used to make research and communication much easier and more simple for people in this current generation.

Most people have heard of the term "internet," and many people use it daily. In fact, the internet may be a very big part of a person's life or job. Many people run businesses directly from their computer. Managing emails and updating a website is crucial to having a successful business. Many people's lives would be drastically changed if they did not have the internet in their lives and so easily available to them. It would make communication and researching arduous and time consuming.

One reason why the internet is a good communication tool is it provides connection to places that would not be easily reached otherwise. The second reason the internet is a good resource tool is it provides access to everything on the web right at one's fingertips at any time of the day. The third reason it is a good resource tool is it provides information on almost every subject one can think of.

The internet is so important to people's lives today since it keeps people connected and allows access to information instantaneously. We are living in a very new technologic world.

Brianna Romero, Grade 9
South Jordan Middle School, UT

To Write

My pencil scratches rapidly on the page. I am transported to a world of adventures, where I walk beside the characters I created: only because I write. Characters are rejoicing over victories, sword fighting to their dooms, or flying spaceships into the unknown, this happening in the same story. Courageous characters stranded on a hot deserted island or pampered characters living in an unreal paradise, maybe both. These warriors and princesses have a purpose, to fulfill their adventures. Their adventures are really stories that are written by me. I watch them think and see them going on these adventures. Little do they know I am their creator. I see the big picture, which is the rest of their lives. I know what will happen: only because I write.

I see the horrible defeats and the glorious triumphs. My ideas splash upon the page with colorful words that revive my characters. I see my characters work together and then split up to fulfill their own purpose. I, the creator, write what they do and how they do it. I create their personalities and how they think, only with pencil and paper. To me the words make them jump off the page and come to life. They don't know their world is made on paper, no clue they have a creator. That creator is me. I am powerful in my writing world. I control everything: only because I write.

Brenna Rhiness, Grade 7
Salida Middle School, CO

Trials Grow Character

I am going to tell you one of my lifetime experiences and how it has taught me determination. My two older sisters were coming home from a soccer game at the Olympic oval one night when they and three other girls were hit head-on by a drunk driver. My sister Shannon was able to get out and call my parents with a shattered collar bone. My other sister, Lauren, was trapped inside the car. After a couple of hours, they finally got her out and flew her to Primary Children's Hospital. Once there, she went through several hours of surgery. She fractured her femur and practically destroyed her ankle. They both went through many gruesome physical therapy treatments, and Lauren went through several surgeries after that. They both were much stronger than I was. I was only seven at the time and I didn't know what was going on, so I was really scared. All I knew was that they were really hurting.

Both of these people shaped me into the determined person that I am. I think that being determined means that you will do something, and you won't let anything get in your way. Anyone can do this by setting a goal and succeeding. I learned that if you go through a tragedy, the attitude you have and the amount of determination that you have helps determine your recovery time.

Andrea Howsden, Grade 8
Excelsior Academy, UT

Cheer

"Life is not about waiting for the storm to pass, it is about learning to dance in the rain." My life revolves around cheer and dance. When I dance I feel like all my problems go away. Dancing makes me feel like I can do anything.

Cheerleading is not as easy as some people think. It is very exciting but also very competitive. One thing I love about cheer is meeting new people. When there is a new girl it makes our family even bigger. We are all very open with each other. Cheerleaders usually work together a lot. If we do not work together, a lot can go wrong.

I love cheer because it lets me be myself. I can bring myself out in competitions. Competitions have always been my favorite. On a competition day I wake up at 6 am. Competition days are always very long. You are with your team the whole day. Every second you get to practice, you do.

Game days are not as busy as competition days. I do like game days very much though. On game days we would practice in the morning. We usually do last minute touches. We work together all day. Team work is a huge thing in cheer. When I'm on the field cheering I feel like I can do anything.

Cheerleading is the one thing I lean back on. When I feel down I get up and dance. When I feel lonely I dance. When I dance I feel like I can do anything.

Jessica Esqueda, Grade 8
Santa Clara Elementary School, CA

My Aunt

Influence, what does that mean to me? My aunt is a person who never gives up and is willing to help people no matter what. She influenced me last summer and showed me nothing is impossible.

The summer of 2011, I went up to my aunt's countryside sky-blue house. That week I learned about taking care of horses and riding these lovely animals. I wanted to care for horses all the time, but I didn't have one. Every day I would groom my aunt's horse, Sissy, who has a white coat and is half saddlebred/half Arab. Then I'd put her saddle on and a bridle. Finally, when I'd finish all the preparations, I'd ride her in the large red dirt arena. Throughout the week I would ride her, groom her, and do everything with her. We would ride through the soft green grass or the brown red dirt. If only I could ride more at home, I thought, but I didn't have supplies; I didn't have a ranch and I didn't have a horse.

Then one day after lunch, my aunt found a club called Pony Club on the computer; it was a place where all sorts of people, young and old, rode these large, strong animals. My parents learned more about it, and later that year around Christmas I received riding lessons at Bay View Equestrian Center. One day, I dream that I'll own a black horse with a white star on its forehead, and maybe I will.

Rebecca Eckhardt, Grade 7
League City Intermediate School, TX

Internet as a Tool

The internet is a modern encyclopedia; it is one of the best ways to figure something out. There are hundreds of different search engines to help you, and many of them you can ask direct questions and get direct answers. This can be helpful with essays for school, no matter the subject. Also you can keep in touch with friends who have moved away. Other times you might need to know some fact that is important for an argument or just out of curiosity. The internet is the very best place for all the above and more.

Not only can you use it for writing purposes but it can be used for social things. An example of this is, once a girl was really good friends with another little girl in about second grade, but the little girl moved away. Eventually, the girls grew into young women and almost forgot about one another. Because they both had a Facebook they became friends on it. Now the two girls are talking more and are good friends again. Another way the internet is useful is it is a great way to stay in contact over short absences. In conclusion, the internet is a very good tool to use for work and essays. Also it can be a very useful social opportunity to find lost friends, help sick friends, and talk with your boss and coworkers. The internet has lots of information that can help you find small facts that you could need.

Brimmley Nielsen, Grade 9
South Jordan Middle School, UT

Asperger's Syndrome

When I was 3 years old, I was diagnosed with an autistic spectrum disorder called Asperger's Syndrome.

Asperger's Syndrome is a developmental disorder that makes it hard for me to interact with other people. For example, it's kind of hard for me to say something to someone without sounding stupid. Sometimes I wish after I say something and people look at me funny that I could erase their memory of what I just said. It's also weird for me to look at someone's eyes when I am talking to them.

School is kind of hard because it's difficult for me to concentrate and to write (I don't like pens because I usually make a bunch of mistakes and can't erase them and I think crossed-out words just look ridiculous). I don't speak, read, or write cursive. And I have a hard time making friends.

I get annoyed easily when someone is breaking rules or doing something that I don't think they should be doing. I like strict routines and it bothers me when there is a change in plans, unless it's a good change, like less homework.

Thankfully, as part of my Asperger's, I also have some special gifts, like singing, drawing, and memorizing. I also have a great sense of humor. Although I may be different, I hope that you will look past those differences and see me for who I am, because, like everyone else, I just want to be loved.

Brenden Krogh, Grade 7
Excelsior Academy, UT

The Wizard of Oz

The crowd clapped; the lights dimmed. My hands were shaking; I was shivering. Would I forget my lines? The seats were crowded with people, all squished together like sardines in a can. My family was in the back, waiting. Everyone was wishing me good luck behind the curtains. It was March 13, 2011. Let's back up. About two months before, the drama club had declared the audition date for "The Wizard of Oz." My family told me that I should try out for Dorothy. I auditioned, unaware that acting was fun. I waited nervously for a week, until the outcomes came. When I saw the results, my mouth dropped into a comical "o." I got the role of Dorothy! For two months, we rehearsed our lines until we memorized them. I became close friends with the actors. A week before the opening show, we got our outfits. When I tried mine on I began to feel like I really *had* become Dorothy. Finally the week of showbiz came. I was really nervous. I went up on the stage and started acting. My worries melted away. It was amazing! We all acted and sang our hearts out. We got a standing ovation, a moment to remember. My friends bring up the memory every once in a while, and we laugh and smile at the fun we had during "The Wizard of Oz." This moment changed my life. So now, I'm always ready to listen for my acting cue — "Lights…camera…action!"

Beverly Fontaine, Grade 8
St Joseph Catholic School, CA

Volleyball + Me = Love

Giving up isn't the answer, trying your hardest is the answer. Volleyball is one of my favorite sports. I have always been very athletic and I have always loved volleyball. It is just a sport I have enjoyed playing since I was young and eventually became really good at it. I am just super excited that I have a sport that I really like and can have so much fun while playing.

Playing volleyball is so much fun I can play all around the court in different positions, like passing, setting, hitting, and although I am short, blocking. My favorite position to play is setter, the reason being that you are always moving and you always get second pass. You also get to play front row and hit. Playing volleyball is a part of my life that I absolutely love.

I started playing volleyball when I was really little. My first volleyball team I played for was at my school in fifth grade. I have gone on playing volleyball for my school for three years now. I will be graduating and going on to high school to play volleyball yet again. I really love volleyball, so last year I started playing for a club team. I have improved immensely and I will continue to play.

Volleyball is a sport that really helped me be the athlete I am today. I love volleyball and all the people I have met while playing! Volleyball is the best sport in the world and I hope to continue to play until there is a day when I cannot play at all.

Alyssa Holtke, Grade 8
Santa Clara Elementary School, CA

The Fatal Glass

The ocean breeze is crisp in the early morning as I walk down the beach. All is serene and calm as a relaxed setting takes its place until…ouch! A piece of glass cuts my foot.

As an Islander, this bothers me because not only must people go to the Emergency Room to get stitches and receive shots, but the glass bottles also affect our wildlife. The Center for Marine Conservation lists most common debris found on beaches with glass shards at the number 5 slot.

When the tides come in at night, all the partying done that day on the beach gets swept away out to the ocean. Glass bottles remain intact until they hit a rock or are crushed by the surf, sending the shards to the ocean floor. The sun, the next day, reflects off the glass bottles pieces and sea life often becomes attracted. In the end, a fish or a sea turtle will eat the remains of the glass bottle and the creature dies.

Statistics show that, on average, 725 glass bottles are accumulated over a week on just one beach. So if a glass bottle were to shatter into perhaps 100 pieces, and only 75 of those pieces were large enough to kill a creature, then about 54,375 sea creatures will die weekly.

It isn't fair to innocent sea creatures to have to live with our wastes. The ocean and the beach is their home, and we are destroying it little by little.

Taylor Roper, Grade 9
First Baptist Academy, TX

A Little Inspiration

Music is a thing that you need in life. It's something that lets you escape; it takes you places you never thought you would go. When I am in a bad mood, I find myself shoving in my headphones and taking a little sweet escape into the world of creative, senseless, inspirational music. To me, it is a matter of how you respond to the world. I honestly think that music can bring a smile to your face, bring you down into the deep, painful torture, or make you feel better in any situation. Music is something that feeds the soul; it brings it to peace.

Music is something that expresses how you feel. For example, think of a scary movie. Something dramatic is happening. They play some dramatic music. Everything gets intense. What I find myself doing when I am mad is playing rebellious, hard rock n' roll. The music you listen to reflects your personality. For example, if you listen to Mozart or Bach, you are probably a hard-working, industrious person who is very successful.

Music is a needed essence in life. It's something humanity cannot live without. Listening to music can get you out of any funk you're in. It always works for me. Music is a ticket to escape from life for a while. People say they wish magic was real, but it is real! It's music and laughter. Music is like medicine. It makes you feel better anytime, anywhere.

Camilla Uphill, Grade 7
Excelsior Academy, UT

My Mice and Me

Mice are extraordinary creatures to observe and have as pets. I have two pet mice: a boy and a girl. The boy gets scared easily and the girl will let you hold her.

Mice can be fun to have around but other times they can be annoying. They both sleep during the day so they are up all night. My mice bite on the bars very loudly. They constantly run on their loud and squeaky wheels all night. They are both very strange; the girl sleeps in her own food bowl. The boy will not let you touch him but he will bite anything.

My mice can be naughty at times. The boy escaped his cage a couple of times. He would stay near the walls and behind the furniture so we could not find him. I tried to grab him but mice can jump high and run fast. I finally caught him but I switched his cage so he could not escape anymore. Mice are escape artists.

Mice can really stink up the house. I have to clean their cages every two weeks. When I try to take them out, it is very hard. The girl grabs onto the cage bars when I grab her tail. I always have to pull her off. The boy will not let me grab his tail. Even when I do grab his tail he grabs the bars, too. Mice are stronger than you think.

My mice may be hard to handle at once, but they are fun to have. They are both adorable and fun to watch.

Samantha Ramos-Barba, Grade 8
Santa Clara Elementary School, CA

What Is Love?

Love is the emotion that cannot be concealed inside the human body. It's a sense of security. It's knowing that you're not alone and then someone will be there to catch you when you fall or to take care of you when something happens. Knowing that someone loves you is more than a feeling, it's something that I can't explain, something you have to find out for yourself.

Love is a force that drives mankind into doing the unthinkable. There's no telling what people will do next when they're in love. Think of a time you were in love. Think of how you felt, how you acted. When you're in love, you act and think and feel completely different than who you really are. Love clouds the mind and makes it seem like nothing else matters. If you have never been in love, it's hard to imagine what it's like. There's no use trying to imagine it, because there is no feeling like it. It's hard to describe. Love isn't just a relationship between two people, it's much more than that. It's a bond of trust expressed in many ways. It's unlike anything you have ever imagined.

Love can be beautiful or a disaster waiting to happen. Love is everything to some and nothing to others. Some people don't believe in love. Some say it's not for them. There are 7 billion people on this Earth and one of them is meant for you.

Mandy Medsker, Grade 8
Excelsior Academy, UT

The Time I Won a Purple Ribbon

My first year in Miners Ravine 4-H, I got a purple ribbon. A purple ribbon is for a Supreme Champion. It was my fourth fair and I was only eleven. To tell you all about it I have to start from the very beginning. My mom was in the same 4-H group as I am, and she showed sheep. When I was old enough to do my own sheep project, my mom gave me her sheep. We registered them under my name, so that I could show their lambs. You can only show a sheep less than two years of age, and she was three. On January 21, 2009, my first lambs were born. Gabby, Reagan, and Kora are their names and their mom is named Sassy. I worked with them all the way through to the Placer County Fair. After Placer County, I worked with them even more. Then Gold County Fair came!!! We washed, sheered, and groomed our four sheep. I showed in market class, showmanship, and breeding. When the breeding classes started, I was nervous because there were more people in this classes than last fair. There were six of us in the ring. The judge felt each animal and placed them first to last. My sheep were first and third. There were only two of us in the Supreme Champion drive. In the Supreme Champion drive the judge chooses Supreme Champion and Reserve Supreme Champion. The judge picked my ewe as Supreme Champion. This means my sheep was best overall this year.

Cheyenne Sanchez, Grade 7
St Joseph Catholic School, CA

The Mystery of Love

Love: one word, many meaning, each different. What is love? Love is a red rose, a burning fire that rages inside of you, a warm hug on a cold, dreary day that makes the world a wondrous place.

Love takes many forms. It is a feeling, an emotion that drives your mind to do the extraordinary and almost impossible. It is shown in our culture, music, and stories. It is also seen in our actions and how we behave with each other. Love can compel us to show the best of ourselves and the worst. To me, there is love in everything. It has no limits and we all share love of something; love of knowledge, love of art, love of nature.

I lay awake some nights wondering about love; why it is so powerful. I stare out the window of my room at the starry-eyed night and its pale glowing moon. Why does love begin ruthless wars, tear families apart and put them back together like the pieces of a jigsaw puzzle, and melt hearts as cold as ice as well as freeze them back? It can give hope and destroy just as easily. Like time, it comes and goes faster than the eye can blink. Why? The answer is different for each person asking the question. For me, the answer is simple: love can only cause us to care, it cannot care itself.

Hannah Bennett, Grade 8
Excelsior Academy, UT

A Girl's Inspiration

Picking out clothes to me is like a fashion designer making a new outfit or a model walking down the runway. Picking out clothes is what I love doing, just like a designer or a model loves his/her job, but to me, it's not a job, it's something I love. In the morning when I wake up, BANG! It hits me. I find myself wondering, What am I going to wear today? I wish I could pick everyone's outfit that they're going to wear that day. Wearing casual jeans or something dressy and nice are two different things. I always get pulled between both of them. It's especially fun because I have a large variety of clothes to choose from. What color? Red, orange, yellow, pink, blue, purple, green or maybe even black or brown, who knows? I enjoy picking out clothes so I can express myself through my outfit. My favorite part of this process is picking out my shoes. Do I want something to match my outfit or make it pop? After I'm done picking out my creation, I put it on, but wait, I'm missing something: accessories. Necklaces, bracelets, earrings, which one? I might as well wear all of them. Finally, I'm done with my choice of style. I look and feel great about my outfit. Once I get to school, it doesn't matter to me what other people think about my outfit. It's who I am, and my outfit represents me and my style.

Aspen Lofton, Grade 7
Salida Middle School, CO

Autumn Nights

There is no night more inspiring than an autumn night with its serene ambiance and its slightly humid feeling. An omnipotent conductor summons his musical ensemble, so that one can hear crickets chirping their familiar song and animals scurrying through the fallen leaves. The crisp air makes the overall atmosphere feel pure and light. Energy wells up inside of me, inviting my nocturnal musings. I feel as if I can distribute my ideals and visions as broadly as the stars scattered across the sky, needing to be recognized and embraced before they extinguish forever into obscurity — a mysterious obscurity that evokes sensations of passion and awe.

The melancholic beauty of bare trees wilting as if in anguish over the loss of their stunning orange leaves is absolutely unrivaled. Each leaf on the ground represents our hopes, disappointments, and displays of perseverance that only we as individuals can identify. These "leaves" of our positive and negative experiences both enrich our lives: the negative ones push us to surpass ourselves; while the positive ones keep us hopeful for the next opportunity to seek in the first place.

There is no better time than an autumn night to resolve to appreciate the splendor of nature, of life — a truly exquisite masterpiece that no painting can fully capture.

Raquel Diaz, Grade 9
Schurr High School, CA

Nevada Vacation

In the summer of 2011, my dad, my brother Max, and I went on a hunting trip to Nevada. My dad had an antelope tag, and Max and I went along for the adventure. We packed up all the things that we would need for the hunt and drove to the Nevada wilderness. About 100 miles from our destination, our ATV trailer broke down; the bearings in the wheel popped out, and we couldn't fix it. This happened on Saturday evening, and all of the shops in the closest town were closed on Sunday. We called a tow truck and we stayed in a hotel for two nights. Monday morning we had the trailer fixed as fast as we could, then we headed back on the road. Our destination was Austin, right in the middle of the state. We found a nearby campground located right adjacent a beautiful stream. The next morning we started to look for some antelope but we didn't see any until it was near dark. We tried to sneak up on them, but they got spooked and ran off. That night, it got really windy and our tent almost blew over. For the next few days we hunted unsuccessfully. We drove our ATV up into the mountains where we met a Peruvian sheepherder named Nico. We also caught some tasty trout and our dad eventually shot a nice antelope buck. Despite the bad weather and trailer breakdown, we drove home extremely happy.

Winston Fitzmorris-Johannes, Grade 7
St Joseph Catholic School, CA

Life Goals

I would love to be very successful in life. I would like to graduate high school with a 4.0 G.P.A. because of my dad. I live very well, I would love to end up as successful as my dad. He graduated college with honors and a 4.0 and I would love to be just as successful and even more, so that I can make him proud to be my father. I want to give my kids the life my dad gave me.

I would also like to go to any college. I would like to go to M.I.T., which is like Harvard for engineers. That would be a dream. All the best engineers come from M.I.T. There I would like to earn my Masters in Material Engineering and graduate with honors and a 4.0 like my father. I would then like to become a scientist for a college, discovering new materials, and also start my own business. I have always dreamed of inventing cars and having them sponsored and built. I also want to have my own brand called C.T.S. and have t-shirts and shoes, etc. I also want to have a golf ball brand.

These dreams are extremely difficult to achieve. I know you need hard work, discipline, and organization. I have already achieved this and work hard every day at school, and I currently have a 4.0. I would like to continue this throughout school. I just need to make sure I don't lose sight of my goals in life.

Tomas Juvera, Grade 8
Excelsior Academy, UT

Board on Snow

When I go down that amazing hill, I feel the wind break in my face with its winter chill. The adrenaline takes over and I go on overdrive. My favorite time to go snowboarding is when the snow hits you smack in the face. Some of the most amazing experiences can come from one soft white surface to another. Also, one of my favorite noises is the hard compacted snow against the also-hard layer of a snowboard. That is just music to my ears. Another great thing about snowboarding is that I live right by Monarch Mountain. My most favorite thing about snowboarding is that I don't have to go to town or the mountain. I just have to wait for it to snow, and that is not too very uncommon, seeing as that we live in Colorado. Colorado can be a great place for a lot of things, but especially snow activities. See, Coloradans were born and raised in snow, and as long as they live in Colorado, they will die in it. So that is a great benefit of living in Colorado. Also, many Coloradans have many spots to do these amazing snow sports. They can also be a very good way for me and family to stay fit and connected. Also, just because it is very fun to me, that doesn't mean it can't be dangerous. It can be very easy to fall off your snowboard and hurt yourself, like I have done many times myself. This is a great activity and sport because of all of these reasons.

Logan Murdock, Grade 7
Salida Middle School, CO

Him

I think I'm in love with my gorgeous someone. His face is so cute, and I love his personality, but his eyes look straight through my heart. I love his baby blue eyes; they make my stomach twist, turn, and flip. His eyes make him the most handsome guy on the face of this earth. When I look into his eyes, it makes me feel like I can't breathe. His eyes just knock the air out of me. His eyes: the perfect shape and color. Those seeing devices always make me smile, even on days were all doom breaks loose. The color of his peepers just fascinate me. They are the most perfect blue I've ever seen. Why did he get blessed with those gorgeously piercing eyes? If he didn't have those eyes, he wouldn't look as good as he does; not saying he would look bad or anything. He wouldn't be the guy he is without those baby blue breath-takers. You can feel them looking at you in a jam-packed room of a million people. Those eyes will make you smile when worst comes to worst. When you feel like you need to cry, just remember those baby blue eyes. His eyes are like pain killers, I just need to look into them, and boom, the pain is gone. The days that he wears blue shirts are when those eyes show their true color. Staring in his eyes for long periods of time makes you fall more and more in love with him. I just can't resist those gorgeous blue blinders.

Montana Moncivaiz, Grade 7
Salida Middle School, CO

Why Jesus Is Important to Me

Even though it could be my family or my pets, Jesus is the most important to me. Jesus came to this Earth to save the sins of the world, and He was born sinless. One day, He was walking along, and spotted John the Baptist baptizing people. When John got to Jesus, he wondered why Jesus wanted to be baptized. But, John baptized Him anyway, and as soon as Jesus came up out of the water, a dove flew down from Heaven and a voice from God spoke. Amazing isn't it? This is truly amazing, because even though Jesus was without sin, He still was baptized anyway.

Jesus did many miraculous miracles, and He told so many parables, (stories), along with His teachings. Everybody that has known about Jesus, and accepted Him, loved Him very much. But one day, Roman soldiers came to arrest Jesus, and brought him to Pilate, (The Roman ruler). People who did not accept Jesus were yelling "Crucify Him, Crucify Him!" So, they did, and they hung Him on the cross. Being crucified was a very horrible thing. Now, Jesus could have walked away, but, instead He chose to stay because He loved us and wanted to save us from sin. But, on the third day He rose from the grave! So, Jesus truly is the most important person to me, because He loves us and saved us from the sins of the world.

Shinaiya Ferguson, Grade 9
First Baptist Academy, TX

The Joy Fishing Brings

Fishing has always inspired me. The skill in catching a fish, and the beauty the creature has, makes me happy just to think about. Fishing has been my favorite ever since I got my first rod and reel. It is the joy of the nice strong tug you get, and the fight you must win to land the beautiful creature. Knowing that I'm catching big old fish on a fly I made inspires me, and fills my mind with joy. The beauty of the bright pink band that runs down the rainbow trout's body or the fascination that comes when I see the dark orange speckles of a big old river brown trout is amazing. There are so many different types and sizes of fish, that the next catch could be a record breaker or a brand new type. It's amazing how smart the fish can be, and how tricky it can be to catch a trout or any fish from a river. You have to have just the right set up. The fly needs to be in just the right position, with just the right depth, and the right length of leader. Fishing seems to be magical. It makes all my stresses of the day disappear. My thoughts seem to wash away down the stream. The only things in life are just the fish, the river, and I. The only thing that I'm concentrating on is the pattern of the water. No matter what the circumstances are, I will always enjoy fishing. The beauty of the fish will always be in my memory.

Kaden Sites, Grade 7
Salida Middle School, CO

My Lyrics

Every note, chord, or word I play is the voice of life. It's the beauty it brings, that makes me want to sing along or write a song. Everybody can write words and turn it into a poem, I can too, but I start from a tune. I love to bring words and a tune together, and ta-da, a beautiful song for you. So you can say I'm a writer, or a song writer. I'm like a great author who can never stop writing. A song is like a flower. When it blooms it can surprise you, and when a bee comes to collect pollen, it takes the song and shares it with everybody else. When rain comes down, it makes that song grow. Like an athlete likes to kick, throw or hit a ball, I like to throw lyrics onto a page. People say I'll never make it, but I always say "watch me." Just like a tune stuck in your head, I have a voice that tells me a tune and words, but I have the opportunity to put them together. I would not be alive without the music I write. When I write a song, it just comes to me somehow, and I know how to put it with a tune. Someday, I will be singing my songs, not somebody else's song, my song, So many choices in life. You can be a math whiz, technology specialist, musician, doctor, makeup artist, or an engineer, or even a super hero, but I choose to be a song writer. Someday, somewhere, somehow, someone will have my lyrics stuck in their head.

Kyndall Newell, Grade 7
Salida Middle School, CO

Being the New Kid

Do you know how hard it is being the "new kid" who doesn't know anybody? I know how that feels, because I have been that kid a couple of times. Like the first day of kindergarten, the first day of school, the first day of school, again, after moving, and then moving again. You should always be nice to the new kid no matter who they are and how they act. Being the new kid is kind of hard, because you don't know how the people treat you and it's scary not to know anyone.

I have friends all over the world. I used to live in Germany for 7 years and I went to German kindergarten. In kindergarten it's very easy to make a new friend by talking to one another and by sharing common interests. That's how I met my best friend, who I visit every summer. We keep in touch by Skype, or by emailing each other.

When I was 7 years old, my family moved to Alabama, where I went to a new school and lived in a new neighborhood. I soon made many friends: we played, and talked, and had sleepovers. I am still friends with them. Leaving Alabama was the hardest, but the best 4 years of my life. The people were very nice to me and my family. Being the new kid can be difficult. So the next time a new student comes to your school, be friendly to them and help them.

Jennifer Howa, Grade 8
Excelsior Academy, UT

My Trip to Monterey

We had a great vacation to Monterey with my cousin Karissa coming down from Washington. It all started when we drove down to Sacramento to pick Karissa up from the airport. After we picked her up from the airport, we headed down to the Carmel Mission. We looked around at all the gardens and took lots of pictures. Then, we went to the Fisherman's Wharf. At Fisherman's Wharf, we went into many different stores and shops. We also went seal watching, and saw five seals and a jellyfish. After Fisherman's Wharf, we went and checked into our hotel. After about an hour of relaxing, we headed down to the Boardwalk. While we were there, we went on lots of fun rides. My favorite ride was the sky ride. You ride it from one side of the park to the other. The view was amazing with the sunset on one side and the beach on the other. Then, we went to Chili's for dinner. I had quesadillas, and for desert I had a brownie. Then, we went back to the hotel. The next day we went to the Monterey Bay Aquarium. There were so many animals, including jellyfish, flamingoes, sea horses, sharks, and my favorite, sea turtles. Then we went to the gift store and bought lots of souvenirs. After the aquarium, we left Monterey. I had such a great time, and the thing that made my whole vacation better was going with my favorite cousin Karissa.

Tori Reyes, Grade 7
St Joseph Catholic School, CA

Are You Thinking About College Yet?

Many students have not given one thought towards college. They have not thought of majors, minors, or even where they are going to go.

Often students hear teachers saying, "Don't wait 'til senior year to look for a college. You need to start now." But how many students have really taken their advice?

Some students may then say, "They are wrong, why should I look at colleges now? I still have four more years." They do not realize how fast four years go by.

So, students, you should start looking even if you don't know their majors or minors yet. If you might be living on campus make sure to check out the dorms, to make sure they are comfortable. Also if you enjoy activities, check to see if there are clubs or organizations around the campus that interest you. So find a place that is comfortable for you because you may be there for many years.

Many students may still say, "Who should I start looking now, I have plenty of time? What is the use in looking if I don't know my majors or minors?" And I, from a personal standpoint, would say, "Everything! If you want a good future, you need a college that is good for you." So start thinking and looking now. You might even enjoy it!

Jasmyne Perry, Grade 9
First Baptist Academy, TX

The Work of Disabilities

I think that people should learn more about disabilities. It is very important to know what a disability is, and people should know that every person living to this day has some sort of disability. Also, everyone should know what their disabilities are.

It is very important to know what a disability is. It could be anything. It could be something that you might be able to change. If you could change it, then it would make your life better.

Every person living today has some sort of disability. Everyone has a disability because we wouldn't learn from anything if we didn't have them. Also, if we didn't have them then no one would have any problems. We all need disabilities because without them, we would not have anything to work on in life.

Everyone should know what their disabilities are. If you don't then you won't know what to work for. If they are extreme disabilities, then you should know what they are because you may need serious help. I believe that disabilities are important, and if you don't, then I hope that someday you will.

Evan Pehrson, Grade 7
Excelsior Academy, UT

Masterful Motivation

We can be inspired to do great things; we just have to find the right motivation. I have been inspired by music. What is music to you? A sound? A feeling? To me, it is that and much more. Music is how I express myself and is a passion of mine. Over the past couple years I have learned to find joy in playing several different instruments. My first instrument was the piano. I played it until 4th grade. During that time, my mom was always pushing me to be better. I was like all children; angry because I wasn't doing as well as I wanted to but not willing to put more time into practice. So the next year, in 4th grade, I started the cello, thinking I would be better at that. I loved it but never had motivation so I didn't do as well as I could have. The next year it was the viola, but with the same result. My mom would not let me quit, but I wasn't getting better. This year, I committed to playing the cello in my school orchestra. I am graded on my practice time and am a perfectionist with my grades, so I practice 100 minutes a week, no matter what. So finally, I have the proper motivation to practice and play as well as I can each day. If you want to be a good musician, I advise you to find the right motivation for you to practice effectively.

Porter Loveless, Grade 7
Excelsior Academy, UT

My Peaceful Terror

His head snapped up. He turned to the right and looked as if he had hit some invisible wall…of smells. My dog walked to the place I had been and followed my scent, or so my dad told me. My dad had taken my wild-eyed, fanatic dog Chase to the lake to swim that day. So this was the reason I didn't expect a muddy dog or my dad back so soon. At that time I was in the woods in my backyard, looking for some solitude and a place where I could sit and think. Chase suddenly came barreling towards me from behind like a runaway locomotive of fur. I didn't see him until he was almost upon me, so I flat-out screamed. How weird it was to see myself scream like a city girl when I have grown up amongst nature. Chase is my fat, one-hundred pound Golden Retriever, and often he forgets his massive size. He has the appearance of a golden lion with large teeth but kind, sensitive eyes, and perky ears. Every day he is the one there, guiding me. Today he charged, happy to see me after being gone. He ran down the hill, leaped over me, and attacked me…with slobbery kisses. The kisses he gave me were like wet, sticky raindrops of drool cascading down my face. That day my solitude had turned to fear, which turned to joy as I wrestled with man's best friend.

Elizabeth Hennessy, Grade 7
St Joseph Catholic School, CA

What Would a Snowflake Do?

The uniqueness of each snowflake spreads out on a layer of dirt and grass. The texture, shape, and size vary between them. Each snow flake is unique, just like you and me. As I watch the small flakes fall to the ground, I ponder them, about their life, which is a lot like mine. They block out the sun and bring dim light to the sky while I dance in joy that they are finally here. The detail in each one is inexplicable. While they fall to the ground I think of all the joy that they have brought me, along with my friends. They go through cycles of life just like we do in our everyday life, change. Sometimes I feel like a snowflake, going from place to place on one big adventure! As I take a second to look and think about the life they bring to our planet, I almost feel like crying, breaking out in tears of joy, sadness, and relief. The feeling that brings me to tears is the feeling that today may be my last day to be myself, to be unique, and to share my love, my love for snow; that one day my uniqueness will die. Yes, I do love snow that much; it is my inspiration to go out and be unafraid to live my life out loud. So I say, "Let it snow, let it snow, let it snow!" The snowflakes that fall so gently are my encouragement to become my own person, to do what I want to do, to become my inner snowflake.

Kyle Johnstone, Grade 7
Salida Middle School, CO

How to Throw a Spiral

Many people throw a football a lot of different ways. My family and coaches have taught me to throw it correctly. This is the way I have been taught to throw it the right way.

For starters, you will need a football to throw with. You will also need something to throw at as a firm target. First, you need to pick up the leathery ball and feel for the rough laces. Your thumb needs to be behind the ball for a good grip on the leather. The pointer finger needs to be right below the tip of the ball for a firm control. Your last three fingers need to be spaced out along the laces. I personally like to lick my fingers, to a leathery taste, for better grip on the ball. Next, find a stance that is very comfortable to you so you don't mess up in the process. After that, bring your arm back and point the ball away from your head. When you're about to throw, make sure to breathe so you can hear your heart pumping slowly. Finally, as you throw the ball bring your arm long over your head for distance. As you release, point your index finger down for the right spin. When you see the ball keep rotating sideways, that's when you feel something inside of you as sweet as sugar.

Now that you know the right way to throw a football. Go outside with a family member and have some fun.

Gage Walters, Grade 7
Lindale Jr High School, TX

A Fragile Leaf of a Memory

When I was 10 I had grasped the nuances of imagination and had come to know every twist of the dried creek bed that edged around my childhood fort, as well as I knew the faces of my own dolls. Although I can remember these green old days full of imagination all that is truly left is a fragile dried up leaf in autumn. My imagination use to belong to a plentiful tree, sheltered with fresh luscious leaves, but had drifted away with the wind, carrying its life with it. I remember the days playing around this enchanted tree as a rough beaten up pirate, at my fort, Tortuga. The days of prowling through the thick dense woods and climbing the highest tree were gone, like the leaves in winter. I still recall the afternoons of being Captain Black Beard and watching the trees towering above me like giants, their limbs, arms trying to reach for the golden goose high up in the sky. The sun projecting a beautiful ray of light, caught by the watchful trees was winking through the limbs down at me. All the creativity of my child-life, the sweet song of innocence, had burned out from the fort. However, the memory of it would never fade completely. Although I cannot remember the details of my fort clearly, I know that the memory of my childish imagination will continue to bring me joy in the years to come.

Rachel Brown, Grade 9
Saint Mary's Hall, TX

People Need Friends

Everyone needs a friend. My friends are there when I need them most. Any time I am feeling sad, they are there. A true friend will be at the bottom of a cliff to catch you. If you have a true friend, then you should love them and be kind to them. A friend is someone you can look up to, someone that will always be there for you, and you will always be there for them. That is a friend. My friends are there when I need them. Be a good friend to everyone.

Some examples of when my friends are there for me is when I am sick and I don't go to school, my friend that is in my same grade will bring me all the things that we did in class that day. When it is my birthday, they give me things that they know I like. When I felt bad because I got a bad grade on my test and I was crying in the bathroom, one of my friends came in and told me what to do to get a better grade.

You can be there for your friends by loving them and giving them what they need when they need it, such as sympathy. Be kind to them. If you know them well enough, then you can joke around and be a little rude, but that is only if you know them well enough. You can give you friend good advice that they will use.

Cherylynne Wayman, Grade 8
Excelsior Academy, UT

My Voice Box Surgery

"Your voice box is paralyzed." How in the world is that possible?! You never hear anyone say: "Oh, hi how are you? How's your voice box?" The point is, you either don't know that your voice box is broken, or you don't care. Well, my voice box was paralyzed for about 10 years, and I didn't even know! I later learned that my voice box paralyzed when I was about 2 years old after having a procedure to fix my heart murmur. I went to about 6 different doctors and they all told me the same thing, "There's nothing wrong with your voice, you just need to speak a little louder." I always believed them until one day I realized that I couldn't scream. I finally convinced a different doctor to have my voice box examined. Well I found out that I was right. I went to regular doctor visits before the surgery, and finally one of the most important days of my life came. I got ready for surgery and finally got the anesthesia. The next thing I knew, there were tubes in my throat. I was awake and I could hear the clash of the metal. My surgeon started talking to me, asking me to talk so they could see my voice box moving. A few minutes later, I fell asleep again. When I woke up, I was in a hospital bed with a new stuffed animal. I recovered, and can now scream and talk normally.

Alicia Gutierrez, Grade 8
St Joseph Catholic School, CA

Softball

"Never let the fear of striking out keep you from playing the game."
— A Cinderella Story

You should never give up on something. You just have to try harder. You cannot let anything get in the way. I have to have good grades to play softball. If I do not then I cannot play because my grandparents think it is because of softball.

I love to play softball. The reason why is because anything can happen. When you hit it far you have to make a good play. You can never stop running only when you feel you're going to get out.

When you hit the ball it is really exciting. Your hit depends on the kind of pitch. It is really fun when you make a home run. When everyone is on base you have more pressure. You have to hit it as hard as you can. Sometimes you even have to bunt.

I like when we make a good play. When you make a good play it means your team is awesome. When we make a triple play it is awesome!

This is why I love to play softball. I would not stop playing or even quit for anything.

Sheyenne Medved, Grade 8
Santa Clara Elementary School, CA

The Beauty of Horses

Each stride is so stunning; his feet keep the right pace and are perfect like a clock keeping the exact time. His eyes move to the direction of your hand. His heart thumps every second. He twitches when a housefly lands on him and bites him. His tail swats away the flies that are on him and he goes back to grazing. His muscles flex, showing strength, agility, and beauty. He keeps his head high and proud when we show, the movement of a horse is breathtaking.

I feel his shiny coat under my hand. Each hair follows the others like a school of fish. His ears turn back to hear what I am saying. His muscles flex in his neck when he turns his head. When he runs, for one split second one hoof carries all the weight of the horse, showing that he is very strong. I see him grinding his food, his teeth far back in his mouth. His eyes are bright and filled with joy. When I look at him, I don't just see a horse, I see a creature that if I didn't have, my life would never be complete. He is radiant, spectacular, and strong as he jumps over the fence, or when he fights off a cougar. I take off the halter while my horse runs to join the other beautiful horses. I watch his hooves hit the ground till I see only the tip of his ears as he canters down the hill.

Ali Hughes, Grade 7
Salida Middle School, CO

Magical Sounds

I'm outside. The wind is warm and blowing my hair off my neck. I hear a sound, my name being called by the wind. Like a whisper, my soul takes flight and I want to chase the sound. I hear it again and again. I run with the wind, trees by my side and grass tickling the skin on my feet. there are so many colors. It's overwhelmingly beautiful. Suddenly I find myself in a place far away from the world of hate, but also far from family and friends, so I can't stay. The call of nature's sweet sound of peace is gone. I lay down in the grass, never to go back again, and close my eyes and listen, just listen, to the beautiful magical sounds of the wind in the trees; can you feel it? The wind being created by the horses running free. When you're in the air, the feel of every color is astonishing, like when the clouds cover the ground below like a blanket. An orange coat just below the plane, made pink because of the sun; that's when you hear the sound, as striking as ever to your heart. If you have not heard these magical sounds, then you need to look for them, listen. Search, because you are nature, born in nature. Unless you like the pain that the real world gives you, the stress that is created, then search for the magical sounds of nature.

Rebekah Clonts, Grade 7
Excelsior Academy, UT

Oreo

Last summer, my father went to the store and came home with a black and white kitten. He wanted a female barn cat because they are good hunters. We named her Oreo because of her markings. She is friendly, energetic, and curious. Oreo became best friends with our small dog, Ferdinand, because they spent a lot of time together. It is fun to watch them play and run around the house. She runs circles around Ferdinand. She hasn't responded well to the other dogs. She usually arches her back and hisses at them before she runs and hides.

Oreo likes to be close to people. She follows me around all over the house and at night she likes to sleep in my bed. Every once in a while, early in the morning, she pounces on my feet and claws at me. It is not a great way to wake up from a deep sleep. I kick her out of my room, but she always comes back to play.

Now that she is older, a decision has been made about her being an indoor cat or the barn cat that my father originally wanted her to be. She recently had a day outside of the house. She hid from the dogs the entire time. Oreo is not ready for "kitty's day out," so I think I am going to have to put up with her attacking my toes in the middle of the night.

Taryn Cox-Stone, Grade 8
St Joseph Catholic School, CA

New Puppies

One day I was sitting in my room and my mom called me out to the living room. She told me that my uncle's dog Chloe was going to have puppies. I was so excited, because I love puppies and think they are adorable and so cute! I was so excited to go to his house to see them, secretly hoping that they all would be cute and none of them ugly. I kept asking and asking my mom to drive me to my uncle's house to see the puppies. Finally, one weekend my mom said that we were going to see them! I was so excited, I was practically jumping up and down. We drove to his house. I made sure I had my camera to take pictures of the puppies. When I got there I immediately went into my uncle's room, where the puppies were. I immediately saw a little spotted puppy. I picked it up and held it for a while. It was my favorite of them all. There were 2 others spotted like her and two black puppies, like Chloe. There was one boy and one girl of each. They were all so cute and I was so happy that I finally got to see them. Then we finally went home, and as I left I said, "Uncle Johnnie, please keep the spotted girl for me." Now I get to convince my dad to get it.

Zoe Greig, Grade 8
St Joseph Catholic School, CA

My Game

As the ball crackles against the back of the plastic netting, there is a moment of total calm before the crowd explodes with cheers and exasperated sighs. This is my moment, the one I crave and relish in every soccer game. The most beautiful thing to me is seeing the faces of my team as I jog back to my side. Happiness and gratitude are on their features as they realize we are finally doing the thing we play this game for—winning. Sure, they high-five me and pat me on the back, but without them, we would have nothing. Soccer has a way of cheering me up; it is my tether, what keeps me from breaking down. The smiles of my team and the heartbreak of my enemies pull me away from troubles in reality. My problems melt away from me like hot wax dripping from a burning candle. At half-time, the perfection is halfway over; thirty more minutes until I will be dragged back to the harsh reality of modern society. The final whistle blows, and my troubles once again start to build around me: parents, homework, and drama with friends. These thoughts threaten to burst out of my head at any moment, leaving me a hollow shell. But soccer is the antidote; it is a way to blow off steam, and it is my handhold. Soccer is my game.

Kevin Murphy, Grade 7
Salida Middle School, CO

The Time I Went to San Francisco

One morning I got up, and went to the church to meet Megan and Elizabeth. Then we drove to San Francisco. We went down there for the Pro-Life walk. We got to San Francisco and went to the place where everybody was to meet. Some people talked about being Pro-Life, and then we started to walk. The walk was about three hours long and Elizabeth, Megan, and I all finished directly at three o clock, it was pretty cool. The walk ended at the pier. Then we walked and skipped down Pier 39. When we got there we went to a restaurant and ate burgers and fries, it was really good. After we ate, we looked around all the shops that were there. We went to the NFL shop and there was an ex-Raider there, his name was Jeff Barnes. We all got his autograph and Elizabeth got a picture with him and got to try on his Super Bowl ring. I also got to try the ring on, it was really heavy and really pretty. He kept making us all laugh and told us we would get bigger rings when we were married. Then we went to the Alcatraz shop and got some key chains. Then we took a light rail train to the car, it took FOREVER!!! We got to the car and headed home for Auburn. We had a great time in San Francisco!

Gabby Anderson, Grade 7
St Joseph Catholic School, CA

Hydie

I used to have a dog named Hydie. It was a while back when she died, but I will never forget her. I was at my aunt's house, and we had been there for a while. After a while, my mom received a call from my sister saying that she was going to take her to the vet, because she was acting strange. Of course, my mom didn't let her because she said it is wasting money. Later, we received another call from my sister, and she said that Hydie was having seizures, and in one seizure, she was paralyzed. After we heard that we hurried home, and when I walked in, I saw Hydie lying on her bed crying. My sister said I should leave, but I couldn't leave Hydie. Later, everybody decided we should take her, but my brother and I couldn't, because it was a school night, so my mom and my big sister went.

In the morning, I asked my mom how Hydie was; she said she was going to be fine. When I came back from school, my mom told me that she lied to me and that they really had to put her down. She said the doctors said she had a disease that there was no medicine for. Meanwhile I was crying. My mom said we could get another one, and I said no dog could replace Hydie. After Hydie died I was never the same.

Jennifer Benitez, Grade 7
Grantham Academy for Engineering, TX

Why Friendship Is Important

Friendship is one of the many things important to me. My friends are always there for me if I am having a bad day at school and my parents can't be there. They are there to cheer me up, make me laugh, and be happy with me. I like all my friends, but there is one of them I live close to and do lots of stuff with. We take dance together, and hang out when we can. Soon I think we will become like sisters. We will start doing everything together. I hope that neither of us will ever move, because my other really good friends in the past have moved and it was really depressing to lose such great friends. Friends help me remember a lot of important things like other friend's birthdays, or remind me to study for a test.

I think that if you choose the right friends, you will always feel grateful to have such good friends in your life that can help you at school. I think really good friends are the ones who defend you if someone says something mean behind your back or starts a rumor about you. Friends are important in everyone's lives because you learn how to interact with other people, and you have someone else besides your family to go to for advice.

Kailee Russell, Grade 7
Excelsior Academy, UT

America Today

Everyone has a dream, whether it be to become President some day or become a teacher. The country we live in, however, is against that for some of us. Most of the country is sexist toward females. That is the reason why we don't have a female President, Vice-President, or we never hear anything about someone unless they are one of the famous singers.

Hey, America, listen up. We girls, who make up a good part of this country, are just as good as all of the guys. Everyone says the girls can't be quite as good as guys at things like sports, supposedly being physically impossible. You just watch and wait though, and some day, some amazing woman will outshine a guy. We will prove that girls are just as good as guys. For a change, all the high up positions of power should belong to all females, no males included. See how fast our country improves. A word of advice to everyone who may happen to read this: change your thoughts, your feelings. For the period of at least a day, have no opinions toward either gender. Try imagining how your life would change if everything was equal to all. Maybe your life would improve some; nobody will know until a change is made.

Jacque Long, Grade 8
Arvada Middle School, CO

People Who Care

Family, to me, means the people who love you and help you. Yes, sometimes it feels like they don't love us and they want us to get out of their lives, but that's not what family is. I have a family of seven, counting me. My dad, who is super smart, helps us with our homework and plays with us. He will always take me to the limit of how well I can play. My mom helps us with everything. She helps us learn our math and our other homework. She can be strict, but she loves us; she's always telling us to be the best we can. My two brothers play with me and embarrass me at the weirdest times. I think that is the way they express that they love me. I know that if I didn't have them, my life would be more boring than a stick in the mud. Then there is me. I am the party in my family. Without me, we would be a normal family. I love to try out new things on my little sister. Sometimes she can be a princess. We love her little laugh. It is cuter than silver bells ringing. My little tiny brother is like a hurricane; always making a mess wherever we go. Then at other times he can be so cute and silent and try to act like an angel. That's what family is to me, the people who love you and will always be there.

Kenzie Moon, Grade 7
Excelsior Academy, UT

The Storm

Last year my brother played baseball at this really fun stadium in Phoenix, Arizona. It was a stormy night but nothing had happened yet. On the news it said that there was a dust storm coming. At the far end of the field, the indigo sky was turning brown. We ignored it until the dust came rushing over the field. All the families were forced to hide in the dugouts, until the storm passed. You could see nothing because of all the dust. All these yucky bugs were being blown at us! Finally, after an hour, the dust had passed. There was dirt everywhere. There was dirt in our eyes, ears, nose, hair, and mouth. Everyone was very unhappy with all the dust covering their cars. My mother was scared to death because my 18-year-old brother was driving in the storm. For most of the game, all we could taste was dirt in our mouths. We knew it was safe so the game started up again. We were so happy to finish the game, and we were going to win when we heard a distant rumble. We thought it was nothing and continued to watch the game. Suddenly, I felt a raindrop. Lightning and thunder started up and the rain came pelting down. By the time we walked to our car, we were weighted down by water.

Lianna Nemeth, Grade 7
St Gregorys Catholic School, AZ

The Story of Gabe

Ring, I was just cleaning my room when a phone when off. Could that be my phone?

Suddenly, I remembered that I forgot my phone downstairs, and I was going to get it. Then my worst fear came into mind, I was going to have to get by the furious cocker spaniel Gabe. When I was at the top of the stairs, I saw him. He looked at me and started to make a strange noise. The look in his eyes seemed like he wanted to tear me up. I tried to go down the stairs, but I was just horrified of what he would do to me. Finally, I had the guts to go all the way down the dark stairs. As I went further down, I heard the noise getting louder. Bewildered and confused, I thought I was losing my mind! Finally I was at the bottom step, and somehow I felt fearless that nothing could hurt me. Confident and secure, I had my hopes up high, because I could see my phone a few feet away! Confident in myself, I made it. Then I noticed, I had to walk all the way up the stairs to my room and get by the dog. When I started going toward the stairs, I heard the noise get softer and softer. I made it to my room; I was glad to be alive.

I am still shaky when I remember that horrible day.

Allison McClellan, Grade 7
Lindale Jr High School, TX

My Older Friend

My older friend is Chad Carpenter. Chad is my eighteen year old cousin. Although he and I aren't related by blood, I think and feel he is my real cousin. To me, Chad is like an older brother to me.

I have learned a lot from Chad, not only physically but also socially. Chad is really funny and also a very likeable friend. He is really good at basketball and attends Caesar Chavez High School. I believe this is what makes us compatible. He is very quiet and shy around people but around me he is funny and cool. I look up to Chad, he is like my role model. He gives me good advice and always pays for me when we drive to places.

For instance, Chad and I were playing basketball at a local park. Some guys without a ball creepily walked up to us and asked if they could play. Of course we let them play. They started to talk dirty and play just the same. They kept on pushing us and grabbing us. They also kept on changing their score. Just as I was about to say something, Chad stopped me. He told me, "It is just a game, let them have it. We have more and we know how to be polite; learn to forget." To me, Chad is very important and a great friend.

George Rivera, Grade 7
St Gregorys Catholic School, AZ

You're It

"Warning: Toilets may cause head injuries." This should be a clearly written label on all toilets.

When I was little, my sister and I decided to play a friendly game of tag. We agreed on making the toilet a base, where you were freed from the danger of being 'it.'

We played and laughed without a worry in the world, just two sisters innocently having fun. My sister had the title of 'it' thrust upon her. In an attempt to clear her name, she began to run after me.

I quickly ran, trying everything I could to make it to the toilet. I was too determined on being safe that I didn't notice the puddle on my bathroom floor from a recent shower.

As I entered the bathroom I began running faster, my eyes locked on my target. My right foot stepped directly on the wet water and as I lifted my foot to take off again, plop! The slippery water shot me forward, face first. The top left side of my head bashed against the edge of the toilet. The force tore my skin to the skull as blood began to splatter out. My parents rushed in, picking up my limp body from the blood-bathed floor. I had to get stitches and still have the scar to prove it.

Shawna Babcock, Grade 9
Woodland Park High School, CO

Piano

Piano is one of the major things that I focus on besides my faith, academics, and sports. I have composed many non-lyrical songs that express the way I like to play the piano. Through learning theory, I am able to know what chords to use and how to approach different notes. I enjoy composing a lot.

With many different markings and symbols, music can be played just how the composer wanted it to sound. Unlike other instruments, the piano can do a multitude of things to make the note sound different. It also has a wider range of notes it can play. These two reasons are why I love piano so much. While playing piano, you don't have to focus so much as instead to solely let the music come to you.

Piano is one of the instruments that can play every genre. It can play classical, rock and roll, blues, boogie, country, ragtime, gospel, and new age. With all this variety, playing the piano for me never gets old.

Piano is a big part in my life, and I don't intend on not using my skills when I'm older. I am attempting to never stop improving, and to always progress with my abilities. Piano will never diminish in my life.

Stuart Buie, Grade 8
Monte Vista Christian School, CA

California Vacation

My name is Ketsia Uwase and my most interesting trip was when I was about 10 years old. My godmother and godfather asked me if I wanted to travel to California with them. I agreed, and my parents let me go to California with my godparents.

When we reached the hotel, my godmother and my godfather told me to change my clothes so we could go to a restaurant. I was lucky to get my own little place to stay, but my godparents were right next door. When we reached the restaurant, my mom and dad called. I was glad to hear their voices. I remember I ordered a Greek salad that night. When we came back to the hotel, my godparents told me the schedule; they said we would go to Disneyland, Lego Land, Sea World, Six Flags, the beach and the San Diego Zoo.

Tuesday was the best day for me because I was able to go on the Tower of Terror. It was the scariest ride I have ever been on. Also, I loved taking pictures of my godparents and me. My second favorite day was Saturday. I had gone to the beach that day. It was awesome. Sea World was so cool because I saw a Shamou show. On Sunday, I saw my favorite animals, pandas and dolphins. They were so cool. I will never forget it.

Ketsia Uwase, Grade 7
St Gregorys Catholic School, AZ

How to Make a Duct Tape Sun Hat

Have you ever wanted to walk around in style? Well now you can with your very own duct tape sun hat. Even you can make it yourself, yes you, all you have to do is follow these simple instructions.

To make a duct tape sun hat you will need an adjustable baseball cap, a roll or two of duct tape, scissors, and yourself. Let's begin, you need to put the baseball cap on and adjust it to your head to a comfortable area. Next tear a piece of duct tape long enough to reach both ends of the cap with slack. Put the sticky side up. After that continue to wrap it around the base with the sticky side up, making sure the sticky side is facing up. Then cover the sticky side with duct tape making the sticky sides connect. You have just made duct tape fabric. When you have finished that take the duct tape off the hat, and grab a piece of duct tape bout as long as a pencil. Connect the piece of duct tape to the base, and make duct tape fabric around the base. Continue to do this until there is a ring around the base.

Congrats you are finished, see since you followed those instructions you created a master piece. Now you can walk around in style.

Haleigh Hopper, Grade 7
Lindale Jr High School, TX

Burnt

It all started three months ago when I moved into an apartment with my mother and father. When we moved all our clothes and furniture in we noticed it was hot, but it was because we were moving. The next morning when I woke up, I told my mother that it was still hot. She called the air conditioning technician to come check it out.

When the air conditioning technician showed up and checked it out, he said our pump broke. It would take two days to fix. When my mother heard that, she called the landlord and asked if we could rent a hotel. He called us back and said we could go to any hotel for free.

Two days later when my bother and I were in the hotel swimming pool, my mother came out and told us that our house had burnt down. The next day my father, mother and I drove to go see the fire marshal to see if anything was salvageable. While we were there, he said that they did not know how it started, but he did know where it started.

When we saw where it started, we knew it was our upstairs neighbors because he would always flick his cigarettes.

After all this happened, we lived happily ever after.

Christopher Villalobos, Grade 7
St Gregorys Catholic School, AZ

Abraham Lincoln

Abraham Lincoln was born on February 12, 1809 to Thomas and Nancy Lincoln in Hodgenville, Kentucky. When Lincoln was a little boy he rarely went to school. All together the time he went to school was about a year. Ever since Lincoln was a little boy he never felt right about slavery. Later on in his life Lincoln decided that he needed to make a difference in slavery, so he started to run for election. While running he said that "If elected I shall be thankful; if not, it will be all the same." He was always such a positive man. He never let anything bring him down. Abraham never cared if people were rude to him he kept moving forward. People didn't like Abraham because he did not believe in slavery. In 1860 Lincoln was elected president. Not even a year after Lincoln was elected president the Civil War broke out. The Civil War was the north and the south against each other. The south, the Confederates, wanted slavery. The north, the Union, wanted slavery to be abolished. In the end slavery was abolished. Five years after being in office, President Lincoln was assassinated at the Fords Theatre by John Wilkes Booth. Abraham Lincoln has helped change the world by abolishing slavery.

Shay Uderjohn, Grade 9
South Jordan Middle School, UT

Making the World Fair

Fairness is mostly about being just to others. Unfairness can take place anywhere. For example unfairness could take place in a school, household, a grocery store, and other places. People should always be fair because without fairness, there would be chaos. Many people grow angry when something is unfair. Unfairness is easily spotted in United States history as well. This is an example of how unfairness has been around for many years. It is never too late to stop unfairness in the world, though. You just have to get involved and make a difference. The world cannot change, unless someone changes it. That person can be you. Of course, though, to stop unfairness, you have to know what it is and how it begins. You also have to know the importance of fairness. There are many ways to solve situations of unfairness. Unfairness may happen in everyday situations. Still, it does not matter how big or how small the situation is, if you really want to make the world fair, you are going to have to start small. First, speak out in your own household, then out in the public, and finally you are ready to speak out to the world.

Jose Aceves, Grade 7
St Ferdinand Catholic School, CA

Grandma Shorty

Oh, my dear grandma Shorty. Your hands are so soft and firm as you touch me. Oh how I feel this burst of happiness inside me. Grandma, you're very kind, caring, and gentle with others. Why did you leave me cold and damp, as tears are shed down my face; why? As you pulled my dad closer and closer, you whispered softly, "Take care of the farm, and your lovely children."

Why did you have to leave us two days before my birthday? I love you so much, and I will always remember the times we laughed. I am very glad that I had time to spend time with you. I always had a close relationship with you. The pain of your death would have burdened me with guilt if I did not know you well. You died before my sister was born. Now I can tell her all the adventures we would have with you grandma.

Now I'm only one of millions of people that have suffered because of a loved one having cancer. Help save the others from the risk of cancer; fill people's hearts with pure joy and settled thoughts. Come join us and help prevent cancer. You can help others by donating just pennies a day.

Paige Boyce, Grade 7
Excelsior Academy, UT

The Little Things

I love Christmas time. It gives my family some actual time to connect. I can't believe that just a few years ago we hardly even talked to one another. That just proves how strong family can be. My family is so strong you can't break us!

Last year had to be the best Christmas ever. It was the first time in a long time that my family was getting along. All of my siblings were at my mom's house. We were all going to bake cookies for the holidays! My brother even showed up, which was a shock to all of us! He ended up not doing anything, but at least he was here! My brother is usually the "no-show" in my family.

We started off with making the cookie dough for the cookies. I think my brother actually helped me out with the mixing. After I made the dough, my oldest sister placed it in the oven. Once the cookies were baked, my mom placed them on a cloth so they could cool down. Once they were cooled, my other older sister brought out the colored frosting. We frosted the cookies and ate them as a family. I guess you could learn to love the little things in life.

Madison Benites, Grade 7
St Gregorys Catholic School, AZ

Cheerleading Is a Sport!

Many people think cheerleaders are made for the sidelines, but in reality we practice and sweat just as much as any football, basketball or baseball player. The only difference is we practice for a two minute and thirty second routine.

Cheerleading is extremely exhausting and challenging, and just because we put on cute outfits and wear a ton of make-up doesn't mean we're not athletic. We work out and practice our routine for hours on end, and we have to run and condition just to stay in shape.

Cheerleaders get injured just as much as, if not more than, anybody else who plays a sport. The reason is because we do dangerous tumbling and even more dangerous stunts, and if you mess up or get distracted on one little thing you could end up with a life-threatening injury.

Even though it's dangerous and challenging, I love to cheer. It gives you more confidence, teaches you self-discipline, and you make friends for life. I wouldn't want to do any other sport in world.

Morgan Campbell, Grade 8
Berry Miller Jr High School, TX

A Game of Peace

Touchdowns and safeties, interceptions and receptions, football is truly the one thing that takes my mind far away from the everyday world. All my mind processes when I am on the field is that this is the one place I want to be. Tackling is like water to me: I can't live without it. Some may think that it is too rough, but it brings my head to peace and harmony. I think of nothing but blissful thoughts as I tackle the wide receiver. Interceptions are like the taste of a homemade cake you just can't let go of. You may perceive it as a "blood sport," but in my jumbled skull it is everything but violent and painful. Without football, my life would be a dreadful mess. Just watching football on TV gives me the exhilarating feeling of standing on the field and playing for your hometown. Adrenaline rushes through my body as I receive the kick and bring my team to a good point on the field, which may lead to a first down or maybe even a touchdown. It may look painful and violent, but your eyes are deceiving you. Recess and gym, lunch and paint ball, nothing comes close to my favorite sport of football.

William Zielinko Grammatica, Grade 7
Salida Middle School, CO

Surprise Catch

Splash! For the second time that day the fish had escaped the hook. I'd been fishing for a long time because I was trying to earn an award for fly-fishing. All this time spent out on the lake had made me hungry so I decided to have a snack of trail mix. Then, suddenly, I had a wonderful idea pop into my head. I was going to use the trail mix as a bait to lure the fish in around the boat. While I was waiting for my Dad to get some trail mix, I got my binoculars and started looking around the lake. My Dad handed me the bag, and as soon as I emptied the bag out in the water, I could see the ripples forming and it started to smell fishy. I quickly grabbed the fishing pole and whipped the line out to the spot where the fish were surfacing. Seconds later I was pulling in a huge trout. I never did get the award for the fish, but I completed my own goal, and that was catching the fish. My Dad was so proud of me that it made me feel pretty proud too. It still occurs today in my mind how hard I worked just to catch one fish. Because of that, I now know to never give up and to strive with all you have left in you one-hundred and ten percent towards your goal.

Dawson Behee, Grade 7
Lindale Jr High School, TX

Getting Back Up

Disability isn't something that I've had to go through personally, but I have witnessed someone who has disabilities. About ten years ago, a family friend of mine named Ryan got in a really bad accident. He used to be perfectly normal. He could walk, talk, communicate, and do everyday tasks without struggling to do so. This was before the accident.

Ryan now has a very hard time communicating with the people around him. He struggles to talk and he has an extremely hard time walking. Ryan is one of the most resilient people I know. He still does what he needs to do and even makes time for things he wants to do. He is not able to drive anymore, but every once in a while one of my family members will see him walking to work. This is about a three mile walk! Every time I see him, he waves and smiles like nothing has happened.

Even though trials come to us or the people we care about, we need to follow someone like Ryan and get back up and move on.

Emma Penovich, Grade 7
Excelsior Academy, UT

Time

Time. We think we can manage it, but we have lost it before we even know where to start. Seemingly everlasting, it is gone in a split second. We wait ostensibly forever, yet before we know what we have missed, we blink and the moment is lost forever in time. Impossibly, we try our best to rewind, to relive the moment over and over again, never letting it slip away into the daunting depths of time itself. Relentlessly, we pour our souls and minds into every second that the day allows us. Yet somehow, as the clock ticks away, infinitely counting, the moment vanishes seemingly into thin air, left solely as a long lost memory in our thoughts and minds. Driven by our creator and stopped only when He sees fit, time inevitably marches on, whether we are prepared for it or not. So we must live each moment to the fullest, capturing it and relishing it forever longer than that brief moment endures. And we must enjoy our precious time while it lasts, for time is of the essence. So easily lost yet so wonderfully shared, time is ours to fill but never to hold. Ceaseless time; oh sweet time.

Katherine Mayfield, Grade 9
Saint Mary's Hall, TX

The Beautiful, Peaceful Place

Nature is so green and alive, but it is so quiet and peaceful. You can think, but at the same time you are distracted by everything. You feel calm and safe while at the same time, with every sound, you get a thrill of excitement. You could go bird-watching or go for a ride on a bike through the forest. You can sleep in a tent and eat food that has been cooked on a fire. You can sit and think in the quiet or watch as all of the green trees whip past your face in the golden sunlight on a bike ride.

After all this daytime fun, you can sit in front of a soft glowing fire, and then put yourself to bed in a tent. You might worry about bears entering your camp until you are so exhausted that you drift into a calm, blissful sleep. The next day you wake up and you do not know where you are until everything returns to your memory in a surreal moment.

As you prepare to leave there is a sadness in the air and all you can think about is what you will miss when you have left. As the green fades away you start to think about the next time, and how much fun you will have.

Katelyn Swasey, Grade 7
Excelsior Academy, UT

Epic Snowboarder

Pitter, patter, pitter, patter! The snow drops like beads on the roof of the lodge as I get ready to hit the slopes. There is an excitement of being with my friend as the warmth of the wood burning in the fireplace and the smell of the hot chocolate makes me feel warm and tingly. The perfectly ridden slopes rise up in front of us like the chair lift going up into the heavens. As we get on the majestic lift to the heavens a man scans my pass. The beep of the scanners made my ears ring.

From the lift, the 'poof' of people hitting the fresh powder made the snow fly on top on innocent bystanders. "Never Summer" are the words on the sign flopping around like a majestic bird at the top of the mountain. On the slope, flakes of silky snow are dancing everywhere. Cold wind mixed with snow hits me straight in the face as my board glides through the snow toward the lodge. Leaving my board, my black boots hit the wet deck as I walk into the lodge. Leaving the cool brisk air behind, the warmth of the lodge and the smell of hot chocolate make my day heavenly.

Michael Wheat, Grade 7
Salida Middle School, CO

Friendship is Life

What is friendship? To me, friendship is the real deal. If I wanted to pick a friend, I would pick someone I can trust. Isn't that what friendship is all about? To most people, it is yes, because friendship means a person who is always there for you, even when you are being a pill bug. My mom says to be a true friend, you have to have a great personality; you have to open up to others, and let them open up to you. You've got to let them know that you want a friend; not just sit there off in the corner and stare at them. I've got many friends, but only a handful of true friends that I can trust and tell anything to. When I'm in a rut they pull me back out. Friendship is one of the best things that a person needs in life, along with love, care, and, of course, oxygen. When you first start a friendship, you have to let them know that you're always there for them, or they may not be there for you someday. Not everything lasts forever, but an ecstatic relationship can last a lifetime. Don't forget to always have a friend you can count on, even if that friend is your mom. It's great to know they're there.

Courtney Loertscher, Grade 8
Excelsior Academy, UT

The World of Books

Books sweep me off my feet on the winds of adventure as I read on in excitement. Like an eager kid waiting, I sit on the edge of my seat wanting more. Mysteries and adventures galore. They are all there waiting for me to read them. I run my hand over the binding of the books, looking for the right one to read. The words of the books call out for me to read them. I finally pick one that's right for me. The words come to take me away from the pain of the world I once knew. Like an old friend, books come and comfort me when I'm sad. They make me laugh like nobody could ever do. Books, like people, hold secrets you will have to search for. To find the meaning I run down a path, looking frantically for something to hold onto. Nestled down deep in the book, I find what I was looking for. I hold the secrets close, never wanting to let them go. Digging down even deeper, the book is finally mine. It becomes a friend. No matter the adventure or problem, books will always be there to take me away.

Kyla Green, Grade 7
Salida Middle School, CO

My Favorite Memory

The bright lights in the stadium reflected off of my helmet as we went in at half time. The coaches said: "Let's learn a new play."

When we got done, the 3rd quarter started, and we ran the first play on offense. Then the coaches told us we were running the new play, and to throw it to me. I looked back, and I could see the ball flying through the air, I could hear the crowd start cheering. I caught the ball and could feel the leather of the new ball. There it was, the end zone 30 yards away. I knew they were behind me so I ran as fast as a cheetah towards the end zone. I was triumphant that I made the touchdown. At the end of the game we defeated the Vandals. When we were shaking hands, I could smell the sweat and see the tears. We were all so happy.

When I made the touchdown, I felt like I was glowing and everybody was staring at me. Now I feel like I'm just a normal kid. This event changed me because now when I make a touchdown, I feel like just a normal kid.

Brayden Bergbower, Grade 7
Lindale Jr High School, TX

Music: The Language of the Heart

Music affects the way you think, act, speak, and your very life itself. Music with an "upbeat" feel will get you bounding and ready to exercise! Music with a slow gentle feel will make you feel sleepy, and ready for a nap. But music can also be degrading, for example, heavy rock music, or rap. This genre of music makes you feel rebellious and plain icky inside, even if you don't notice. So it is best to choose your genre carefully, and make sure it is appropriate for the activity that you will be participating in. I find that classical music is the best type of music out there. It has songs with bounce, and peaceful songs, like waltzes, or minuets. The best part is none of them make you feel unpleasant. In fact, quite the opposite!

Along with this, I think that music, specifically playing a musical instrument, is very good for the mind. It involves math, reading, exercise, science, and so forth. It (as my music teacher, Mr. Innis, said) has the potential to be the pinnacle of knowledge!

Broderik Craig, Grade 7
Excelsior Academy, UT

The Time We Got Our Puppy

One summer day in August, my family and I went to the Nevada County Fair. We went on so many rides and had lots of fun. We thought that going to the fair was the best part of the day, boy were we wrong! When we got home and walked in the door, we saw this brown furry thing running down the hall. We had no idea what it was at first. Then, when it stopped to sniff us, we saw it was a small, brown puppy. She came with the name Lola. She is half Chihuahua, half wiener dog. She is so cute. We played all day with her until she climbed on to my mom's lap and fell asleep. She is adorable. We had never expected to get Lola at all, so it was a real treat. Our last dog was a big dog so we had to get used to our small new puppy. No matter how big she is, we love her just the same.

Darby Carrillo, Grade 7
St Joseph Catholic School, CA

Grades 3-4-5-6 Top Ten Winners

List of Top Ten Winners for Grades 3-6; listed alphabetically

Christian Alcantara, Grade 5
Woodland Intermediate School, IL

Aubrey Beard, Grade 6
Odessa Middle School, MO

Zoe Brown, Grade 6
South Middle School, MO

Patrick Dang, Grade 4
Outley Elementary School, TX

Henry Hooks, Grade 6
Baylor School, TN

Kelsey Lin, Grade 5
Woodland Intermediate School, IL

Virginia McEvoy, Grade 6
Baylor School, TN

Peyton Norris, Grade 6
Selma Middle School, IN

Kayla Repko, Grade 5
All Saints Catholic School, PA

Kristine Velez, Grade 6
Woodcreek Middle School, TX

All Top Ten Essays can be read at www.poeticpower.com

Note: The Top Ten essays were finalized through an online voting system. Creative Communication's judges first picked out the top essays. These essays were then posted online. The final step involved thousands of students and teachers who registered as the online judges and voted for the Top Ten essays. We hope you enjoy these selections.

Soccer

Soccer is a sport people play on a field. There are a few rules: No pushing, and no using one's hands. Those are the two basic rules. If a player pushes, the other team gets a free shot. If he uses his hands the referees give the ball to the other team.

In soccer there are two goals and two goalies. The goalies block the goal if a player shoots. If the goalie does not get the ball, then the opposing team receives one point. If the goalie does get the ball, he will pick it up, drop it, and then kick it across the field to one of his team players.

In England soccer is called football. The rules are still the same. Players dribble with their feet. When they dribble they just pass the ball back and forth between their feet.

A pass is where players kick the ball with the inside of their feet towards the player they wish to receive the ball.

If the player wants to shoot, he can do a shoelace kick. A shoelace kick is where a player kicks the ball with his shoelaces. Just so people know no one ever kicks the ball with his toe.

Sounds really fun right? Just wait until you start playing.

Ava Van Maren, Grade 5
St Pius X Catholic School, TX

The Ocean Institute

I was in 5th grade when my class went to the Ocean Institute in Dana Point, California. Our class went twice. It was the second time that was super nerve-racking and scary. I was in a group of six people and we all had our own individual speech. I had to speak about the Scientific Method. We all dressed very fancy in dresses and suits. My group and I had to get up on stage in front of about 50 kids from other elementary schools.

I had a microphone in my hand and my speech memorized in my head. I was the second person to speak and I was extremely nervous. I was so stiff and scared, but at least I could remember my speech. I was looking at everyone in the audience and I started talking. Once I started, I wasn't even scared or nervous anymore. My long speech seemed pretty short to me. Now, I do not have as much stage fright as I did before.

Stephanie Spatz, Grade 6
Margaret Landell Elementary School, CA

My Artistic Flair

My artistic flair is painting. Painting is fun because you can be creative and paint what you want. I got interested in painting because my mom was an artist when she was younger, and there are paintings she made around my house. People say I am very good at it, since I have been painting and drawing since I was little. I hope that when I am older I can have my paintings in an art show and people will buy them.

I like to paint nature and animals. I put lots of detail and work into my paintings. I also like bright, vibrant colors because it brings out the picture. Supplies I will need are paintbrushes, different colors of paint, and a canvas. I will enjoy being an artist when I am older.

Annie Langmade, Grade 4
St Thomas the Apostle School, AZ

Inspiring Others to Grow

"Inspiring Others to Grow," I feel that term has been lost over the years. We have been sucked into the technology age, and helping others has been thrown in the trash. We do whatever pleases us and not what pleases others. Social networking has taken the place of being nice to others.

Imagine that you are in New York, the Big Apple. You are just walking along and then suddenly someone bumps into you and you spill your drink on yourself. What would you say to that person? You would probably get really mad at the person, but you can't get mad at the person! You need to be nice to the person because if you are not, that will only encourage being mean to others. I know this is hard to do, but put yourself in that person's shoes. Would you like being yelled at? If not, reflect on what you would actually do if this happened to you. This is a lesson on being nice to others, and helping others to grow.

If we continue to not get so mad at others, we can make our community a better place. So remember it is okay that we are going into the technology age, but remember to not move the nice things we do into the trash bin.

Wade Varesio, Grade 6
St Raphael School, CA

I Have a Dream War Will Stop

I have a dream in the future, war will stop. War is very violent to me. First of all, it can hurt and kill people. I dislike it when I hear on the news that people from the war just died. They risk their lives for us! I'm very delighted that they risk their lives for us, so we won't get injured. But I'm very tearful that they risk their lives. It makes me sad as a puppy crying in the rain. I really wish I could do something that could help the war stop. I'm very happy that they get to wear protective suits! It makes me as joyful as a star finally shining up in the dark blue sky! Some day, I wish I could stop the war and stop people from risking their lives for us so we don't get hurt. Thanks to the people that are in war, we will never get hurt and nothing bad will happen to us! Although they still get hurt, we will always appreciate them!

Janelle Nutche, Grade 5
Foothills Elementary School, CO

Diversity Means More Work for My Mom

When it comes to dinner time at my house my mom asks "What do you want for dinner" I say grilled cheese then my sister says yuck and my little brother say's yum cheese. I ask my mom why everyone is so different. She said everyone has things they like and don't like. There is not one meal I can think of that my whole family likes. This means more work for my mom. She has to make one meal for the people that like what she's making and another for those who don't like what she's making. In my house diversity means more work for my mom. We are all different in some way from what we like to eat to what we like to do for fun. I am glad we are all different because if we were the same that would be pretty boring.

Natasha Shaw, Grade 4
Eagle Valley Elementary School, UT

A Horror Story of Fish Proportions

Any pets I've owned have ended up dead. I'm convinced it's been through no fault of mine, but my parents may beg to differ.

I'll travel back in time to my first experience as a pet owner, well, fish owner. My doomed fish, Sloppy Joe, was won at the annual carnival at my school. He pioneered the newfangled idea (for me) of naming pets after food. Confined in a plastic bag the first few days of his short, concise life, Sloppy Joe quickly moved into new housing. He lacked companionship, so, to battle that, Broccoli came into his life. Sloppy Joe and Broccoli were two peas in a pod. Well, for the few brief weeks they knew each other. That's right, you already know the end to this tragic tail. Broccoli died and Sloppy Joe followed him in a tragedy that combats *Romeo and Juliet* in terms of grief.

You would think after my first botched attempt at fish-ownership, I would know better than to adopt another fish. Apparently not. Fettuccini Alfredo (Alfie for short) swam into my life after an article deluded me into believing that beta fish were unkillable. Practically immortal if you like. Well, whoever wrote that article was dead wrong. Pun intended. After Alfie was transported back to my abode, he lived in splendor there for a few months. I really thought I had found an everlasting fish. But no, of course not. Alfie died. I'm blaming his death on a (possibly toxic) square bowl I stuck in his fish tank. R.I.P. Alfie

During my lifetime I have had a tumultuous affair with fish. So, in conclusion, keep your fishy friends far, far away from me.

Esmé McMullan, Grade 6
St Pius X Catholic School, TX

My Memorable Dream

Once I had a candy dream. On my birthday, we were driving in the car. I was very excited because my family was going to go to the store and buy lots of candy and supplies for my candy party. We went over a stream and through the hills. We crashed through a shrub and then we saw a supermarket.

We went into the shop and bought a whole cart full of candy. It was so tempting to eat it but I remembered it was for the party. We shopped for cookies, buttercups, cake, Butterfingers chocolate, candy corn and all sorts of candy.

We were about to go when mom said, "Let's get ready for the party." So we got candy decorations and sweet tablecloths and tempting chairs. Our second cart got full so we had to stop shopping!

We paid at the cash register and headed back for the car. While we were going back to the car we went over a speed bump and the heavy cart tipped over! We started to clean it all up. Once we'd finished, we heaved it into the car and started to drive home.

We drove home and all my friends were there! We sat down and in front of me there was a humongous pile of candy! I was about to share and eat it until I woke up! Boy was I grumpy!

Joshua Kim, Grade 3
Top Kids Center, CA

My Pet Peeve

Do you know what a "Pet Peeve" is? A "pet peeve" is something you dislike. My name is Godia Boyden; I come from a large family. I have an amazing mother, a hardworking father, two lovely sisters, two annoying brothers and one joyful nephew. Though I have such loving family members, there are things that I just need them to understand about me; I have "pet peeves."

My main "pet peeve" is when someone just comes in my room without knocking. I consider that to be extremely ruse. One should knock because people need their privacy. You should knock because they might be getting dressed, and you just open the door. Why is it so hard for them to just knock before entering?

Another thing that I don't like is when people take stuff without asking me. Like my brother for example, when he comes into my room and takes my controller to my Wii without asking me. Then he walks out as if that is all right. Maybe if he asks me next time, I may not mind and he may not experience my anger.

How about this "pet peeve?" When I'm at school and people are mean to each other, I get quite bothered. When this happens, it's just plain rude and disrespectful. First of all, we should all get along with each other at school. We should all try to be much nicer to each other because you might need the exact person who you were mean to when facing tough times.

In conclusion, it's all about respecting one another as well as respecting what someone has. If something occurs that you do not feel comfortable with, don't respond to that individual, just back away and tell an adult.

Godia Guillory-Boyden, Grade 4
DeQueen Elementary School, TX

Yaks

An interesting animal is the yak. Yaks are longhaired animals that look like bulls. Most of the yaks now are domestic or raised on a farm. Wild yaks are most commonly found in Northern Tibet and Western Qinghai. Wild yaks might even be found in Southern Xingjian, but most domestic yaks are found in the Himalayas.

There are many uses for yaks. Most people use yaks for carrying food and other items while traveling, but yaks can also be used in games and competitions. The most famous yaks' game is yak skiing. Some others are yak racing and yak polo. Yak games are usually place din Central Asian countries. Yak skiing is a sport practices in the Indian Hill resort of Manila and is used as a tourist attraction. Yak skiing is when a skier waits at the bottom of a slope and a yak is at the top. The yak and the skier are connected by a rope going around a pulley at the top of the slope. When the skier rattles a bucket of pony nuts, it makes the yak run down the slope while the skier skies up the slope. Yak polo is just polo but on a yak instead of a horse. Yak racing is where ten to twelve mounts race, usually a short distance. In addition to games, yaks are also used for their hide, meat, and milk. Yaks are very stimulating animals.

Quarter Morrison, Grade 6
St Pius X Catholic School, TX

How Diversity Is Important in Our Community

What traits and personalities would we have if we were all the same? The same ones as everyone else. We are all amazing just the way we are. Disabilities, strengths, and weaknesses are some things we differ in, and we all need to come to the understanding that they are great. Our differences make us all unique and special. If we all knew the same information, who would be there to help us with our troubles and conquer our fears? When people say obnoxious things such as "You're stupid," they are completely wrong. In I-Spy we usually spy something different each time. If all of us always spied the same thing each time, the game would be completely pointless. The differences in the game make it fun.

If we were all alike, everybody would be in the same place all at once, doing the same thing. For instance, in the mall we would be all buying the same thing at the same time. I would hate it because it would be way to crowded. We all have our strengths and weaknesses, but we should all be fair about that. We shouldn't make people feel like they are worthless, because we all have value in us. Try walking in their shoes a couple times and ask yourself "Would I like that?" before you say anything mean about someone else. If everyone was nice to each other the world would be a better place to live in.

Karlee Hanson, Grade 6
White Pine Charter School, ID

Leaving Germany

Leaving Germany wasn't easy for me. I had to leave my friends behind and I had to leave my house.

I went to my room as a tear fell down my face. I saw my empty room fade away into the sky, because a tear fell down my face, which made it blurry. I walked down the stairs with my mom. My dad honked the horn; I walked sadly toward the car. I gently opened the door to the car, and got in and so did my mom. I waited for my dad to start the engine. While he did, I looked at my house for the last time and thought of all the good times I had there. I remember the first time I entered this house when I was four year old and how my kite got stuck in our tree when I was six. You could probably still see a piece of it hanging there today. I loved it there; but, then I had to leave.

I felt like that was the best home I will ever have but now I know that home will always be where my family is.

David Hernandez, Grade 4
Horn Academy, TX

Are You the New Kid?

I started to go to Landell in fourth grade. I had just moved from Riverside and did not know anyone. I was very nervous. When I was lining up for our class, this kid in a tie-dye shirt walked up to me and said, "Are you the new kid?" I nodded to him and replied, "Hi my name is Rogelio. What's yours?" He told me his name is Nick, and he also told me to sit near him. After finding my seat next to him and his other friends, I wasn't so nervous anymore. I met all his friends, and the rest of the day was a blast.

Rogelio Sonza, Grade 6
Margaret Landell Elementary School, CA

The Great Fall!

It was a hot, sunny day at my old school. I was in kindergarten that time, and only five years old. Our teacher had given us a coloring page to color, so we could stay busy for a while. Everyone was laughing, and talking with their best friends. I had a question to ask, but I was shy to ask my teacher. So instead I went to my best friend, and asked her but she did not know. Finally after deciding for a long time whether I should ask my teacher or not I did ask her. My teacher was nice, and gave me the answer.

I do not know who did it, but someone had pushed my chair far away from the desk, and I did not notice. I just came to my desk, and I sat down. However since there was no chair to sit on, instead I fell down with a huge "BOOM!" My face was all red, and I was really mad at myself. Some kids started laughing, and other nice kids helped me. My teacher came over, and asked me if I am okay. After what seemed like a long time everyone forgot about what had happened. However I still remember, and whenever I think about it I laugh, or feel more embarrassed!

Jahnvi Panchal, Grade 6
Margaret Landell Elementary School, CA

Leaving

It was the day my dog, Max, had to be sent away. My tear leaked down my cheek as I was saying goodbye to Max. I asked if there were anything we could do, but then I realized that my baby brother was going to get hurt by Max. I couldn't imagine my baby brother getting scratched by Max. I fell asleep silently waiting for the next morning. At dawn I quietly snuck out to the living room looking for Max. I looked all over the house and didn't hear a single sound. I knew that Max was nowhere to be seen in the house. I went back to sleep and heard a bark outside. It was my uncle walking with Max on a leash. My smile became bigger and bigger when I saw Max. I didn't have to worry about Max being sent away. They jogged away slowly, still hearing the sound of my favorite dog. I don't care if my dog does not live with me, he will always be in my heart.

Kirby Wei, Grade 4
Horn Academy, TX

The Best Place to Be

Sugar and flour is strewn all over the floor but I don't care, for the good smell of cookies wafts up to my nose. In the good place of home, this is the part my heart is.

When the mess is cleaned up, and the cookies baked, I put them on a plate and head to the TV room where I find the rest of my family.

As I walk in with the plate of cookies, my mom, dad, and brother start to laugh. I look up and start to giggle, too. They're at the funniest part of the movie. I snuggle down next to my mom in her big armchair then pass the plate of cookies.

"That was funny!" my brother said.

"Yes, yes it was." I say. Then I smile because this is the other place my heart is.

Rachel Iliev, Grade 4
Horn Academy, TX

Moving Out

It was a beautiful June day, and my family and I were swimming in the pool. My mom had gone inside to talk to her company. Her company had just been bought. When she came back outside, I swam over to say hi. She looked very worried.

Then she gave us the news that we were going to move to Houston. I thought to myself, "She wouldn't make you do this if she didn't have to do this, too." I was furious! This was not a very good end to a beautiful June day.

"That's not fair!" I said.

I called my dad later on that night, and I could tell he was about to cry when I told him the news. I could imagine the look on his face…so sad…not being able to see me that much anymore.

After the rest of my family was told, we started to see each other more, or at least it felt like it to me. When my mom and step dad started to travel to look at a house, I knew that this was permanent, we were really moving. When the movers came, I was heartbroken, I was moving the next day and leaving all my family behind.

Now I love my house and my friends that I've made here. I have a great life here in Houston. I'm sad that I can't see my family anymore, but it's okay to miss the people you love.

Isabel Alvarado, Grade 6
Woodcreek Middle School, TX

The Beach

The hot sand squished between my toes as I jumped out of the car. I am finally happy. I run to the water. When it touches my toe, I jump and run further. I run until the water reaches my waist. I can't run anymore so I walk until it reaches my neck. I swim back to where it reaches my waist.

After a while I remember the sand village my dad helped me and my sister make the last time we came. I asked him if we could build another one, and he said, "Yes!" We started to work as soon as he replied. I ran to get buckets, shovels, and my sister. It was hard to steer her away from the seagulls eating our food. Eventually when I told her about it, she dropped her whole bag of Cheetos.

Once the sand village was made we got buckets of water and poured it in the hole that lead to a path to the ocean. The next time we went to the beach, it started all over again.

Abby Perkins, Grade 4
Horn Academy, TX

Pizza Delight

Every Friday night I eat my favorite food, a cheesy delicious pizza. My sister and I make them at Papa Murphy's, where she works. Once she threw a cheesy pizza at me, because I messed it up and put the wrong toppings on it. It was so funny! She and I even make mini pizzas for my brothers. They're as big as a soccer ball. My favorite flavor is cheese and pepperoni, and my favorite part of eating pizza is the crust because it is so crunchy. We get the pizza for free through my sister's job. I feel so lucky to get such good pizzas every week.

Callie Horne, Grade 3
Vista Charter School, UT

Capitol

We were sitting at the dinner table laughing and talking like nothing could go wrong, until my parents told my brother and me the bad news.

When we moved to Europe, we had to leave our dog, Capitol, at a home for dogs. We had been living in Europe for two years and we had not seen her ever since. At the home for dogs, Capitol got cancer. Capitol died a little while after she got cancer. She was my first dog and she meant everything to me. She would never get mad at me even when I pulled her tail or jumped on her back. She never bit me and she comforted me when I was sad.

When I heard the news, it felt like the end of the world. It felt like I would never be happy again. I stared at my parents in disbelief as they sat there quietly. Everything was silent until my parents told my brother and me to go upstairs and take our showers. We quietly walked upstairs trying to forget about everything that happened that night.

"I did not even know that dogs could get cancer," I said to myself.

After that day I realized that sad, bad things might happen but you just have to move on. I realized that even sad things are important.

Lauren Faust, Grade 4
Horn Academy, TX

My Stuffed Animals

My huge stuffed lion that I love sits on the tall, white shelf and smiles at me every day. I can't remember too well how long ago I got him, but I know I got him at Christmas, and that was a really fun time. I named him an original name, Lio. I love to jump on his soft, squishy body and pet his fantastic, furry hair.

I named another stuffed lion after him. He sits in a packed box, patiently waiting for me to get him out of the packed garage. We barely moved here, so sadly, he is still packed up. He is like a mini Lio, so I named him Junior Lio. I got him from a kind lady named Judy Scott after my mom's friend died.

I also have a gorilla the size of Lio. He has curly black hair. I got him from the hospital when I almost died. I was very young, about 5 years old. It was scary at that time. So my mom bought me my big gorilla to make me feel better.

I love my stuffed animals and I would never replace them.

Zoe Odom, Grade 3
Vista Charter School, UT

My Special CD

I have a CD that my daddy made of him reading, and I admire it! Written in marker on it is "For the kids." I got this CD when I was little, when my daddy had to travel a lot with the army. It has stories my daddy knows we LOVE, like "Roll Over," "Crayons," "Ants Go Marching," and two others. It is so super-de-duper special! I love listening to it at bedtime when I am sad and whenever it is my turn to choose the CD. I love that my daddy thought of me and my family that way. I feel a happy and grateful feeling deep down when I listen to it.

Sarah Grace Jones, Grade 3
Vista Charter School, UT

Sharks

Sharks have attacked surfers' surfboards, so most people think of sharks as killers.

Most people might think of sharks as killers, but most sharks attack because people have been mistaken as food. A shark's main source of food is seal, bird, octopus, crab, squid, salmon, cod, dolphin, marlin, ray, sea otters, turtles, tuna and dead whale.

Sharks do not have many predators. Orca whales feed on great white sharks. Sharks live all over the world. The first hybrid sharks have been found off the coast of Australia, which is a sign that sharks are adapting to climate changes. Sharks have been also found in cooler seas.

Sharks can be small or large and huge. The smallest shark is the dwarf lantern shark, which is 17 centimeters. But, the largest is the whale shark, which is 14 meters. One was found at 46 feet, the biggest fish in the sea so far. Bull sharks, another breed of shark, can live in fresh water.

People can find sharks in some aquariums. Sharks are not man-eaters and they can be appreciated.

Brian Kostoch, Grade 5
St Pius X Catholic School, TX

Man Up

I asked in a tired voice, "Dad how much longer till we're there?" Dad replied, "The hotel's just around the corner." Two minutes later we were driving into a hotel parking space. We piled out of the car and go in to check into the hotel. The people at the counter were done in a flash. As we trudged to the hotel room with all our stuff, I asked my dad, "How far is camp from here?" Dad replied, "I don't know but we will find out in the morning. For now, though, just get some sleep." The next morning I woke up with my dad shaking me yelling "WAKE UP." Then he said we only had an hour till we had to leave and we still had to eat breakfast. That got me going. Soon we were driving off to camp. It was about a thirty minute drive. When we got there, we got introduced to our counselors, and went to our cabins to get settled. Soon my dad left. I was on my own from that moment on. I knew I was going to have to grow up and face my problems on my own. I felt homesick during that time but I grew up.

Allison Clarke, Grade 5
Horn Academy, TX

The Change

When I was five, I went through a change of schools. I first was in St. Nicholas when I was in preschool. After that I went to Horn Academy. I felt different because there were so many different kids I hadn't met before. The first kid I knew was Austen. Then I met a few other kids. I decided I would hang out with Austen the rest of the day. I also met this funny kid named Abraham. These were the only kids I knew. I thought all of them were nice except for one who was kind of mean sometimes. But Austen was the most fun to play with. At least I knew some people in school. That was the time I changed.

Wesley G. Cummings, Grade 5
Horn Academy, TX

My Dogs

My dogs are Maggie and Vince. Maggie is a Golden Labrador. Vince is a Border Terrier. We feed them Beneful every day about twice a week and I give them walks every day.

Vince is an energetic dog. When I open the door, he jumps on me and starts licking me. Vince is lovable in so many ways. When I come home, he also follows me. Then when I sit down, he jumps and lies down right next to m. Vince is also a mid-sized dog who has big ears and follows instructions very well. For example, Vince used to run to Ocean Drive when he got out of the house, but now he comes back when we call his name.

Maggie is a calm dog. Maggie is also a big dog who has big ears and has a big nose and I love to be around her. Maggie is always lying down either next to me or in our living room. Maggie is a very fluffy dog. When I'm petting her, I get hair all over my shirt and my pants because she is so fluffy.

Those are my dogs. Both of my dogs mean so much to me because we picked Maggie up as a stray and we got Vince from Pee Wee's which is a rescue and stray dog place. I'm glad they live with me now.

Charlie Uecker, Grade 5
St Pius X Catholic School, TX

Alex

My mother had a dog and her name was Alex. She was a black Labrador and never bit anyone, ever. I only knew her for about 5 years. On a Christmas morning when Alex was very old and sick, she had to be taken to the veterinarian. Mom left with Alex in the car. Dad, Paul, and I waited and waited for what felt like hours and hours. We all hoped Alex would be okay. When Mom finally got home, she was alone. I was the first one to speak. "Where is Alex?" I asked. Mom answered with the one thing I feared, "Alex is gone," she said. I understood that Alex was old but it was still so sad. Now we have a dog named Cici. She is not as smart as Alex but she is fun. There are many things that make Alex and Cici different but there are also things that make them the same. I will always remember them both.

Merrell Goza, Grade 5
Horn Academy, TX

My Great Grandmother

My great grandmother was very sick and in the hospital. We visited very often, but I had a massive project and we needed to work on it so we stopped for a little while. I was at my dad's side of the family's grandmother's house doing my homework. Then my mom walked in and said that my great grandmother had died.

She was the first person that died when I was alive. I cried a lot when she died. It was hard to stop crying. My mom tried to help me stop but I couldn't stop crying. Then I remembered how religious she was and that she was sick. *The Bible* is all about how God loves us and that everything happens for a reason. Then I realized that she was happy in Heaven. She just was in a different place.

Trey Pokorny, Grade 4
Horn Academy, TX

Best Friends

You might have a hundred friends, but you only have a few true friends. I call them best friends or BFF's. I think that BFF's are supposed to be loyal, true and caring. Best friends are supposed to be there for each other. If your best friend turns her back on you, then she is not a true best friend. BFF's can be guys or girls.

Best friends are loyal because they can keep a lot of secrets. BFF's are true because they will always tell you the truth no matter what it is. BFF's are always at your side at all times.

They are always there for you and you are always there for them. If she falls, the other is there to help her up. If something bad happens to one friend she has a shoulder to cry on.

Best friends are friends in good times and in bad. If someone passes away in your family, your best friend is there for you. If a family member gets married, she is there to congratulate the married couple.

People have many friends, but you only have a few true friends.

Melissa Alaniz, Grade 5
St Pius X Catholic School, TX

My Parents Are Important to Me

My parents are important to me. They take good care of me. They help me with my school work. They also take me to places.

My parents take care of me a lot. When I get sick, they give me medicine. They take me to the doctor and to the dentist. My mom makes hot food for me every day. My dad buys me everything I need. They dry my tears when I am crying.

My parents always help me with my school assignments. My mom helps me with my math and English homework. My dad assists me with Arabic homework. Both of them help me create wonderful projects for school.

My parents take me to amazing places. One time, they took me on a cruise. It was the Disney Cruise. There were great music and lots of activities for kids to do. The cruise was huge, I ran everywhere. It was fun.

My family is significant in my life. I can always count on them. I love them and they love me too.

Sara Farah, Grade 3
Islamic School of San Diego, CA

Leaving

I skipped down the old brown sidewalk for what would be the last time in a long time. I turned around quickly to see my grandmother's small house. I knew I did not want to leave but I had to. Skipping gracefully, I sat down on an apple red bench. Teardrops slid slowly down my cheeks. I saw a figure approaching me. It was my gloomy mom. She placed a lime green suitcase in the car. I asked her why we had to leave. She placed her small hand on my shoulder and told me that I have school tomorrow and that we will be back. I moved my head slightly to say bye and I stepped in the car.

Arielle Nates, Grade 4
Horn Academy, TX

Louisiana Forest Change

When I was little, I lived in New Orleans, Louisiana. I lived in a neighborhood called Forest Brook which was an apt name for it since it had a little brook full of ducks and a forest colored by varied shades of green…I haven't seen a more beautiful place. But one day, something shattered its beauty.

Hurricane Katrina was on its way to New Orleans, so the plan was to evacuate…fast. We went to a friend's house in Dallas, Texas and stayed for the night. Maybe more than a night – but it was until the hurricane blew out, that we dared drive back home. The houses I saw while driving home were pitiful. Most of them were damaged and split open by nearby trees. My house was totally undamaged – nearby trees only toppled on top of each other. Fortune was with us, but not the forest surrounding our neighborhood. Almost all of the trees in the forest were all crushed. It could've been a giant that trampled the trees, for all I knew. I'll never see this forest straight again. This changed put a dent in my childhood, a dent that I try to straighten out but will never be the same ever again.

Michelle Miao, Grade 5
Horn Academy, TX

Skim Boarding

Whoosh! The waves crash as I skim along the water. Splash! I fall into the water. My skim board lays on the sand as I watch my older brother skim across the water. I try to do the same, but I slip and fall and hit the edge of the skim board with my back. AH! AH! AH! Blood gushes out into the water. I scraped my back. My mom took me up to the hotel to get it bandaged. That really changed what I did at the beach for the rest of the day. I didn't skim board. I just built sand castles. After my back was all better, I went back to skim boarding but I changed so that I was more careful. Although skim boarding is my favorite activity at the beach, I learned that there were other fun things to do at the beach like snorkeling, building sand castles and boogie boarding. This changed what I usually do at the beach.

Joseph Times, Grade 5
Horn Academy, TX

Leaving School

School ending was hard. We had to leave our beautiful outdoor amphitheater. The trees around our classroom with a minimum amount of sunlight was so graceful. It was so peaceful when you went outside and read while a slight breeze went by. Sitting on the amphitheater with the sun blazing in your eyes was not the best, but I still enjoyed it. Summer ending was weird because we had a new school, but at least the new school was a little nicer. The old school was a great school but the new one is just a little better. I know that some people, like me, still miss and hate that we had to leave the delightful old school.

I wish we could have stayed in the school that everyone misses. It was a creative and fun school.

Riley Harrison, Grade 4
Horn Academy, TX

Nose Rings

Last year I had to do a report on American Indians in different regions. We got to pick what Indians we got to do. Looking at pictures in our social studies book of which Indians we could do I instantly I knew which ones I wanted to do. When we picked, Ms. Planje, my teacher, would choose a student to go up and write their name on which tribe they wanted to do. When I was called I quickly found which one I wanted to do and wrote my name down. I picked to do it on the Pacific Northwest Indians. I picked them for a silly reason that eventually became our chant. As I was looking at the pictures of the Indians the nose ring that the Pacific Northwest Indian was wearing amazed me.

For the project I was with Lee, Ryan, Jeffery, and Dana. We all had to research a specific thing that those Indians did. I forget what I did, but I think it was the food. When we started to make up our project Ryan and I thought that we should chant at the end, "We are the Pacific Northwest. Nose rings, nose rings, nose rings, nose rings." We actually did it too! Yet, only Ryan and I did it. Lee, Jeffery, and Dana held signs that said, "We Are The," "Pacific," and "Northwest." They held these up as we chanted. It was hilarious, and made everyone laugh.

Jason Pontillas, Grade 6
Margaret Landell Elementary School, CA

Ding Dong Ditching

"I'm so bored," complained my friend, Seth. Seth lives down the street from us. It was a dull, Monday afternoon. Monday was probably the worst day of the week. "Hey, I got an idea!" Seth suddenly said. "We could ding dong ditch people's houses!" Well, first of all, neither of us could run faster than a turtle. So I wasn't in the "ding dong ditching" business. Seth walked up to a random house and rang their doorbell, and I couldn't believe my eyes once he rang that doorbell. For the first time in my life, I actually saw Seth run. He was as fast as a jackrabbit. An old man opened the door and said, "I must be losing my mind." And as soon as he closed the door, I burst out laughing. "Ha-ha-ha! That was so funny!"

That was probably one of the funniest moments of my life. But what was most important was that I had created a friendship with my best friend, Seth.

Enrique Cardenas, Grade 5
Horn Academy, TX

Friendship

What I like most in a friend is a kind heart and trust. A true friend doesn't put something less important before you, they don't tell secrets, and they don't lie. A friend would be someone you've known for years and have trusted them throughout those happy years, a friend would be someone who protects you and cheers you up when you're down, and especially a friend is someone who loves you and you love them. The most special thing you can have is a friend. Going to a friend's house proves friendship and trust, and a friend doesn't abandon you. What I like in a friend is that I'll remember them forever.

Daniel De La Fuente, Grade 5
Castle Hill Country Day School, AZ

My Trip to Las Vegas

My uncle came to visit for a week. This meant that we could go on a trip. For a long time, I had been waiting to go on this trip. At last, the moment has arrived. We were on our way to Las Vegas.

Before the trip, we prepared. My mother packed our food, water, and clothing. My father made directions and got the car ready. I helped look for a Masjid. Everyone went to bed early that night.

At the morning of the trip, we were on our way to Las Vegas. Everyone helped put stuff in the car. My father drove us there. We kids were playing in the back with my uncle. On the way, we saw interesting things.

We have arrived at Las Vegas safely. The first thing we did was go to the hotel and put the stuff there. Next we visited Bellagio. There were lots of trees and many shops. At night the city was shining. There were lights everywhere. Some were colorful, and had beautiful shapes. It felt like the stars came down.

The trip was amazing. I had fun with my family. I would love to go back one day.

Abdurrahman Arif, Grade 3
Islamic School of San Diego, CA

Where Tranquility Reaches Earth

"Everyone is asleep but me," I sighed. I stepped into the family library, and took a deep breath of the warm summer air. The musty smell of books seemed soothing and natural, yet ancient. I strolled over to a corner covered in soft carpeting, which tickled my feet. My forehead formed tiny salt water droplets, but before I opened the window I noticed that the sun's rays glinted on it making it seem luminescent. When I finished gaping out the window I tried opening it, yet it always had a glitch. Today it was a tree branch scraping against the window pane. Struggling to open it, I lifted the transparent, plastic window a crack, so I heard blue jays and robins chirping in unison. The tranquility quickly spread through the room, and I curled up in a ball on the pearly-white sun-warmed matted carpet and dozed off.

Isabella Hsu, Grade 4
Horn Academy, TX

Moving

The whooshing breeze soothed my mind as I was on the musty-smelling bench on our front porch. I thought about how much I would miss my friends and neighbors who helped me through all my troubles. I felt so miserable just thinking about it. Our family was moving because we had a small house and we were about to have another brother which was fine but I wanted to keep all my friends and did not want to move. I just wished that somehow everything would move with us so I wouldn't be lonely at all and have some company. "Let's go!" my father said in a stern voice waiting for me to get into the car. Without showing any emotions, I got into the car still dismayed on the inside.

Leigh Vo, Grade 4
Horn Academy, TX

High Merit Essays – Grades 3, 4, 5, and 6

Moving to a New School

It was my first day of 2nd grade in a brand new school named Outley Elementary. As I went through the big doors, my heart started to beat fast, and even though my mom was by my side, I was still very scared. Will the other kids laugh at me? Will I do the right thing? Will I do the wrong thing? Will I be popular? Will the others ignore me? Will I make a good impression. All these questions were going through my head, but I thought, if I don't try I won't succeed so I guess we'll just have to see!

As I went to my new class I realized I was 3 days late from the first day of school, so I was behind on a lot of work! As the day went by I did all of my work and made absolutely no trouble. It turned out I was not popular, the other kids did ignore me, and I made the worst first impression possible. During specials and class I tried to start a conversation with some of the kids at my table, but when I talked they listened to a word, and then went to talk to someone else.

After lunch (on the second day of school) someone from the front office came to transfer me to an AIMS class since I qualified for the gifted and talented class. I packed my things and went to my new class. My new class was a lot more welcoming than my first class and I was able to make new friends right away. They were so kind to me even though I knew none of them. Maybe coming to this school wasn't such a bad idea!

Elizabeth Ogolo, Grade 4
Outley Elementary School, TX

My Sand Dollar Collection

My favorite thing to collect is sand dollars. A sand dollar is shaped like a flower and is smooth. It has a hole in the bottom. It is shiny and a whitish color. You find them at the beach in Hawaii and California. I collected some of the sand dollars from San Diego. My aunt got some for me. I have 20 of them and they have sand inside. When you shake them, they sound like a rattle. They can break if you hit them because they are fragile. My sister's friend sat on one of them and it broke. They can only be found at certain beaches.

My brother and I keep all our shells together, and he gave me all of his sand dollars. I can only put my collection on soft blankets. It is up high, so my cousins can't get it. I have all my sand dollars in a box with my seashells. My favorite sand dollar is big and is not shaped like a flower, which is why it is my favorite. It is round and large and is the only one that is not cracked. I have five small sand dollars, five medium-sized ones, and ten big ones. I named my sand dollars after my relatives, like Betty, Jeremy, Lydia, Tony, Lizzy, Deran, Dylan, Lisa, and Curtis.

I can play with my sand dollars sometimes, but not all the time, because if I play with them too much, they will break. Sometimes I clear off my dresser and decorate it with my sand dollars if there is a blanket on it. My sand dollar collection makes me feel like I am at the beach. I love my sand dollars because they are a treasure to me!

Jasmine Mock, Grade 3
Vista Charter School, UT

The Day I Got a Certificate

The best time in my elementary school year was in 2nd grade. It was near the end of the school year and everyone was at the last assembly of that school year. They were announcing awards for the students that had perfect attendance and had not pulled a card or gotten a pink slip for the whole year. I sat anxiously on the floor, waiting for them to call Mrs. Forgione's name to go up and present the awards. There were butterflies in my stomach as I sat there, praying that I would get at least one award that day. Finally, the principal of Landell called Mrs. Forgione's name and asked her to come up and present the awards to the students that had perfect attendance or didn't pull a card or receive a pink slip.

Name after name was called. I was fidgeting with my shirt as I tensed. Had she called my name? I realized she had called my name! I proudly stood up and walked up to my teacher. I received my certificate and stood next to the other students that had gotten a certificate. That whole day, I had a smile from ear to ear. I was so happy I had gotten certificate! After that day, I have always set my goal to not miss a single day of school and not receive a pink slip or pull a card.

Katelyn Huang, Grade 6
Margaret Landell Elementary School, CA

The Speech

It was in 5th grade when Ms. Chung's class (the class that I was in) was getting ready to go to the Ocean Institute. We were practicing for two or three months getting ready for this day. Everyone was on the bus chatting and laughing and having fun. After about a two hour drive on the bus we had arrived. When our class got off the bus some people from the Ocean Institute came to greet us and give us name tags. Next, they brought us into a room and separated us into groups.

My group was in the biggest of the three rooms. After watching two other schools give their speeches it was our turn. I was all excited and happy till it was my turn on stage. When I got the microphone I did not know what to do so I froze for a little bit. But then, I told myself to just relax and read your notes. I read my notes and after my part was over I felt relieved.

Kekoa O'neil, Grade 6
Margaret Landell Elementary School, CA

Big E

The Navy's aircraft carrier Enterprise is the longest in service carrier. It has served 51 years.

The carrier Enterprise, nicknamed, "Big E," was the first nuclear-powered carrier. It was also the longest naval vessel in the world, with a length of 1,123 feet long! Enterprise has participated in summer surge and provided support in operation "Iraqi Freedom."

Carriers are the "Capital Ship" of the fleet. This means the U.S. has 21 carriers, but is only operating 11. We need carriers so that they can deploy and recover aircraft from missions or for sky checking. If we didn't have carriers, a lot would be different. For instance, we might have lost a lot of wars.

Ben Mikulencak, Grade 5
St Pius X Catholic School, TX

New Way of Life

"Bang, bang, bang." I look out the door. There's the principal walking down the hallway with a possum running in front of her. That was the old Horn Academy with dust on the wall, colors on the desk, and the smell of coffee and caramel in the air. Sure that's not what you might call a perfect school, but I would. It was like home.

Now the modern Horn Academy has gray paint on the walls, smart boards, and it smells like dust in the air. There's no principal chasing a possum down the hallway for sure. Boring, right? At least it is when you have been in a school with 80-year-old trees shading you when you walk outside your classroom door, and a hawk that flies through your classroom window.

I miss my old school. This school feels like jail. When you look outside your window you see houses. When you walk outside your door you see other classrooms. When you change schools you lose passion. I loved my old school with colorful walls, huge trees and beautiful wildlife, like birds and bunnies. I guess that is what you have when you get all new stuff; you get a new way of life.

Ashley Clarke, Grade 5
Horn Academy, TX

When I Moved to Bellaire

About six months ago, I moved to Bellaire, Texas. I really didn't want to move. My mom told us to come into the living room. There was a plate of doughnuts in the middle of the table. She told us slowly, "I brought you here because we are moving to Bellaire in July." There was complete and utter silence.

It was July 21st the day we moved. My whole family jumped in the car and my mom started driving to Bellaire. It took two whole days! When we got to Bellaire, we went to our hotel and settled in. When we left our hotel the next morning to go to our brand new house, I was really scared. As we walked in, my mouth dropped open. Our house was amazing inside and out.

On the first day of school, I walked in and sat down. I was very nervous that day. When I got back home, I felt great. The day had been fantastic. At the end of the week, I told myself, "I might end up having a good time here in Bellaire."

Charlotte Goldenberg, Grade 4
Horn Academy, TX

My Jewelry Box

My jewelry box looks like a purple leopard. When it opens, you can see all my sparkly jewelry. I have about…hmm…say…tons? It has a leather handle and the whole thing is overflowing with my shiny baubles. I even keep my special baptism necklace in it to keep it safe. The box is all made of tough leather. The shape is kind of rectangular and the size is about nine inches tall and seven inches wide. Do you want some of my jewelry? No — mine! If you lift up a latch, then the whole thing opens. It was a very special gift from my mom that I will give to my daughter someday, if I have one.

Arianna Madsen, Grade 3
Vista Charter School, UT

Stargazing

Stargazing is when you look out in the night sky and observe what is going on. You can see many star patterns like the Big Dipper or planets like Venus. Stargazing is a hobby for some people, especially if they have a telescope. Stargazing is better when done at a certain place and time.

Some people think nighttime is the only time to stargaze. However, that is not true! The best times to stargaze are also sunset, dawn, and sunrise. To get the best views, look from certain places, such as a mountain campsite. For best results, look from a place where there are no city lights. Special instruments are a must for stargazing. Use your eyes or a telescope.

To get started, look at a specific direction in the sky. Constellations are placed all over the sky. The place of the constellations will also change throughout time. Some constellations or planets will need to be seen with effort. Others can be seen easily.

It requires effort to look for some constellations. That is because they are arranged in groups of stars. A common constellation is the Big Dipper. It looks like a big spoon. Others are Orion, Pegasus, and the Little Dipper. Pegasus is a winged horse. Some constellations represent different mythical characters.

Planets can also be seen in the sky. Since Venus is the closest planet to us, it is the first planet to be seen in the night sky. Other planets that can be seen are Mars and Jupiter.

Stargazing may be done for a long or short time. If you are done looking at the stars, think about the night sky. Maybe one day you will be able to find a new constellation!

Yusuf Amanullah, Grade 3
Islamic School of San Diego, CA

Diversity

We are all different in our own way. The difference in our personalities and gender attracts us to each other. If we all looked alike and wore the same clothing, it would be pretty tedious in this world. Some believe that they need to look like everybody else, when it's just best to be ourselves.

If we all had the same talents and hobbies, we wouldn't be that amused in each other. Having unique talents makes you feel special about who you are. For example, I am a dancer that performs and competes. I have practiced dancing since I was three and now I can share my talents. One of my friends likes to paint and I think she is really proficient at it. She can express herself in art. My friends are more divergent than me and that's what I like about them. My family is all divergent in our own ways, but we accept each other for who we are.

Race is a major difference here in America. My family recently had a foreign exchange student. Even though she looked different and acted different, we welcomed her into our family. I learned that they have a lot of respect for those that are older and wiser than them. I also learned that their education is very important as a culture. I had a fun time discovering how different she was than us.

Daycia Lee, Grade 6
White Pine Charter School, ID

My Miracle

I was in the car half way to Oceanside, California, where I thought it would be the best weekend ever. My father and I were going to Oceanside so we could go see his girlfriend and one of my closest friends Sydney, her daughter. When we first got there, we all said our hi's and got settled in. An hour later Sid and I went bike riding around the beach, AWESOME! The next day was complete chaos trying to get ready for the beach. We found my dad on the couch sleeping, Lynne, his girlfriend said we should wake him up so, we did! Immediately, Sid and I hit the waves, we weren't surfing. Sydney wanted to go really deep, so she took me with her. She promised I'd be fine, but I was still really freaked out. I had never gone out so far before. In the end I was right. I shouldn't of gone out so far. About two minutes into it I lost all contact with Sydney. I was petrified, what could I do? When I was thinking about all this, the next thing I knew I couldn't breathe, underwater, trying to get up, and couldn't yell! A couple seconds later I saw seaweed around my legs and arms, I couldn't get up or breathe! Finally, I heard Sydney's voice. I still have no idea how I got tangled or untangled but, I was lucky I had a real miracle!

Raechel Schmidt, Grade 4
Pepper Tree Elementary School, CA

Motion of Dance

You silently walk on stage. You see the millions of eyes watching your every move. You are nervous and scared, until you hear the music and you feel the beat in your soul. Your nerves vanish and you feel wiggly. The feeling grows and suddenly you burst into dance. You start to frolic across the stage in a graceful motion. You mess-up, but you do not care. You are in another world, the world of dance, and you are free there. You spin and spin, circle and circle, twisting and twisting, in an endless tornado. The crowd is dizzy just watching you, but you are not.

As the music slows down so do you. All your feelings come back as you quietly walk off the stage. Though your body is still, your soul is still dancing to the beat of your heart. Now your heart is engraved with dance. You are a dancer.

I feel this way when I dance. You may not feel it, but it is my motion of dance. I am a dancer. Watch me dance.

Annika Zoetmulder, Grade 5
East Sandy School, UT

Sad Things Are Important

While I was at my grandparent's house, the hospital called my grandpa and said my great uncle had died from a brain tumor. My grandpa got off the phone and said that your uncle has passed away. I felt water in my eyes and I ran to my grandma and she asked me what was wrong and why I was crying. I was so sad I could not speak. So she went to my grandpa and asked why I was crying and before you knew it my grandma was crying. A few days later there was a funeral service in memory of him. It was the saddest day I had to go through. But I know he will be in all my memories.

Madison Olds, Grade 4
Horn Academy, TX

Dolphins

Dolphins are beautiful creatures. They are very playful and cute. if you see a dolphin he will make your day.

Did you know that every dolphin has a different and unique dorsal fin? That's how people can tell them apart. Some dolphins have holes in their dorsal fins.

Dolphins are very social animals. When dolphins are in an aquarium, they need to be with other dolphins so they won't feel alone.

Did you know that dolphins' ears are so sensitive that sonar from ships makes their ears bleed? If their ears bleed, they could die. Sometimes dolphins beach themselves to get away from the sonar. When a dolphin beaches itself, it gets really close to shore and then the waves wash the dolphin on shore the rest of the way.

Dolphins talk a lot by making clicking sounds to speak. They make different sounds for danger too. Dolphins will make warning clicks and slap their tails on the water to warn other dolphins and tell them they are in trouble. For example dolphins will warn against sharks. Sharks are their natural enemies.

The tail is a very important part of a dolphin's body. If something happens to a dolphin's tail, it will probably die, which is very unfortunate because dolphins are so amazing in the way they move. The tail is connected to the spine, which means if it gets fractured, the dolphin will be paralyzed. After a couple of minutes, they will drown. The blowhole is very important too. That is how they breathe. if they don't come up from the water to get air, they will drown.

Dolphins are very strong, powerful, and gorgeous.

Taylor Skrobarczyk, Grade 5
St Pius X Catholic School, TX

Moving to San Diego

It was a gigantic theater with a big stage. The show was almost over I though glumly. I had to go to an airport and fly to San Diego. My mom was checking her watch every minute. "Sai let's go and call your dad and there you could say bye to your friends," my mom whispered. My legs wobbled. My heart beat faster and faster. My hand ached as they stretched and wrapped around my friend, Anisha. Every tear was as big as an elephant, every word was a painful ache. We both knew that we weren't going to see each other every week. We gave each other hugs and my family departed.

We got in the car and from Orlando we drove to the airport. I slept in the car thinking about my friend and thinking about San Diego. After about 35 minutes, we were at the airport, ready to get on board, but not ready to leave my friends and the house behind. We waited in the super long line and went on board for our new adventure. A few tears dropped. "No, I shouldn't cry. I am a big girl," I thought a hundred times. But the tears escaped. I knew that I would have new friends and have fun in second grade. It was painful leaving your best friends. The line moved and I gave my tickets to the air host. I never knew that one step would change my life forever.

Prasanna S. Padmanabham, Grade 5
Dingeman Elementary School, CA

Fishing

Fishing is my favorite hobby because it's exciting and I'm able to relax by listening to the sound of water splashing safely and the bubbles gurgling. Of course, people need patience but whenever they catch fish, it pays off.

Our family competes for records. For example, I hold the record for the biggest flounder and for a huge crab that accidentally got stuck on my line. My brother and I caught one fish together when it bit the bait on both of our lines and our lines got tangled.

Once my brother caught one unusually small catfish and I wanted to keep it. So, I filled an empty Gatorade bottle with saltwater and then my brother held him over my hand. He was still hooked in his lips, but then the hook slipped. So, the catfish's sharp fin went an inch into my wrist, narrowly missing one of my arteries, and causing much pain. I didn't bleed, but it hurt when my dad pulled it out. Then I became nauseous and because I was passing out, I don't remember much. But, I do remember going quickly towards the dock, getting carried into the truck, and rushing into the hospital emergency room. I woke up to my dad, brother, and cousins all around me. I was in a bed with my hand in freezing water when my mom arrived. My family code named this new record as the "fishing accident."

Sometimes fishing leads to more than catching fish. Either way I still like fishing and all the adventures that come with it.

Kyle Pekar, Grade 6
St Pius X Catholic School, TX

Pluto

I find Pluto very interesting. Pluto is one out of the nine planets. Pluto is a planet that was first called Planet X. Its Greek name is Hades. It is 4.5 billion years old and it was the smallest planet until August 2006. It was discovered by a Nazi scientist. Pluto is the 9th planet and it is 3.67 million miles from the sun. It also crosses the Neptune trail in a swarm known as Kuiper Belt. It takes light 6 hours and 30 minutes to get there. It can be closer than Neptune, and has an egg-like orbit.

Pluto has three moons. One is named Charon. Charon is neutral gray. The second is called Nix and the last one is named Hydra. Nix is blue and Hydra is greenish-red. Pluto, a dwarf planet, is -360 degrees Fahrenheit, has a rocky silicate core, and contains nitrogen, carbon monoxide, and methane. It is also made of rock and ice, has no people on it, is green, has a mass of 1.31×10^{22} kilograms, and is two-thirds the size of our moon. It also has lots of poisonous gases.

In conclusion, Pluto is an interesting planet. Even though it is a dwarf planet, it is still interesting. It has three moons, and is very cold. Many more fascinating facts have been discovered about Pluto. It also is 3.66 billion miles away from the sun. In fact, it takes 247.7 years to orbit the sun once. Even though it is so far away and nobody has ever set a foot on it, the scientists still know all these amazing facts. I hope this will teach you new facts about Pluto.

Jonathan Wang, Grade 5
Top Kids Center, CA

My House

My house is very big. I get very many compliments about it. My room is pink; when we moved back in 2007, I had a theme of princesses. My room is connected to my sister's room by our own bathroom. The bathroom is themed after frogs because my mom loves them. My sister's room is themed after Tinkerbell, and is purple. She never really liked Tinkerbell, but my mom wanted a theme.

Across the hall from my room is the guest room. My mom wanted one so that when we have visitors, they don't have to sleep on our new couch. The guest room is a very tan kind of room. There is no actual, or permanent, theme for it.

Next to the guest room is the guest bathroom. That room is themed after Texas. The towels are dark blue with red and white stars at the ends, along with the hand towel and the carpets. There is a framed piece of construction paper that has red, white, and blue pieces of torn up construction paper in the form of a Texan flag.

At the other end of the hall is my mom and dad's room. It doesn't have a theme. Neither does their bathroom. Their bathroom is humungous. It is awesome! My hall is the shape of a capital T. At the end of the hall, is my living room, with a television in the corner next to the windows showing the yard with our three dogs. Then we have the couch in the shape of a right angle. My kitchen is also very big, and it is attached to the dining room. We have about six chairs and a bench. That's my house!

Sara Bryant, Grade 6
Lampasas Middle School, TX

Because It Counts

"Why do You have to go?" I tried using my big girl voice, but only tears came out. Dad was leaving in two days for Iraq. He was missing my sixth birthday. My heart felt like it had hit an iceberg and sunk.

My dad tried to console me, but his soothing voice didn't work this time. It wasn't the first time we'd had this conversation and it wasn't going to be the last. I thought to myself *I just want my dad. Don't those boss guys have daughters too?*

The next day, he said that he was going to take me out to Barnes and Noble. My face lit up and my mouth started speeding very fast. I could have gotten a ticket. I got dressed like a race car and flew down the creaky, soft carpet steps like there was no tomorrow. Or that's what I wished. But I pushed that thought out of my head. We picked out a book, went to Starbucks and had a great time. I wished the day would never end.

On the following morning, I smelled my favorite breakfast, pancakes! I saw Mom and a tear rolled down her cheek. I remember that he was leaving today. A hurricane started in my mind. My dad hugged me and I hugged him back so hard. I never wanted to let him go. I felt a little sad, but I knew he was going for a good reason. I couldn't wait for him to come back. I knew he'd be back soon!

Alexandra Kotsos, Grade 5
Dingeman Elementary School, CA

Confrontation in Imagination

"Loot detected!" I, a first grader, yelled.

I was playing the game of Pirates, which was based solely on my imagination. Sailing on my pirate ship, I had found loot, a tennis ball.

"Full speed ahead!" I commanded, dashing to the "treasure."

As I darted toward it, I noticed a rival pirate, another first grader, scampering toward the ball.

"The loot shall be mine!" I bellowed.

I, Captain Joshua, was determined to obtain the loot!

Both of us scurried to the tennis ball, but I had beaten him to it. I crouched over to pick up the tennis ball, when a figure snatched it. I looked up and locked eyes with my rival. Clutched in his hand, was the treasure. Glaring at him, I wildly swung my "sword" at him. I smacked his arm and his expression showed soreness. With eyes full of fury, steam seemed to rise from his head. Unexpectedly, he violently scratched at the air, clawing my face. The cut stung, and my heart became overwhelmed with rage. This was not an imaginary game anymore. It was a furious fight. I tackled him and both of us lay sprawled on the ground.

At that moment, our teacher appeared and saw the tackle. She looked cross, for a frown was planted on her face. After we were lectured about the danger of fighting by our teacher, we apologized to each other and were punished. What's more, I didn't get my loot! My teacher took it!

Joshua Moon, Grade 6
Margaret Landell Elementary School, CA

My Eighth Birthday Party

On the morning of July 31, 2008, I woke up early in the morning. "Mom! Dad! Wake up! It's my 8th birthday!" I ran to my parents' room and jumped up and down. I've been waiting for this party for months and it was finally here! "Your party is starting at 1:00, Shinwho! Don't get too excited!" my mom said. I had forgotten my friends and neighbors were going to come in the afternoon. Still, I was excited.

Once my parents woke up, we started getting ready. My dad set up the table and got the big chocolate birthday cake. My mom made balloons and got the pizza. I helped them and put on a pretty dress that was for special occasions. I was grinning happily the whole time.

We were all ready when the guests started coming in. I greeted my neighbors and my friends with a friendly smile. They were holding large boxes. They looked heavy and big. I couldn't wait to open them! We sang a short happy birthday and I blew out the candles with a wish. The cake we ate was delicious. It was very sweet though. We ate until we were full. My friends and I played and played until it was time to open the gifts. I got pretty dresses, fun games, and cool crafts. Time flew by and the party was soon over.

When the guests left, I was disappointed that the party was over. I'd wanted the party to be longer. But I enjoyed it and the party was fun and exciting.

Shinwho Kwun, Grade 5
Dingeman Elementary School, CA

The Dangerous Gate

"Ericka, it's time to go!" my mom called. I ran downstairs. It was the second day of tennis camp. Soon, we got to the tennis courts.

"Good job," cried Chelsea, our tennis teacher and assistant to the coach, Richard. "I'll go ask Richard if we can go to the walls."

"Let's play tag!" cried my friend Bailey, as we waited for Chelsea to come back.

"I'll be it," another friend, Emily, replied Emily tagged Bailey who ran after me.

"Tag!" Bailey cried. I chased her and Emily. They shot through the fence door. I ran through after them but stopped as pain shot through my head and scarlet blood dripped down my face. I was screaming inside my head. I almost cried. Soon, my cut was clean and I was going home.

At home, my mom checked the cut. She told me I needed stitches. I started crying again. "I don't want to get stitches!" I wailed. My mom told me I might get sick if I didn't get stitches so I finally gave in and let my mom take me to the hospital.

At the hospital, we followed a nurse into a room. Soon, a lady came in and started preparing to give me stitches. The doctor started to numb the place around the cut and started doing stitches.

"I put in four stitches," the doctor told my mom.

Richard told me I opened the gate the wrong way. I learned to always be careful with gates.

Ericka Li, Grade 5
Dingeman Elementary School, CA

Bathtub Trouble

Burble, burble! Water splashed from the faucet into our bathtub. I watched, excited.

I waited. Finally Mom dumped in the bubbles. Her golden curls fell against the bathtub. Pop! Mom turned off the water.

Mom turned on the jets. Bubbles oozed out.

Winslow poked his head over the edge. His eyes glittered with envy. He wanted to lay in the bath.

"No, Winslow, get your nose back," Mom teasingly scolded. Winslow turned around and laid down.

"I think it's ready," Mom said. The bath looked luxurious. The bubbles foamed, the bath steamed. Suddenly, ring. Mom ran to get the phone. I followed her. We left the room, leaving Winslow alone with the bath.

Mom got off the phone and walked back while I bounced behind her. When she looked in the bathroom, her eyes got big. I looked around her and gasped.

Winslow was lying in the bathtub. He was covered in bubbles, lying down.

We both laughed. Winslow looked up guiltily. Some bubbles dripped down his muzzle.

"Well, since he is in there, we might as well give him a bath," my mom said. She poured the shampoo on Winslow. I joined her. Winslow loves baths, at least the way humans take them.

Lauren Garcia, Grade 5
Dingeman Elementary School, CA

Mind Game

It has been said that baseball is 95% mental. There is a lot of truth to that statement. Certain situations sometimes arise that require a player to have ice in his veins. This happens regularly, but one time really stands out in my mind.

During this particular baseball game, we were up 8-0 going into the final inning. We thought we had it in the bag, but we were quickly reminded that a baseball game isn't over until it's over. Our opponents had first bat going into the inning. They definitely found their bats and quickly closed the gap in the score. The game was now tied at 8.

With bases loaded and only one out, the coach pulled the pitcher and called me over. He was putting me in to pitch out the game. I knew I needed to be perfect and shut down their bats. My mom later said that she was sweating bullets, but I felt confident in myself.

The first batter stepped to the plate. I pitched three perfect strikes that had him swinging and missing. Whew! I had one down, and one to go. "I can do this," I told myself. The next batter stepped up. I felt a little bit of nerves creeping in, but pushed them down. Again, I was able to place my pitches well and strike him out. What a relief! I was so glad that I was able to help my team by switching the game's momentum.

Luckily, we were able to keep our bats going and pull out the win. While much skill is required in baseball, it is extremely important to learn to remain levelheaded throughout the game. It can be the difference in winning and losing.

Marshall Kellner, Grade 6
Lampasas Middle School, TX

Creature of the Night

The sun was glaring down on us and sweat covered our faces. I felt the hot rays of the sun burning the back of my neck. The football felt good in my hand. I chucked the ball. The wide receiver caught it and rushed down the field. He tossed it back to me. I ran my hardest and avoided the safety. I went into the end zone. Touchdown! I began my slow walk down the field, unaware of the creature in front of me. I felt a tiny prick and looked down and saw a three-inch spider crawl away from my foot.

The first thought that came to me was oh dang, I just got bitten by a spider. So I ran for my mom. My foot started to swell up but I pushed on. The pain soon became so great that I had to slow down to a fast walk. But even that didn't last long. I pushed on hopping on one foot. Finally after 30 seconds I collapsed. My foot felt like people were stabbing knives in it. My eyes were getting heavy. After seconds I closed my eyes.

My sister was crowing over me. I jumped up only to fall down again. I looked at my foot and almost fainted again. My foot was purple, it looked like the rainbow hosted a party and invited all of his color friends. I limped over to the pool and showed my mom the bruise. She gave me an ice pack and said to hang in there. After 2 hours my foot returned to normal size. I realized then that this was the day that I was going to remember for a long, long, time.

Joshua Castellitto, Grade 5
Dingeman Elementary School, CA

Knowing Your Cat's Behavior

This is a subject I've always known. I've had 3 cats before, and just got my 4th. So, let's start with the basic behavior: meowing.

If your cat likes the outdoors, and isn't fixed, you should expect it to be yowling, or, in other words, having the "call of the wild." This means kitten season is soon, and you cat is calling for a mate. If your cat prefers to be indoors, long, loud meows mean, "I want something!", whereas short, quiet meows mean "Hello!" I'm sure you all know what hissing means, if you don't, too bad, but when your cat is purring, and lashing its tail, it means "Cut that out!"

Next, beware of the threats and anger. When your cat is angry, remember one thing: "anger" is one letter short of "danger." If your cat is angry, leave it alone for a while. Otherwise, it will start to bite and scratch. If you have ever seen two cats, who hate each other and stare into one another's eyes, you will know that cats take staring as a threat.

And last, but not least, cats' behavior during the night hours is lively. Have you ever been awoken at night because your cat was jumping on you under the covers? Don't get mad, it's just following its natural instincts. Cats are nocturnal, and it's going to get frisky from sundown until late in the morning. It'll calm down at noon or so. Until then, be careful.

If your cat is meowing, angry, or frisky, just remember all that I told you about your cat's behavior. Especially, remember that angry part.

Katherine Atkinson, Grade 5
Washington Elementary School, CA

Old Hickory

Who was called Old Hickory? Who was one of the most important Presidents in our American History? This leader was called Old Hickory because he was tough as hickory wood.

Andrew Jackson was born on March 15, 1767 in the South Carolina colony. He lived with his cousins since birth because Andrew's father died six days before he was born. His cousins' family asked Mrs. Jackson and her children to stay with them. When Andrew was five, his mother enrolled him in a small academy at Waxhaw Church. Andrew did well in that school. However, he did not like being picked on by other children. Since Andrew was so little and thin, he was easily knocked down in the wrestling matches.

In July 1780 when he was only thirteen, Andrew joined the army. He was once captured by the British. When he refused to clean an officer's boots, his hand and head were slashed with a sword; the scars remained visible his whole life, but he was proud of them. Then Andrew started to teach school in Waxhaw. In December 1784, he went to North Carolina to study law. When Andrew was twenty years old, he became a full-fledged lawyer. In 1796, Andrew became a member of the House of Representatives. Afterwards, he joined the Senate and served as governor of Florida Territory.

I admire Andrew Jackson for his courage and deep love of America. The seventh president is my hero.

Tony Nguyen, Grade 5
Montessori Learning Institute, TX

Going to Chile

My heart was pounding like a bunch of basketballs. I couldn't believe that I was about 30,000 feet in the air! But at least I was going to meet my grandfather for the first time ever.

About two hours had gone by and we ate until we never wanted to eat again. Then we waited and waited and waited and waited...until finally our plane was ready and it was time to go to Chile! 3, 2, 1 blast off! We were 30,000 feet in the air again. I played video games, watched movies, heard music, and even had sort of a good drink because it was kind of dry. I felt as if I were the queen of the plane since they were attending me so well.

My head felt as if it were about to explode with swirling thoughts all over the place. But then BAM! I was sleeping the night away. I was awakened by the shaking of the plane about ten times! Finally, I found my ear plugs and stuck them right in my ears and back to sleep I went. I was awakened by the shaking of my dad telling me that we were there! I was so glad to hear that. I popped out of my seat and I was excited to hear that.

Then I saw him, My Grandfather! I cried with joy. I saw so many of my relatives waiting for me and my family. I missed them so much! I've been dreaming about this mostly my whole life and it has finally come true. I wondered to myself, "Why do my uncles and cousins love me so much?" Then my grandmother answered that right away, "Family is in the heart." And I couldn't agree more.

Francisca Centron, Grade 4
Outley Elementary School, TX

The Decisive Championship Game

It was a dark night that I will see for the rest of my life. Screech, in came our coach's car. He drove up to the soccer field with a big smile.

The championship game started in a rough way with people committing fouls. The score at half-time was tied 3-3. Late in the game they scored a goal and everybody lost hope.

Our coach gave us confidence by telling us all about the good memories we had and that we could still win the game. After we were recharged, I started forward with a kid named Trevor. Trevor and I lost the ball quickly. The sound of the crowd was too deafening to bear.

Then Trevor made a surge by stealing the ball on a puny pass. He and I traveled down the field as fast as cheetahs. Unfortunately, we lost the ball.

Unexpectedly we got the ball back and our whole team was chasing at the ball like wild dogs. When Trevor got the ball and shot, he missed. Fortunately I was there for the rebound and scored.

The referee said that we would have a golden goal overtime. it didn't take long to get down the field, but we couldn't score. We stopped the ball. It was a 2 on 1 opportunity for me. He passed to me and I scored. We had a big celebration. This was a very memorable moment for me, and we jumped around and celebrated like crazy.

Sahil Wadhwa, Grade 5
Dingeman Elementary School, CA

Harry Is a Girl?

One night, my whole family was watching television, when I went to go get a snack from the fridge, without knowing that my cat, Harry, followed me all the way to the fridge. When I got the snack, I guess he kind of snuck into the fridge.

He didn't get out when I left the fridge, so he was stuck. I went back to watch TV with my family. About an hour later the movie started to get interrupted by a strange, eerie, almost ghost-type sound. I figured something big was going to happen, like we find out that our house is haunted by some wicked ghost or something. My dad told me to stop worrying, that we have a bad pipe or something. We all started to believe him, because the sink in the kitchen was pretty bad. I think that might be why he thought it was too.

Another hour later, the sound was back, but it was extremely loud. Last time, it wasn't that loud, but not this time. This time it was real loud. I told my dad that something is wrong, really wrong. We all, except dad, who thought it was a bad pipe, started to get kind of scared, because we knew it wasn't a bad pipe. I started to look for the noise. It was in the kitchen. Dad thought that proved him right. I knew that it wasn't the sink, so I kept looking.

Finally, I looked in the fridge, and there, on the top shelf, was Harry. I gasped and my family came to the kitchen to see what happened. Harry had had three kittens. We call them Mores, Henry, and Lily. We don't see them a lot because they're outside cats, but we know they're there.

Larry Queen, Grade 6
Lampasas Middle School, TX

Great-Grandmother's Death

I was at my house when I got the horrible call from my mom. My great-grandmother, Nanny, had just died the day before. Next week was her funeral and I had to miss a day of school.

While I was at the funeral home, I saw everyone laughing and having a good time. I was confused, so I asked my mom what they were doing. "They're remembering the funny moments of her life," she said.

When I went over to the coffin, I started to sniff, and my eyes started to get watery. I could see Nanny's body in the coffin, one lid open with bunches of flowers on top. I tried to focus on the sparkling gold painted handle or the shiny white covering on the coffin. The body was just too overwhelming. When my mom steered me away, I started to thank her for getting me away from that terrible moment.

When we went to the graveyard, her coffin was already ready for lowering. I went over and paid my due respects to her. I took a seat in one of the many fold up chairs set up around the coffin. Everyone sat down as a priest walked up. "It is now time for Nanny to leave us, but before she does, we need to say a good-bye prayer."

As my family was leaving, I saw the last glint of sunlight reflect off the gold handles, and at that moment I swore I would never forget her.

Boomer Beasley, Grade 4
Horn Academy, TX

Scholars' Fate

Why should teachers and students experience such a severe consequence? What is it? Well, teachers are getting laid off as rapidly as can be here in the U.S. Especially California, which is suffering severely regarding this ongoing issue.

Around 19000 teachers were given pink slips in the year 2011 itself. So many teachers losing their jobs each year certainly impacts its scholars. Every teacher getting laid off will cause kids to be squished into tighter classrooms. Each individual may not be able to receive enough attention from their teachers when there are so many other students experiencing the same situation. Secondly, teachers are a vital part of every scholar's learning and education. Think about the amount of respect we are providing to the teachers. They have chosen this career to offer children the beauty of learning. It would be a shame to lose them, don't you think? Last but certainly not least, teachers should keep their jobs because of the lack of staff members there will be in school, excluding them. During emergencies and lock-downs, who will protect the children? Safety is first, right? Right now, teachers are first!

In conclusion, teachers shouldn't lose their jobs because of the impact that will happen without them. Also, since the teachers offer their precious time and energy to help children, they deserve the right to stay in their position. If you believe in teachers and their importance, join in to make the difference for millions of parents, thousands of students, and hundreds of teachers. So come on, let's 'Make the Change'!

Shriya Padigepati, Grade 5
Top Kids Center, CA

Diversity Makes Life Fun!

Our differences make our community a better place. Diversity keeps our community from being boring and dull, it allows for a variety of occupations, and the diversity in Idaho Falls attracts visitors and tourists. It is important that people are not the same.

First, if there was no diversity, life would be dull and boring. All music would be the same and not fun to listen to. All sports would be the same. Plays and concerts would all be the same. That would be boring.

Without diversity, there would not be a variety of jobs. Everyone would want to do the same job. Everyone might want to be a lawyer. There would be no doctors, firemen, or policemen. Society couldn't work that way.

Without diversity, places would not have visitors. Every place in the United States might be famous for gambling, not just Las Vegas. Museums and amusement parks would all be the same. There would be no reason to go on vacation because every state would have the same tourist attractions.

It is important that people aren't the same. I wouldn't want to look or sound like everyone else, or have the same personality as everyone else. I like being my own person. All places would be very crowded because people would all want to do the same things, eat the same things, and play the same things. Diversity is important.

Jordan Maughan, Grade 6
White Pine Charter School, ID

Stuck on 78

Putt! Putt! Putt! The vehicle wailed. I was stuck in the middle of the highway coming back from a fun trip at Wild Rivers Waterpark in a long, white limo. What had started out as a joyful adventure with swim team friends soon transformed into a frightening experience for all of us.

We were happily driving home with air conditioning blowing hard and music playing through the surround-sound speakers. Suddenly, the car pulled over to the side of the road and we knew something was wrong. We were trapped, sitting in the car waiting for news to come. Waves of nausea washed away everyone's good feelings, and the constant sound of people sighing and yawning became repetitive.

Hot rays of sun that were shining down earlier now started to disappear behind billboards and fast-food signs. The sky turned to faded orange construction paper. Some of us counted the cars driving by. Others tried to take a nap.

We all took turns sitting on the front steps, for breathing in the fresh evening air helped us escape the hot, stuffy nightmare inside. After what seemed like days, another car arrived to bring us back. The ride home was about forty minutes, but I had fun toying with the controls for music, lights, and AC with my friends.

When we arrived, all our anxious and caring parents were already waiting for us. Until then, I had never thought about how wonderful the feeling of home was.

Valerie Ho, Grade 5
Dingeman Elementary School, CA

Reptiles and Amphibians

Reptiles and amphibians are not very well known to the world. The tiger salamander is usually less than a foot long and is found in the U.S.A., Canada and Mexico. Lungless salamanders are the largest family of salamanders. They breath through their skin and they spend most of their time in damp places.

The big headed turtle sounds like it naturally has a big head, but that is because it is heavily armored. This turtle is smaller than eight inches. Another example of a reptile is the Nile crocodile. It kills big animals by dragging them into the water, but the Nile crocodile has no enemy except other crocodiles. It has a brown pointed snout and can grow up to 20 feet long.

Lizards are another type of reptile. The frilled lizard is a very neat lizard. It can hiss as a warning. Another warning is that it picks up a flap on its neck. It goes up on its feet and if its attacker does not run, it will strike with poison. One of my favorite lizards is a leopard gecko. I have one in my house. It has a short fat tail. It mostly moves at night and in the days it mostly stays in the shade.

Another interesting reptile is the reticulated python, which can grow up to 33 feet long. It has no poison, but it kills its prey by very tightly squeezing it. When the egg of this python hatches, it is two feet long.

Reptiles and amphibians are interesting to study.

Rock Anderson, Grade 6
St Pius X Catholic School, TX

Awareness for Fairness

"These men ask for just the same thing, fairness and fairness only. This so far as in my power, they, and all others, shall have," said Abraham Lincoln. Fairness is what we should show others. To be fair means to great people with justice and in the same way. Being fair is a good thing to do because you'll make the people around you feel good. Fairness can be simply displayed by giving someone a turn in the game or by treating people equally. To you, being fair might not be a big deal, but to others it may be. They could have had a bad day and when you were fair and considerate, they would be happier and appreciate what you have done for them. You can make people not feel like outsiders, outcasts, or separated from others, and they would feel like they belong by just being fair. People will think you are a kind person and you will know you did something right, just and good. People may or may not thank you, but inside they are grateful, even if they do not seem like they are. Treating people unequally would be mean and unfair. When you are unfair, people might have low spirits, be sad, have their feelings hurt, or maybe even get angry. You cannot be kind to one person then not to another. Fairness would be a great value, habit, or virtue to have.

Cassandra Cantu, Grade 6
St Ferdinand Catholic School, CA

The Dream

Do you have a dream? Well, I do, it's about the trees, let me tell you about it.

First of all I think the rainforest is a beautiful place, but probably not for long? The reason why is because they cut them down. Do you know why? if you don't know why it might feel like some one stabbed or pierced you right in the heart. Those people cutting the trees are like fire breathing dragons burning down the rainforest and all the other trees in the world in a very fast way, but the reason why they cut them down is for money. I think I know what you're thinking — that cutting down trees might be awesome but it isn't. Cutting down trees is a horrible thing to do because if all those trees are cut down there probably won't be enough oxygen. If you have something to do help them do it while you still can and save our beloved trees.

Tara Tripp, Grade 5
Foothills Elementary School, CO

Somebody Dying

Eight years ago my great grandmother died. One day I went to my great grandparents' house. My great grandfather was still alive. When I got to my great grandfather's house, I tried on some of my great grandmother's make up. Then I tried on some of my great grandmother's jewelry. Then my great grandfather gave me some Big Red gum. I almost cried when I chewed the gum because I kept thinking of her and I only knew her for two years. After I was done, we had to go. I was very sad when we had to leave from her house. I wish she never had died. I miss her with all my heart.

Sally Shaw, Grade 4
Horn Academy, TX

Inspiring Others to Grow

How can we inspire others to grow in everyday life? When we inspire others to grow, we can do the little things that can help any person, anyone! Encourage others to grow in their faith. Encouragement really inspires others to do their best in what they do, or grow. You can encourage others to do the right thing. You can encourage them with God.

Growing in your faith, a friendship, and school are just some ways you can grow. We can encourage them and inspire them to grow in everything they do. you can help them grow in their faith with God by going to Mass with them, praying for them, or reading the Bible to them.

Sometimes people really forget to give thanks to God for our lives, to live another day! Maybe we need to encourage others, so at the same time you encourage yourself to be closer to God. We need to know that God loves us so much that He gave His only Son; He gave us a faith, a faith that we can truly believe in.

Instead of focusing on what we don't have, we should focus on what we do have. Instead of focusing on ourselves, sometimes we should think about others. We can do the little things that can be something big for someone else.

Kimberly Lac, Grade 6
St Raphael School, CA

Circus Fun

When people go to the circus, it's amazing. One favorite thing to get is cotton candy. It's an awesome fluffy delicious candy that melts in your mouth like a snowflake…aahhh.

At the circus there are some unusual things that people don't normally see. For example, there are clowns, a fat lady shaving her beard, and a striking striped tiger with its mouth showing mighty sharp teeth. In addition, there are dogs jumping through hoops of fire. It's so much fun!

At the circus there are games to do like fishing for plastic fish, sack races, and sometimes pin-the-tail on the donkey, and don't forget the super exciting and funny egg races. One time a clown flung an egg in the air and it landed on his head, which was hilarious.

Now run along and go tell your best friend, to go to the circus next time it's near.

Hannah Marie Claudio, Grade 5
St Pius X Catholic School, TX

My Small Place

When I take a step into my room after school, I sit down in my favorite chair. The chair is hot pink with peace signs of all different colors. When I sit in the chair, I fell the pink fluffy fur rub against my skin. I love that warm cozy feeling I get when I sit in my special chair. Whenever I'm going to read and I have to pick a spot in my room to read, I always pick my special chair. It helps me focus because of that warm comforting feeling I feel when I read in my pink fluffy peace chair. Feeling the fur when I am in my special chair could put me to sleep. Just looking at it you now, it's very comfy.

Emily Herbst, Grade 4
Horn Academy, TX

Inspiring Others to Grow

I feel that I inspire others to grow in different ways. The most powerful way that I can inspire others is by my actions. Acting like a Christian is a stronger way to inspire others to be better. I believe in God, and try my best to follow His Ten Commandments.

My parents have taught me that actions speak louder than words. They inspire me by leading a Christian life. My school has a Christian environment and I am always learning from others how to be a better person. This environment teaches me to treat others with respect and kindness.

Another important way I inspire others to grow is to treat others as I would like them to treat me. I believe that I cannot ask to be treated a certain way unless I am willing to treat others in that same way.

A Christian act that I have learned from my faith is forgiveness. When I go to church and tell God about my sins and ask for forgiveness, I feel relieved and inspired to keep trying to be better. By learning about forgiveness, I am able to forgive others. This action is the most important because it reminds us that we are not perfect, that we always make mistakes, and that we learn from our mistakes.

Anthony Borgatello III, Grade 6
St Raphael School, CA

My Stuffed Animals

When I wake up, the first thing I see is one of my stuffed animals. I like to lay them out on the floor and play in them, especially by jumping off my bed into them. Some of my favorites are a turtle, a teddy bear, and an angry bird. I love my cute, fuzzy, fluffy stuffed animals. I have 150 stuffed animals, and I have to keep them in big bags because I have so many. I have fluffy teddy bears, funny monkeys, some fuzzy dogs, crazy designed snakes, BIG lions, and lots of others. Some of my stuffed animals are presents from people for my birthday and Christmas. Some of them are trip souvenirs, like the turtle from Hawaii that is wearing a lei. That is my favorite one. My brother has some stuffed animals, but only 13. He sometimes gets jealous of my collection. We are trying to collect as many stuffed animals as we can so we can set a world record. I love my stuffed animal collection.

Jacob Robertson, Grade 3
Vista Charter School, UT

Grandma Died

I was at a hospital waiting for my dad and mom, hoping for good news. I did not want my grandma to die. All my family and I were waiting for the doctor to come. The doctor called Mom and Dad to go to my grandma's room. My mom told me she was alive. All my family started to celebrate. The next day one of my cousins came running and crying. He told us "Grandma died," then all my family started to cry. I thought she was going to survive. I thought the doctor did not want to do anything to save her. I always thought I was going to have her next to me.

Gael Aguilar, Grade 4
Horn Academy, TX

Grace to P.A.C.E.

One of my most memorable moments was this year at the P.A.C.E. Graduation Ceremony. It was a humongous part of my life.

After the bell for the last recess rang I raced to the front of the school. Everything was perfect so far that day. I didn't leave anything at home or get into any trouble. Plus I looked great with my black jacket and my black fedora on. Some of my classmates were joking about my outfit. Before we went in, jackets had to be taken off. Now I was just a boy in a hat as one of my classmates said. Finally it was time to go in. I walked in smiling through the streamers hanging in the doorway. When the class bowed I did a fancy bow with my fedora and then I sat down like everyone else.

I was smiling and paying attention to everyone on stage and the officers in the crowd. Then it was time to announce the contest winners. I was sitting on the edge of my seat hoping to be called up. I had a really good project. First, Robert was called, then, Nick, and then me, I got 1st place. I was so happy as I walked to the end of stage and up the steps. I shook hands with Ms. Morin Loren, Officer Young, Ms. Beatty, and a couple others. I proudly accepted my medal and read my poem aloud.

Amiel McDonald, Grade 6
Margaret Landell Elementary School, CA

Hello Obama!

I started to go to Landell when I was in third grade and of course like many new students would have felt, my stomach felt as if Google butterflies were inside my weak stomach. As my mom escorted me into my new class, I noticed that the lights were turned off, and that my classmates were watching something intently, but that intentness was soon broken. All eyes went on me, as if they were expecting me to do a back flip with a perfect landing.

My teacher Ms. Cornwell asked me to take a seat in the front row. I asked one of my neighbor peers what they were watching and this is what she said, "We're watching a speech our President Obama said to his citizens." I look up at the smart board and see Obama's face. Smiling to myself, I think that maybe this year won't be that bad after all. (And it wasn't bad, it was great!!)

Jane Lee, Grade 6
Margaret Landell Elementary School, CA

Ice Skating

Ice skating is really close to my heart in many ways. I taught myself as I grew older. When I started taking lessons a few months ago, I got a Russian coach that was funny and taught me how to do cool tricks that I would never forget. I take public lessons, and I was so happy when my mom said she would be taking me to private lessons for my hard work on the ice. I hugged her so much. I also was happy because my friend takes private lessons! Now I'll have twice the fun! I will always have a great touch with ice skating, and it's also my favorite sport!

Erika Marinin, Grade 4
Outley Elementary School, TX

What Would We Do Without Computers?

What would people do without computers? They would be lost. Computers are very helpful in people's lives.

Without computers, people wouldn't have e-mail. They would have to hand write everything, buy stamps, and put the envelopes in the mailbox. Think about how easy and fast just typing some words and pressing send is as compared to handwriting a letter.

If a student has a really long report due tomorrow, he might spend several hours writing it. With computers, he can type a really long report in much less time. In addition, more copies can be printed instantly as needed.

With computers, whenever someone wants to know something, he just goes to Google and types in what he wants to know. Then in a few seconds, there's several choices to find the answer. Without computers, people would have to rely on common sense and books whenever they wanted to know something. Computers are much faster than looking up information in a book.

People use them for research, communication, games, entertainment, news, weather, and to collect data. NASA and hospitals also use computers for research and many, many other reasons. See how much computers do for us?

Evan Pangilinan, Grade 6
St Pius X Catholic School, TX

Free

Swish, I opened the car door. Jordan and I busted out of the door. We were finally in San Antonio. The hot, humid, summer air surrounded us. Even though it was hot, it felt good to be free. After we got all of the luggage, we checked into our room. The air was cold and the room looked like it was made for us. There were two humongous beds we could jump on. There was food and drinks we could eat or drink, anything that my dad would let us. We freely ran around like the children we are. We felt the wind through our hair as everything just seemed to disappear. Worries, trouble, and homework all slipped away from Jordan, Jacob and me. We felt as free as can bee. We had the best time. We played, enjoyed, and acted like we were supposed to without getting in trouble or getting yelled at. After an absolutely amazing day, we had to go to bed as dreams and visions filled our heads.

Olivia Lavorini, Grade 5
Horn Academy, TX

My First Fifth Grade Experience in Landell

On my first day of Landell, I was in fifth grade. It was a new experience for me because I didn't know anyone except for Raymond because we went to the same church together. I didn't want to be a loner on my first day because people would think I'm a nerd or something. But later, I started to make new friends. Jasper and Dana were my best friends ever since we met. We did have some fights, but it always got better and we all knew that we were B.F.F.L. (Best Friends For Life). And we always had a good time even now.

Emily Byun, Grade 6
Margaret Landell Elementary School, CA

The Amazing Cruise Ship

My family was going to a cruise ship. To get to the cruise ship, we had to drive. A couple hours later, we saw the outline of our cruise ship. After we got through security checks, we got inside the cruise ship. When my family got into our cabin, we were very surprised at its size. It was the size of a small living room. The cabin had one bathroom, one closet, one television set, and four beds. Two were on the floor, and two smaller ones were attached to the walls. We put our luggage on the red, furry floor, and plopped onto the beds and watched some TV. A few minutes later, we explored the cruise ship. There were big swimming pools, four restaurants, and many shops filled with clothes.

The next day the cruise whip was headed for Mexico. When we arrived at Mexico, we saw a flea market with people selling food, shirts, and other merchandise. We also saw a geyser, and a statue made out of bones and metal wire. It was in the shape of a giant. After many attractions, my family came back inside the cruise ship.

The last day on the cruise ship felt like forever. I was a little sad when it was time to leave. I watched the cruise ship shrink into a small dot as my family drove away from it. I wish my family could go on a cruise ship again.

Kevin Yoo, Grade 5
Dingeman Elementary School, CA

What I Want to Be

When I grow up I want to be many, many, many things! But my three focuses are being an artist, pianist and a veterinarian.

I want to be a vet because I really love animals such as dogs and cats. I also want to make all of the animals' feel better and get strong and healthy. The more I take care or make the animal feel better, the more I learn about the animal I'm taking care of. Besides a doctor never stops learning.

I also want to be an artist. I get to paint pictures and portraits. An artist also gets to express themselves by showing what they feel and their personality by drawing or painting. There are many, many beautiful colors you can use and patterns too. It will make your art even more beautiful.

Being a pianist is also very great. You can play many songs and learn different notes and play different tempos too. It is a wonderful instrument.

Elizabeth Luu, Grade 4
Outley Elementary School, TX

My Teddy Bear, Sparkles

I love my teddy bear, Sparkles. I sleep with her every night. She is soft and a sparkly purple. She wears an "iCarly" shirt and a skirt with diamonds in the shape of a camera on it. Sparkles is very furry and is about a foot tall. I got my bear from my grandma, and she got it from Build-A-Bear Workshop. I got it on my seventh birthday. When I opened it, I loved it so much. I am glad I got Sparkles. My grandma is so nice. She rocks, and I'm glad she is alive. I hope she will get me another stuffed animal. I love my teddy bear and my grandma.

Carlie Blair, Grade 3
Vista Charter School, UT

Fairness: A Characteristic Within Us

Many people aren't fair to one another because they are angry. Fairness is the act or state of being fair. We should all have the right to be treated equally. We were all made by God so we should all be treated the same. We should all be fair to one another. Fairness can change a part of our everyday lives. Some of us are taking fairness for granted. Other children around the world are not being treated with respect because of their skin color. If this keeps happening we could go back in time to like what happened to Dr. Martin Luther King Jr. Fairness is a very important characteristic we all have within us. If you want to be treated fairly, then you should treat others fairly. Just like what the golden rule says, treat others the way you want to be treated. Fairness is something we all need to remember to do every day of our lives. In school if you are treating someone without respect there will be a consequence. We should be fair everywhere we go, like at the mall, in school, at the park, and at the library. We should be fair to our teachers, pets, parents, siblings, friends, aunts, uncles, and grandparents. Your life can really change when you become fair. We should be fair every day of our lives.

Jayleen Mercado, Grade 6
St Ferdinand Catholic School, CA

Daisy

When I wake up, the first thing I see is my stuffed puppy... Daisy. Her face is a gorgeous black. I can't think of something more beautiful than her. She makes me happy when I touch her because she feels a lot like my real puppy, which she was named after. Daisy's B.F.F. is Saidy, my best friend's dog. I got Daisy for Christmas, so she wears a red and white Santa hat. She is probably the most special thing in my life I have had so far. Every night of the week I get in bed and sleep with her. My puppy is not real, but she really looks like it. She is the best present I have ever gotten for Christmas. She is soft and furry as a leopard in the dark. Her whole body is a pretty khaki with a sliver of brown on her spine. I got Daisy from a really good friend named Cameo. Daisy's tail is the curliest tail I have ever seen. She is the cleanest puppy. I love my puppy, Daisy!

Aliya Cleverly, Grade 3
Vista Charter School, UT

A Sad Moment

"Let's go," said my dad as we put our luggage in the car. I said, "Wait, I want to look at the house for the last time." I looked at my bed, my room, and how my life was going to change, but my dad didn't let me see any more. "COME ON," he said with impatience. I went to the car and as we passed the life changing house, I said bye and imagined it saying bye back. As we passed the house, I couldn't take it. My tears were dripping faster than my hose at full speed. My heart was beating as fast as my computer loading. Then, I thought in my head, now I know how it feels like to move from a house that you will never see again to a place you will probably love even more.

Preston Jong, Grade 4
Horn Academy, TX

Breaking Bones

Have you ever broken your ankle? It's actually a tiring experience.

When I spent the night at my grandma's house, I always loved playing on her tall front porch. That hobby of mine changed when I fell off the porch. I was climbing on the outside railing, and I guess I didn't pay attention and I let go of the grip I had. I fell right into the garden below and landed flat on the side of my foot. It hurt, but I didn't cry. But I did have to scream and yell, "Emily! Emily! Come help me up!" until somebody helped me.

They finally got me up the stairs and into the house. I sat on the bed and I had to put ice on my ankle, but it swelled up as big as a watermelon! When my mom saw that the swelling didn't go down, I had to take a twenty minute drive, with my sister poking at my ankle, to the hospital.

When we finally got there, I was exhausted. How could I be so tired when I didn't even walk that day? I have no idea.

The doctors had to take x-rays of my foot. They really hurt me, because they kept on poking at my foot and turning it around and poking at it some more. I was glad to get out of that place!

I felt like a princess because everybody, except for my sister of course, always asked me if I was okay or if I needed anything to eat or drink.

That entire experience was a little bittersweet, stating the fact that I broke my ankle. I sure hope that I don't break my ankle again, though I wouldn't mind the pampering!

Sarah Lingle, Grade 6
Lampasas Middle School, TX

Planting Seeds of Faith

Planting seeds of faith is easy in a hard way. Just doing the simplest thing is planting seeds of faith. Planting seeds of faith can be fun. You can go to church with your family and friends.

One way I can plant seeds of faith is to take little kids to church. I do that now on Wednesdays. I love taking little kids to church because in church you learn about Jesus' time. One example I set for the little ones is that if I go to church, then they will probably go to church more and get closer to God.

Another thing I could do is read the Bible. I could also read the Bible to people in class. The Bible is interesting because I get to learn what Jesus' life was like and that he loved us so much he died for us. I think learning about Jesus is fun and important. This is fun and important because he loved us so much that he took his life for us.

Talking about God at school is fun because I get to talk about God with friends. I don't just talk about God in school, but also in church. I am not just planting seeds of faith in people, but I am also planting seeds of faith in myself. That is helping me learn about God too.

That is how I plant seeds of faith. I am not just planting seeds of faith in myself, but in people too. I think learning about God is helpful and special. I think planting seeds of faith is special to everyone.

Olivia Jewell, Grade 6
St Raphael School, CA

Volleyball

Volleyball is a fun and active sport for anyone.

Volleyball needs twelve players, six on each side. When the net is up and players have the volleyball, they're ready to play.

Players line up, three in the front and three in the back. When a player serves it over the net, the back player on the other team will try and hit it back over the net.

If the back player hits the ball and it doesn't go over the net, his team players in front of him will try to hit the ball over the next two more tries.

If that works, the players on the other team will try to hit back. If that doesn't work, then the other team gets the point. Of course, there has to be a referee to make sure the rules are fair.

When players play, there are two or three quarters in the game. The team that wins is the one who makes twenty-five points first. If one team wins both quarters then that team wins. if one team wins a quarter and the other team wins the other quarter, then there is a third quarter. The third quarter only goes to fifteen.

As a result there is a team who loses and one who wins. All that counts is that you did your best.

Emilee Flores, Grade 5
St Pius X Catholic School, TX

My Artistic Flair, Designing

My artistic flair is designing machines and vehicles. I always liked drawing little diagrams of spaceships. I like to build small things, like prototypes. So I've kind of already started designing.

I would need a few things to be a designer. I would need a master's degree in engineering, and maybe a degree in math. I would have to use things like pencils, paper, computers, calculators, and small building materials to make prototypes. I would gradually build the prototypes bigger until they reach full scale. I might improve cars and helicopters, and possibly invent a new vehicle, such as a monocycle. I would need to get a patent if I had a new design built. You can do so many things as a designer.

My artistic flair is designing. I would like to get paid, and have it be my real job. I would really like to become a designer of machines and vehicles.

Gray Cuevas, Grade 4
St Thomas the Apostle School, AZ

Bye-Bye Horn

One bright summer day, I really went deep into my mind and thought, "I'm really going to miss that old school. It's just so great." It was just so sad that it was about to be violently crushed before my eyes. The school was so great because it was so small, and you feel so free when you walked outside with the trees towering over you. It was just so perfect. When it is demolished, the construction workers will build a new school that is enclosed and two stories. When we move to where the new school is, you won't feel one with nature. I really miss that school a lot.

Nathan Reichert, Grade 4
Horn Academy, TX

Birth of a Franchise

Thirty years ago today, January 10, 2012, is the day when something very special happened to this ordinary franchise. This was the birth of an unstoppable West Coast Offense, which was led by Joe Montana and the San Francisco 49ers.

Thirty years ago the 49ers were playing in the NFC Championship, trailing the Dallas Cowboys by six points in the fourth quarter with three minutes left. Joe Montana and Linville Elliot marched the Niners down field by running the ball to set up a pass, which is now called the West Coast Offense. They ran the ball to the six-yard line with fifty-one seconds left on third and three, they could not settle for a field goal and Joe Montana knew that. As the ball was snapped, Montana notice a blitz coming right at him. He rolled right, moving backwards as four Cowboys came right at him. He launched the ball from the twenty-yard line to the back of the end zone where Dwight Clark leaped up and pulled it in. The Niners made the extra point field goal and took the lead with forty-seven seconds to go.

The crowd roared as the time ticked away and the San Francisco 49ers won the NFC Championship game. They went on to win the Super Bowl. That game proved the 49ers were a hardcore football team using the concept of running the ball to set it up to throw, which is now called the West Coast Offense. That game gave birth to all five Super Bowl wins the 49ers have now. Now the Niners have made it to the playoffs for the first time in seven years. Belief and luck is not all they have, but only the history of the dominant West Coast Offense, which drives them.

Drew Schivo, Grade 6
Madonna Del Sasso School, CA

All About Me!

Unless you go to school with me or you're related to me, don't talk about me. I've decided to tell three things about me. The three things are my B.F.C. club book, my dog's bone, and a marker.

Obviously I love art. Art is fun and a little bit hard. Art is fun if people compliment you, and you try, also if you let your mind go to something you like and paint it. Art is only hard if you don't try and if you aren't passionate. It's hard if you don't try and don't paint something you like.

My dog's bone tells you that I'm an animal lover. Being an animal lover is fun but hard. It also costs tons of money. Being an animal lover is fun because you get to take care of cute animals. It's hard because most animals need to be trained and are hard to walk. It's fun to take care of animals but it costs hundreds of dollars. You have to buy food, toys, treats, and bathing supplies for the animals.

Finally, my B.F.C. club book. There are positions and club books. Depending on your personality you set up a room full of stuff you like to do. In the B.F.C. meetings, the club welcomes new members, makes club books and does fun activities.

That's all the things I'm going to tell you about, and that's what everything means.

Karen Miller, Grade 5
Fremont Elementary School, CO

How to Be a Good Friend

I can be good friend by caring for my friend with compassion and kindness. When my friend is in need, I will reach out and offer a helping hand. I will forgive my friend whenever he does something wrong. I listen to my friend intently whenever he's trying to tell me something. I give my friend compliments. When my friend is frustrated, I use positive words to cheer him up. I am trustworthy by always keeping my promise, and I stand by my friend in all situations. I will not do anything to hurt my friend's feelings.

You can be a good friend by helping your friend when he faces difficulties. You can offer your help before he asks for it. If your friend has a different opinion, you should show respect by listening patiently to your friend. Accept your friend for who he is, with both his positive and negative qualities. You should always be pleased to share your stationery and snacks. You should treat people the way you want to be treated. If your friend wants to be alone, respect his privacy and freedom. If you borrow something from a friend, take good care of it and then return it without being asked.

Matthew is being a good friend by treating people equally. He demonstrates fairness by always taking turns when playing with others and by not taking advantage of the weaknesses of others. He keeps me company and accepts me for who I am. He respects me and does not interrupt me when I say boring things. He always offers his snacks, even before I ask him. He does not criticize others behind their backs. He cares genuinely for me by sharing generously. He is truly happy for me when I win a race or any award.

Ian Lee, Grade 5
Top Kids Center, CA

A True Friend

A true friend is always there for you. I am so happy I have one. When I have a problem, she is always right next to me. When I fall, she is always there to pick me up. A true friend will never leave your side, even through the toughest parts of your life.

When I see her, she always smiles and it makes me smile. Every time she smiles she has a twinkle in her eyes. When I see that twinkle, it gives me hope that we will be friends forever.

When I talk to her, I feel like the happiest person in the world. Every time we talk we come up with something to laugh about. Our conversations are so random. Most of the time the people sitting around us have no clue what we're talking about. That makes us laugh.

When I'm at her house or she's at mine, we always have so much fun. At night we prank call people. It's so much fun. Then, if it's in the summer, we go outside and get a sprinkler and start running through the water. It feels really refreshing on a hot day. Sometimes when I'm at her house her mom takes us to places like Pizza Hut, the movies, and other fun places.

I am so glad that I have a friend like her. She is one of the most amazing people in the world. I hope we will be friends forever.

Leah Hooper, Grade 6
Lampasas Middle School, TX

Abby

My favorite best friend, Abby, is very good at Tae-Kwon-Do. For her birthday party last year she brought me and a few other friends to the Tae-Kwon-Do studio that she goes to. We all met her master. He is called Master Beisel in class. Once Abby and I got to the studio, Abby showed me where to put my shoes. We waited on the mat until everyone arrived. When everyone got there Master Beisel tied bandanas around our heads. Abby was a black belt for the day! After the party, Abby and I had a sleepover.

Just a few weeks ago, Master Beisel paired Abby up with a sparring partner about her size. She was paired up with one of the strongest boys in the class. She started training for weeks and she was sparring every Friday. Last weekend she was in a tournament and she won a trophy about two feet tall! She told me it went great and she sparred with two people and won both times. Abby might not know this, but she is magnificently incredible at Tae-Kwon-Do. Abby is my friend, and I believe she can do anything that is possible.

Katie Artura, Grade 4
Pepper Tree Elementary School, CA

Bullying

Bullying is really a tragedy. That is why a lot of schools have a no-name-calling week. My school does.

Dwarf tossing abuse, (which is a type of bullying), is when you pick up a dwarf and toss him around. It may be funny to imagine, but it is not in real life.

If you see someone bullying another person, tell an adult. Take the adult to the scene. Make sure the adult takes care of it. If a bully is bullying you, don't start crying or get annoyed. The bully wants to make you feel bad. So just walk away.

All these reasons show that bullying is a tragedy not to be ignored.

Aarti Kalamangalam, Grade 3
Roberts Elementary School, TX

Nature Photography

My artistic flair is nature photography. I first got interested when I was looking on the internet for pictures of nature. Once I saw the beauty of the pictures I started taking pictures of my backyard. I have done lots of nature photography already, and I love the outdoors, with the wild animals, the plants, and the sunshine.

My photos can help others too. Others can enjoy nature without even going outside. They can learn a lot from my pictures. They can learn the color of different plants or animals. They can learn many other things also.

I'm going to need a lot of things for my photography to become a success. I'm going to need a good camera and several different lenses for it. I'm going to need to take several classes on photography, and I'm going to need a lot of practice.

Nature photography is a fun and interesting thing to me. It can help me and others. I can enjoy nature, and learn things at the same time. It can become a career. It is my artistic flair.

Lauren Engelthaler, Grade 4
St Thomas the Apostle School, AZ

Boxers

Boxers are one of the most beautiful dogs in the world. God must have spent a lot of time making these beautiful creatures. The boxer's body is compact and powerful. Their muscular, front legs are straight and parallel when viewed from the front. The back legs are well muscled.

In addition, the boxer is happy, high-spirited, playful, curious, and energetic. But, sometimes, they don't live long because of health problems. Some major concerns are cardiomyopatha and other heart problems. From age eight on, they are more likely to get tumors. Some white boxers are prone to deafness. Despite these issues, boxers may life 8-15 years.

Furthermore, boxers also will do well in an apartment if sufficiently exercised. Boxers need daily work or exercise, as well as a long daily walk. (It will get the owner exercising too!)

Finally, boxers need lots of human leadership. One thing you have to teach a boxer is to not jump on people, and not to be boisterous. Training a boxer can be easy, if the owner learns how to train dogs. Boxers make a great family pet. If the owner has children, they will love to play with these dogs. Boxers are wonderful dogs.

Acadia Tamez, Grade 5
St Pius X Catholic School, TX

The Scare

One fine morning, I was going to visit my grandma and grandpa. It was a very cheerful day, until I was sitting with my grandpa and he said, "I will miss you." I said, "Why did you say that?" He said, "Because I have a serious case of cancer, that could kill me." I remembered all the memories we had together. The next day, I went back and spent all day with my grandpa. Three days later, he went to the doctor, and the doctor said, "The news is very bad and that you have stage 4 lung cancer." I stayed up all night, crying. I was sad that he would leave me, but I knew he would be in a better place. Then a few months later, he got really bad. I knew he was going to die soon. The next day, he was a lot better, and he was laughing and telling jokes, but then that Monday, he died. I knew in my heart that he still loved me a lot. I also knew that he would still have a place in my heart.

Hanna McCann, Grade 4
Pepper Tree Elementary School, CA

New Things and New Friends

When sixth grade first started I was with my friends Erin, Madison, Lauren, Kristen, and Shannyn. Then I started making friends that were in my classroom, like Aeji, Hyunah, Rachel, and so on. I also started playing something that I've never played before. Handball. It might be the best thing I've played in my whole life. I never thought that trying something new would be so fun.

Now, I'm still playing handball every day every recess. Sixth grade is better than I thought it would be. Now, I want to try new things every day, and try to make new friends as well!

Catherine Chao, Grade 6
Margaret Landell Elementary School, CA

Leaving Honduras

We had to leave Honduras because my dad's friend hired him as a doctor to work at Houston, Texas. The last day in Honduras, my mom let me play with my friends. I rode my bike to Maggie's house. Maggie, Stacy, Trixe, Hannah, and Daisy led me out to the yard. "We heard that you are leaving to go to Houston," Daisy said. "Yeah," I replied sadly. We walked to the tree house and climbed the ladder. We played Green Light and Red Light, Hide and Seek, and Freeze Dance. At 1:00 p.m., my mom picked me up from Maggie's house. I looked out the car window. My friends started to wave to me goodbye. Tears started to fall from my eyes. I didn't know if Houston was going to be fun. I wondered if I would be going to a new school. I wondered if all the new kids would laugh at me. After I made it home, I started to pack my things. I will miss Honduras, but I think it will be OK. When we were at the airport, I waved good bye to my friends. The plane took off. I will miss everyone in Honduras because they were special to me.

Amy Fonseca, Grade 4
Horn Academy, TX

Forever

My cave crystal looks like gold lightning. My sister Kamee gave it to me because she was moving. I put all my crystals in a special spot that no one will find out at all. They are on a white shelf that is really tall. I keep my crystals underneath my new helmet. My cave crystal is hard as glass. I have a lot of crystals and rocks. The one I'm talking about is called the big baby crystal. The crystal has a little stick to stand it up so that it doesn't tip over, and some of the other crystals have a stick too. The cave crystal is about medium sized. The color is a dark gray and it has sharp ends. When I go to sleep, I always hug it. It is a special gift that I will keep forever.

Kylee Terrell, Grade 3
Vista Charter School, UT

John

One day my grandma and grandpa got a divorce. Then my grandpa got remarried and had a son named John. One day we all met up at my brother's basketball game. My grandpa, his new wife, and John had to drive all the way from Modesto because of John's disabilities. He is in a wheelchair because he can't walk. He goes to a special school in Modesto.

After my brother's game, we all drove to Red Devil's Pizza. I asked my mom for a few dollars to play games while our food got ready. My mom gave me a few dollars and I made a beeline for the claw machine. I had decided to win a stuffed bear for John. I inserted a dollar and moved the claw towards a green bear. I took a few tries but finally I got the bear. I cheered. I grabbed the bear and rushed to the table. I thrust my hand out and handed the bear to John. He hugged the bear and said thank you. I felt really good giving the bear to John. I had wanted to give him something special. Something he would remember forever. And that is what I did.

Ashley Rondomanski, Grade 4
Pepper Tree Elementary School, CA

Teaching Tolerance

According to kidshealth.org, every day one out of every six children is ridiculed because of their race or ethnicity. Many children refuse to go to school because they are bullied about their race. Have you ever wondered what we could do for the people of different races, to stop the bullying directed towards them?

No one, child or adult, should have to endure the racist comments that people go through each day. The problem is that some children think they are superior to other races and are ignorant about other cultures or refuse to learn anything about other cultures. They think this gives them the right to discriminate against other children.

Racism has always been a big issue throughout history. To solve the problem of racism, children need to learn about, understand, and respect each other's cultures. For example, there could be a Racism Awareness Month at the schools. During this time speakers would come and teach students about how damaging racial bullying can be to children's self esteem. They could also teach the students about other cultures and help the students become more accepting of other races. Finally, the school could hold a cultural festival. Students from different ethnic backgrounds could share food, stories, and clothes from their country. This may take time away from classes and be expensive to hire speakers, but this will be worthwhile and make school a safer place for everyone.

This solution may seem like a lot of time and work, but it will make many people happier. Racism has been a big problem in America for over a century, but we will be the ones to end it by appreciating other cultures, and respecting everyone, no matter what their ethnic background.

Sophia Danzeisen, Grade 6
Vacaville Christian Schools, CA

My Fifth Birthday

Everyone came to my party. The inside of me bubbled like a scientist's test tube as I placed the gifts on the rectangular table. We were at Chuck-E-Cheese and it was almost lunchtime. My mom gave us all shiny gold coins. Jing! My coins rang out as I shook them. As I wandered around looking for a game to play I saw it, the basket shoot.

The purpose of the game was to drop coins down the slot trying to get it into a hoop. My eyes fixed on a certain basket — the jackpot. I took a gold coin and dropped it in. It fell off the rim. I took another coin and missed. I was about to give up when I became so desperate that I grabbed a coin and tossed it in. Ding! Tickets were spilling out of the machine like a kid squeezing a bottle of chocolate syrup.

"Cake time," my mom called.

Everyone rushed back to their seats. I sat at the end of the table and the cake was placed in front of me. The farmhouse was scarlet red and snow white. The animals were in the perfect place. The sweetness of the cake made me shiver with glee. This was the best day. I looked at the candle and wished that my birthday would be the best and it was.

Katie Pham, Grade 5
Dingeman Elementary School, CA

Dyslexia

Have you ever wondered about dyslexia? Did you know that anyone can get dyslexia? Dyslexia is mainly found in children from birth to the age of five. You can learn to live with it by going to your doctor or by getting therapy.

Dyslexia is a learning disability. In some children if they get frustrated it makes their dyslexia worse. Often it creates a comprehension problem. Dyslexia can cause trouble reading because letters can mix up and make you confused. Scientists say it can be a genetic thing, if a family member has it it is most likely where children get it from.

Fortunately some find that medication can help control their dyslexia. Forty-five million people have dyslexia in the United States. Some people who have dyslexia are: George Washington, Thomas Jefferson, and Orlando Bloom.

Support from family and friends is encouraged. It helps to know that people care about you no matter what happens. If you or someone you know has dyslexia then join a support group. Support groups are nationwide so you can go get support from other people like you. Also you will learn how to deal with dyslexia.

Dyslexia is a gift. Lots of people think it is a challenge but people who have dyslexia are very artistic and are very smart. My sister is dyslexic and I am so proud that she is learning to deal with it at such a young age. My family is so supportive of my sister. She gets therapy to help her to overcome it. I love my sister and she knows I am so proud of her every day and I will help her every day. Every step of the way I will be there for her.

Gillian Cooke, Grade 5
Faith Lutheran School, AZ

Life Coming Undone

I was in my room, cleaning up the mess. Right outside my door all I could hear was my parents shouting at each other. I saw a small shadow at the bottom of my door. That's when my sister came in to help me clean. When all the screaming ended, my dad slowly walked into the room.

He asked us to take a seat on the bed. When we sat down, he got on one knee, and he told us the most devastating thing. He said "There is no easy way of saying this: your mother and I are getting a divorce." Once those words reached my ears, I was heartbroken. I just couldn't bear the idea of them getting a divorce.

Tears started streaming out of me. I ran to him for a comforting hug. Then he explained why they were separating. I wasn't really paying attention. "Why, why do they have to get a divorce?" I kept asking myself.

At that very moment, I realized that this was really happening. I didn't want to believe it, but I had to. I had heard of kids living with both parents. I never thought that would be me, though. I had a hard time with everything, but now I'm kind of glad. There is no more fighting between them. Through this experience, I have been formed into a better person, inside and out. I've learned that sometimes things can get difficult, but in the end everything turns out all right.

Kristine Velez, Grade 6
Woodcreek Middle School, TX

Poseidon

Have you ever wondered who the god of the sea is? The mythological god of the sea is: Poseidon, a Greek, and Roman god. His Roman name is Neptune. Poseidon is the god of the sea, horses, and earthquakes.

Poseidon was born to Kronos and Rhea. Kronos heard a prophecy that his children would overthrow him so he ate his children. Then Zeus, Kronos' son, grew up and then made Kronos throw up his children. Together all the children defeated Kronos their father.

Poseidon has very little patience, is quick tempered, and is greedy. He once dried up all the rivers to another goddess' city because he was angry at her. Though he restored one river that was home to a nature spirit that had once helped him.

Poseidon built his own palace under the sea. It is called, Aegae. It is very large and marvelous. Poseidon is known for, causing earthquakes, people drowning, and large storms. Poseidon's nickname is the Earth-Shaker because he can cause earthquakes.

Poseidon is married to Amphitrite. She is the queen of the seas. Poseidon had many children. They were not all Amphitrite's children. One of his children was Triton. Triton is a merman, but instead of one tail he has two. Poseidon once liked Medusa and this created Pegasus the flying horse.

There are books written about Poseidon, and the other Olympians, both fiction and nonfiction books. One fiction series is the Percy Jackson series by Rick Riordan. I recommend this series if you like Greek mythology, with a twist!

Robert Railey, Grade 6
Faith Lutheran School, AZ

Rainy Days

The rain falls down like little droplets of melting crystal. The warmth and pleasure inside feels so soothing and relaxing. I enjoy rainy days because I enjoy sitting and reading, gazing at the rain, and playing classic board games with my family and friends.

First, I like to sit and read when it rains. It makes me feel cozy snuggling on the couch and reading an adventurous book. This relaxes me and reduces my tiredness and stress. I can feel enjoyable and entertained too.

I also like to gaze carefully at the rain. This makes me discover the beauty nature has to offer us. It also clams me down and makes me think of game times. It's so peaceful and is very relaxing. The rain also has a beautiful sound and has so much tranquility.

Lastly, I adore playing board games with my family and friends. It allows me to enjoy my time and have a simple laugh. I can enjoy the game and have a humble togetherness time. We can smile and cozy up with cups of warm drinks.

I will always appreciate rainy days because I like to sit and read, gaze at the rain, and play board games with the family and friends. It allows me to bundle up, relax, and feel humble. The refreshing feeling of raining days wraps me with a curtain of warmth too.

Patrick Dang, Grade 4
Outley Elementary School, TX

An Unearthly World

In "The Raven," Edgar Allan Poe uses rhyme, unique characters and setting to establish the eerie and depressing mood. To begin, the beat Poe develops encompasses the reader, making it almost impossible to pull away: "From my books surcease of sorrow — sorrow for the lost Lenore / For the rare and radiant maiden whom the angels name Lenore" (lines 10-11). The beat is not only strong, but it is also twisted like the narrator's mind. Poe makes one feel the narrator's loneliness and despair. The characters in the poem are unique in that they are almost the antithesis of each other. One is the quiet, watchful raven that comes to this man silently and observes and waits. The other is a sad, lonely man who has a mysterious bird talking to him, reminding him of his lost love: "'Wretch,' I cried, 'thy God hath lent thee — by these angels he hath sent thee / Let me quaff this kind Nepenthe and forget this lost Lenore!' / Quoth the raven, 'Nevermore'" (lines 81-84). The narrator is driven mad by this bird, and terrified. The raven is gentle and observant, carefully assessing this man. Lastly, Poe creates the setting with a midnight time and wintry season. "Ah, distinctly I remember it was in the bleak December, / and each separate dying ember wrought its ghosts upon the floor" (lines 7-8). Poe creates the setting by not only describing the mood, but also detailing the outside world. When he describes an empty, lonely December, there is the feeling that the man is grieving over someone whom he has lost who was very close to him. This is extremely depressing. Edgar Allen Poe uses rhyme, characters and setting to create an unearthly world, descriptive of a lost, mourning lover.

Milena DeGuere, Grade 6
The Mirman School, CA

Yosemite Magic

Raindrops glistened like jewels on the treetops as I stepped out of the car into the beautiful hotel. Ice stuck to the doors and the red carpet was smudged with dirt and neon yellow signs that read "CAUTION." The tile floor was slippery on my clunky black boots and the suitcase I held suddenly felt heavy with gear for the snow. A blue chair with green velvet stood in front of the welcoming gift store and a crackling fire warmed the room. The lights, which were somehow unpleasant, shined on to the tile floor. We could not check in right away, so our whole family made their way down to the mezzanine. Our plastic coffee cups burned, so I wrapped five napkins around the cup and the cocoa was delicious. By four o'clock, we snatched the keys from the front desk and went out to the tea room. There were 13 flavors of tea and I selected Moroccan Mint, my dad selected Orange Pico Black tea, Grandma got classic Green Tea and I practically lost count of what everybody else picked. All I knew was that it was bedtime. The next day, I peered out the window and I saw fields and fields filled with snow. After we ate in the dining room, my brother and I put on our snow gear. Dad, Andrew and I exited the hotel, our black and gray sled trailing behind us. All in all, this vacation was really fun and I wouldn't trade it for the world.

Abigail Barrett, Grade 4
Pepper Tree Elementary School, CA

The First Is the Worst

"Daniel, pull your card!" hollered my teacher. Hearing her scream, I glanced up from my coloring sheet. But being unable to catch her scowl, I persistently colored. Obtaining no reply, my first grade teacher shrieked, "Daniel, pull your card this instant!" That got my attention. I figured she was screeching at me.

"Did she mean what she stated?" I cogitated frantically.

But before she opened her infuriated mouth at me again, I gradually arose from my chair. Although I was stunned, I staggered towards the behavior chart. The room was silent, and I sensed that countless pairs of eyes were gazing at me. Somberly, I yanked and shoved my green card to the back, which then revealed the hideous yellow card. Subsequently, I tottered back to my desk and slouched into my chair. Then with one distressing attempt, I peeked at the behavior chart. I, Daniel Park, was the only student who had a yellow card.

At first, I was irate at the teacher.

"Why did she give me that obese, insignificant yellow card?" I muttered.

But after pondering for a minute, I figured that it was my fault. I didn't hear the teacher state, "Stop what you're doing, and put your eyes on me."

Now, when I consider about this miserable phenomenon, I can chuckle easily. However, this memory never departs from my head. Maybe the saying "first the worst" is true, since in first grade, I obtained my first and worst card pull.

Daniel Park, Grade 6
Margaret Landell Elementary School, CA

Leather vs Plastic

First, I would like to say that I think that leather soccer cleats are better than plastic soccer cleats. Almost all of my soccer friends think the same thing. This is why.

Okay, so one of the reasons that, in my opinion, leather soccer cleats are better is because they are breathable. I cannot stress it enough; soccer cleats that are breathable help you so much when you are on the field. I have had some experience with this sort of thing because I am a soccer player. When you're on the field and you're running, jumping, and kicking, it is so important to be able to have a good feeling in your feet. Plus, when you're on the field trying to play with plastic cleats, you may see people booing at you because you have to bend over just to itch your foot. And for what, so you have a shoe that is shiny.

Of course there are some people that think that they are so cool because they have a shiny shoe. They may also say that some of the best soccer players in the world wear plastic shoes. But what they don't know is that the only reason that professional soccer players wear plastic cleats is because they are getting paid to wear these. Some people might also say that their plastic shoes can withhold water and not get damaged at all, but it's not true. All soccer cleats can't take in that much water at all because of the fact that they are supposed to be a little stiff.

CJ Wilson, Grade 6
Beacon Country Day School, CO

Outrageous Surfer Girl

"We are early, don't rush, you might trip!" Mom advised. Still, I ran like a cheetah to the cool sand of the silent beach. I saw Alexandra and Alyssa's moms. A light bulb went on over my head. Alexandra and Alyssa should be here somewhere.

Suddenly I felt a wet hand. It was Jenna!

"Come on, let's get your wet suit on."

"OK." I skipped to the edge of the ocean water. Then I saw them, playing in the waves. As I raced over, sand went flying through the air like pixie dust.

I slipped on a wet suit and ran to the water's edge. The icy water touched my toes. It felt like little spiders crawling up my legs. Goosebumps went up my spine.

"Circle up girls," said a lady with a black wet suit and a heartwarming voice.

We all sat in a circle on the silky ground, then stretched.

Smack, bang, splash! One by one the kids fell into the sea like dominos.

"Jodie, it's your turn!" Alexandra chuckled.

Right then, I could taste fear in the air, yet, I hopped onto the surfboard while the instructor pulled me into the water. A huge wave came my way.

"Go Kodie! You're doing great!" Cheering entered my ears. I was standing on a surfboard! For the very first time! Afterwards, I jumped off the board and ran to my mom. "Did you see that?" Her warm hands stroked my cheeks.

I've felt like a surfing pro ever since.

Kodie Sanders, Grade 5
Dingeman Elementary School, CA

Scraping My Eye

It was a Saturday morning and I was going to my cousin's house. When we got there, she was getting ready to go for a jog. I asked if I could come with her and she said that if I came, I would have to keep up with her.

When we started jogging, I started to get tired. I stopped for a break and when I looked, I saw that my cousin was way ahead of me. I started running as fast as I could and when I caught up to her, I tripped on a rock. My cousin screamed when she saw that I was on the ground. She pulled me up and asked if I was okay. I looked up at her to answer, when she cried out in despair. She pointed at my face; I was bleeding out of the corner of my eye.

There was no doubt I was going to the hospital. My mom and my cousin rushed me there. When we entered the hospital, they took me straight to the emergency room. It turned out I had pieces of rock in my eye. After they took the pieces of rock out, they put this special medicine on it and made me wear an eye patch for three weeks.

Those were the worst three weeks of my life. I couldn't wait to take that eye patch off. The next time I went to the doctor, they took it off to see if I had gotten better. My eye had healed in such a short period of time. Even though it had healed, I had to be careful with it. I learned an important life lesson that day: always pay attention to what you are doing!

Rosa Alonso, Grade 6
Lampasas Middle School, TX

Chernobyl

Nuclear power plants do more harm than good. Would you want a nuclear power plant blowing up near your house? If it did, you would not be happy. The Chernobyl disaster, a nuclear accident, occurred in 1986 in Ukraine. It had four reactors. This accident started with an experiment. The crew was to find how long the turbine would spin after a major loss of electricity. Although these tests were carried out a year before, the power had gone down too fast, making it necessary to design a new voltage regulator. This day in 1986, the technicians planned to test it. They began to set up for the test. Unfortunately, an operator failed to program the computer to keep power at 30%, so there was not enough power to do the experiment. To get more power, the operator pulled a few rods. There was still too little power. This was because of xenon poisoning. To keep the reactor from shutting down, the operator disconnected many automatic circuits. If a disaster occurred, it could not be prevented. By the time the operator moved to shut down the reactor, it was in a very unstable state. Since there was a flaw in the control rods, there was a power surge at the time they were inserted in the reactor. Under intense heat, the reactor burst and blew the top of the building away, spouting radiation into the atmosphere. More than 100 firefighters arrived to put out fires. The nearby people were evacuated because of contamination with radiation. This was one of the worst nuclear disasters. You would not want a nuclear power plant near your house, right? If it blew up, you might be contaminated with radiation. We should take effort and action to try to get rid of Nuclear power plants.

Andrew Wang, Grade 6
Stratford Elementary/Middle School, CA

My Worst Nightmare

Bullying is about the worst thing that can happen to you. I know this from personal experience, because I was always getting put down and bullied ever since I was in kindergarten. Now I am in fifth grade. I used to cry every day and every morning when my mom dropped me off. I was terrified by the words that filled me with sadness.

Everyone has the right to be respected, because everyone in this world has feelings. When you're respected, it makes you feel important, and you feel brave, and you can stand up to that person that is putting you down.

Everyone is beautiful in their own way. Even though you probably might not be as pretty or as popular as everyone else, you are still unique in your own way. When someone teases you, it's usually about your looks or how you dress; but what they don't see, is how you are on the inside. You can be nice, sweet and adorable; but they don't see that, they just make fun of your style most of the time

I always tried everything for people to like me, but it seemed like my school was a world full of hatred over me, when I didn't even know what I did wrong. But now I am the happy girl I am today because I have a lot of friends, teachers and my parents that support me.

Jaqueline Alvarez, Grade 5
Washington Elementary School, CA

Competition

One of my favorite sports is softball. I also like track. When I play these sports I want to be the best I can be, and to do that I have to get competitive. Some people think competition is bad. They think competition hurts self-esteem and causes jealousy. Those people want to get rid of competition so everyone can have fun.

Without challenges our world would be less advanced. Competition is good because it pushes us to get better. Challenges brought us technologies, medicines, entertainment, and tons of other stuff. Competition is part of our life and has made the world better.

Competition pushes us to grow and become stronger. For example, find others that are better than you and challenge them. To achieve great things we have to focus. Competition helps to make us better and helps us to try new things, which leads us to build character.

Competition is natural to all living things. Everybody wants to be good at something. Competition helps us to find that one thing. Little kids want to do things like people that are older than them. This makes them push themselves and try new things. Animals want to be leaders, so they bark, growl, and fight to prove who the leader is. Challenges help us to learn from our mistakes, which makes us better.

Competition can be negative and harmful. The key is to teach positive competition. When we lose, we need to be good losers and be happy for the winner. We need to encourage others to get better and not always focus on winning. Winning isn't everything, but being happy for others and improving ourselves is what the goal of competition should be.

Regan Dunn, Grade 6
Lampasas Middle School, TX

Young Author's Tea

When I was in kindergarten, I was chosen to read my story about dolphins in the multipurpose room. At first I was really happy and excited. Then I was really scared. How can I get up there all by myself and read a story into a microphone? I didn't know what to expect, so all I did was practice at home because that's all I CAN do.

On the evening of the Author's Tea, I was dressed in a blue dress. My mom kept fixing my hair as we were waiting outside. Usually, I would complain, but I was too nervous to say anything. I was so nervous I almost ripped my essay from holding it so tight. The next thing I knew, I was sitting in the chair on the stage. They put a microphone that went on your head on me. I stared at the audience while a whole room of kids and adults stared back with their eager eyes and ears. I started reading my dolphin story really slowly and softly. Barely anyone could hear me. I talked so quietly that a man in the crowd yelled, "LOUDER PLEASE!" I got really embarrassed. Then, I realized that it wasn't so hard! I started to read with more expression and feeling. At the end, everyone clapped and I bowed and hurried down the steps with a really big smile and a heart filled with pride.

Belinda Kang, Grade 6
Margaret Landell Elementary School, CA

Differences Make Us Beautiful

It is important to be different because variety, surprises, and color make us happy and make the world beautiful. What would be the point of being human if we were the same? We would have the same skin color, faces, clothes, jobs and homes. We would be called "billionths" instead of twins or triplets. If everyone in the world looked and acted the same, life would be robotic and boring. Our differences identify who we are and where we come from.

If you imagine a world without these things, you can understand why we should always adore our differences. For example, picture us all green. It would be dull. How could we see beauty and enjoy beauty if there was nothing to compare things to?

When I play soccer, I am one of the smallest players and it isn't always easy to play against the tall players on other teams. However, the more I play the sport, the more I learn that being small can be an advantage, like dribbling the ball around players. We also need tall players on our team because they can guard the goal and kick the ball far. Without players with different skills, we wouldn't have an excellent soccer team. We are all stronger when we work in teams that have people with special skills and abilities.

Sometimes we want things to be the same because we have been hurt or excluded by others. Sometimes we feel that we want to act and look like others. However, our differences make us stronger and make our community a better place.

Eden Crisler, Grade 6
White Pine Charter School, ID

My Big Change

"Swooo...hasss" I started breathing heavier than usual. I could feel sweat slide down the side of my cheek. I blinked my eyes three times for good luck. My eyes zoomed from side to side across the narrow passageway. A sign of doubt swallowed me as my car drove away. It was...my new...SCHOOL.

Even thought it was my first day and I was already introduced and was in my seat, I was completely nervous. My eyes tried to scan and find someone to talk to. I got a few "hellos" and a lot of "Hey Chris" comments. As I listened to my teacher blabber away, I couldn't shake off the nervousness, I couldn't even talk.

The transition has been pretty rough, especially for me. All my friends were in Austin. Here in Houston, I don't know anybody. The only thing I have here is family. I lived in Houston most of my life, but sadly the new school isn't even in the same district as my old school. This means I don't even know the area!

The first time I stepped into the front office, I saw the stairs and couldn't believe it was two stories! As I scanned the area as they showed me to my class, I noticed they had lockers. Sure they were made of wood and didn't have a door, but they were still lockers!

I am writing this on my third week of school. So far, it's been getting better. I've made at least nine friends and counting. It's been pretty good. I just hope I don't have another...BIG CHANGE!

Christopher Castro, Grade 5
Horn Academy, TX

New Puppies

We have a six year old yellow lab named Kloe and she would always run off. One night during the summer, my grandmother came over and she started looking at Kloe funny and then she said "I think Kloe is going to have puppies!" My mom started staring at Kloe's belly too, and then it was confirmed...Kloe was going to have puppies. As days passed I watched her belly get bigger, then one day I was home alone with Kloe, I went to check on her and saw a little black shape in her box. I called my dad, but all I got was his voicemail. I called my brother and I said "Bubba, I think Kloe had a puppy; 'cause when I checked on her I saw a little black shape in her box." My brother said "Ok. Just stay out of the washroom till I get home!" When my brother got home, he called my grandma and told her what was going on. She rushed right over, and she saw that Kloe already had two puppies. My grandma was calling my mom to tell her about Kloe. We already had seven puppies! My mom stayed up all night with Kloe. The next morning we had eleven little puppies, but when everybody left, Kloe was still acting strange... and then came one more puppy. As the puppies got older, my parents decided that they're going to give away the puppies, except the two me and my brother got to keep. We named our dogs Buddy and Oakley. But to sum it all up, seeing Kloe have the puppies was a beautiful and wonderful experience.

Bradi Branham, Grade 6
Lampasas Middle School, TX

Fairness in Our Lives

Showing fairness by example is when a child watches what his or her parent does. For example, my mom and dad wanted us to watch a movie as a family one Friday night. I wanted to watch Christmas Vacation, my brother wanted to watch The League of Extraordinary Gentlemen. Since we did not agree my parents told us each to pick three movies, shuffle them and put them on the table so they did not know who picked what and they would not be picking favorites. They both agreed on Grease. This was fair because they did not pick favorites and did not know who chose that movie. You can show fairness through your thoughts, how you think and feel about another person, or when you have an opinion about something. Some people think others are not cool because they do not have a leather jacket, skinny jeans, a cell phone, or the latest style of shoes. This would not be giving a fair opinion about that person. She could be really cool, smart and fun. It is important to really know somebody before you make an opinion about them. You can't just say, "Oh, that person is not good with fashion," or "That person gets stuck on a math problem so that makes them not good at math." In conclusion, fairness about being an important person in someone's life and making the right decisions. Your actions, thought and examples can tell others that you're a great, funny, cool, honest and fair person. Fairness can be contagious, just like a smile.

Mckenna Robles, Grade 6
St Ferdinand Catholic School, CA

The Gandhi of America

My hero was a peace-loving man, born in Atlanta, Georgia, on January 15, 1929. Do you know who he is?

As a child, Martin Luther King had two friends: they were both white, Thomas Legdan and William Garneter. One day, he went to visit his friends. Their mother said that they could no longer play together. Martin was very sad. Martin's father was a minister and Martin loved to hear him speak in church. He had a kind mother who was a teacher. Martin started school a year early and soon became the best reader in his class.

When he was only 15, he started college at Morehouse College in Atlanta, Georgia. Both his father and grandfather had gone there. There he studied Henry David Thoreau and Mohandas Gandhi. He married Coretta Scott and became a minister like his father and grandfather. He led many marches to earn equal rights for black people through nonviolence. He led the boycott on the Montgomery, Alabama buses. King led the "March on Washington" on August 28, 1963 and gave his "I Have a Dream" speech at the Lincoln Memorial.

He was awarded the Nobel Peace Prize, but four years later on April 3, 1968 in Memphis, Tennessee, he was assassinated. In 1983, the third Monday in January was declared an annual federal holiday by the United States Congress to honor the life and ideals of Martin Luther King, Jr..

I admire him because he was determined and unstoppable. He wanted to help others.

Sebastián Peña, Grade 4
Montessori Learning Institute, TX

I Love Sports!!!

I love sports! I do six sports. My favorite sports are running, baseball, and soccer. Everyone in my family does sports. I am going to show you what you need and what there are in these three sports.

I love to run! There are rocks, dirt, grass, and hills in cross-country running. My team is called Oak Hill Racing and I run in the bantam age group. There are also other age groups such as sub-bantams, the age group below me. The ones above me are midgets, youths, intermediates, young men and young women, and the oldest age group is open.

Baseball is a sport with a ball, a bat, and a glove. When you are up to bat you have to hit the ball or walk to get on base. If you hit the ball you can get a single, double, triple, or home run! However, you only get three tries to hit the ball.

Soccer is played with a ball, a goal, and two teams. To get a point, your team has to score a goal by kicking the ball over the line and into the goal. To be offense, your team has to have possession of the ball. To be defense, the other team has to have possession of the ball.

Everybody should participate in sports because they keep you healthy. If you want to do sports you have to eat healthy foods. Unfortunately, you can't really drink a lot of soda and eat a lot of junk food. If you want to be good at sports, you have to always practice and try your hardest!

Miles Worthen, Grade 5
Two Rivers Elementary School, CA

The Trip of a Lifetime

How many times do you get to take a trip as amazing as this? Last summer my grandparents invited my family to travel around Germany and Denmark. I just couldn't wait to go.

My grandparents live in the city of Bremen, Germany. We spent a lot of time touring the city. It is a beautiful place with many old buildings.

Our next destination was a Danish island in the Baltic Sea called Aero. There are only four little towns in Aero; the town we stayed in was called Marstal. The island was beautiful, and all of the little towns had tiny houses painted all different colors. It was such a beautiful place.

Our next stop was Berlin, Germany, but on the way we stopped in Schwerin. This is a town that has a large and impressive castle, and I just had to see it.

We finally got to Berlin. What a huge city! We went on a tour bus, which showed us some of the main sites. On the ride we saw the Brandenburg Gate, parts of the Berlin Wall, and Checkpoint Charlie. Checkpoint Charlie is where people could get into the eastern part of Berlin, because East Berlin was shut off to westerners. The Berlin Wall separated East Berlin from West Berlin. One part of the Berlin Wall was painted by famous artists; the remaining part is known to be the largest outdoor museum. In the streets of Berlin there are little cobblestones that show where the wall once was. I learned a lot that day about Germany's history.

This trip was the most amazing trip I've ever taken! I got to go so many places that most kids my age have never been to. What a life changing experience.

Nora Lawson, Grade 6
Lampasas Middle School, TX

Fairness in Our Lives

Is fairness in your life? Well, it should be because fairness is what gives us rights, justice and equality. Just imagine a world where everything was unfair and based on greed. Taxes would be very high, everyone would be put in jail for being different and the world would always be at war. Every country and its people would always want more and more. A robber would get off scot-free because there would be no fairness in our justice system. Without fairness, it is difficult to tell the difference between right and wrong. Without fairness our world would have no peace. Imagine teachers grading unfairly. What if they gave everyone grades based on favoritism and not based on a fair grading system? The favorite students would stop trying and learning, knowing that they would always get good grades. The non-favored students would also give up because no matter how hard they worked, they would always receive bad grades. The effects from lack of fairness can have a great impact on everything. Let us say you are an important person in government and you were not fair. Then the laws you create would only be used to help yourself. You would not consider being fair to others. There would be criminals running around free, without punishment, simply because the law that would put them behind bars might impact you in a negative way.

Joshua Salcido, Grade 6
St Ferdinand Catholic School, CA

Music Helps

My science project has to do with the mobility of running. Mobility is the ability to move or be moved freely and easily. An athlete will need to recognize the importance of running for every sport. The problem is, when they are running, they start to feel the pain and fatigue. That is why my science experiment is to see if music helps an athlete ignore the pain and fatigue. Music is not only a source of entertainment; it can be a motivational and a relaxation tool. Music also helps with moods. For instance, if you listen to lively music it can perk you up and motivate you to increase the intensity of your training. If you listen to slow paced music, it can calm you down before a competition such as a marathon. It synchronizes to the rhythm of your body movement and can help our muscles in the learning of new motions. Music plays a vital role in enhancing creativity. Music triggers the brain centers, which deal with the development of creativity, thus benefitting him/her in the performance of other creative tasks. In general, responses to music are able to be observed. This experiment was done to show the effects that music has on an athlete's performance by comparing two participants who ran around a track twice. They ran on the first day without listening to music and on the second day with music. Having music in the background seems to make time pass more quickly, therefore music can be an effective tool in training an athlete's stamina, confidence, and performance.

Doralisa Lopez, Grade 6
Immanuel Christian School, TX

Paintball Experience

Paintball is so fun. It's an adrenaline rush. I love paintballing

Before we go paintballing, all of my friends meet at my house. We get in the car and go to the desert. When we arrive, we make two teams. The paintballs can sometimes hurt, so you have to wear layers and a mask to protect yourself.

When the teams are ready to play, the ref will count down and the teams will run and hide. Some people like to spread out; some like to stay together. I like to spread out. Once you see the other team, you shoot.

When you get ready to shoot, you aim down your barrel. The barrel is where the paintball comes out of the gun. So wherever you point your barrel, the paintball will go. When you find your target, you close an eye, look down your barrel and pull the trigger.

Always remember to dodge when you play paintball. You dodge by going side to side or up and down. A paintball can also be dodged by getting on the ground or running to a different cover.

Stealth is helpful in a match because it will help you to not get shot. When you are on your belly, you crawl to get closer to your opponent without them noticing.

At the end of the game we pack up, get in the car and go home. When I am done paintballing, I feel exhausted, calm and happy. You should try it someday, it is so amazing.

Christian Vasquez, Grade 4
Home School, AZ

My Favorite Animal — Cats

My favorite animals are cats. There are many kinds of cats in the whole world besides domestic cats. We are so familiar with domestic cats, but sometimes we don't know that lions, tigers, leopards, caracals, margays, cheetahs, jaguars, pumas, lynxes, servals, bobcats, ocelots and other cats also belong to the cat family — the Felidae. Unlike domestic cats, other cats can thrive without humans. They are wild cats. They are often larger than the domestic cats. Unlike domestic cats, some wild cats, such as lions and tigers, attack and eat people. You should never pet them. Normally, the cats which attack people are not the strongest. They are weak, old or sick.

Cats live all around the world, except the Antarctic and the Arctic. Lions, caracals, cheetahs and leopards all live in Africa. They don't have thick fur, so they don't overheat. Cheetahs are the fastest mammal in the world, they can run up to 70 miles per hour. But they can't run for very long. Leopards like to lounge in trees because of the heat. Jaguars, margays and ocelots live in the South America. They all have spots for camouflage. Wherever cats live, they have learned to adapt.

I like cats because they are beautiful and graceful. They have long and sleek bodies with large bright eyes. They also have strong paws and legs for gripping and jumping. I like how they look, how they act, and the way they are. I like the way they pounce and play with their food before they eat. I think it is quite cute. If you just say the word "cat," I would say I like it. It would take a millions years to explain the reasons why I like them. They are just what they are.

Sydney Liao, Grade 3
Top Kids Center, CA

Inside a Hot Air Balloon

In the first and second week of October, for 9 days, there is a balloon fiesta. It's the Albuquerque Balloon Fiesta. Every balloon pilot from Texas to Paris, France wants to fly in this amazing event. Once you get there, the nonfictional magic begins!

Before the sun rises, you get out of bed to go to the balloon park. Then a beautiful morning glow starts. The pilot's balloon glows. It's caused by a part of the hot air balloon called the burner. The balloons light up; when it's dark it makes the balloons look like fireflies! After the morning glow is the mass ascension. The mass ascension happens when all of the balloons get inflated and go into the sky at once. When I was there, they broke the world record for the most hot air balloons in the sky (345 hot air balloons!).

A balloon pilot does not only fly a balloon, but can walk inside the balloon! No one else other than the balloon pilot or his crew can walk inside, unless you are very lucky. I got to be one of the lucky people! Mind-blowing, eye-popping: I couldn't believe what I saw. Also, there are a lot of ropes, so I had to be careful. The balloon seemed as large as a galaxy. After I went to the balloon fiesta, I discovered that I want to be a balloon pilot. I want to be like that balloon — free, majestic, and peaceful.

Bridget Lynch, Grade 5
CHILD Montessori School, TX

My Dad's MS

The moment I was told that my dad had multiple sclerosis, I became terror-stricken. I started asking my mom if I would ever see him again or if he can die from it. She told me that multiple sclerosis or MS can cause arms and legs to lose function. She also reassured me by explaining that there are many therapies available to help someone with the disease. I couldn't wait to see my dad and find out for myself.

The first time I visited my dad after hearing the news, I noticed he wasn't as strong as usual. He also gave himself a painful shot in his leg that caused a terrible headache. He explained he had to give himself the shots every Saturday to combat the disease.

To show support for my dad, I try to help out around his house. He becomes tired easily. I also participate in MS walks with my dad when I can. He always makes the walks fun. He has a scooter he has decorated and he does silly things like pretending to race.

My dad and I can never get enough fun. He is stationed at Ft. Sam Houston in San Antonio, so we get to go to Sea World at least three times a year! Isn't that awesome?! He tries to make our time together special and fun, even when he is not feeling well.

I'm really proud of my dad. He really tries to stay strong for me and keeps a positive attitude, even though I know he is tired and hurting.

Taylor Yates, Grade 6
Lampasas Middle School, TX

The Time I Went to Florida

We were packing for our trip to Florida to visit our grandparent's house. It is an eight hour trip so we packed lots of toys and games to entertain us on the way. When we got there we were greeted by many relatives; it was very late by then so we went to sleep. When we woke up we brushed our teeth, ate breakfast, and played with our cousins: Conner, Rose, and Chris. Our grandparents don't live that far from Sea World, so we all went there. The first ride we rode was the Steel Eel, we rode it thirteen times in a row. I had found where the camera was, so I waved as we passed it on the highest drop. The next ride we rode was the Manta, it raises you up like you're on the belly of manta. Later, we saw Shamu and sat in the Splash Zone, so we were all very wet when it was done. After that we went to the water park. We got in the tubes and went down the waterslides. Then we went back to Grandma and Grandpa's house and went to bed.

The next day, we were going to Disney World, so we got ready. The trip was a bit longer this time, so we brought our iPods for entertainment. When we got to the park we saw one of the shows at the Enchanted Tower. We rode some of the rides, like Tower of Terror and Rock and Roll Coaster. We brought food and drinks, but I just had a soda. When we were all done we went back to our grandparent's house and went to bed. The next day we played outside for a while and said our goodbyes; then we started out trip back to North Carolina.

Robert Madden Jr., Grade 6
Lampasas Middle School, TX

Texas Independence

It all started on October 2, 1835, when conflicts between Texas and Mexico started to pop up like bubbles from a scuba diver's mask. The battle of Gonzales started it all. It set flame to the fuse which led to the bomb, and the bomb blew up with an ear-shattering sound and a gigantic boom.

Davy Crockett fought at the Alamo with a group of volunteers from Tennessee, including James Bowie, who invented the bowie knife. They fought hard and long for Texas' freedom, sending many pleas to Sam Houston asking to send backup. Sadly, the dust cleared and the band of Texan volunteers had been defeated in that tragic battle. Sam Houston, the leader of the Texan Army (who I happen to be related to), may be remembered by his battle cry, "Remember the Alamo! Remember Goliad!"

The epic feud between Sam Houston and Santa Anna raged on. Many bloody battles continued to take place at different scenes. But, they all came down to one important attack.

In the attack in San Jacinto, Santa Anna and his men were taken, some were killed, some surrendered. The Treaties of Velasco ended the war between Mexico and Texas. The treaties were signed, saying that Texas was free from Mexico and was its own country.

Houston (the city) was the first capitol of Texas. They later moved it to Austin. Texas joined The United States in 1845. Texas is now booming with people. Houston happens to be America's third largest city. As I like to say, "Once a Texan, always a Texan!"

William Tucker, Grade 5
St Pius X Catholic School, TX

School

School is a very educational and fun place. School teaches us many things we have to do to get a good career and a successful life. Without school, we wouldn't know anything at all. There are schools all over the world.

There is elementary, middle and high school. It goes from kindergarten through high school. Sometimes we might have tests. Every school in America takes a standards test. If you finish high school, you might want to think about going to college or the university.

Some students love school, like me, and some students don't want to learn or want to get a good career. It hurts me when I hear students saying they hate learning and don't learn. It makes me sad when I hear that some kids don't have any school and don't know how fun it is to learn new things. Many successful people, like President Obama, and our teachers, went to school.

There are many things we have to learn in school. We learn math, reading, and English language arts. My favorite subject is writing. If I didn't know how to write, I wouldn't be writing this essay right now!

We should appreciate that we have schools all around us. Learning can brighten our future. It is really wonderful to learn new things in school.

Emily Sanchez, Grade 5
Washington Elementary School, CA

Football

Football is a sport all about heart. Just like the analogy, it is not the size of the dog in the fight, but the size of the fight in the dog.

For example, in one football game, both our quarterback and backup quarterback were hurt, so the coaches put in Seth Cockrell. He is one of the smallest kids on the team, but he is so good.

We ran the same play over and over, just in different directions. Finally, the offense coach told us to run the go-pass, in which the quarterback takes a five-step drop and throws to a receiver that runs a far and straight route.

I was waiting for the word "go" and my heart was pounding. "GO!" That is when I ran as fast as I could and turned around. Seth saw me open and threw it hard and high. The cornerback and I jumped in the air. I hit the ground hard and felt a sharp pain in my back. It hurt! Seth was also hurt. He got hit after he threw the ball. The other kid got a flag, giving us an extra fifteen yards.

We were pushing through the pain and time kept passing by. Finally, the fourth quarter was over and we lost 0-14. Our coaches were proud of us, though, for not giving up and continuing to fight. Even though we didn't come away with a win, we were able to walk away with our heads held high because we didn't let the pain get the best of us. We showed a lot of heart that day.

Mason Bumpus, Grade 6
Lampasas Middle School, TX

Chamisal Novice Girls 12 Singles Tennis Tournament

My tennis tournament took place at Chamisal Tennis and Fitness Center in Salinas, CA. I was really excited to play against girls my age and test my skills. Once I arrived at the court I was ready to play but I was so nervous I felt like I didn't want to play the match anymore. But my family gave me courage to play. I won my first match: 6-2/ 6-4. The director yelled, "Is April Rose Maniwang here?" I ran all the way to the tennis court.

The last match I played was against a girl named Mila. When we were practicing I noticed she hits the ball very hard. I knew that she was better than me by her serves and consistency. I was ready to play the finals and served first for the match.

I struggled to hit the ball back because she hits the ball so hard. I knew I had to step up my game but it was too late. She won the first set by 6-3 and this time she led the set by 4-1. I was serving and the score was love-40. She won that game and the score is 5-1. I knew if I lost this game the match was over. I tried and I tried but it wasn't good enough. She won 6-3/ 6-1.

I thanked her for playing the match. She said that I was good and I almost had it. We shook hands and I said, "See you next time!" I was the finalist in the Division Novice Girls 12 Singles. I was so thankful and happy that I had the opportunity to play this tournament. Even though I wasn't the champion it was a good experience overall. I learned a lot and hopefully I'll be a champion someday.

April Rose Maniwang, Grade 6
Madonna Del Sasso School, CA

My Sad Memory

One afternoon Ms. Cheryl had called me to the office because my dad was there. When I got to the office, my dad knelt down to explain that someone had died. When he said that my Great Grandpa Charlie had died, I burst into tears. He told me to stop crying and squeezed me because he know I felt bad.

As I walked back to my classroom, my head started to hurt. I tried to think of happy things, but all I could think of was playing with Great Grandpa Charlie. I stopped abruptly in front of my classroom door, and listened to everybody playing.

I felt my chest burn and tears swell up in my eyes. I could feel them rolling down my already tear-stained face. I knew that I was never going to see him again. The only happy thought that showed itself to my mind was that he would always be in my memories.

We went to his funeral in Louisiana the following weekend, in celebration of Great Grandpa Charlie's lifetime. He was a retired veteran.

Haylie Sims, Grade 4
Horn Academy, TX

Road Trip to Chicago

"Ready?" my dad said. "Yup!" We were leaving our house and about to go to Chicago!

We were in the middle of the country (which is Kentucky). What I saw outside my window was breathtaking. there were fields of flowers everywhere! I opened my window and the breeze went through my hair and my face. It felt so relaxing. When the moonlight touched my face it was getting really dark. So we had to spend the night at a hotel to get some rest. Once we got a good night sleep, we were on the road again. When my dad said we were only a few miles away I was so excited and nervous at the same time. I was excited and nervous because I never met my cousins and I didn't know what they would think of me. When we finally got to my great grandparent's house all my cousins were outside. They all yelled, "SURPRISE!!" My smile was from ear to ear. I was so happy.

After the family reunion, we went to the park and watched the fireworks light up the sky. It was the best July 4th!

Emily Sanchez, Grade 4
Outley Elementary School, TX

My Brown Box

I l-o-v-e my brown box because my brother made it for me for Christmas. But I just got it on February the 20th. I do not know how long it took my brother to make it, but it is so special anyway. My brother made it up in Salt Lake in his woodworking class before he moved back with us. It is smooth on the top half and hard on the bottom half. Inside it is rough and he carved my initials on the lid. On the bottom of the box he carved his name like an artist. I am going to fill it with special treasures I find, like rocks and seashells from the beach. When I open my box, I feel happy because it reminds me of memories with my brother. I love it so much!

Kiley Brinkerhoff, Grade 3
Vista Charter School, UT

Never Trust a Doctor

The office smelled like rotten tomatoes. I walked past a kid in his mom's lap, and heard him sob, "I wanna go home!" I found myself shivering, not because it was cold. I grasped my mother's hand tighter. She chatted with the lady at the counter. She had Mickey Mouse scrubs on, but that was just the act. My mom rushed me into another room. The room had red containers containing red stuff. BLOOD! My stomach did a quadruple flip as my eyes filled with tears and my face filled with fear. The doctor sat me down as she took a vile filled with a greenish liquid. She came over with a huge needle that looked 3 feet long and 4 millimeters thick. The doctor saw my fear, and quickly tried to help by saying, "Only one little prick…" She grabbed my arm and jammed the needle through my skin. Red engulfed my eyes, and made me nearly puke. The pain was like a bullet through my skin. Finally it was out, but then she said "Oh wait I didn't get the vein." I wanted to cry my eyes out. After the 9th stab, my mom started getting mad with the doctor. I could see it now; "Welcome to ABC News! Today, our top headline is bout our trustworthy local doctor. Did she murder her patient? Stay tuned!" She finally put the greenish stuff in the right place, and I could barely get up from the chair. You can never trust a doctor.

Erica Altman, Grade 5
Horn Academy, TX

A Magical Moment

I let the butterfly crawl up my hand. Its little feet tickled my fingers. Then the little butterfly flew away. I was probably about four.

A few months before, I had planted milkweed with my mom. Then I saw a small striped thing crawling on a leaf. I ran inside to tell my mom about it. She said that it was a caterpillar. I asked if it would turn into a butterfly. She said, "Let's keep it and see!" She put some of the caterpillars in the cage with some milkweed. Meanwhile, my sister, Natalie, was playing outside in the garden. I heard her scream, "There are rainbow worms on the new plants that we put in!" It turned out that they were caterpillars. We raised them and they turned into "J" shapes. Then they turned in beautiful chrysalises. After a long time of being a chrysalis, they opened up as butterflies.

Kate Faris, Grade 5
Horn Academy, TX

Dusty

I was at home when the owners of the apartments we lived in told us that we were no longer able to keep our cat. He was a gray tabby tom cat with green eyes. His fur must have been the softest fur I have ever felt. I named him Dusty, and he was the first cat I've had. We had to give Dusty away. He did not like other cats. He would hiss and try to pounce on them. He kept the mouse population down. Dusty meant everything to me. Whenever a bug or mouse came near me, Dusty would pounce on it. I loved Dusty a whole lot.

Nadia Wackerle, Grade 4
Horn Academy, TX

Children of the Fallen Soldiers

Throughout the year children of all ages lose their parents. This can be a really hard thing to go through. Children everywhere are losing their mothers or fathers, because of military wars. Children are left alone thinking they are to blame. The stress they face is enormous. There are many events that remember the fallen solider, but what about the children of the fallen soldier? It is a known fact that children without fathers are more likely to get in trouble. The thought of growing up with one parent or none at all is just horrible. Can you imagine growing up with no mother or father? Kids can become evil and mad at the world. This could lead to jail, or harming themselves or others around them.

There are a few programs for the children of the fallen soldiers. However, I believe they should make an entire day dedicated to these kids. The children deserve a day just to know people care about them no matter what happened. Kids that lose their parents might never be the same without parents; some though might not show any changes. They might just hold all their feelings inside. Some programs help them to release their dread and doubtfulness in their mind and heart. This doesn't have to be just about kids with military parents but anyone who has family or friends in the military: grandparents, uncles, nephews, nieces, aunts, and anyone else who has served.

I know it's hard to just get over it. The children of America's fallen soldiers deserve a day dedicated just for them to show them even though they have lost someone special that they shouldn't just give up on life or themselves but to let this better them for the future.

Jimel Drayton, Grade 6
Lampasas Middle School, TX

The Most Special Place to Me

I walk out into the snow, in an outstanding, beautiful place: Utah. I love going there when they have snow so I can play in it as the glorious softness of the snow falls on my body. It's like flying, or falling through the clouds. When I am in Utah, I also like to go skiing. There is a big hill the size of three elephants stacked on top of each other that I love going town every time I am in Utah. I go down it as fast as I can. The soft, cold, ice snow goes flying on me while I'm skiing down the humungous hill.

When I get back to my hotel, we have to ride the gondolas. When you're in a gondola, there are windows and you get to look at all the sparkling snow from three hundred feet above the ground.

The last time I went skiing in Utah, I saw a deer by the trees! The deer was so glorious and wonderful; I couldn't stop staring at it. Then in the morning, we had to go home. It was very sad going back to my very warm hometown, just leaving the beautiful cold sparkling snow. I love going to Utah so I can have some time being cold and not so warm all the time. When I was in the airplane, already I was feeling it get warmer and warmer as I got sadder and sadder.

Kaitlyn Metzger, Grade 4
Horn Academy, TX

All About Me

When people ask me to describe myself it is difficult because there is a lot to tell. But I am going to tell you about three little items. A book, a rock, and a quarter.

Well, you see a mystery book, but I see time and energy. So much energy it's like a bunny running through the meadow. Me, myself, I like to solve mysteries. I like figuring out the answers. They seem rewarding to me, and after the mysteries are solved you see the smiles and the happiness in the family's eyes, like an orphan finally, getting something to eat.

Creativity means a lot to me and this rock shows just that. I love the color it has. It reminds me of the sun. The sun is yellow. So without colors, we wouldn't be able to see during the day. Your creation can be personalized the way you want it. It can be beautiful and unique.

From where? I am from Las Vegas. Two years ago I moved from Las Vegas to California. A year later I went back to Las Vegas for two years. Then I came to Colorado. Basically what I am trying to say is that you never know where your money came from. I could be from far away and you would never know. It went from one place to another. That is how a quarter represents me.

Whenever people ask me to explain myself, I tell them about these three items, as maybe these three items will change. It will just take time to see. But for now, me and these three items are stuck like glue.

Kaihla Warner, Grade 5
Fremont Elementary School, CO

Luna Moth

The Luna moth is a very rare species. You would be lucky to see one because they are endangered. We are polluting their habitats, causing them to die. Many scientists are trying to find good homes for them so that they won't become extinct. The Luna moth is mostly found in China, Canada, and North America.

The Luna moth has very beautiful wings. Its wings are pale green with eye spots and a long tail. Its wingspan is approximately four and a half inches, and that may not sound big, but for a moth that's huge!

The Luna moth as a caterpillar is considered a part of the silk worm family. It makes its cocoon out of silk and leaves. They will stay in the cocoon through all of spring and summer sometimes, even through all winter.

The adult female Luna moth lives for only a week. During the week it lives, it can't eat it, has no mouth. When they come out of their cocoon they crawl over to a tree, climb up, and rest there for a day. At first their wings are not yet strong enough to be in use, so they stay in the trees. The only thing the Luna moth does in its week to live is mate, lay eggs, then die. As it flies, it sends out a chemical that attracts a male. It lays its eggs on the leaves of trees. It lays up to 200 eggs!

In conclusion, the Luna moth has many unique features about it, whether it's having no mouth, being very large, and being endangered. This is a very interesting bug.

Jubilee Johanneman, Grade 6
Faith Lutheran School, AZ

My Trip to Death Valley

I went to Death Valley during my winter break. Two families also went with us. It took about three hours to go to the hotel. It was nighttime by the time we arrived. I couldn't wait for the adventure for the next day.

When I woke up the next morning, I got dressed and we started our journey to the Death Valley. It took two hours to reach there. It was a very long trip. The first point we stopped at was the Mesquite Sand Dunes. They are huge mountains made up of sand. The color is like light yellow.

The next point we stopped at was called Artist Drive. This name was given because the mountains are different colors. Colors like red, purple, brown. Artist Drive is also really steep. Then we went to the Devil's Golf Course. It isn't a real golf course though. Instead, it is a field covered completely in salt. I looked for salt crystals. Some of the boys tasted the salt. The salt looked good on the rocks.

Finally we went the Bad Water Basin. It was land covered in salt, but the salt looked like snow from the far horizon. It felt unusual walking on salt. Bad Water Basin was my favorite point from the whole journey. The place was made because parts of the ocean were closed up, creating seas and salt lakes. Death Valley was one of these places, but because of the extreme heat of Death Valley, the water dried up, leaving behind the salt.

I loved this journey the most. The journey was really exciting. This was the best journey ever. It is fun to go on adventures like this.

Fatimah Siddiqah, Grade 3
Islamic School of San Diego, CA

My Phone

On the day before Christmas Eve, my mom told me that I was going to get a phone. I was really excited because my mom told me that the earliest I was going to get a phone was my 11th birthday.

When I got home, I did my homework as fast as I could because my mom said I wouldn't get my phone unless I finished my homework before she got home.

When my mom got home, I raced downstairs and I said, "Come on Mom, let's go." Then my sister asked, "Where are you guys going?" Before I could say anything, my mom said, "We're going to buy some clothes." My sister stared at us for a second and then said, "OK." In the car, I though about why my mom had lied about where we were going. Then I realized my sister might be jealous that I'm getting a good phone.

When we got to the phone store, my mom said, "Pick any phone that you like." After some time, I decided to get an Android. My mom bought the phone and we took the phone home.

When we got home, my mom went into the house before me. When I did get home, my sister said, "I can't believe that I got a phone!" Then I realized that my mom had tricked me. I didn't want to tell my sister about it because then she would feel guilty. To this day, she still doesn't know about this.

Andrew Yang, Grade 5
Horn Academy, TX

The Story of Jake

My cat Jake is a strong cat. This is the time I almost lost him. It all started…when my godparents came over to have dinner with my family. We had let the cats out, but it was time to get them back in because it was sunset. My brother and I could only get Finn in (who was Jake's brother). Where was Jake? We didn't know! Me, my dad, my godfather, and my brother searched EVERYWHERE! Everyone took a break to eat…except for my brother. He was determined to find his cat. After everyone ate we went back to searching for Jake. We yelled his name for about 15 minutes, and then he finally scampered in. I tried to catch him. I couldn't catch him, but my Uncle Murray could. While I was chasing him I thought that I saw him bleeding. It was true! It turned out that his lower eyelid was bleeding. I started to cry. I was freaked out and scared. My brother and godmother tried to calm me down, but it only helped a little bit. My mom held him like a baby in a blanket and put a hot towel over his eye. Meanwhile, I was still crying my eyes out. I was constantly checking on him. It was getting late; we had to go to bed. Happily after that night he made it. That night was very scary, but I'm so lucky to still have that adventurous cat.

Alana McKinnon, Grade 4
Pepper Tree Elementary School, CA

My Favorite Place

Seeing the water rush into the river makes me want to jump into the ice cold water. Running through the thin, tall grass feels like getting tickled on my feet. Hearing the birds chirp makes me relaxed and I never feel stressed or depressed. You always smell the fish from the river. This is my favorite place where you always have fun doing chores no matter what. You always want to go exploring every time you wake up in the cold breezy morning, when the mist hits you. But out of all that, the front yard is my favorite place. It is where my mom got married. Every time I go out there I stand right where my mom said "I do." Every time I go out I put my chair where my parents stood and listen to the birds chirp. Sometimes I can picture my parents kissing in the sunset and running together down the carpet to start partying with everyone. Sometimes I cry when I think about their wedding because they did not get to have love for long.

Gabi Coleman, Grade 4
Horn Academy, TX

My Business

I want to own a "Subway" business in Indonesia because they don't have one and they probably don't have great tasting foods that are healthy for them. since it's a new business over there, I want a lot of cheap and good stuff that the public can have access to. This is important to me, because I want the best and most successful business in Indonesia. Also, I have lots of relatives that I can visit and they can come to my restaurant for refreshment while they visit me, so it is beneficial for both of us.

Ardian Kuswanto, Grade 4
Outley Elementary School, TX

Being Fair Is a True Way to Act

Fairness is a really good way to be friendly and respectful. We use friendliness in fairness by sharing things with a second person that needs it the most. We are respectful when we share with a person even though we do not like them. We are fair at school when we let everyone kick the ball when we play kickball. We are also fair when we play the game right. We also are fair with our family members at home. We share our electronics with our brother or sister by taking turns. Our moms are fair by giving each person in the family the same amount of food at each meal. Being fair can help us with keeping our friends and family with us. We are fair to God's creation by giving all plants water and not just one. God's creation needs to be treated fairly because it is a living thing that was made by God. Each living thing should be treated fairly just like you want to be treated fairly. Even on holidays, people need to be treated fair. During Halloween, giving your friends the same amount of candy is a way to be fair. On Christmas, you should give your cousins gift cards that all have the same amount of money in them. Fairness takes place anywhere, at any time. Fairness is sued by everyone, even preschoolers.

Allegra Mia Romero, Grade 6
St Ferdinand Catholic School, CA

Odd Memory

Before I came to Landell, I went to a private school for kindergarten. Every Tuesday after school, they would sell snacks on a cart. What I really loved on the cart was a raspberry and blueberry slushy. So my mom gave me a dollar every Tuesday. One day, a girl that I did not know came up to me and asked me for fifty cents. I replied that I did not have extra money. She kept on begging me, and it was extremely annoying. I really did not know what to do, so I thought. I said, "Okay…fine…I'll give you fifty cents." So I ripped the dollar in half, thinking that ripping half of the dollar is fifty cents.

We went to the lady who was pushing the cart. We asked her if we can buy anything from the cart with the ripped dollar. She constantly laughed, and the girl I gave the ripped dollar to was puzzled. Finally, the lady said that ripping the dollar cannot buy anything. I was disappointed, and sad that I just wasted a dollar, and could not get my slushy.

Yessel Jheong, Grade 6
Margaret Landell Elementary School, CA

My Room

On a brisk fall day, I wake up and open my window. The wind blows into my room. There are leaves on my bed and leaves in my bookshelf. I smell the fresh air in my room. It smells crisp and autumny. I sit in my gray fuzzy reclining chair. I feel like I could sit back and relax. All of a sudden I hear a "Boom!" Then I hear a "Crash!" I quickly got up and looked out my open window. Water started to get inside my room! Soon enough it ended. My opened window is now closed.

Jessica Hoechstetter, Grade 4
Horn Academy, TX

My Friendships and Hardships!

"What?!!" I was mortified as I looked at the long lists of who was going to be in whose class. Almost all of my friends were in Mr. Loeffler's class. I sat on the bench and pouted. I wished I was with my friends. "At least I had Hannah," I thought, although, I didn't really know her that well. Shannyn, Kristin, and Erin were all together, except me. I walked around and sulked for the rest of the day. When school finally came I realized it wasn't so bad. So, as the year went along, I grew to make new friends. I became friends with Aeji, Hannah, and so many others. I still kept my friendship together with the others, but I didn't feel so alone any more. The year ended with marvelous memories, and Hannah and I were best friends that looked forward to 5th grade!

"Nooooo!! Not again!" As I looked at the lists for fifth grade I found my name on it all alone! Now I wasn't with Shannyn, Kristin, Erin, Aeji, or even Hannah!! As I got through the hardships, I met Leyna. Leyna is a great friend and was there for me. During my last year at Landell, my friends weren't in the same class as me again. I always felt left out and forgotten. Since my close friends weren't in the same class as me, it taught me to make new friends, and it made me stronger. I'll never forget being here at Landell!

Madison Tanaka, Grade 6
Margaret Landell Elementary School, CA

Friendship

What I like most in a friend is a friend who doesn't let you down.

I like a friend who treats you nice because the most important things that make a good friendship are trust, kindness, and loyalty. You can tell a friend things that you don't want others to know and they will not tell anyone. Friends never kick or hit each other unless they are playing, because a friend does not hurt you. A friend never talks about you to others or makes fun of you. Friends are always there to help each other and cheer each other up.

Another important thing about a good friend is someone who likes the same things you like. I like playing video games, talking with my friends, playing board games, and shooting airsoft guns. The last thing I really like in a friend is humor. I like a friend who tells jokes and makes me laugh. Friends are special people.

Cody Allen, Grade 5
Castle Hill Country Day School, AZ

My Tree House

I walk home from school through green grass. It warms me up when I think of my tree house. I walk up to my house and I see my tree house in the back ground. It is beautiful, I say to myself. Walking to my tree house, I think of what I am going to do. Maybe I will play Monopoly or Twister, or maybe I will just sit and watch the leaves blow away. I just love watching the leaves blow away. I should do that because that is what my hart wants to do. This is my perfect place.

John Taper, Grade 4
Horn Academy, TX

Mad Science

Last Friday after school, I went to a program called Mad Science. Mad Science is a one-hour after-school program where we can learn different kinds of science. It was my third class at Mad Science. I can't believe we are already halfway through all the classes! During the past two weeks, we'd learned about robots and energy. We learned about what robots are and what kind of robots are there. We also learned about the different types of energy. This week we learned about the basics of chemistry.

When I joined the other students at our group's table, I had no clue what we were going to learn. I hoped it was chemistry, because the "You Be the Chemist" contest is coming up, and I was right! However, it wasn't the type of chemistry I was expecting. He talked about physical mixtures, solutions, and suspensions. I expected him to talk about the periodic table or molecules, but class soon got interesting when he brought out liquid timers that were similar to hourglasses. After that, he showed us a bottle with beads, water, and sugar. The blue and white beads were huddled together in the middle of the bottle. Whenever the teacher shook the bottle, the blue beads would go to the surface while the white beads would go to the bottom. The beads would then gradually float together again. After that, we built our own take-home suspension bottles and took them home.

I learned a lot about science that I had never learned about before. The teachers all made science fun. I wish I had classes like this every day of the week.

Sheldon Zhu, Grade 5
Top Kids Center, CA

Globetrotters

There's a basketball team named the Harlem Globetrotters. I have been to two of their games. I will remember both of the games forever, because the Globetrotters are the funniest people ever. Last year I went to one of their games and there was a guy named Squirrel. He would jump on the hoop and put his head in it. The Globetrotters acted up so much the refs had to have a penalty box. There was also a guy named Special K. Special K once pantsed a guy while he was trying to make a free throw, then that guy came and pantsed him, but he was wearing another pair of shorts. Special K once told the ref that he had a mosquito on his head, so the ref yelled "Don't let it bite me," then Special K smacked the ref on the head and got put in the penalty box.

This year the Globetrotters had a girl on their team for the first time ever. Her name was TNT. The Globetrotters had a guy named Stretch who was 7 ft. 2 in. tall. There was a guy named Tiny that was 7 ft. 8 in. tall. In the beginning of the game a guy named Bones made about ten slam dunks. In the middle of the game a guy named Big Easy made a player mad, so that player tried to pour water on Big Easy, but Big Easy picked up a kid and used him as a shield. At the end of the game I got a ball signed by some of the team. Those were my two trips to the Harlem Globetrotters.

Trevor Blackburn, Grade 6
Lampasas Middle School, TX

A Girl's Best Friend

I was in the 3rd grade and I was sweet and kind to others. I was very good at making friends and had lots of sleepovers. I had cousins, friends and relatives. Still, there was something missing in my life. I needed someone I could go to when I got hurt, and who would cheer me up when I was bored. One day, all of this stuff changed for me.

It was a Friday night and I was bored. My mom was at work and I was at home with my dad. The next morning it was totally cool and surprising moment in my life. When I went downstairs, my mom said she had a special surprise for me. When she said that, I was already brainstorming ideas of what I was going to get. Was it a notebook, a new bike, a dress, a toy?

When my mom came home she had a box of blankets. I was shocked. I didn't want blankets as a gift. Then something magical happened. My mom told me to look through the box and I found a black furry little creature. It was a pug puppy. It was a boy and he was cute and black. I named him Pepper. I had a new best friend.

Letycia Lynch, Grade 4
Wiederstein Elementary School, TX

The Basketball Tournament

About a month ago, there was a basketball tournament. Well, Emily, Jasper, and I decided we should all enter so we could have fun since it's our last year at Landell. So we played our first game and we lost. We versed three sixth graders from Mr. Gary's class. None of us were basketball players so we weren't good. I guess we were also very nervous because everyone was yelling and staring at us with their eyes wide open which was really creepy. Since we lost our first game we were in the loser bracket. We versed another team, a group from Mr. Gary's and lost again. We were laughing a lot after the games because we knew we weren't good.

Dana Son, Grade 6
Margaret Landell Elementary School, CA

My Cousin's Prize

I'm walking to the House of Representatives to accompany my cousin, Sara. I hope she gets one of the top ten. The top ten get to have their art work in the president's office and get to meet him. When we go in, the halls are very silent. We find the auditorium. Some last seats are left for us to sit at. Then the announcing starts. The people started to announce the competitors of the competition. Thirty minutes passed and I was getting bored and was about to fall asleep when they started to say stuff that didn't make any since to me at all. Then they started to announce the top ten (or winners of the competition). I let out a sigh of relief. "Maybe this trip wasn't going to be so bad after all." I leaned forward, crossed my fingers to call Sara's name. "And one of the top ten is Sara!" I was so proud of Sara, I was gong to congratulate her once we got out of the auditorium. I was going to give her a gigantic bear hug on the way out. She told me that she got a camera, books and more. I hope I get to win a contest someday soon.

Diana Marquez, Grade 4
Outley Elementary School, TX

The Importance of Having a Family

It is very important to have a family because if you don't, you can be very lonely. If you don't have a family, who will you be with for the rest of your life? If you don't have a family, then who is going to take care of you? You need to be loved by someone. If you don't have a family, who will be able to hug and love you? How would you survive without a family? If you don't have a family, what will you eat? How will you sleep without a nice and warm house? If you didn't have a mom, then who would you be able to hug in the morning when you wake up? Who would make you nice, yummy brunch, lunch and dinner? Who would tuck you in bed at night? It would be sad without a mother. How would you be if you didn't have a dad? If you didn't have a dad, who would maintain a house for you? If you didn't have a dad, then your mom would've had to get a job to maintain you, and then you would barely be able to see your mom because she would be working. If you didn't have any brothers or sisters, who would you play with if you didn't have any friends? If you didn't have a family, who would you be able to hug, to talk to, and most importantly, love? It is very important to have a family.

Jonathan Barron, Grade 5
Washington Elementary School, CA

The Barn Owl

A silent flier soars upon a starry sky and hunts down its prey.

Owls are very mysterious, yet fascinating creatures. Each owl has a scientific name with its normal name. The scientific name for a barn owl is tyto alba.

The barn owl is usually 16 inches long, medium sized with very long legs. Its heart-shaped face has been said to show love and wisdom. The tyto alba has dark, brown or black eyes, a white face with an edge of tan, and a tan back with fine streaks of pale gray. There is also white cinnamon beneath and on the wings.

Lastly, the tyto alba lives everywhere except Antarctica, and in many places; barns, old buildings, cliffs and trees.

The owl flies home to its hollow as the sun creeps up. The barn owl sleeps a good sleep.

Hero A. Dahlman, Grade 5
Mary E Pennock Elementary School, CO

Cozumel

Blue-green elegant peacocks sashayed across the path as I walked with my friends past them through the resort in Cozumel. Tiny hummingbirds flew through brightly-colored flowers, making this experience seem like a dream. Cats, iguanas, and parrots also roamed freely and gracefully here. Even a camera could not capture these animals and flowers as perfectly as I saw them. My friend stopped, picked up a red-pinkish flower and put it in my hair, which already shone and sparkled in the burning and blazing sun. Tears filled my eyes when I remembered that I would be leaving this place, but my eyes shone with realization that I would have this place etched in my heart forever.

Sophia Perepelitsa, Grade 4
Horn Academy, TX

Stand Up for Our Differences

In our country, you see unfairness and prejudice. People do things they like to do; our community is made up of interesting things. There are many people in the community: people of different races, religions, ages, genders, and personalities.

It would be dull if people were identical. You can explore the world by meeting people from other places, trying foods from different countries, or learning to speak another language. Differences make our life more uplifting.

In 1955, Rosa Parks said that black people shouldn't be treated unfairly. It was horrible when they couldn't take a seat in the same place or drink from the same drinking fountain. Now the law protects everyone.

If everyone had the same religion, people wouldn't understand their religion as much. When you have different religions around you, it makes you think more about what you believe.

Everyone has a different personality. We bring out our personality by doing the things we like to do. If you were just like everyone else, no one would have a favorite color, sport or food.

Some kids think they always have to hang around people their age. Older people know things you don't know. Younger kids are fun and crazy, but they always have new ideas. You learn different things from your dad, mom, grandparents, uncles, and aunts; but everyone teaches you a lot.

If there were no differences in the world, it would be dull and less fun. Differences make us stronger, because we can all add something to our community.

Emily Day, Grade 6
White Pine Charter School, ID

Selfless, Caring and Just

Being fair is challenging at times. Foremost you have to be selfless, caring and just. Fairness means equality. We try to be fair every day and however hard it is, at least we still try. For example, there were four children waiting in line for their mom to give them cake, but there was not enough for everyone. The first three kids received a piece of cake, but there was no more for the fourth kid. The fourth kid was very disappointed. If the mother knew that there was not enough cake for everyone, she might have cut smaller pieces. This is an example of unfairness because she was careless. To make it fair, maybe she could have given the fourth kid something else in return. Happiness should be what matters most to the child's mom. The mom could have given the child a cup of ice cream or something; even though it's no cake, the child would still be happy and not feel left out. Fairness comes up in everyday life, from discipline at home to the silly things such as not sharing a toy. Fairness is the kind of action you want to keep up with because it is the good thing to do. The more you aim to be, the more people will look up to you. Fairness is difficult to do for many people, even for me, especially for those of us who have younger siblings or family relatives that are younger than us.

Christina N. Perez, Grade 6
St Ferdinand Catholic School, CA

Our Differences Make Our Community a Better Place

If you look at a group of people, no two are exactly alike. There are many differences between them, like gender, race, and characteristics. There are also differences you cannot plainly see. Differences are the best thing that can happen to us. The first and most obvious reason is that you can tell two people apart. And if everyone was exactly the same, there would be no variety in life. Everyone would be doing the same things, and life wouldn't be very interesting.

There are many physical differences, like race. Whether your African, Mexican, or Caucasian, your skin always says it. Then there are our physical attributes that set us apart. Your eye color, hair style, glasses, etc. There are also differences that can't be seen, just as there are those that can. There's your mind. How much you know, the way you think, your ideas, and so on.

The biggest difference that truly changes our character is the goodness of your heart. The only way to truly be famed wonderfully is to be goodhearted and nice. This can truly make you different from anyone else. There are many ways to stand out with goodness, but the best ways by far are to be kind and flawless or intelligent and hardworking. Whatever the case may be, I'm sure there's a way to be different.

Jared Hansen, Grade 6
White Pine Charter School, ID

The Lego Plane

I was on lego.com looking at Legos when I saw a really cool airplane, and I wanted it so badly. That Christmas my aunt and uncle gave it to me as a present. We usually open presents on Christmas Eve so we built it that day. I kept building things that were not in the instructions but my aunt fixed it. When we finished building it I was so happy. The next morning my sister said I could have her origami paper because I had a creative mind. I didn't hear that part but she was already gone so I decided to put some use to it and what came out was the best thing that I ever made (besides my Lego plane). The next day I dropped my Leo airplane. As I was trying to rebuild it I noticed that some of the pieces were gone so I built it differently. I made some really big changes then the outcome was entirely different. I really liked it and I thought about it then it came to my head my sister said I had a creative mind and I felt happy that I had a talent, a talent for creating things.

Travis Wu, Grade 5
Horn Academy, TX

My Blankey

When I wake up, the first thing I see is my cute pink blankey. My blankey is very special to me. It isn't soft at all, but I can still handle it. I love its yummy smell after it gets washed. It has little fluffy dogs on it and I love to stare at them. I think I got my blankey from my mom or grandma. First, my sister had it, but then she passed it down to me. I would always feel the soft fringe edges around it and I still do, even though some of them have ripped off. I know I will always have this blankey forever!!

Aubree Rodgers, Grade 3
Vista Charter School, UT

Bang!

I was walking to the school on the road with my Tae Kwon Do friends in Korea. We were talking about lots of stuff when BANG! I was walking backward, and I got tripped by the vase with flowers in front of the flower store and it hit my head on the back. I slowly got up, and I saw my friends telling me "Are you okay? Are you okay?" Then, I saw my friends, but there were two of my friends each. One of my friends told me, "How many fingers am I holding up?" Then I said, "Four," but my friends were staring at me. She was only holding up two fingers!

Even though the world seemed weird, I finished walking to the school. Then, the bell rang and I had to go to my classroom, but instead, I went to the phone station in our school which was there for emergency. My eyes were weird, but I could still see the numbers. I pressed my mom's number, and said, "Mom, if my friend holds up two fingers, it looks like four." My mom was confused, so I told her everything. She then came to pick me up, and made me sleep. After sleeping for two hours, my eyes were getting better. That day, I wasn't able to go to school and I learned not to walk backward. This was one of my embarrassing events because my friends asked me questions the next day about what happened.

Rachel Kim, Grade 6
Margaret Landell Elementary School, CA

My First Sighting of the Blue Angels

Fwooosh! Neeeoooow! Blue Angels flew over me! It was Friday, October 1, 2005. The San Diego Air Show had started. I was standing at the end of our cul de sac with my dad. I saw Blue Angels #2 and #5 flying over my house. They were loud. They had almost popped my eardrums. I could smell smoke from their engines. I held up my little toy Blue Angel and pretended to fly with them. Kapwing! I could imagine that I touched a Blue Angel. It felt HOT!

I was so excited because I am a big fan of the Blue Angels. I learned that the Blue Angels are F-18 Hornets. I was so impressed by what the pilots did. They performed different formations. They shot up high into the sky, separated from each other and then swirled down. They did all the tricks. I like airplanes and pilots so much because they are both skillful at flying. When I grow up, I want to be a pilot and fly Blue Angels, S-3 Vikings and passenger jets.

Lance Gallwas, Grade 5
Dingeman Elementary School, CA

The Bee Stinger

I remember the time in first grade I was saying goodbye to my friend. I accidentally stepped on a bee. He said "Why did you step on the bee?" I said "It was an accident." He said "Okay." The next day he said to the teacher that I stepped on the bee.

The teacher said "What? Why did you do that?" I was afraid to say it was an accident and I got in trouble, but not big trouble. She just told me why bees were important. I was still sad on why he told on a thing like that.

Ethan Soriano, Grade 6
Margaret Landell Elementary School, CA

My First Day of School in Third Grade

As my mother guided me to my classroom, my mind was full of mysterious thoughts. I just came back from my one-year trip to Korea, and had forgotten almost all of my English. While the rambunctious noises traveled through my ear, it came straight out of the other. I had no idea what the students were talking about and it made me wonder why I had to come back to America. Right as I reached my classroom, the bell rang for school to start and I pondered about what I should be doing. My mother then turned to me and told me in Korean, "Do well at school and behave properly!" I wasn't sure what to do, so I just stood still until a teacher came up to me and brought me inside a classroom.

The teacher introduced herself and told me that her name was Ms. Meadows. She was very nice and kind to me. As she led me to the classroom, a countless number of eyes stared at me with wonder. Ms. Meadows directed me to my seat, which was between my first two friends, Sophia and Belinda. Sophia and Belinda helped me with every problem I struggled with and they helped me get used to my surroundings. During recess, they would play with me by hanging on the bars or showing me around the school. Sophia and Belinda helped me realize that staying at Landell wasn't so bad

Kathy Min, Grade 6
Margaret Landell Elementary School, CA

On Eagle's Wings

The plane lurched at my every movement. I could feel the power of the 300 horse power carbine chamber engine in front of me. I snapped back into reality. When the control tower gave me clearance to fly, my uncle helped me taxi to the runway. When we got there, I increased power and the wheels lurched. I sped down the runway. The plane bounced once and lifted up off the ground. I was flying! As I pulled up on the joystick and I flew up into the wild blue yonder, I felt as carefree as a bird. The people on the ground looked like ants. Suddenly I heard my uncle say it was time to land and he was going to take over to land. I snapped back into reality and I watched as the plane soared as mighty as a hawk back to the landing strip. As I walked away with my uncle, the plane looked sad and a bit like it had a missing piece, like a bird in the zoo. I felt the same. I felt as if I left a piece of me in the sky that day. Someday I will go back and get it.

Jacob Schmalz, Grade 5
Horn Academy, TX

My Special Dress

I have a special dress that I got for my 7th birthday. My mom's friend gave it to me. That dress has 3 fairies and 6 flowers on it. My dress is a purple color, dark purple and light purple. It goes down to my knees and is made out of cotton. When I wear my dress I feel so pretty. I wear my dress all the time. This is my favorite dress. When it was summer, I wore my dress all the time too, because it was very, very hot. My dress is the best present I have ever gotten on my birthday.

Oleksandra Zahara, Grade 3
Vista Charter School, UT

Beautiful Corpus Christi

I have lived in Corpus Christi, Texas, my entire life, and it is such a beautiful place. In Corpus Christi there are always tourists. The main tourist attraction is the gorgeous Gulf of Mexico. Whether it's a hot summer day for building sandcastles or a freezing cold day for sitting on the edge of the water drinking hot chocolate watching and listening to the seagulls, Corpus Christi is a fun place to meet new people and have a great time.

Another reason why people love Corpus Christi is because of the various activities they can chose. For example, people can be a member of the birdwatcher's club, participate in the Beach to Bay marathon, or simply adopt a beach to help the environment. There is also fishing, Hooks baseball, windsurfing, water-skiing, and boating. In addition, there are upcoming attractions too, like Schlitterbahn on the island and a water park by Whataburger Field. Whatever a person chooses, he's bound to have the time of his life in Corpus Christi.

In Corpus Christi there are several different beaches on the bay and the gulf, including: Mustang Island State Park, J.P. Luby Surf Park/North Packery Jetty Beach, South Packery Jetty Beach, Upper Padre Island Seawall, Windward Beach Access, Padre Island National Seashore, Padre Balli Park/Bob Hall Pier, Whitecap Beach, Corpus Christi Beach and McGee Beach. They are all great for family times for picnicking, scavenger hunts, surfing, and playing in the sand, or just enjoying the scenery.

In conclusion, Corpus Christi is a fabulous place to live or retire and is the coolest city ever!

Victoria Humphrey, Grade 6
St Pius X Catholic School, TX

Medieval Times

The Medieval Times spanned 700 years from 800-1400. There was no electricity. It was a hard life. Also, they had many wars with other kingdoms.

These wars were usually in the countryside or in places where the townspeople would not get hurt. The wars were fought for land or material possessions such as gold, clothes or food. The weapons used were blunt such as clubs, swords, spears, bows, arrow, catapults, and rocks. The armor they wore was metal, leather, cotton, and wool. The people who wore metal armor were knights, and the people who wore leather, cotton or wool were archers, assassins, and townspeople.

Blacksmiths made weapons and armor used for war made of metal, cloth, herbs, and stone. Blacksmiths made swords a basic weapon. Also, they made blunt weapons such as a club or mace. a Two-handed weapons were a long sword, spear or battle ax. The last weapon is a bow, which shot an arrow. Armor made for knights were plain metal or made into chains and then into a chain mail. Archers and assassins' armor was made into hoods, leather chest plates, leather caps, and other leather armor. But, blunt weapons could easily damage the armor.

The townspeople had many jobs. Some families were farmers and sold crops to merchants in town or to travelers. Also, a town seamstress made or repaired clothes. last, a kingdom had an inn for friendly travelers. Almost every citizen had a job even if he was a child.

In conclusion, life in Medieval Times was very difficult, had many wars, and all citizens had jobs back then.

Sang Hoang, Grade 6
St Pius X Catholic School, TX

Traitor

Have you ever been tattled on for a piece of fruit? Maybe not, but I have. It all happened in Florida while I was in Pre-K. It was a sunny day and my Pre-K classmates and I were walking towards my classroom. We were coming back form lunch. I was sucking on a piece of pineapple. (They didn't like you having food in your mouth after lunch). I was sucking very slowly so no one would notice. Unfortunately, the boy next to me did. He asked me, "What are you sucking on?" We were nearly to the classroom and the teacher was outside, so I knew I had to be quiet. I whispered, "I'll tell you inside." After we got in, I said to him, "Promise not to tell anyone?" He replied, "Yes." "Swear?" I asked. He stuck out his pinky and I took it. Unfortunately, I didn't see him crossing his fingers behind his back. I showed him the little cube of pineapple I was sucking on. I expected him to tell, but he didn't. He just nodded and went back to work. After I finished my work, something terrible happened! He told the teacher! I was still sucking, so I had to think quickly! I hid the cube under my tongue. I wasn't smart enough to think about eating it. "Open your mouth," she commanded. I showed her. "Let's see under your tongue!" I was discovered! Not only were my parents mad at me, but I didn't get to go outside for a week!

Abhaya Chopra, Grade 5
Horn Academy, TX

Planting Seeds of Faith

When a baby is baptized, they take their first step towards God. They'll grow closer to God in the future, because the baptism is just the beginning. I think that the parents of Catholic children have planted seeds of faith in them through their baptism. Also, when you plant seeds of faith, you inspire others to grow, since that seed you planted, will blossom into a spiritual Catholic.

I think one way to plant seeds of faith is to simply go to a Catholic school. If your parents send you to a Catholic school, they're planting seeds of faith in you. I think this is because Catholic schools teach about God and the Ten Commandments, and they teach us to try and follow in Jesus' footsteps.

Also you could take someone who doesn't believe in God, to Mass. You explain to them the readings, sing spiritual songs with them, and take them to communion. You could explain what the host represents and why the Eucharist is important. I think if you take some to Mass, his or her faith in God might expand.

Lastly, when you plant seeds of faith in other people, you're helping yourself. When you help other people, God will be proud. Our mission as Catholics is to be missionaries, to spread God's words, and explain the values of God.

Tiffany Nguyen, Grade 6
St Raphael School, CA

New Year's Resolution

I have some New Year's resolutions I have saved up last year so I would achieve more things in life. To me, a New Year's resolution is basically a goal that you would want to achieve the next year.

I have 3 New Year's resolutions. My first one is that on school days I want to wake up early because once I come downstairs I don't even have enough time to eat breakfast and I just end up going to school with an empty stomach. I would eat breakfast at school but I usually eat at home. For example a kid wakes up late and gets ready for school, but he wants to eat breakfast.

I want to finish my homework on Monday and Tuesday without having to worry about any of the other days that I need to do my homework. But this goal is kind of hard because there are more distractions in my house then there are at school.

My last reason is that I need to stay on task and stop day dreaming so I can finish my work and get on with the other things. It's important to get these things done and improve my education so I can grow up to be a great person.

That is why you have New Year's resolutions, so you can achieve in your life!

Tiffany Akwarandu, Grade 4
Outley Elementary School, TX

Who Am I?

As I walk on the beach on a cool, crisp day, I watch as these kids laugh at me. Are they laughing at my skin? Are they laughing at my clothes? Are they jealous of me? I don't know. So I ask myself, "Who am I?" I am a boy who was born on December 27, 1999. I am a boy who is growing into a teenage body. I am a boy who watches MTV and plays Xbox all day. I am a boy who still shares a room with his little sister. I can be a slacker sometimes, but I am a boy who loves his family and teachers more than himself. It changed my life forever to watch as they laughed at me. Why am I this way? Because I do have dignity in myself, but sometimes you just have to grow up. Just because I changed my life doesn't mean you have to change yours. Like Michael Jackson once said, "It doesn't matter if you're black or white. We are all beautiful in every single way." It's not right to make fun of anybody, because it doesn't matter who or what they are, we must love them anyway.

Frederick Lee, Grade 6
Woodcreek Middle School, TX

My Special Flower

One of my favorite special things is my glossy, shiny, glass flower. It is a knickknack with a little bit of sparkling glitter in it. It is very smooth. It is very clear, so clear that I can see right through it. My cousin Abby, who lives in Salt Lake, gave it to me. I really miss Abby. My flower helps remind me of her. She gave it to me when she came to visit us. She gave it to me at my house. When my mom saw it, she said it is not just play jewelry. My flower is very important and special to me.

McKenna Turner, Grade 3
Vista Charter School, UT

The Big Point Winner

It was a boiling hot June day and a Friday, which meant Mr. Loeffler was about to announce the point winner and it was the last couple days of school. I have won four times and so have my other classmates Aaron and J.J.. If a student wins for the fifth time, he or she gets a free book order up to four dollars, a homework pass, lunch from any restaurant (McDonald's, In-N-Out, etc.), and a ticket to Disneyland. My hands were trembling, my knees were shaking, and I was jumping up and down quite a bit.

Mr. Loeffler was tallying up the points and I saw Preston, Jovanna, J.J., and Aaron written on the board with tally marks under our names. "Drum roll please...," Mr. Loeffler proclaimed, "And the point winners are...Preston and Jovanna!!!" Inside I was excited, elated, enthusiastic that I had won five times and some students whose desks were near mine congratulated me. J.J. was putting his head in his arms and pounding on his desk. Aaron was disappointed, but he was a good sport about it. That was the best day ever!!!!

Jovanna Mai, Grade 6
Margaret Landell Elementary School, CA

Lake House

We were driving down the steep concrete hill surrounded by chestnut brown spiky pine cones. I jumped out of the car and ran over to my favorite tree. The branches were lowered just enough for me to get on. I climbed up to the tip top of the dark brown tree with lime green leaves. I knew where to sit every time because there is a spot that is shaped like a chair. I laid back to watch the beautiful different shaped clouds. One cloud was shaped like a teddy bear doing a black flip, and another one looked like a frog on a boat! In my mind I could hear the motor and the sound of the water splashing. I love weekends at the lake house!

Allie Baker, Grade 4
Horn Academy, TX

Help Save the Manatees

I believe manatees should be free. Free from harm and death. Manatees don't hurt you, so don't hurt them. Manatees need your help badly. They're living creatures. God made them.

Every year there's less, and less, and less, because of the boats that hurt them. Manatees are joyful loving creatures. They enjoy life! That's what's great about them. These animals suffer every year. Soon, these animals will be extinct, like dinosaurs. I would be really sad, would you? These people need to stop before all the manatees are gone. You're hurting them.

First, I think we should put up signs where manatees live, so people will know. Then, I think that if people see the sign, then they should NOT ride over there. Finally, I think people should help the manatees get better or be loving to them. This is what I believe and always will. I hope people will be more careful around manatees.

Cori Campbell, Grade 5
Foothills Elementary School, CO

Cancer

When I started preschool, I was scared because I didn't have any friends, until I met Ashley. When I met Ashley and knew more about her, I figured out we had a lot in common, like drawing, playing, and singing. Whenever we played we played outside, where the breeze would hit our face and we could draw with chalk on the hard floor. A few months later, I found out she had cancer. It was horrible because the other kids made fun of the way she looked. Sometimes she cried when they teased her, but she tried to hide her tears so they wouldn't tease her more. Soon our class became so calm, and I realized Ashley was not there. She was in the hospital. I couldn't help wanting to know about her. My mom called her mom and her mom told my mom that Ashley had passed away. My mom and I couldn't believe it. When my mom hung up the phone, she quickly hugged me and I began to cry. Even my mom let down some tears, too. A year later, when I was in kindergarten, I was still depressed about Ashley's death. Even the kids who once teased her were sad. I made a new best friend. Even though I made lots of new friends, none of them were the same as Ashley.

Samantha Hernandez, Grade 5
Washington Elementary School, CA

The First Day of School

The first day of first grade was interesting. The attendance list was not perfect. One girl, Rachel was absent. So, I knew that the girl I did not recognize was Rachel.

The next day a tall girl with brunet hair walked through the door. I knew that was Rachel, because she wasn't familiar. I wanted to greet her on her first day of school, but I couldn't. We had work to do.

By the time we lined up for lunch I was ready to say hello. "Hi, Rachel," I greeted. Her eyebrows we up as her curiosity grew. "How do you know my name?" she asked. I explained that she was the only person absent on the first day of school.

The second day of school was a great day because without that day, I wouldn't know my good friend, Rachel.

Shae Fox, Grade 4
Horn Academy, TX

Point of View

When I was 8 years old I went to a family reunion in Nebraska. After everything died down we finally had time to go look at some cattle in a pasture off to the side of everything else. While we were walking over I saw a snake off to one side. I told my mom and she said to just stay away from it. A few minutes later we were walking back over and I saw the snake again! This time we showed everyone but of course my uncle didn't see it so he started walking toward it! My mom yanked him back from the snake. We all backed away from it but not my grandpa. He started throwing sticks at it to see if it was a rattlesnake! It got really mad and finally stuck its rattle out. Then I pointed out that it looked like it had diamonds on its back. Now I look more carefully where things might be hiding.

Bennett Howell, Grade 5
Horn Academy, TX

Precious Procession

People probably have a valued object in their life, mine is the music trophy. It might not be expensive or valuable, but it is very special to me.

My trophy was given to me by a very special person, my piano teacher. My teacher is a well known and famous music composer in my Vietnamese community and has put a large amount of his time and effort to teach me to reach my full potential.

A few years ago, I had an enormous opportunity to play on an expensive brand new grand piano. At the end of the recital, I was astonished when my teacher presented me with a trophy for my outstanding performance.

My trophy means the world to me. It represents my accomplishment of mastering piano and it also makes my parents proud. My trophy signifies that all of my practice and hard work paid off. It has encouraged me to never give up and to always do my best to achieve my goal. Whenever I look at my trophy, I am reminded of the graceful movements of playing piano and hearing delightful music.

Vu Nguyen, Grade 6
St Cecilia School, CA

If I Had a Dream

I have a dream that poverty will end. What would you feel if you went to bed every night and were hungry? I feel like we need to stand up and make sure children get food every night. It makes me feel so sad. I know how it feels to be in poverty. I think if every one would be less selfish, every one might just have a home to live in and have supper every night. Would you like to live out in the snow? No, I bet you don't, so just think of what you can do to help. Sometimes it makes me want to stand up ad scream. I bet you're wondering why. First, because not many people want to help. Second, because these days not a lot of people can help others out with money. That is why we should help the people in poverty. That dream for poverty is we should donate more food and money for people in poverty.

Skylar Gipson, Grade 5
Foothills Elementary School, CO

One of the Most Dangerous

Even though there are a lot of things going wrong around the world, I choose to write about war. First, war is dreadful to me. Whenever I hear that a war is going to happen, I just want to zoom up to my room, and sob my heart out. Next, it isn't fair. When I just concentrate about war it crushes me because I think of the color red and the innocent people living there getting harmed. I wish we could put an end to it. Finally, I don't understand. Why do they have to harm innocent people? Then we have to put our lives on the line and probably we will get seriously injured or die. It just breaks me. Watching the news and seeing an innocent soldier, fighting for our country just die. As you can see, war is like a flytrap that you have to get out of so you can fight for your life.

Malcolm Gomez, Grade 5
Foothills Elementary School, CO

The Lion Tree

One day my dad and I were walking on a trail near our home in Auburn, when our dogs started barking at something higher up on the trail. As we approached, we found that in a big pine tree there was a mountain lion!

The lion had climbed 20 feet high up in the tree, and it was lying on a branch, looking calm. Even though our two dogs were barking at the base of the tree, he didn't seem to care. This was a full-grown mountain lion, colored light brown, with some black markings around its eyes. He didn't make a sound, but just looked at my dad and me curiously.

My dad and I started talking to the lion, saying things like, "How are you doing?" and "We're just like you, enjoying the day." The lion just looked at us peacefully, as if he understood.

After about five minutes of this conversation, my dad and I walked back up the trail to our home, followed by our two dogs. We never saw the lion again.

Every time we walk on this trail, we get excited when we come to the part of the trail where we saw the lion. And we smile when we look at The Lion Tree.

Austin Rawlings, Grade 6
St Joseph Catholic School, CA

Kindergarten Song

I was in kindergarten, and we were getting ready to sing our 1st grade song. We practiced and practiced and practiced and practiced for about 2 weeks. The night had snuck up on us, and we were entering the MPR. All of the kindergartners were dressed nicely and cute were about to began their song. I was very scared, because there was a crowd and I had to sing in front of that crowd.

The teachers went "Ready begin," and all of us began to sing: "1st grade, 1st grade, we learned to share, and care, and love with our friends. I want to be a part of it, 1st grade, 1st grade." There were cameras flashing, red lights on for video taping, and laughs or smiles from the crowd. I felt really special that night, and it was a good night.

Elayna Roberts, Grade 6
Margaret Landell Elementary School, CA

My Treasure Chest

My uncle gave me a very special wooden chest. It holds special charms, a mood ring, hawk feathers, a golden owl, quarters, and a diamond rock that my grandparents gave me. The rock is like the chest and is special because it is very valuable to me. My chest is very special. It is brown and black, and it is about 15 inches wide and 7 inches tall. I like how it is very soft on the inside because of the fuzzy material in it. The lid of the chest does not come off; it opens up like my laptop. It is my second best gift after my laptop. I know my uncle loves me and the chest. He tells me that I'm special, and he texts me or calls me to check on the chest to make sure it is okay. It touches my heart often. I will never betray it and I will treasure it my whole life.

Bodey York, Grade 3
Vista Charter School, UT

When the Cows Come Home

The last weekend in the month of November, something terrible happened at my grandpa's ranch. All of my grandparents' cows got sick and he had to go to Tucson to buy a specific medicine for his cows. The cost of the medicine was approximately $4,000 dollars. The worst thing about the medicine is if you were to poke yourself with the needle, it would stop the blood from flowing through your body and you would die instantly. Before we could give the cows medicine we had to herd them into the corral.

We had to get on our horses, herd the cows together and take them to the corral. It was tough because the cows have a mind of their own, and it's very annoying. The cows sometimes go where you want them to go, but not all the time, and this time it was tough to get them into the corral. Finally, we got the sick cows into the corral, and now were going to start giving them the medicine. They were all in the chute, now all we had to do was give them the medicine. We had to be extremely careful with this certain type of medicine, only one mistake and someone could die. We pulled the cows' neck skin out and gave them 2 doses of the medicine, we were very close to being halfway finished and it was going great. Luckily, no one had poked themselves with the medicine. We finished the last and final cow and were through for the day. Just like all the stories, this ended happily ever after.

Rylan O'Brien, Grade 6
Faith Lutheran School, AZ

Houston, We Have a Problem

I was leaning on the wall in the kitchen when it all started. My dad was sitting down at the kitchen table and so was my brother. My mom was leaning on the wall along with me. The fog outside was distracting and very gloomy. It was the perfect weather for what was about to happen to me and my family. My mom and dad were nervous to tell us, the look on their faces said so.

My dad said, "I have some news for you guys. We're moving to Houston!" My brother and I were devastated! I couldn't believe what I was hearing. I was completely flabbergasted!

My brother started balling! My head just felt like a coconut that had fallen out of a palm tree. I was overwhelmed. Moments passed and my brother was still crying frantically. I was shocked. I didn't know what to feel.

Once my brother finally stopped crying, my parents told us in a couple of weeks I would have to go through my things and sell the stuff I don't want. So weeks passed and I started to sell my things even though I wished I didn't have to.

I thought my life was over! I was devastated to levels I can't explain. I was completely disappointed. I stayed up for hours at night crying myself to sleep. It was the truth and it changed my life forever! I learned that no matter what life throws your way, you keep going and pushing through the pain, and then you will eventually find your way to the sunny side!

Lauren Parrish, Grade 6
Woodcreek Middle School, TX

An Unforgettable Moment

My unforgettable memory happened at Oakland, California, in winter 2008. I had just come back from another boisterous day of kindergarten. I was suffering a large amount of leg pain. My leg was throbbing and the pain was oppressive. My mom told me I was five-star perfect.

Things weren't going good for me. I was still having excruciating pain. Mom and Dad started to worry. They brought me to a hospital. The doctor said I had something bad and I had to go to children's hospital, so we did. I was worried to death.

Ugh! My leg hurt a lot. So anyway, I was in the Oakland Children's Hospital. My leg had a disease that's name was so long. Then the affectionate nurses brought me to a new room. It turned out I would have to stay there for a week. Was my leg really this bad?

It was my fifth day there, and my 4th day of missed school. In school, they were making cards for me. I couldn't believe that my class was making cards for me.

The doctor tried this macabre medicine on me, but I threw up. That night, I was woken up by a chummy nurse. She told me I would have to have surgery if this medicine didn't work. I was totally paralyzed. I didn't want surgery, so I took a large gulp and drank down the medicine. And you know what? I didn't vomit. That was an unforgettable moment.

Roshan Kannan, Grade 5
Top Kids Center, CA

The Patient Road

I couldn't believe it, I was going to Florida. I'd always dreamed of going. "Disney World," I murmured. From the fast rushing rides to the little twirls, I immediately started to pack.

I woke up the next day with a startled look. "Today's the day," that phrase kept repeating in my head over and over again. Then, I busted out of the house like a volcano. As soon as we got in the van, the trip started. Then it was night. Then I heard that we had only gone form Texas to Mississippi! I was shocked. On the road, I could feel the rocks and the bumpy road. That irritated me.

It was the middle of the night when my dad suddenly dragged the van to the grass in the middle of the highway! A moment later, he started snoring. Then, he snored louder. And to me, his snores sounded like a pig snort. "This is going to be a disaster," I thought. Later on, I decided that I was impatient. "Hurry up!" I yelled. It took a while before he drove out, and kept going.

The sunrise was up and was beautiful as gold. I knew at that moment it was morning. Then I realized that I had stayed up all night just on being excited. Finally we were in the hotel. The moment I stepped in, it was like a palace, shiny floors, clean rugs, and servants in uniforms!

We were now in Florida. My dream came true, and maybe my trip with my family wasn't so bad after all.

Jessica Vu, Grade 4
Outley Elementary School, TX

Sushi

Have you ever tried sushi? Sushi is delicious and a tasty treat. What is sushi? Sushi is rice wrapped in seaweed with some topping like cucumber, egg, crab meat, avocado, shrimp, etc. Another type of sushi is sashimi. Sashimi is like sushi, except there is raw fish in it and it doesn't have seaweed. If you think raw fish sounds bad, you'll be surprised. Sashimi tastes awesome! The most common types of raw fish are salmon, tuna, yellowtail, octopus, shrimp, etc.

Where did sushi come from? Sushi was invented in Southeast Asia as a way of preserving fish. Later, Japan made it as more like a cuisine. If you're on a diet, don't worry, sushi is one of the healthiest meals. Sushi has many different types. For example, there is the California Roll, the Dragon Roll and many others. Sushi is eaten with wasabi and soy sauce. It is a spicy combination. The wasabi is to kill all the germs on the raw fish, just in case. The soy sauce is an easier way to mix the wasabi up, and it tastes good, too.

Here are some interesting facts about sushi. Did you know that the term 'sushi' doesn't really mean sushi at all? It means rice seasoned with vinegar, sugar, and sauce. Also, when people eat sushi they mostly drink miso soup. However, they drink it at the end of the meal, not at the front, because of digestion. If you're scared to try sushi, don't worry. Sushi will satisfy your mouth!

Samantha Long, Grade 6
Top Kids Center, CA

A Determined Leader

Who was blind and deaf but still succeeded in her studies? Who was the first handicapped woman to graduate from college?

Helen Keller was born in Tuscumbia, Alabama, on June 27, 1880. Helen's mother was Captain Keller's second wife, and Helen was the first daughter in the family. Helen learned to walk at an early age and was very smart. In 1882, Helen got very sick with a very high fever. The fever finally went away, but unfortunately Helen became blind and deaf. Doctors could not do anything. Soon Helen found ways to communicate and followed her mother everywhere. She absolutely loved to feel plants outdoors. However, she had many tantrums so the Kellers went to a different doctor who was an eye specialist. He advised them to see Alexander Graham Bell. Mr. Bell told them to write to the Perkins Institute. A teacher named Annie Sullivan came on March 3, 1887. On April 5, Helen finally started listening to Annie and learned from her teacher. When Helen was almost 8, she visited the White House to meet President Cleveland! Helen attended college and was the first lady to graduate. During college years, Helen wrote many books to help handicapped people and give them hope. Helen Keller died on June 1, 1968.

I admire Helen Keller for her strength and perseverance. She is my hero.

Pia Shah, Grade 4
Montessori Learning Institute, TX

What Would Your Kids Think of You?

You know when your parents are embarrassing trying to act cool, or "hip" as they would say? They would try to say, "That's messed up," or, "What's up man?" Do you make fun of your parents for something about them like their laugh or their snore? Have you ever thought what your kids would think about YOU?

When you're older, you might not know about all the new technology. You'd be the one who sounds lame when you say, "What's up?" You're also going to be the one that will always forget your kid's name. You might be the type of parent that always asks, "How do you do this?" You then have the power to ask your kids to do anything.

What your kids think of you won't be so bad if we end up like the cool parent. They would be okay with you saying what we say now. They wouldn't be weirded out or embarrassed when we're with their friends. We'd get to be with them without them saying, "You can go now!" It's seems hard to plan how you are going to act if you want to be cool parent.

As you grow older, think about how you'll treat your kids, how you're going to help them, teach them, and help lead them through a good life. You don't want to end up a mean parent, or lead them into a bad future. You'd want to listen and support their dreams. So, what kind of parent do you think you are?

Hannah Rebancos, Grade 6
Madonna Del Sasso School, CA

Football

My favorite sport is football. It is my favorite sport because I love to tackle other people. Also I like to run, and the last thing that I like to do is throw the football.

I would like to talk about tackling. The best game to play when you want to learn how to tackle is Oklahoma. it is a game where two people start on the ground one of them with the football. Then the coach will blow a whistle. Then they will both get up and sprint at each other. The person without the ball will try to tackle the person with the ball. That is a very fun game to play. I remember my first time playing the game. it was me against my friend BJ. I was the person with the ball. Coach blew the whistle and we got up and BJ tried to tackle me and he just was pushing and pushing until coach said next group because our time was over. The reason why I think you should play this game is because it can improve on tackling.

I want to talk about running. it is a really fun thing to do. It can keep you healthy and in shape. Did you know that running in place is healthier than running to the corner of the street? I run so much that I almost like track more than football but football beats track by a landslide.

I want to talk about throwing the football. I love to throw the football so much that one time I fell asleep with a football in my hand.

Charles Robins, Grade 4
Outley Elementary School, TX

Orange Leaf

When I walk in I see the lime green tiles and smell the fresh fruity yogurt. My favorite place is Orange Leaf. I can't wait to try all the different flavors and topping. I always choose the mango machine first and can't wait to pull the lever. My favorite topping is the Popping Boba. It explodes with flavor when you spoon it into your mouth and then pop it with your teeth. As the yogurt comes out of the machine, it swirls into the cup that is supposed to be below the machine. Their Popping Boba comes in two different flavors which are mango and strawberry.

Their yogurt is very flavorful. The flavors taste like fruit. The yogurt is very soft. You can put fruit on your yogurt as a topping. Topping make the yogurt a little more flavorful. Once you get your yogurt, you can get toppings. The topping are self served so you can go get what topping you want and also how much of it you want. They price the yogurt by weight. You can also get the amount of yogurt you want. If you wanted to, you could get different blends of yogurt. Sometimes I get blends of yogurt but not all the time.

Rebekah Wong, Grade 4
Horn Academy, TX

A Day to Remember

In fourth grade, my class went on a field trip. This field trip was almost at the end of fourth grade. While we were in the bus, Jenny, my friend, and I started playing "Would You Rather." We made a lot of silly jokes and played some games we made up. Once we arrived, all of our classmates were jumping for joy. We ate lunch once we arrived and then got separated into groups. We bought pans, shovels, and pots at this fake shop so that we could mine for gold in a river nearby. I found a lot with my group members. Also, my group members and I had to help dig holes in the dirt and make bricks for fun. On a rock, we all ground corn to make flour and afterwards, we made tortillas and ate them. I will never forget this fun, hard, day.

Hyunah Yeom, Grade 6
Margaret Landell Elementary School, CA

Mt First Day at Cawthon

Three years ago, my family and I moved to Cypress from Long Beach. So I had to move to a different school. My first day at Cawthon Elementary school was frightening and exciting. It was frightening because I didn't know anybody, new teachers and I missed my old friends. I was also sad because things were not the same with my friends and I. We used to have fun together, but now we didn't even get to see each other anymore.

Then, things became more exciting when I made new friends and I got to know some teachers, especially Mrs. Houck. She was wonderful to me. She helped me when I needed her. She was very patient with me and I appreciated her very much. I will never forget that first day at Cawthon.

Justin Leng, Grade 6
Margaret Landell Elementary School, CA

Fairness

An example of fairness is two people breaking a law and both of them go to jail, serving the same sentence. People need to be fair no matter the time. If a person commits a crime, and innocent people go to jail, that would be unfair. If you were to see someone not being fair to others, you should say something to that person. Being fair is being kind to everyone in your life equally. With all the things you do in life, you need to be fair with everyone you interact with. Fairness is thinking about others first in your life. The Declaration of Independence claimed that all men are created equal. To do that, America has worked hard and come a long way trying to make things fair for everyone. The Civil War was important because it affected African Americans and one of the main causes of the Civil War was to fight for the end of slavery. It took African Americans a long time to receive fair treatment. It took many African American leaders like Martin Luther King Jr. who fought for the people's rights and fairness for others with a different skin color. Cesar Chavez was a man who stood up for the fair treatment of the Mexican farm workers. A hero is not always famous or has super powers, but many are willing to risk their lives to save others, which leads them to do actions of good towards other people. A hero believes in equal rights and doesn't discriminate; he shows fairness to all.

Matthew Rubio, Grade 6
St Ferdinand Catholic School, CA

The Fair in Fairness

Fairness is a very substantial virtue because it helps people be on the same terms which lead to others getting along. If fairness can get people to see beyond their problems, they can learn to accept others for who they are. In this way, everyone can be able to express themselves freely. It is also important in respecting other people by giving them a chance to say what they have to say to do what they have to do. In doing this you give them attention when they are given the opportunity to speak. This gives them more confidence to let their feelings and ideas out. Fairness leads to other valuable virtues that make us have a stronger personality to become better people that we know we can be. It leads us to other valuable virtues by letting others know that by being fair we can be good leaders. It also shows others that we can be reliable when they need us. Sometimes to learn to be fair, you have to experience it yourself or try and put yourself in another person's shoes. Putting yourself in others' shoes would give you the experience to know how they feel when they are being treated unfairly. Fairness should be about being considerate and thinking about others. It should also be about being reasonable in making decisions in which you can make others included. Others can be included by being welcomed and accepted others. Its role in helping get humanity through life is what makes it so essential.

Kymberly Franco, Grade 6
St Ferdinand Catholic School, CA

The Day My Dog Died

It was Christmas Day, I had just woken up and walked out of my room. I noticed that Alex, the family dog, did not come greet me as she usually did.

"Dad, where is Alex?" I asked my father.

"She had to go to the vet," my father replied.

"Why?" I asked him.

"She got very sick," he replied, "and so they put her to sleep."

"What does that mean, Daddy?" I asked.

"It mans that they had to kill her in a painless way," he replied.

At that moment my heart shattered into tiny pieces that it could not rejoin completely. I ran into my room and stuffed my face into my pillow and screamed so loudly my parents could hear it clearly. A few hours later, my mom came in and told me that they had waited for me to come out and open presents with them. I did and got lots of good presents, but I still could not fill up the rest of my heart.

Paul Goza, Grade 4
Horn Academy, TX

My Music Box

When I wake up, I carefully open my beautiful music box. The lovely beautiful music comes out as I sit and listen. The music is from the movie *Swan Lake*. It is decorated with lovely ballerinas. When you open the box you can see a ballerina spin around and around. I got it from Christmas when I was seven years old. I used to call it my treasure box. I loved running around, saying "I have a treasure box." It is very special to me and I love it very much. My baby brother tries to steal it and tear it apart! It is my prized possession. Once my friend accidentally tore off the ballerina's wings. I got really sad, but I forgave her. I think that my music box is the best present ever!

Brenna Gunnell, Grade 3
Vista Charter School, UT

My Little Cave

When I was six, I lived in a yellow house by a lake. Behind that lake was a cave. I always went in it when I was wanting my alone time. The cave looked like a bright beautiful adventure. There was room for only 1 person, and one animal. It had a smooth layer to sit on, the cool water splashed on my toes, the warm breeze ran across my face, and the cave was the only time I got to be alone. Sometimes I brought my dog Emily. Emily is the sweetest dog ever. One day my parents said we were moving and I was very sad. I thought that I would never see my cave again. When Emily saw me cry she came to me, and cheered me up. Now, I remember the cave, and remember how peaceful it was.

Lauren Zieske, Grade 4
Horn Academy, TX

My Zoe

Zoe's eyes were as droopy as ever. I was laying down on the floor listening intently to my parents talk. "Reagan you're going to have to get it out." It made me sob even harder.

This morning was the morning she was going to die. "Go with it Reagan," my mother kept telling me. The only reply I could bring myself to say was a hushed, "okay." "Let's go," my mother whispered, trying to soothe my feelings.

I went into the dark kitchen. It was filled with gloom. I walked over to her and reached into my pocket. My hand came out with a treat enclosed in it. As I fed her the last treat I would ever give her, I felt sadness. I gave her the last hug I would ever give her. This would be the last. I looked into her eyes. She looked back at me. I felt forlorn like an abandoned dog.

"Reagan," my mother nudged me, "time to go." I looked at her one more time. This time she walked over to me. "Goodbye, Zoe," I whispered. "Goodbye."

I thought, my family is broken. She is gone. She is my sister. She is me. My life would never be the same without her.

Reagan Kimzey, Grade 4
Horn Academy, TX

Friendship

What I like most in a friend is humor, loyalty, and kindness. I like nice and funny people. I like friends who are encouraging and help you out when you're hurt. A good friend is nurturing and gives you strength when you feel defeated. They want you to do your best and have fun. They stand up for you if you're being bullied. A good friend wants you to be yourself because that is what they like about you. You can be a good friend too, by helping your friend out. If you're both nice to each other, you'll probably end up being friends forever. The most important thing about friendship is that you can be friends with anyone. It doesn't matter how old you are. Even the most different people can be friends.

MiKyla, Grade 5
Castle Hill Country Day School, AZ

The Cobra

It sits proudly upon the Lexington's flight deck with its damaged rotors. As the drilled rotors lay there, something else shows what hardship it's been through: the battered decals with razor sharp teeth and gleaming eyes. The weapons stand out to show how powerful it used to be. The cockpit has shattered windows. Controls that are now malfunctioned used to control the helicopter. The seat's old dry leather is cracked to where you could see the cotton inside. The parachute was so battered it only had one strip of worn out cord still attached to the chute. It's white numbers still stood out boldly so tourists could see. This helicopter may still be old, but it is the most fascinating to me.

Gene Gopon, Grade 4
Horn Academy, TX

There Is Such a Thing as a Kindergarten Dropout

Imagine this: little girls in cute dresses and bows, boys looking shy and, for some reason, guilty. The alphabet hangs on one wall, the number chart on another. The smell of dry-erase markers hangs in the air, having been there forever. Yep. You've just taken a time machine back to kindergarten. But here's something you don't know: you don't have to go to kindergarten to get into grade school.

In kindergarten, children learn how to read. If they don't go to kindergarten, they aren't prepared for grade school, which could impact their whole life. Some parents don't send their kids to kindergarten, which is basically child abuse. It should be a written law that if children don't go to kindergarten, they don't get in to grade school. This could have a big impact on the educational standards of America.

On the other hand, some people think that kindergarten is like advanced preschool, and maybe that was the case a while ago. But nowadays, things are getting more and more advanced in school curriculums. It would be hard to go into grade school and be expected to know things that they would if they had gone to kindergarten.

In conclusion, I think it should be the law that all children must go to kindergarten, if they want to proceed to grade school.

Abigail Wehrman, Grade 6
Beacon Country Day School, CO

My Tremendous Sleepover

Have you ever been in a situation where you were late for something exciting? That's how I felt the day of my first sleepover. All I could think of during the basketball game was how fun the sleepover would be.

I rushed from the court of my successful basketball game into the pitch-black night. I got home and streamed into the house. I finished my usual ten-second shower and hurried downstairs, ready to go to my friend's house. This would be my first sleepover. "Hurry up," I yelled as I zoomed into the car. Finally, I sped to the door of my friend's house and rang the doorbell. When the door opened the bright light blinded me. I ran through the hall to join my friends playing the wonderful and entertaining game of Mario Kart Wii. We finally stopped and settled down for the night.

We rose from bed quickly so we could get the day started early. We were up before anybody in the house. We played the Wii and moved like we were really in the game. By the time we were ready to eat, I was almost sweating and it felt like the Wii remote was still in my hand. I rushed into a chair and saw the pancakes. The maple syrup from the pancakes washed my mouth and the pancakes were as soft as butter. I was disappointed when the sleepover was over but it was still the best sleepover of my life.

Andrew Kim, Grade 5
Dingeman Elementary School, CA

My Bearded Dragon

My bearded dragon named Spike is a lizard that has spikes all over its body and can grow to two feet long. This reptile sometimes puffs out its neck, so it looks like it has a beard. If it is attacked, it uses its spikes to defend itself by shipping its tail and scratching with its sharp claws.

I feed Spike crickets, food pellets and mealworms. In addition, I give him water and I take him out daily into the hallway. I close the doors and put towels on the bottom of the doors. I let Spike run up and down the hall until he is tired. Then I put him back in his cage. Bearded dragons are desert animals, so I keep two heat lamps on Spike during the day and one UV light on him during the night. He likes taking baths in warm water. I give Spike a bath about once a week. Moreover, I built him a tower and he somehow gets to the top of it; but I have never seen him get to the top.

Furthermore, it is fun to watch him chase and eat the crickets. I put a whole box of crickets in his cage and the box has a clear top, so Spike tries to eat the crickets from the top of it because he cannot see the plastic covering. Some crickets are dead, which he won't eat. I move them around, so he thinks they are alive and then he eats them.

Finally, my bearded dragon is unusual as a pet, but also it is fun to own.

Aaron Martin, Grade 6
St Pius X Catholic School, TX

My Trip Downstairs

"Give it back," I screamed. "No," she yelled and slammed her door. My sister took my piggy bank with all my money. I had gotten it for my birthday and had spent hours painting it. I ground my teeth, clenched my fists, and wanted to scream. I needed a drink.

I started down the stairs. My face was red, damp, and frigid. Icy, wet tears swelled up in my eyes and dripped down my face. I stomped down the stairs not looking where I was going. I tripped.

The world around me spun and swirled. I slid and my legs struggled to find something to stand on. My arms flailed as they scrambled for something to hold. I felt the cold handrail rush past me. Swish! I picked up speed. Crash, thud! I hit the floor.

I felt the cold tile. I lay there hardly able to breathe. My back burned like it had been scorched by a blazing fire. My muscles ached like a snake just bit me. I could not budge. I tried to scream but my mouth was parched. I tried to roll into the family room, but my muscles ached.

After what seemed like forever, my dad walked in. He carried me to the couch and iced my back. It sent chills up my spine. I shivered. Ouch! The bouncy couch soothed my body. I was tired so I took a nap. I dreamed of the wonderful days to come.

Naya Menezes, Grade 5
Dingeman Elementary School, CA

Surprise Crash

Snap, pop, crack! The ground balls sped past me. This was the 20th practice since the start of the off-season. Boom!

Dad swung the black synergy softball bat. I picked up the yellow ball and threw it to first base. A loud grunt popped out of my mouth and flew into the air. I could feel the warm sweat slide down my face.

The crack of the ball disguised the loud crash on the burning street. Before I know it, Dad was down the hill, and not very happy. I was as confused as a kindergartner in a middle school.

After Dad left, Annie, Jackie, and I froze as if we were statues. It seemed like hours before we decided to grab our things and walk down to the street where our car was sitting. The light post was bent into a strange shape. A man with a black BMW was talking to my dad. The rear end of our GMC was smashed into the middle of our car. Before I knew it, my mom was crossing to the side of the street that we were on. I wasn't sure she was coming but I was so glad when she got there because I felt very safe. Mom works at Geico so she called one of her car repair people to come to Scripps Ranch High School's softball field. Since mom drive there, Jackie drove Annie and I home. After that, I had a feeling inside me that everything would be okay.

Sophia Scarangella, Grade 5
Dingeman Elementary School, CA

Oops, Wrong Turn!

Wohoo! I thought, this was going to be fun!

"Are you sure you can do it?" asked my dad.

Of course I can, I thought but I only replied with "Yeah." I pedaled my bike towards the hill, my heart pounding. I reached the hill and zoomed down it, wind whipping my face.

I still felt the wind on my face for a second, then, whump! The ground was under me, and bushes were on top of me. I had fallen into the bushes that lined the one-way road leading down a hill in UCSD.

When I got out I was scratched and scraped and I hurt. But I was just glad that we were not in one of the more public parts of UCSD.

We somehow managed to get back to the car. When we got there I was tortured, in a way that involved being washed with rough paper towels. At first it hurt like getting thrown into a nest of piranhas and getting fished out a little too late, but after a few minutes I felt good enough that we could leave the parking lot and go home. After about two weeks I was all healed and I knew that I would be more careful next time I rode down a hill on my bike.

When I remember what it felt like, I imagine 100 shots all at once. Then the corners of my mouth slightly lift into a small smile, as I know that will never happen again.

Rachel Banister, Grade 5
Dingeman Elementary School, CA

Our Differences Make Our Community a Better Place

We all benefit from having a variety of opinions, attitudes, and cultures to learn from. This is what makes our country diverse, and it helps us in understanding and accepting others that are different from us. We learn from others every day, and I think we all benefit from diversity in our society.

Being different helps us to respect others for their individual capabilities, and contributions in our community. We need to feel special because of our differences, and appreciate others for what they add to our life experience.

Each of us has special talents. No one is good at everything, so we depend on others in our society to help us when we are struggling with something. If we were all the same, we would all share the same weaknesses. Because we are all different, we have a wide variety of talents to assist us in becoming a success in our lives. These differences also give us a variety of personalities that can help us understand something better. I think being diverse makes us stand out in some way, helping us to feel good about ourselves, while appreciating others.

Our differences make our society a better place to live. We all need these differences to grow and learn if we expect to be successful in our own lives. We should all embrace our differences and be happy we have them. A healthy society needs to have a diverse group of people living in it to succeed.

Parker Stilwell, Grade 6
White Pine Charter School, ID

What Is That?

There was a cool, crisp breeze in the air as I was walking to school for another day of Kindergarten. Right next to my mom, I thought nothing could go wrong, until I felt something under my shoe. When we stopped at the crosswalk, I lifted my shoe from the ground and looked. There I saw was a big blob of dog waste. Sad, scared, and embarrassed, I told my mom and asked if we could go back home and change my shoes, but we were already late and we had to keep on walking. When we got to the classroom, I was hoping Ms. Clair would be late so I would still have time to wipe off this disgusting, disgrace to all nice shoes. Sadly, she was on time as usual.

"Okay class, make sure your shoes are nice and clean because the janitor just cleaned the room yesterday," Ms. Clair said. Blazing past my mind I thought that I would get in huge trouble if I walked inside with this gook on my foot. Right after she said that, my eyes started to water. Then I started to cry. Then I started to bawl. "What's wrong Shannyn?" Ms. Clair questioned me.

"I...I...stehiped in dohog pooohoohhhhp!!!!" I shouted, trying to speak clearly without large gasps in between my words. We tried to have a straight conversation after that, but I was all worked up. Thankfully, my mom brought a second pair of shoes.

Shannyn Karasawa, Grade 6
Margaret Landell Elementary School, CA

Ely!

I was at my little brown house, helping with dishes in my small town of Wilsonville, Oregon, when I heard a mumbling sound outside. I was a little confused at first, and then I heard Grandpa shout out, "Come here, I got you something." I ran out, but grandpa said, "I'll lead you, keep your eyes closed, no peeking."

After walking for a bit, I finally got to open my eyes. I looked and saw that my dreams had come true. I couldn't believe it, only in dreams had I seen such a beautiful horse. Grandpa actually got me my very own horse.

Grandpa said that I needed to name him, train him, feed him and clean up after him. I named him Ely, fed him his favorite foods (apples, carrots and celery) and did everything else to take care of a horse. I did so well training Ely that we won the horse race championship in the summer of 2010. My pal Ely and I even made the front cover of an awesome sports magazine. My whole family was so proud that we celebrated for two days!

Whenever I go back home to Wilsonville, I always ride Ely as if it were my last time with him. I'm still training the old boy, and if you ever get to meet him, I hope you love him the same way I do. Remember that if you do what you're told and follow your dreams, they just might come true.

Brittanie Garthe, Grade 6
Woodcreek Middle School, TX

How Our Differences Make Us Special

I think it's good that we're not all the same. Life would be uninteresting if we were all the same we would wear the same clothes every day. We would all have to feel the same feelings as everyone else. We would be like robotic zombies, and that would just be scary! I think it's good to be alike in some ways because if we were all different from each other then we probably wouldn't like each other, because we would have nothing alike.

I think it's important we're not all the same because then there would be no excitement, no "sparkle" in life. Life would be boring if we were all the same. We fight with our friends and siblings because we are different from each other. But if we were all the same then you wouldn't be able to be unique.

You wouldn't be able to be the first person on the moon, because everybody would have already been to the moon. There wouldn't have been a unique Albert Einstein because everybody would be Einstein. We would look like him, we would like what he likes, it would be planet of Albert Einsteins! Our differences are what make us special. They're what make you...you!

In conclusion, I think that being different makes us mentally stronger. Sometimes it's hard being different. We might get picked on for being different, but in the end I think it matters most that YOU are proud to be you.

Hannah Weber, Grade 6
White Pine Charter School, ID

Hurricane Ike

My dad was making dinner, my mom was helping him and my sister was doing homework. Suddenly the lights started to flicker. My sister screamed (ok, we both screamed, but she screamed her head off). My dad finally shut my sister up. We all stayed in the kitchen with the glow of the fire from the stove. Suddenly our back door opened and water poured into the kitchen. My sister started screaming again and my dad quickly ushered us upstairs with the water getting to my ankles. We stayed upstairs in my parents' bedroom. My sister and I feel asleep to the sound of rain patter.

When I woke up nothing was too badly damaged, but everything downstairs was soaked. If you couldn't' swim you'd drown in the water. When the wave moved it hit the ceiling; it looked like the wall of a cave. I sat down on the top step, water soaking into my mismatched socks. I figured might as well make the best of it. I ran to my room, put on a bathing suit and goggles, ran back to the stairs, and cannonballed straight into the water. I sank like a rock and climbed the stairs slower than a turtle when I didn't have that much breath left. I used the stair to propel myself forward to the surface. My family came rushing to my aid, even though I was fine. When they saw me they burst out laughing. The put on their bathing suits then joined me in my fun.

Christina Watson, Grade 5
Horn Academy, TX

5th Grade

I loved the 5th grade. I got the teacher I wanted, and it was so fun! I was in Ms. Planje's class, and it was awesome. After lunch she would read us a few chapters in a book, and she also had stuffed animals that we could put on our desk at that time. Also during teacher read time, we could draw, or write notes to our friends, or listen to the teacher. I liked math because I got to stay in my class, so I did not have to pack up my books before I left. Yippee. Sometimes in math we would play games. Although we had math homework every day (except for test days) I got used to it. Surprisingly, I kinda liked to take the states quizzes. Me and Tia would make up little methods so we could remember them for the quiz. Like for Annapolis, Maryland, we thought of Anna and Mary went to Polis land. Sounds crazy but we remembered it.

Lunch was fun. We usually went before the 6th graders in the lunch line (but not this time). We would come late sometimes but we still got lunch first (sometimes). I also liked the Ocean Institute. It was cool because I got the hypothesis for my job and it was fairly easy. I loved picking out my outfit for the presentation, but we got a weird room to present our presentation, and our flash drive would not work. That was not the highlight of the year.

Paige Magee, Grade 6
Margaret Landell Elementary School, CA

A Snap to the Future

I have a dream for the future…that our oil spills will stop, that our animals and plants will stop dying form that.

Our oil spills will eventually stop, but we need them to stop soon. The water creatures (ducks, swans, birds) get killed every year from boats spilling oil in the water. It's not right for people to go by the water, spill oil in it, and let the birds die from that.

Our plants are also in danger. Animals need those under water, just like we need trees out of the water. Animals need plants to keep the water fresh and clean. They also need to have a home where no one bothers them there. Oil spills can cause every animal in the lake, ocean, or river to die. Who needs the animals to die? Who wants people to get in trouble like a robber robbing a bank? Next we need to fix a problem! We need to stop bringing oil to the ocean!

When we kill fish, they go meandering to the bottom, just like a bird getting hit smack in the head by a car going zoom, zoom, zoom! Let's snap out of oil spills!

Maddie McDonough, Grade 5
Foothills Elementary School, CO

The Junior High Change

Next year I will be going to middle school. I'm wondering what changes I will have to make. I wonder what I will have to read, and how much homework I will get. The changes will take a while to get used to but I know I'll get used to them. I'll have to make new friends and meet new people. I will be the youngest in the school instead of the oldest. I'll also get new teachers. I am nervous about it but I'm also excited. I will get to play sports and other things that I can't do now. Perhaps I will even have a male teacher. I have never had a man for a teacher before. I am definitely looking forward to middle school.

Conner Kornmayer, Grade 5
Horn Academy, TX

Tingles

Tingles is a tiny teddy bear with a blue shirt and a hat. Tingles has flowers on his clothes. He has a tiny bow tie around his neck and suspenders on his back. I got him from Ai-Young. She is Korean. Ai-Young is really pleasant. She told me that he is a lucky doll. I think that Tingles is so popular that I am writing a book about him. Tingle's arms are shaped like wings so he can soar through the canyons (between the cracks in the sidewalk). Tingles is sleeping in my sack boy's hat. My favorite thing to do with my spare time is write in Tingle's book. My relative has one, too, but it is a girl version. Tingles is my best friend.

Truman Holt, Grade 3
Vista Charter School, UT

How Could You

I was at the dentist; I was surprised I even had to be there. The dentist said it wouldn't hurt at all, but he was wrong. He took out this wrench and I knew what was going to happen. I did run but they got me and held me down by both arms and legs. He took the wrench and fixed it on my tooth. Yank! Yank! He had just torn out both of my front teeth one by one. The pain was like sticking two needles through your gums. Then they had put some medicine in my lip which made my lips larger than a duck's bill. They had said I could go and I jumped off the bed like a ravenous leopard. Once we got home I was so mad at my toothbrush (which I used every day) that got me into this and I threw it outside. Once I was in bed, my mom said that if I put my teeth under my pillow, I would get twenty-five dollars. When I woke up, there were the same lousy teeth that got torn out. Not even one cent was under my pillow. I was in a state of denial about the fact that you can't trust anyone or anything even if they're your parents. I sill loathe the Tooth Fairy for she did not pay her debt.

Hammaad M. Sayyed, Grade 5
Horn Academy, TX

I Could've Won

My favorite memory would be when I won first place for photography in 6th grade. Everyone was saying that my picture was really good but all of the other pictures looked really cool and I thought that mine was plain and dull. When the day came for the people to announce who had won I was so nervous because I hate getting up in front of a lot of people and this was the whole school. By the time they got to the sixth grade photography part I was a nervous wreck. First, they announced all of the runner ups and then they said the places from 3rd to 1st. When we were at the second place award they did not call my name so, I had to assume that I won it.

After, they announced that they would reveal the winner of all the schools at the dinner party they were having with the mayor. Sadly, my mom forgot about the party and made plans for me to hang out at my friend's house. When I got home the next morning I looked at the calendar and yelled at my mom for 5 minutes for forgetting my important dinner. I might have won first but, now I will never know. Thanks a lot Mom.

Viki Voragen, Grade 6
Margaret Landell Elementary School, CA

My Necklace

My mom and I have a shiny gold necklace from my dad to remind us of my brother. My gold necklace is in a clear box with the shape of a shimmering star on it. My brother's name is Garrett, and my necklace was a present from his memorial. Everyone that goes to my church was there. My great-grandma and my grandma and my other grandma and grandpa were there. My gold necklace has Garrett's shining ring and a cross on it. It hangs on my neck gracefully, like a crystal hanging from a star. My necklace is amazing, fantastic, awesome and super fabulous! I think the necklace is the best necklace in the world because it reminds me of a very special person.

Shay Peterson, Grade 3
Vista Charter School, UT

My Own Space

My favorite place is on the top of my glorious bunk bed. I go there most of the time because I am frustrated, mad, sad, or I want some time alone. I chose that spot because my little sister can't get to it. My mom and dad cannot get to it because it will break. When I was 8, I built it with my grandpa's help. The top of my bunk bed is made out of polished wood and huge nails. The nails are as black as a moonless night sky. The wood is as straight as a wall. The top is as tall as the clouds. The ground looks as if it is a mile away. It is the only place I can be alone and let my feelings out. The top of my bunk bed is my favorite place.

Amir Hesomatipour, Grade 4
Horn Academy, TX

Moving Day

The sun shines through my window, and I wake up. At first, I didn't know what day it was, but then I remembered. A smile stretched across my face. It was moving day! I quickly got out of bed, and ran to my parents' room and yelled "Mom, Dad! So you know what day it is?" "Sunday, at 6:30 am?" my mom asked. "Wrong! It is moving day!" I shout.

A couple of hours later I saw a moving van. "Yay! They're here!" I shouted. I was so happy! My room was finally going to be humongous, and I'll have my own bathroom.

The next day we moved in completely. I got to paint my room by myself. Moving is great!

Zoe Brezner, Grade 4
Horn Academy, TX

My Cat Charley

My family's cat is very special to me. I got my cat at my mom's friend's house. We decided to name him Charley. Charley grew and grew. He ate kitty treats and he loves them now. Charley is orange and white and has long hair. Every night Charley jumps on my bed and curls up against me. One time he fought a black cat in my backyard. When I went to my backyard, there was black hair everywhere, and I never saw the black cat again. I think he won the fight. Now I can't find him. Where are you, Charley? We have another cat now. She is okay, but she scratched me on the eye. I hope I can find a really good cat that is similar to Charley.

Houston Birch, Grade 3
Vista Charter School, UT

My Family

I have a great family. My family is the best family on earth. They love me and I love them. My parents give me lots of presents. They are always there for me no matter what.

My parents love me the most in this world. Whenever I am hurt and crying, they wipe my tears and comfort me. They tell me everything will be okay. Every day, both of my parents give me lots of hugs and kisses. They keep me safe and protect me from harm.

My family buys me many presents. For example, during my seventh birthday, my mom gave me a remote control car. It was big and fast. I played with it all night long. My dad gave me money. Some of the money I bought toys with it and the other I gave it back to my family. Every time I do well in school, they give me presents or take me to places.

Most importantly, my family is there for me all the time. Once I was in the playground, and I was about to fall. Suddenly, my father appeared and saved me from falling. They never missed any of my school projects and presentations. They take good care of me when I am sick.

As you can see, my family is the best family on Earth. They love me and I love them very much. They spoil me with presents. They are always there for me when I need them.

Reem Awad, Grade 3
Islamic School of San Diego, CA

Midway

The car stopped. The sky was blotted out by dark clouds. We walked up the metal stairs and made a sound like banging pots and pans. The cold wind blew as hard as a stampede of rhinos running toward us. The hangar door we walked through was big enough for a thousand men. Jets and planes were everywhere. Some had missiles on the bottom of their wings and some had machine guns on top of them. We went into three planes. "Follow me," said my chaperone.

We strolled down the hatch and looked at the galley, which had models of cooks. We walked into the engine room. The steps were close to each other, so I had to be very careful. I was trembling, thinking I would fall. The engine was so loud; it could wake up a lazy person forty miles away.

After several more rooms, including the brig, which had a fake jail (we took a picture in it), we walked onto a glass sheet and "floated" 40 feet above the loading area, with two models carrying missiles, and nothing else. We walked on deck and went into the captain's quarters. It was warm enough to thaw frozen food in less than a minute.

It was now time to go. I walked into the car, and it took off. I can't wait to go again.

Alex Rinder, Grade 5
Dingeman Elementary School, CA

The Best Family Ever!

I have a great family and they are all different. They are nice to everybody in the family.

Sarah is the oldest and first to move out of the house. She loves to be in community plays and sing pop songs and show tunes. The second oldest is Max. He has a snake and a lizard. He is always listening to music in his room.

Paul has a lot of friends and is very tall. he is sometimes in plays too and he is really funny when he changes his voice. Bill loves to play games and be with his friends. He is also really trustworthy and nice.

Emily is the second youngest. She is smart, funny, and nice. She is good at drawing and playing piano. She likes to be in plays and sing also like Sarah.

I am the youngest kid in the family. I like to play volleyball and jump on my trampoline. My mom is funny and nice. She has been in a lot of plays and always helps me when I need it. My dad is the king of the house. He is an engineer at work, but at home he plays the drums and still works really hard on the things that he needs to do like chores and repairs.

I think that my family is very good. Everybody is kind and funny.

Benny Myers, Grade 6
St Pius X Catholic School, TX

Inspiring Others to Grow

I feel that everyone has turned away and forgotten about these four words, "Inspiring Others to Grow." I want to inspire others to grow in their faith as Jesus did and I want them to enhance their faith towards God. I will help everyone, young and old, to love God, to become a part of God, and to spread the word of God and Jesus to everyone.

I can help everyone become a part of God by becoming a Catholic and receiving the Eucharist. Being a Catholic means to be baptized in the church and receive first Holy Communion. Communion is when we receive the body and the blood of Jesus Christ. By receiving the body and blood of Christ we become a part of God.

I think it's important that people spread the word of God. I could encourage everyone to read the Bible. I would read scriptures and explain their meaning. Some people will become excited and want to learn more.

I have been inspired by others to grow in my faith with God and I hope I can do the same to others. Through my actions, I hope my love for God will rub off on other people. Sharing my love for God with others, I hope I will create a new faith for them to follow.

Dax Galvan, Grade 6
St Raphael School, CA

Sad Things Are Still Important

When I learned my grandfather died, I was heartbroken. It all started one morning in my mom's car. She was driving me to my grandmother's house for a visit. While we were driving, my mom said, "Don't mention your grandfather to your grandmother."

"Why?" I asked unhopefully.

"Because," my mom sighed. "He's dead." A 10 second silence started that not even the sound of the car roaring down the highway could penetrate. I went into shock. When we got to my grandmother's house, I didn't dare mutter a word. I isolated myself in dead silence. It was 10 days until the funeral, 10 sorrow filled days. When the funeral finally came, a lot of people were already over it. I was not one of those people.

This was the first time I've ever experienced a death in the family. Honestly, I can't really remember the funeral service. All I can seem to remember is that it didn't seem to take place in a church. It looked more like an old house. Even if I was too young to understand what they were saying, it still lives sorrowfully in my mind. I will never forget my grandfather. Goodbye, Grandpa.

Logan Gill, Grade 4
Horn Academy, TX

Going to Texas

"Sweetie, we have good news!" my mom said anxiously. "Uh, what?" I asked casually. I dragged my feet to the stairs and walked down. "Well, long story short, we're moving!" My mom smiled faintly. "What?" I screamed and felt as if steam was coming out of my ears. I pounded up the stairs, marched to my room, and slammed the door behind me. I bundled up in a ball under the covers and cried.

The next day, the movers came and carried all of the stuff out of my house. The house looked so empty that I felt like yelling at the movers even though it was not their fault. My whole house looked dull and empty. The only thing that was colorful was my room painted with little purple flowers. As my family loaded in the car, I went upstairs and kissed the walls like a million times. I ran outside and hugged my friend so many times. I tried so hard to hold in the tears but they easily escaped. I felt bad because she was crying too. As we left I looked through the back window and watched my friends until they eventually disappeared.

We arrived in Texas a day later. I still felt disappointed but a smile grew on my face as I looked at my house. "Wow, I really think I am going to like it here."

Reagan Draper, Grade 4
Horn Academy, TX

The Hidden Underneath

A man walks in. You know immediately who he is. The thick white powder, the laughing smile, the red nose tells us. He is a clown.

But is he really who you think he is? A person portrayed as one who is always happy, cheerful, who laughs; of course that's who he is. You don't even have to think about it. Or does he have a hidden underneath?

People aren't always who you think they are. One moment happy, the next grieving, it's easy to mask what you really feel. Or, when there is a common stereotype about who you are, it's even easier. If you are supposed to be outgoing, you'll change to fit the description, because that's who you are, right?

On the other hand, say you are meeting someone new. They have nerdy glasses, look down at their feet, say hello in a whisper. They are obviously shy and you are going to treat them like that. But what if they are different? What if they are really outgoing, but it takes them a while to open up? Will you recognize them for who they are, or will you continue thinking of them as the person they are supposed to be?

The clown shows his face, his real face. Will you accept it? Or will you say, "That's not who you are?"

Rukmini Kalamangalam, Grade 6
Sidney Lanier Middle School, TX

Until the End

This school year couldn't be such a wonderful year without my friends. I might not have had too many friends, because I usually hung out with this friend all year. Even through everything that we've both been through, we went through it together. This was something I really appreciated. One memorable moment this year was when my friend and I worked on a science project together. This might not be so memorable to many people, because they have more friends and more memories, but this showed our friendship bond and trustworthiness towards each other.

My friend researched information while I was creating slides for the PowerPoint we were making. I was almost done with the PowerPoint, and saved it. I checked it again, and all my progress was gone. I was devastated, because it took me about 2 hours, and all that work was now gone. My friend told me to persist, and not give up. Although it was hard, I memorized how the format was and which designs were on the slides. After a while, I finished the PowerPoint and was ready to send it. This showed how my friend and I really trusted and encouraged each other even through the hard times.

Kristen Kim, Grade 6
Margaret Landell Elementary School, CA

Preserving Our Environment

Pollution is bad for our environment. Littering is bad for animals and humans. Recycling is important to conserve our natural resources. The pollution is very bad for the environment because the gas in the air causes global warming. For the air to be fresh, we need to stop using our cars and having so many factories create smoke when making their products. The worst thing about pollution is that it is filling the air with some things that are toxic. Littering is a big problem in all communities because it is something that cannot be stopped. It is something that people think does not matter; but it does matter. It kills animals and makes everything look ugly. It also takes years to disintegrate.

Recycling helps preserve our environment. It helps us reuse things; for example, paper is reusable and it is better to use than plastic, because it is not harming the environment. We all need to preserve our environment to prevent global warming and all the undiscovered bad things for our environment. In conclusion, we all want to keep our environment safe so our future people and animals will have a better world to live in.

Fernando Cruz-Esparza, Grade 5
Washington Elementary School, CA

9/11

Ten years have passed since that tragedy. Many people helped, for us, they are heroes. Some people even died: 2,996 people in total past away. Some of them were firefighters, policemen, and people walking through the streets, and also workers that worked on the highest floors. Many people felt sad because they lost their families and friends. Other people felt angry with the ones responsible for causing the tragedy. Everyone still remembers that catastrophe. It will always be in our hearts, the people who passed away and the tragedy. Everyone wonders who was responsible for the tragedy. Some people say it was Osama bin Laden, other people say it was the government. Also, why did the responsible person for the catastrophe do it? Was he or she mad with the US? Did he want the economy to go down? And also, who helped him or her do it? Many people said that the people from where Osama bin Laden was from, stole four airplanes, two hit the Twin Towers, another one was going to hit the White House, and the last one crashed into the Pentagon Field. I wonder what life would be like if the tragedy didn't happen. I imagine that the economy would be good if the war would have never begun.

Nallely Villalpando, Grade 5
Washington Elementary School, CA

A Symbol of Faith, Freedom, and Family

I have an extremely special object that I consider my most treasured possession. It is impossible to put a value on a gift that is so precious. My Godparents, Fred and Barb Scarpello, gave me an American flag as a Baptism gift.

No ordinary flag, it flew over the United States Capital building in Washington D.C. on January 23, 2000. Whenever I look at my American flag, I can hear Fred's booming voice and hardy laugh. I can feel Barb's gentle, loving touch.

In addition to my flag being sentimental because who gave it to me, it is a symbol for all Americans. Inspiration comes in many forms in our society. Faith and freedom inspired the founding fathers of America, yet our country has been at war for most of my life. The flag inspires me to make a difference later on in my life to make our country a better place. This flag shows how our country cares for us and how the people overseas are fighting for our protection, which makes me glad to be an American. I know that Fred and Barb are always going to be there for me just like my flag and my country represent strength and honor. The pride I feel whenever I admire this symbol of freedom is extraordinary.

Luca Scarpello, Grade 6
St Cecilia School, CA

Planting Seeds of Faith

"Planting Seeds of Faith" is always a way to inspire people in their faith. Lots of people forget that we should love and spread the word of God. I always try to plant seeds of faith with my family and my friends. As it says in the Bible, God wants us to spread the word of God all around the world.

I will help "Plant Seeds of Faith" by reading the Bible to others if they can't read. Or take people to Mass if they can't get there on their own. This would plant seeds of faith because it would help both of us to learn more about our faith.

I plant seeds of faith by having discussions about God. This would help people learn about our Lord. This would plant seeds of faith because it is always good to learn something you didn't know. When people say, "You learn something new every day," the best thing to learn about is God.

I chose planting seeds of faith because it is something I do in my everyday life. My last way to plant seeds of faith is to be nice to others. If someone is down or sad you can cheer them up. It is always okay to be nice to a person. It's also okay to "Plant Seeds of Faith."

Izabelle Ruehlman, Grade 6
St Raphael School, CA

A Strange Little Ritual

I have a strange little ritual. Over the summer months, I get up every morning, just after some of my friends have gone to bed. It's 4 a.m. and I am awake, alert and excited. I squeeze into my swimsuit. My body is used to the tight feel of Lycra; it's my 2nd skin. I have 28 of these 2nd skins, all with matching hats. On the way to the pool I hear nothing; not even the birds are up at this silly hour! The pool water is perfectly still, smooth as glass and shimmering in the light. The powerful smell of chlorine I find comforting. With my cap and goggles on, I share a passion with twenty other mad people in the pool; I am not alone. We share a bond. There are no breaks, no recoveries, and no half-times. They understand me. To an outsider, though, we must seem psychotic. I swim because I love it. I love a great challenge. Swimming teaches me to find my limits and surpass them. To feel the lactic acid build up in my arms, my legs turning to blocks of wood and my heart pumping fit to burst, I propel myself through the water, finishing a practice totally exhausted, knowing that I have put my all into it. A swimmer is what I am. The pool is my home.

Liberty Chanin, Grade 6
North Hills Preparatory School, TX

Inspiring Others to Grow

There are many ways to "Inspire Others to Grow." I try and do that a lot. I try to put happiness and faith in everyday situations. I love to help my friends by being positive all the time. There are many things I try to do to "Inspire Others to Grow" in faith. Many people underestimate the power of having faith in God. We need to appreciate God. This is the way the world should be: filled with faith.

I try to set a good example by getting good grades and helping others to try their hardest in school. I also try not to do things that might get me into trouble. Hopefully when I do these things it will inspire others to do the same. I like to talk to my friends, but if something that they're talking about is not the right choice, I will try to talk them out of it.

I hope that I can continue helping and inspiring others. It won't always be easy, but I will do my very best. At my school, we learn about our faith. This is a great way to stay in touch with being a Catholic. My faith is all about treating others like you would treat God. This is very important in life, to stay true to your faith, I will do that.

Gemma Sturgeon, Grade 6
St Raphael School, CA

Inspiring Others to Grow

Today, in the modern world, we are too caught up in electronics and tattoos. We are pretending to be friends with people just because of their money, looks, or popularity. We are forgetting what a real friend really is. We're not being kind to people and people aren't being kind to us. We're putting them down, rather than inspiring them to grow.

One way to do that is to be a helpful and loyal friend. You should encourage them to grow in their faith. That doesn't mean that you always have to do what they want and never what you want. You can try to switch off, compromise, and be fair. Also, if you make a promise to a friend, you should keep it. A good friend is not one that gives you answers on a test. You should do your own work and not cheat.

I found out that people these days don't appreciate what they have, because they always want more. We think we always have to do bad things that aren't good, just to impress our friends. A real friend won't want to change you, because they should like you just the way you are. And remember, don't try to follow others and live in their shadow. Be your own person.

Anna Coronado, Grade 6
St Raphael School, CA

Friends

People may ask, "What is a friend?" because maybe they have never been filled with love from someone. Friends do not only fill up your heart like water fills up a cup, they are also the people who hold your hand when nobody else understands you. They want to heal you and "see" the real you. But in order for friends to "see" the real you, you have to open up. Friends have a shoulder for you to lean on. They keep your tears in their pockets and keep them from escaping. Friends are always worth being with because they help you have fun and have a fabulous time when you need one. Also, when I'm depressed and sad, my friends make me forget what depression and sadness means, because they put a huge smile on my face. Friends are good helpers. Our life is like a sunflower. The sunflower grows and grows until it is time for the petals to perish, but the leaves stay like your friends that help you have a beautiful life. Everyone deserves a friend because friends also help you go in the right direction towards a good future, and they would always love you, help you, and "have your back" no matter what.

Marelyn Aguirre, Grade 5
Washington Elementary School, CA

My Dog's Death

My dog's death was a tragic sight. It really was a bad thing for me because my dog had been with me every since I was born. She stuck with me all the way until she died. I didn't know what happened to her because the ran freely in the yard. Nothing was wrong with her until that Saturday night where she bled. Something had hit her or struck her. We didn't know what had, but my dad and I were very shocked. We took her to the vet. When the vet came out she told us that there was no way to cure her. We were sad that happened. I was heartbroken. They burned our dog into ashes. The ashes were in a box with her name on it. "Bogo."

Bowen Thi, Grade 4
Outley Elementary School, TX

Index

Aceves, Jose ... 131
Adams, Christian ... 38
Adams, Cody ... 45
Afanasieva, Daria ... 30
Aguilar, Gael ... 154
Aguirre, Marelyn ... 191
Agusala, Veena ... 54
Aijala, Matthew ... 46
Aiken, Aaron ... 50
Akwarandu, Tiffany ... 177
Alaniz, Melissa ... 143
Alberts, Alex ... 13
Allen, Cody ... 172
Allen, Michael ... 41
Alonso, Rosa ... 162
Altman, Crystal ... 66
Altman, Erica ... 169
Alvarado, Isabel ... 141
Alvarado, Kayla ... 79
Alvarez, Jaqueline ... 163
Amanullah, Yusuf ... 146
Ancira, Sofia ... 62
Anderson, Bailee ... 63
Anderson, Gabby ... 127
Anderson, Madison ... 76
Anderson, Rock ... 152
Angell, Ashleigh ... 39
Anguiano, Alyssa ... 55
Applewhite, Savannah ... 110
Arif, Abdurrahman ... 144
Aromin, Krisianne ... 99
Artura, Katie ... 158
Atkinson, Katherine ... 150
Awad, Reem ... 188
Babcock, Shawna ... 129
Baker, Allie ... 177
Baker, Josh ... 77
Baldecchi, Cole ... 41
Banister, Rachel ... 184
Barandas, Kailey ... 92
Barker, Kasey ... 87
Barnes, Caleb ... 91
Barney, Katie ... 8
Barrett, Abigail ... 161
Barrientos, Elyssa ... 97
Barron, Jonathan ... 173
Bartholomew, Alisa ... 71
Bateman, Megan ... 85
Beasley, Boomer ... 151
Beckham, Madison ... 57
Beckstrand, Kassidy ... 22
Beem, Hunter ... 61

Behee, Dawson ... 132
Beltran II, Xavier ... 35
Benites, Eliana ... 95
Benites, Madison ... 131
Benitez, Jennifer ... 128
Bennett, Hannah ... 121
Bennett, Sarah ... 83
Beres, Jaqui ... 115
Bergbower, Brayden ... 134
Berrett, Alexandra ... 22
Berry, Ashley ... 53
Bi, Austin ... 72
Birch, Houston ... 187
Blackburn, Trevor ... 172
Blackmore, Katie ... 17
Blair, Carlie ... 155
Blair, Nicole ... 106
Bognar, Nathan ... 53
Bohman, Spencer ... 57
Boneta, Evan ... 19
Bonilla, Cristian ... 104
Borgatello III, Anthony ... 154
Bowman, Joseph ... 26
Bowman, Reese ... 36
Boyce, Paige ... 131
Bradeson, Logan ... 68
Bradford, Christopher ... 38
Brandt, Karlee ... 104
Branham, Bradi ... 164
Braza, Kevin ... 56
Brezner, Zoe ... 187
Bridgers, Rachel ... 13
Brinkerhoff, Kiley ... 168
Bronchick, Abigail ... 52
Brooks, Shelby ... 19
Brower, Natalie ... 74
Brown, Anya ... 114
Brown, Brooklynne ... 67
Brown, Erica ... 24
Brown, Rachel ... 125
Bryant, Sara ... 148
Buie, Stuart ... 130
Bullock, Shalee ... 94
Bumpus, Mason ... 168
Burnett, Kayla ... 45
Bustos, Mireya ... 93
Buttars, Daz ... 12
Byun, Emily ... 155
Caldwell, Brianne ... 73
Camacho, Samuel ... 57
Campbell, Cori ... 177
Campbell, Morgan ... 132

Cantu, Cassandra ... 153
Cantu, Eric ... 60
Cardenas, Enrique ... 144
Carlson, Eric ... 65
Carney, Adriana ... 39
Carrillo, Darby ... 134
Carter, Taylor ... 38
Castaneda, Elizabeth ... 30
Castellitto, Joshua ... 150
Castro, Christopher ... 164
Catapusan, Diana ... 74
Centron, Francisca ... 151
Ceron, Maria ... 109
Chadwick, David ... 28
Chandler, Courtney ... 53
Chaney, Cayla ... 30
Chanin, Liberty ... 191
Chao, Catherine ... 159
Chapman, Taylor ... 11
Chase, Alicia ... 38
Chavez, Jake ... 36
Cheney, Carly ... 39
Chopra, Abhaya ... 176
Chrane, Theron ... 24
Christensen, Zachary ... 41
Clark, Keely ... 92
Clarke, Allison ... 142
Clarke, Ashley ... 146
Clarke, Stephenie Kirsten ... 35
Claudio, Hannah Marie ... 153
Cleary, Jake ... 116
Cleverly, Aliya ... 156
Clonts, Rebekah ... 126
Cobb, Trevor ... 107
Cohen, Tiffany ... 40
Coit, Evan ... 61
Coleman, Gabi ... 171
Colton, Brynn ... 104
Composanto, Carl ... 48
Conder, Hailey ... 69
Connors, Brett ... 20
Cooke, Gillian ... 160
Cooley, Michael ... 97
Coronado, Anna ... 191
Cowan, Hadley ... 49
Cox, Ester ... 110
Cox-Stone, Taryn ... 127
Craig, Broderik ... 134
Crane, Cassidy ... 79
Crews, Kelsey ... 78
Crisler, Eden ... 164
Croft, Kira ... 64

Crosby, Sarah 90	Foreman, Alexandra 61	Heath, John 57
Crossley, Cody 68	Fox, Shae 178	Hedges, Ross 13
Crowley, Jesse 83	Franco, Kymberly 182	Hendricks, Caitlynn 53
Crump, Brendan 70	Futagawa, Emili 95	Hennessy, Elizabeth 124
Cruz-Esparza, Fernando 190	Gaborko, Piercen 97	Herbst, Emily 153
Cuevas, Gray 157	Galeano-Buggs, Jesse 71	Hernandez, Anthony 33
Cummings, Wesley G. 142	Galindo, Bianca 25	Hernandez, David 140
Curatola, Natalie 44	Gallwas, Lance 175	Hernandez, Katelynn 72
Curtis, Mason 59	Galvan, Dax 188	Hernandez, Pamela 96
Dahlman, Hero A. 173	Garcia, Francisco 63	Hernandez, Samantha 178
Dammeyer, Ashley 37	Garcia, Lauren 149	Herzog, Katelin 20
Dang, Patrick 161	Garner, Zoe 23	Heshmatipour, Amir 187
Danklef, Bailee 101	Garrett, Ashley 14	Hill, Robert 99
Danzeisen, Sophia 160	Garthe, Brittanie 185	Hinojosa, Julia 89
Dasilva, Patricia 11	Garza, Sierra 24	Ho, Valerie 152
Davis, Grant 15	Gibbons, Tehya 115	Hoang, Sang 176
Day, Emily 174	Gill, Logan 189	Hockersmith, Brittney 95
De Jesus, Fernando 16	Gill, Ricky 74	Hoechstetter, Jessica 171
De La Fuente, Daniel 144	Gimblet, Morgan 100	Hoffman, Jessica 110
De Los Reyes, Angel 85	Gipson, Skylar 178	Hoke, Madison 78
DeGuere, Milena 161	Giron, Athena 65	Holland, Hailey 88
Diaz, Kassandra 18	Glenn, Mia 58	Holt, Truman 186
Diaz, Priscylla 22	Gobin, Lauren 72	Holtke, Alyssa 119
Diaz, Raquel 121	Goddard, Andrew 61	Hood, Magdalena 68
Diaz, Samantha 8	Goldenberg, Charlotte 146	Hooker, Douglass 76
Done, Ana 80	Gomez, Malcolm 178	Hooper, Leah 158
Draper, Reagan 189	Gonzalez, Ashley 81	Hopper, Haleigh 130
Drayton, Jimel 169	Gonzalez, Gabriel E. 66	Horne, Callie 141
Dunn, Regan 163	Gonzalez, Michael 24	Horrocks, Eleanor 49
Dylla, Justin 55	Goodsell, Kym 30	Horst, Josephine 78
Ebert, Amanda 58	Goodworth, Spencer 104	Howa, Jennifer 123
Eckart, Kaitlyn 44	Gopon, Gene 183	Howard, Ren 27
Eckhardt, Rebecca 118	Gorabi, Varesh 91	Howe, Bailey 99
Emmons, Cody 112	Gordon, Emily 12	Howe, Kelsea 31
Engelthaler, Lauren 158	Goza, Merrell 142	Howell, Bennett 178
Escot, Bella 36	Goza, Paul 182	Howsden, Andrea 118
Esqueda, Jessica 118	Grawe, Lizzi 33	Hsu, Isabella 144
Estrada, Bailey 102	Greaves, Linda 29	Huang, I-Chia 9
Estrada, Lila 32	Green, Kyla 134	Huang, Katelyn 145
Fairbanks, Ben 86	Greenberg, Nicole 83	Hugelen, Alexia 70
Farah, Sara 143	Greer, Nicholas 115	Hughes, Ali 126
Faris, Kate 169	Greig, Zoe 127	Humphrey, Victoria 176
Farren, Alex 99	Griffith, Saydies 117	Huppert, Scott 87
Faust, Lauren 141	Gudgel, Austin 84	Huriega, Alec 77
Ferguson, Shinaiya 122	Guillory-Boyden, Godia 139	Hurley, Kayla 39
Figueroa, Daniel 112	Gunnell, Brenna 182	Iliev, Rachel 140
Fisher, Jordynn 51	Gutierrez, Alicia 126	Imad, Desirae 107
Fitzmorris-Johannes, Max 105	Guzman, Josiah 87	Iohmeyer, Kayla 54
Fitzmorris-Johannes, Winston ... 121	Hales, Joshua 116	Ishak, Peter Ghassan 44
Flaherty, Alexandra 75	Hall, Sarah 109	Jensen, Kyra 18
Flores, Adriana 62	Hall, Tyrell 40	Jewell, Olivia 156
Flores, Ashley 52	Hansen, Jared 174	Jheong, Yessel 171
Flores, Emilee 157	Hanson, Karlee 140	Jin, Sangyeon Sean 25
Flores, Rajel 74	Harden, Emma 110	Johanneman, Jubilee 170
Fogle, Angela 31	Harrison, Riley 143	Johnson, Abigail 56
Fonseca, Amy 159	Harvey, Vanessa 61	Johnson, Maddi 113
Fontaine, Beverly 119	Hasbun, Monique 84	Johnson, Savanna 37
Forbes, Kylee 29	Hayes, Tyler 34	Johnstone, Kyle 125

Index

Jones, Kelsey 34
Jones, Sarah Grace 141
Jong, Preston 156
Juvera, Tomas 122
Kaila 94
Kalamangalam, Aarti 158
Kalamangalam, Rukmini 189
Kang, Belinda 163
Kannan, Roshan 180
Kao, Lillian 28
Karasawa, Shannyn 185
Keathley, Avery 69
Kelleher, Danny 64
Kellner, Marshall 150
Kelso, Alexus 106
Kendall, Jaden 90
Kenyon, Hailey 46
Kessler, Carson 99
Kilgore, Rebecca 15
Kim, Andrew 183
Kim, Joshua 139
Kim, Kristen 189
Kim, Rachel 175
Kimzey, Reagan 183
King, Leah 91
Ko, Sarah 38
Koehler, Alec 40
Koonce, Drew 91
Kornmayer, Conner 186
Korrapati, Aashika 69
Kostoch, Brian 142
Kotarski, Madeline 14
Kotsos, Alexandra 148
Kreitlein, Lindsey 19
Krivanek, Savannah 109
Krogh, Brenden 119
Kuo, Ivy 32
Kuswanto, Ardian 171
Kwun, Shinwho 149
LaBas, Jayden 89
Lac, Kimberly 153
LaCroix, Rebekah 108
Lam, Vanessa 10
Laney, William 15
Langmade, Annie 138
Laquian, Joshua 16
Lavorini, Olivia 155
Lawrence, Cort 101
Lawrence, Tim 21
Lawson, Nora 165
Leavitt, Cathy 52
Lee, Caitlin 35
Lee, Christina 114
Lee, Daycia 146
Lee, Frederick 177
Lee, Ian 158
Lee, Jane 154
Leng, Justin 181

Lennon, Katie 49
Leopold, Nina 115
Lew, Ysabel-Rose Vargas 71
Lewis, Gabrielle 48
Li, Ericka 149
Liao, Sydney 166
Lima, Raya 26
Lingle, Sarah 156
Linz, William 27
Liu, Johnny 106
Liu-Zarzuela, Jasmine 89
Loertscher, Courtney 133
Lofton, Aspen 121
Logan, Amanda 80
Lona, Alyssa 47
Long, Jacque 128
Long, Samantha 180
Longoria, Camryn 76
Lopez, Doralisa 166
Lopez, Lisa 16
Lopez, Paige Livingston 113
Loveless, Porter 124
Lucas, Merrick 27
Luna, Daniel 103
Luong, Caroline 51
Luu, Elizabeth 155
Lynch, Bridget 166
Lynch, Letycia 173
Lyndes, Noah 31
Lyne, Eric 86
MacCarter, Tatum 115
MacCleary, MacKenzy 108
Madden Jr., Robert 167
Madsen, Arianna 146
Magaña, Diego 75
Magee, Paige 186
Magwili, Mikaela 100
Mai, Jovanna 177
Malveaux, Krystyn 27
Maniwang, April Rose 168
Mansour, Meghan 110
Marinin, Erika 154
Marioni, Marco 22
Marquez, Cassandra 98
Marquez, Diana 173
Marquez, Rueben 11
Martin, Aaron 184
Marvel, Amanda 44
Matero, Brianna 16
Matero, Dante 105
Matthews, Jordan 64
Maughan, Jordan 152
Mayfield, Katherine 133
McArthur, Conner 63
McCann, Hanna 159
McCarty, Tanner 115
McClellan, Allison 129
McClellan, Megan 54

McClellin, Katelynn 58
McConnell, Sammi 34
McCray, Casey 37
McDonald, Amiel 154
McDonough, Maddie 186
McGrath, Morgan 9
McKinnon, Alana 171
McLauchlan, Duncan 102
McMullan, Esmé 139
McMurray, Avery 114
Medsker, Mandy 120
Medved, Sheyenne 126
Megahey, Zoey 25
Meline, Andrew 67
Menard, Donavan 50
Mendez, Cristina 10
Menezes, Naya 184
Mercado, Jayleen 156
Methot, Nils 88
Metzger, Kaitlyn 169
Miao, Michelle 143
Mikulencak, Ben 145
MiKyla 183
Miller, Karen 157
Miller, Madeline 112
Min, Kathy 175
Minor, Seth 102
Mitchell, Kaylah Rose 45
Mock, Jasmine 145
Moltz, Callie 16
Mommer, McKinley 110
Moncivaiz, Montana 122
Monson, Nicolo 63
Moon, Joshua 149
Moon, Kenzie 128
Moonesan, Leah 18
Mordue, Madeleine 41
Morris, Briana 92
Morris, Monique 21
Morrison, Quarter 139
Morrow, Megan 35
Muhlestein, Morgan 25
Mumford, Serena 72
Munar, Lindsey 60
Munn, Shannon 104
Munoz-Saldana, Sharon 37
Murdock, Logan 122
Murego, Danny 100
Murphy, Kevin 127
Murugesan, Akilan 56
Myers, Allyson 40
Myers, Benny 188
Nastala, Olivia 113
Nates, Arielle 143
Nemeth, Lianna 129
Newell, Kyndall 123
Nguyen, Tiffany 176
Nguyen, Tony 150

Nguyen, Vu ... 178	Rakestraw, Alexiss ... 67	Santacruz, Mario ... 103
Nichols, Devin ... 9	Ramirez, Viviana ... 93	Santiago, Mandy ... 105
Nicholson, Skye ... 34	Ramos, Nicolas ... 96	Sayer, Laney ... 8
Nielsen, Brimmley ... 118	Ramos, Pedro ... 109	Sayyed, Hammaad M. ... 187
Nunmaker, Kylie ... 18	Ramos-Barba, Samantha ... 120	Scanga, Kristen ... 44
Nutche, Janelle ... 138	Rao, Kiran ... 92	Scarangella, Sophia ... 184
Nuttall, Kendra ... 51	Rawlings, Austin ... 179	Scarpello, Luca ... 190
O'Brien, Rylan ... 179	Reardon, Kayson ... 60	Schallenmuller, Caleb ... 13
O'neil, Kekoa ... 145	Rebancos, Hannah ... 181	Schechterle, Zane ... 82
Oakley, Stephen ... 85	Redmond, Derek ... 80	Schivo, Drew ... 157
Ocon, Ava ... 113	Redmond, Kayla ... 102	Schmalz, Jacob ... 175
Odom, Zoe ... 141	Reger, Megan ... 73	Schmidt, Raechel ... 147
Ogolo, Elizabeth ... 145	Reichert, Nathan ... 157	Schmitt, Shelby ... 23
Olds, Madison ... 147	Renteria, Juan ... 73	Schoenfeld, Jesse ... 67
Ortega, Ashley ... 30	Reyes, Tori ... 123	Schuchardt, Kendall ... 113
Owen, Brenna ... 54	Rhiness, Brenna ... 117	Sciascia, Donna ... 106
Owen, Madison ... 12	Rich, Sarah ... 26	Scott, Madison ... 14
Pack, Maddie ... 66	Richards, Emily ... 100	Senatro, Steven ... 91
Padigepati, Shriya ... 152	Ridge, Kale ... 98	Senter, Ben ... 96
Padmanabham, Prasanna S. ... 147	Rienhoff, Colston ... 84	Shacklett, Seth ... 94
Pagette, Caroline ... 35	Riggio, Danielle ... 96	Shah, Pia ... 180
Palmer, Allie ... 95	Rinder, Alex ... 188	Shatell, Stephanie ... 94
Panchal, Jahnvi ... 140	Ringwood, Erika ... 105	Shaughnessy, Makena ... 86
Pangilinan, Evan ... 155	Rivera, George ... 129	Shaw, Natasha ... 138
Park, Daniel ... 162	Rivera, Sammy ... 84	Shaw, Sally ... 153
Parrish, Lauren ... 179	Rivera, Sierra ... 47	Sheesley, Skyler ... 49
Payne, Allison ... 104	Robbins, Brianna ... 82	Shih, Ivonnie ... 17
Pehrson, Evan ... 124	Roberts, Elayna ... 179	Shin, Owen ... 62
Pekar, Kyle ... 148	Robertson, Jacob ... 154	Shull, Madi ... 32
Peña, Sebastián ... 165	Robins, Charles ... 181	Siddiqah, Fatimah ... 170
Penovich, Emma ... 132	Robinson, Taylor ... 44	Sims, Haylie ... 168
Perepelitsa, Sophia ... 173	Robles, Mckenna ... 164	Sims, Morgan ... 52
Perez, Christina N. ... 174	Robles, Trino ... 40	Sites, Kaden ... 123
Pergande, Elias ... 46	Roche, Katie ... 108	Skelton, Nate ... 84
Perkins, Abby ... 141	Rodgers, Aubree ... 174	Skrobarczyk, Taylor ... 147
Perry, Jasmyne ... 124	Rodriguez, Elizabeth ... 10	Smelser, Victoria ... 48
Perryman, Caroline ... 18	Rodriguez-Soto, Sarah ... 90	Smith, Avery ... 32
Petersen, Shelbie ... 59	Rogero, Melissa ... 83	Smith, Bonnie ... 107
Peterson, Aubree ... 11	Rogers, Mikelle ... 116	Smith, Caleb ... 108
Peterson, Gabby ... 111	Romero, Allegra Mia ... 171	Smith, Cameron ... 45
Peterson, Shay ... 187	Romero, Brianna ... 117	Smith, Olivia ... 65
Petnicki, Olivia ... 90	Rondomanski, Ashley ... 159	Snyder, April ... 79
Pham, Katie ... 160	Roper, Taylor ... 119	Son, Dana ... 173
Pham, Matthew ... 37	Rosilier, Aubrey ... 78	Song, Min-Jun ... 60
Phan, Nathan ... 82	Rubio, Matthew ... 182	Sonza, Rogelio ... 140
Phot, Rachel ... 33	Ruehlman, Izabelle ... 190	Soriano, Ethan ... 175
Pina, Joseph ... 98	Russell, Kailee ... 128	Spangle, Travis ... 103
Pinto, Shaloni ... 85	Rydberg, Robin ... 75	Spatz, Stephanie ... 138
Pittman, Layney ... 111	Sajja, Amulya ... 36	Spicer, Jessica ... 31
Piziali, Emma ... 81	Salazar, Kimberly ... 116	Sprunk, Blake ... 59
Pokorny, Trey ... 142	Salazar, Samantha ... 64	Stanislaus, Mishta ... 83
Pontillas, Jason ... 144	Salcido, Joshua ... 165	Stashyn, Katarina ... 50
Poole, Kylie ... 93	San Miguel, Jordan ... 19	Steere, Megan ... 23
Potts, Ella ... 70	Sanchez, Cheyenne ... 120	Steffes, Eric ... 112
Powell, Harper ... 101	Sanchez, Emily ... 167	Stephens, Matthew ... 84
Price, Tristan ... 19	Sanchez, Emily ... 168	Stilwell, Parker ... 185
Queen, Larry ... 151	Sanchez, Sophia ... 55	Stinson, Zoe ... 62
Railey, Robert ... 161	Sanders, Kodie ... 162	Stoddard, Diana ... 70

Index

Stolze, Crystal 58
Stone, Tristan 73
Stover, Ben 15
Sturgeon, Gemma 191
Sullivan, Ella 114
Suminski, Naomi 88
Suri, Abhinav 77
Swasey, Katelyn 133
Tabasco, Kolleen 28
Tadros, Justin 91
Tadwalkar, Sujay 29
Tamez, Acadia 159
Tanaka, Madison 172
Taper, John 172
Tapken, Molly 12
Taylor, Rachel 41
Taylor, Stelth 59
Teresi, Katie 103
Terrell, Kylee 159
Tharp, Rachel 40
Theis, Alexandra Rae 111
Thi, Bowen 192
Thomas, Jenna 117
Thompson, Michael 8
Tilford, Nicole 46
Times, Joseph 143
Tipirneni, Pooja 108
Titzman, Devon 81
Tontz, Annamarie 69
Topham, Alexis 81
Tran, Jamie 20
Tran, Ruby-Ann 17
Tripp, Tara 153
Trujillo, Alexa 14
Truong, Pauline 28
Trusevich, Madison 75
Tucker, William 167
Turner, McKenna 177
Uderjohn, Shay 131
Uecker, Charlie 142
Ugalino, Margaux 66
Uphill, Camilla 120
Ursano, Nick 70
Uwase, Ketsia 130
Vaghjiani, Nikisha 9
Valadez, Eleasar 107
Van Maren, Ava 138
Vance, Rachel 50
VanderHeyden, Kyle 21
Varesio, Wade 138
Vasquez, Christian 166
Vecchiola, Vincenzo 47
Veeravelli, Suhitha 20
Velasquez, Gia 97
Velasquez, Sidney 111
Velez, Kristine 160
Vickery, Nathanael 71
Vigil, Phillip 106
Villalobos, Christopher 130
Villalpando, Nallely 190
Virani, Amaan 55
Vo, Leigh 144
Voragen, Viki 187
Vu, Jessica 180
Wackerle, Nadia 169
Wadhwa, Sahil 151
Walker, Chase 105
Walker, Morgan 109
Walters, Gage 125
Walton, Miette 81
Wang, Andrew 163
Wang, Jonathan 148
Warner, Kaihla 170
Wary, Summer 89
Wasson, Emma 71
Watson, Christina 186
Wayman, Cherylynne 125
Wayman, Holly 53
Weatheread, Madison 8
Weaver, Brady 47
Weber, Hannah 185
Wehrman, Abigail 183
Wei, Kirby 140
Wells, Matthew 82
Welter, Brittney 88
West, Katie 11
Whatley, Olivia 62
Wheat, Michael 133
White, Veronica 93
Whittington, Hallie 48
Wicks, Heather Alexis 11
Wille, Alex 86
Wille, Nick 56
Williams, Anthony 33
Williams, Breanne 34
Williams, Faith 98
Wilson, CJ 162
Wilson, Denali 111
Winnert, Joshua 80
Winward, Samantha 26
Womack, Emma 101
Wong, Rebekah 181
Wood, Kaitlin 10
Word, Bennett 76
Wordelman, David 70
Worthen, Miles 165
Wu, Travis 174
Yang, Andrew 170
Yanni, Maiah 87
Yates, Taylor 167
Yeom, Hyunah 181
Yoo, Kevin 155
York, Bodey 179
Young, Lane 68
Yu, Shuyin 21
Yuan, Allison 77
Yuen, Allison 23
Yung, Justin 51
Yung, Nathan 79
Zahara, Oleksandra 175
Zaruba, Jordan 65
Zhao, Ke 17
Zhu, Sheldon 172
Zielinkc Grammatica, William 132
Zieske, Lauren 182
Zoetmulder, Annika 147
Zuniga, Ana 29

Author Autograph Page

Author Autograph Page

Author Autograph Page

Author Autograph Page

Author Autograph Page

Author Autograph Page

Author Autograph Page

Author Autograph Page

Author Autograph Page

Author Autograph Page